THE END OF THE WORLD IS JUST THE BEGINNING

ALSO BY PETER ZEIHAN

Disunited Nations: The Scramble for Power in an Ungoverned World

The Absent Superpower: The Shale Revolution and a World Without America

The Accidental Superpower: The Next Generation of American Preeminence and the Coming Global Disorder

THE END OF
THE WORLD
IS JUST THE
BEGINNING

Mapping the Collapse
of Globalization

—

PETER ZEIHAN

HARPER
BUSINESS
An Imprint of HarperCollinsPublishers

HarperCollins books may be purchased for educational, business, or sales promotional use. For information, please email the Special Markets Department at SPsales@harpercollins.com.

FIRST EDITION

Designed by Kyle O'Brien

Library of Congress Cataloging-in-Publication Data has been applied for.

ISBN 978-0-06-323047-7

22 23 24 25 26 LBC 16 15 14 13 12

For me, dedications are difficult because I'm . . . lucky.

I was born in the right country at the right time to grow up in safety.

Simultaneously old enough and young enough to recognize the disconnects
and opportunities in the shift from duck-and-cover to 5G.

I've been blessed with more mentors than I can count,
something only possible because they *chose* to play the role.

I'm in my field only because of those who have come before,
and I'm able to read the future only because of the questions
I'm asked by those who will come after.

Without the village, my work—my *life*—would not be possible.

So thank you.

Thank you all.

This is the way the world ends
Not with a bang but a whimper.

—T. S. Eliot

Should we be so lucky.

—German proverb

CONTENTS

THE END OF THE WORLD IS JUST THE BEGINNING

INTRODUCTION

The past century or so has been a bit of a blitzkrieg of progress. From horse-and-buggy to passenger trains to the family car to everyday air travel. From the abacus to adding machines to desktop calculators to smartphones. From iron to stainless steel to silicon-laced aluminum to touch-sensitive glass. From waiting for wheat to reaching for citrus to being handed chocolate to on-demand guacamole.

Our world has gotten cheaper. And certainly better. And most definitely *faster*. And in recent decades the paces of change and achievement have accelerated further. We've witnessed the release of more than thirty ever-more-sophisticated versions of the iPhone in just fifteen years. We're attempting to shift wholesale to electronic vehicles at ten times the pace we adopted traditional combustion engines. The laptop I'm tapping this down on has more memory than the combined total of *all* computers globally in the late 1960s. Not long ago I was able to refinance my home at a rate of 2.5 percent. (It was stupidly awesome.)

It isn't simply about stuff and speed and money. The human condition has similarly improved. During the past seven decades, as a percent of the population, fewer people have died in fewer wars and fewer occupations and fewer famines and fewer disease outbreaks than since the dawn of recorded history. Historically speaking, we live in an embarrassment of riches and peace. All of these evolutions and more are tightly interwoven. Inseparable. But there is a simple fact that is often overlooked.

They are artificial. We have been living in a perfect moment.

And it is passing.

The world of the past few decades has been the best it will ever be *in our lifetime*. Instead of cheap and better and faster, we're rapidly transitioning into a world that's pricier and worse and slower. Because the world—*our* world—is breaking apart.

I'm getting ahead of myself.

In many ways this book is the most quintessentially "me" project I've done. My work lands me squarely at the intersection of geopolitics and demography. Geopolitics is the study of place, exploring how everything about us is an outcome of *where* we are. Demography is the study of population structures. Teens act different from thirty-somethings versus fifty-somethings versus seventy-somethings. I weave together these two disparate themes to forecast the future. My first three books were about nothing less than the fall and rise of nations. About exploring the "big picture" of the world to come.

But you can only speak at Langley so many times. To pay the bills I do something else.

My *real* job is a sort of hybrid public speaker/consultant (the fancy marketing term is geopolitical strategist).

When groups bring me in, it's rare that they want to ruminate over the future of Angola or Uzbekistan. Their needs and questions are closer to home and their pocketbooks, wrapped up in a series of economic questions about trade and markets and access. What I do is apply geopolitics and demography to *their* problems. Their dreams. Their fears. I peel out the appropriate parts of my "big picture" and apply them to questions of electricity demand in the Southeast, or precision manufacturing in Wisconsin, or financial liquidity in South Africa, or the nexus of security and trade in the Mexico border region, or transport options in the Midwest, or energy policy during the turn of American administrations, or heavy industry in Korea, or tree fruits in Washington State.

This book is all that and more. So much more. I'm once again using my trusty tools of geopolitics and demography to forecast the future of global economic structures, or, to be more accurate, their soon-to-be lack thereof. To showcase the shape of the world just past the horizon.

The crux of the problem we all face is that, geopolitically and demographically speaking, for most of the last seventy-five years we have been living in that perfect moment.

At the end of World War II, the Americans created history's greatest military alliance to arrest, contain, and beat back the Soviet Union. That we know. That's no surprise. What is often forgotten, however, is that this alliance was only half the plan. In order to cement their new coalition, the Americans also fostered an environment of global security so that any partner could go any*where*, any*time*, interface with any*one*, in any economic manner, participate in any supply chain and access any material input—all without needing a military escort. This butter side of the Americans' guns-*and*-butter deal created what we today recognize as free trade. Globalization.

Globalization brought development and industrialization to a wide swath of the planet for the first time, generating the mass consumption societies and the blizzard of trade and the juggernaut of technological progress we all find so familiar. And *that* reshaped global demographics. Mass development and industrialization extended life spans, while simultaneously encouraging urbanization. For decades that meant more and more workers and consumers, the people who give economies some serious *go*. One outcome among many was the fastest economic growth humanity has ever seen. *Decades* of it.

The Americans' postwar Order triggered a change in condition. By shifting the rules of the game, economics transformed on a global basis. A national basis. A *local* basis. *Every* local basis. That change of condition generated the world that we know. The world of advanced transport and finance, of ever-present food and energy, of never-ending improvements and mind-bending speed.

But all things must pass. We now face a new change in condition.

Thirty years on from the Cold War's end, the Americans have gone home. No one else has the military capacity to support global security, and from that, global trade. The American-led Order is giving way to Disorder. Global aging didn't stop once we reached that perfect moment of growth. Aging continued. It's still continuing. The global worker and consumer base is aging into mass retirement. In our rush to urbanize, no replacement generation was ever born.

Since 1945 the world has been the best it has *ever* been. The best it will *ever* be. Which is a poetic way of saying this era, this world—*our* world— is doomed. The 2020s will see a collapse of consumption *and* production *and* investment *and* trade almost *everywhere*. Globalization will shatter into pieces. Some regional. Some national. Some smaller. It will be costly. It will make life slower. And above all, worse. No economic system yet imagined can function in the sort of future we face.

This devolution will be jarring, to say the least. It's taken us decades of peace to suss out this world of ours. To think that we will adapt easily or quickly to such titanic unravelings is to showcase more optimism than I'm capable of generating.

But that's not the same as saying I don't have a few guideposts.

First comes something I call the "Geography of Success." Place matters. Hugely. The Egyptian cities are where they are because they had the perfect mix of water and desert buffer for the preindustrial age. Somewhat similarly, the Spanish and Portuguese rose to dominance not simply because of their early mastery of deepwater technologies, but because their location on a peninsula somewhat freed them from the general melee of the European continent.

Toss industrial technologies into the mix and the story shifts. Applying coal and concrete and railways and rebar en masse takes a *lot* of money, and the only places that could self-fund were those with a plethora of capital-generating navigable waterways. Germany has more than anyone in Europe, making the German rise inevitable. But the Americans have more than anyone in the world—than *everyone* else in the world—making the German *fall* just as inevitable.

Second, and you may have figured this out for yourself already, Geographies of Success are *not* immutable. As technologies evolve, the lists of winners and losers shift with them. Advances in harnessing water and wind eroded what made Egypt special into history, providing room for a new slate of major powers. The Industrial Revolution reduced Spain to a backwater, while heralding the beginning of the English Imperium. The coming global Disorder and demographic collapse will do more than condemn a multitude of countries to the past; it will herald the rise of others.

Third, shifting the parameters of the possible impacts . . . pretty much everything. Our globalized world is, well, global. A globalized world has one economic geography: the geography of the whole. Regardless of trade or product, nearly every process crosses at least one international border. Some of the more complex cross *thousands*. In the world we are (d)evolving into, that is relentlessly unwise. A *de*globalized world doesn't simply have a different economic geography, it has *thousands* of different and *separate* geographies. Economically speaking, the whole was stronger for the inclusion of all its parts. It is where we have gotten our wealth and pace of improvement and speed. Now the parts will be weaker for their separation.

Fourth, not only despite the global churn and degradation, but also in many cases *because of it*, the United States will largely escape the carnage to come. That probably triggered your BS detector. How can I assert that the United States will waltz through something this tumultuous? What with its ever-rising economic inequality, ever-fraying social fabric, and ever-more bitter and self-destructive political scene?

I understand the reflexive disbelief. I grew up during the age of duck-and-cover. I find it galling that issues such as "safe spaces" in colleges devoid of divergent viewpoints, transgender bathroom policy, and vaccine benefits have even crossed into the proverbial town square, much less all but crowded-out issues such as nuclear proliferation or America's place in the world. Sometimes it feels as though American policy is pasted to-gether from the random thoughts of the four-year-old product of a biker rally tryst between Bernie Sanders and Marjorie Taylor Greene.

My answer? That's easy: it isn't about *them*. It has never been about them. And by "them" I don't simply mean the unfettered wackadoos of contemporary America's radicalized Left and Right, I mean America's political players in general. The 2020s are not the first time the United States has gone through a complete restructuring of its political system. This is round seven for those of you with minds of historical bents. Amer-icans survived and thrived before because their geography is insulated from, while their demographic profile is starkly younger than, the bulk of the world. They will survive and thrive now and into the future for similar reasons. America's strengths allow her debates to be petty, while those debates barely affect her strengths.

Perhaps the oddest thing of our soon-to-be present is that while the

Americans revel in their petty, internal squabbles, they will barely notice that elsewhere *the world is ending*!!! Lights will flicker and go dark. Famine's leathery claws will dig deep and hold tight. Access to the inputs—financial and material and labor—that define the modern world will cease existing in sufficient quantity to make modernity possible. The story will be different everywhere, but the overarching theme will be unmistakable: the last seventy-five years long will be remembered as a golden age, and one that didn't last nearly long enough at that.

The center point of this book is not simply about the depth and breadth of changes in store for every aspect of every economic sector that makes our world our world. It is not simply about history once again lurching forward. It is not simply about how our world ends. The *real* focus is to map out what everything looks like on the other side of this change in condition. What are the new parameters of the possible? In a world *de*-globalized, what are the *new* Geographies of Success?

What comes *next*?

After all, the end of the world really *is* just the beginning. So, it's best if we start there.

At the beginning.

SECTION I:
THE END OF AN ERA

HOW THE BEGINNING BEGAN

In the beginning we were wanderers.

We didn't wander because we were trying to find ourselves; we wandered because we were *HONGRY*. We wandered with the seasons to places with more abundant roots, nuts, and berries. We wandered up and down elevation bands to forage for different plants. We followed the animal migrations because that's where the steaks were. What passed for shelter was what you could find when you needed it. Typically, we would not stay in the same place for more than a few weeks because we'd forage and hunt the yard to nothing in no time. Our stomachs would force us to start wandering anew.

The limitations of it all were pretty, well, limiting. The only power source an unaided human has are muscles, first our own and later that of the handful of animals that we could tame. Starvation, disease, and injury were common and had the unfortunately high likelihood of proving lethal. And any provided-by-nature root or rabbit that you ate was one that someone else would *not* be eating. So, sure, we lived in "harmony with nature" . . . which is another way of saying we tended to beat the crap out of our neighbors whenever we saw them.

Odds are, whoever won the fight ate the loser.

Pretty exciting, eh?

Then, one miraculous day, we started something new and wondrous that made life less violent and less precarious and our world fundamentally changed:

We started gardening in our poo.

THE SEDENTARY FARMING REVOLUTION

Human poo is an odd thing. Since humans are omnivores, their poo boasts among the densest concentrations of nutrients in the natural world. Since humans know where their poo gets, er, deposited . . . let's call it "inventorying" and "securing fresh supplies" was a simple process.*

Human poo proved to be one of the best fertilizer and growth mediums not just in the pre-civilized world, but right up until the mass introduction of chemical fertilizers in the mid-nineteenth century—and in some parts of the world, even today. Managing poo introduced us to some of our first class-based distinctions. After all, no one really *wanted* to gather and inventory and distribute and . . . apply the stuff. It is part of why India's Untouchables were/are so . . . untouchable—they did the messy work of collecting and distributing "night soil."†

The Great Poo Breakthrough—more commonly referred to as humanity's first true technological suite, sedentary agriculture—also introduced humans to the first rule of geopolitics: location matters, and which locations matter *more* changes with the technology of the day.

The first Geography of Success, that of the hunter/gatherer era, was all about range and variety. Good nutrition meant being able to tap multiple types of plants and animals. No one likes moving house, so we wouldn't relocate until an area had been picked clean. Since we tended to clear out an area pretty quickly, and because hunger would mercilessly nudge us to greener pastures, we needed to be able to easily relocate. We tended to concentrate, therefore, in areas with a great deal of climatic variety in a fairly dense footprint. Mountain foothills proved particularly popular

---

* Important geopolitics lesson. History—*real* history—is not for the squeamish.
† For those of you fascinated by this topic, I'm afraid this is all my and my editor's stomach can handle. I'll happily refer you to Jared Diamond's *Guns, Germs, and Steel* for its at-times train-wreck-fascination level of detail on the econo-biological implications of the Gardening-in-Poo Revolution.

because we could access several different climatic zones in a relatively short amount of horizontal distance. Another popular choice was where the tropics bled into the savanna so we could tap game-rich savannas in the wet season, and the plant-rich rain forests in the dry.

Ethiopia was particularly favored by hunter/gatherers as it blended savanna, rain forest, and vertical striations into a single neat package. But that was utter crap for (poo) farming.

Getting all the food you needed from one place required a single large-ish chunk of flattish ground—not the sort of spread or variety that could sustain hunter/gatherers. The seasonality of movement of the hunter/gatherer diet was largely incompatible with the constant attention requirements of crops, while the seasonal nature of harvesting crops was largely incompatible with the needs of humans' desires to eat year-round. And just because *you* were staying put and farming didn't mean your neighbors were. Without proper disincentives, they'd tend to forage right through your garden and you'd be out months of work and back into starvation mode. Many tribes started farming only to abandon it as unworkable.

Squaring these particular circles not only required that we learn a different way of feeding ourselves, it also forced us to find a different sort of geography from which we could source the food.

We needed a climate with a sufficient *lack* of seasonality so crops could be grown and harvested year-round, thus eliminating the starving season. We needed consistent water flows so that those crops could be relied upon to sustain us year-in, year-out. We needed places where nature provided good, sturdy natural fences so that the neighbors couldn't just walk in and help themselves to our labor-fruits. We needed a different Geography of Success.

THE WATER REVOLUTION

The only places on Earth that sport all three criteria are rivers that flow through low-*latitude* and low-*altitude* deserts.

Some parts of this are obvious.

» As any farmer or gardener knows, if it doesn't rain, you're screwed. Yet if you set up shop on the banks of a river, you'll never run out of water for irrigation unless some bearded dude starts writing a Bible.

» Low-latitude regions get long, sun-filled days all year; the lack of seasonal variation enables multi-cropping. More crops at more times means less hunger, and hunger sucks.

» High-elevation rivers flow fast and straight and cut canyons in the landscape as they go. In contrast, low-altitude rivers are more likely to meander through flat zones, bringing their water into contact with more potential farmland. As an added bonus, when a braided river overflows its banks with the spring floods, it leaves behind a nice thick layer of nutrient-rich sediment. Silt is a *great* poo enhancer.

» Being in a desert region keeps those pesky foraging neighbors at bay. No sane hunter/gatherer is going to get to the edge of a desert, gaze into the endless mass of heat ripples, and dreamily opine, "I bet there are some awesome rabbits and rutabagas that-a-way." Especially in an era when loose sandals were the most durable footwear available.

Rivers also hold a couple of less obvious advantages that are just as critical.

The first of them is transport. Moving stuff around isn't all that easy. Assuming you have access to an asphalt or concrete road—the sort of road that didn't even exist until the early twentieth century—it takes about twelve times as much energy to move things on land as compared to water. In the early years of the first millennia BCE, when a top-notch road was *gravel*, that energy disconnect was more likely in the neighborhood of 100 to 1.[*]

Having a slow-moving desert river running through the hearts of our first homelands enabled humans to relocate everything from where it was in surplus to where it was in demand. Labor distribution enabled early humans to exploit more fields and so increase plantings and food supplies,

---

[*]   We didn't even get *cobblestones* until the third century BCE.

and to do so in places that didn't need to be within a short walk of where we lived. Such advantages were often the difference between spectacular success (that is, everybody doesn't starve) and equally spectacular failure (everybody *does* starve). There was also the not-even-remotely-insignificant issue of security: soldier distribution via the waterways enabled us to fend off those neighbors dumb enough to cross our desert lawns.

This transport issue, all by itself, separated the early agriculturalists from everyone else. More lands under more secure production meant more food produced, which meant larger and more stable populations, which meant more lands under more secure production, and so on. We were no longer wandering tribes, we were established communities.

The second issue rivers solve is one of . . . digestion.

Just because something is edible does not mean that it is edible right off the plant. Things like raw wheat can certainly be chewed, but they tend to be hard on every part of the digestive system, contributing to bloody mouths, bloody stomachs, and bloody poo. Not good things in any age.

Raw grains *can* be boiled to make a gruel that is disgusting in taste, appearance, and texture, but boiling both wrecks the grains' nutrient profile and anyway requires substantial fuel. Boiling might work as a supplementary food stream for a tribe that wanders from place to place and often has a supply of fresh firewood and only a few mouths to feed, but it's a complete nonstarter in a terminal desert valley. Deserts never have many trees in the first place. Where deserts and trees overlap would of course be along rivers, putting fuel sourcing in direct competition with farmlands. Anywho, the point is that successful riverine agriculture generates *big* local populations. Boiling food for a lot of people—for a community— every day simply isn't feasible in a world before coal or electricity.

Bottom line? Clearing land, digging irrigation trenches, planting seed, tending crops, and harvesting and threshing grain are the *easy* parts of early agriculture. The really brutal work is getting two pieces of rock and grinding your harvest—*a few grains at a time*—into a coarse powder that can then be prepared into easily digestible porridge (without needing heat), or, if you lived with a foodie, baked into bread. Our only available power was muscle power—both humans and our critters—and the sad physics of the grinding process required so much labor that it kept humanity in a technological rut.

Rivers helped us flush this problem. Waterwheels enabled us to transfer a bit of a river's kinetic energy to a milling apparatus. So long as the water flowed, the wheel would turn, one big rock would grind against another, and we just needed to dump our grain into the grinding bowl. A bit later, presto! Flour.

Waterwheels were the original labor saver. At first nearly all that savings was simply folded back into the backbreaking work of irrigated agriculture, bringing more land under cultivation, enabling larger and more reliable yields. But with the farm-to-table process becoming somewhat less labor intensive, we started generating food surpluses for the first time. That too freed up a bit of labor, and we had inadvertently come up with something for them to do: manage the food surpluses. Bam! Now we have pottery and numbers. Now we need some way to store our urns and keep track of the math. Bam! Now we have basic engineering and writing. Now we need a way to distribute our stored food. Bam! Roads. All our *stuff* needed to be kept, managed, and guarded in a centralized location, while all our *skills* needed to be passed on to future generations. Bam! Urbanization and education.*

At each stage, we pulled a bit of labor out of agriculture and into new industries that managed, leveraged, or improved the very agriculture the labor had originally come from. The steadily increasing levels of labor specialization and urbanization first gave us towns, then city-states, then kingdoms, and eventually empires. Sedentary agriculture may have given us more calories while deserts provided better security, but it took the power of rivers to put us on the road to civilization.

During these early millennia, there . . . wasn't much traffic.

River-driven agricultural systems could—and did—pop up all along the world's many rivers, but cultures enjoying that crunchy desert coating

---

* Yes, this is all very *Civilization* by Sid Meier. Dude did his research.

were rare birds. Our first good choices for sedentary agriculture-based civilizations were the Lower Tigris, Euphrates, and Nile, the mid-Indus (today's Pakistan), and to a lesser degree, the Upper Yellow (that's today's north-central China), and . . . that's about it.

Cultures may have been able to carve out niches—or kingdoms, or even empires—for themselves along the Missouri or Seine or Yangtze or Ganges or Kwanza—but none of them would have enough insulation from the neighbors to persevere. Other groups—whether civilized or barbarous—would wear these echo cultures down with unrelenting competition. Even the biggest and most badass of all those echo empires—the Romans—"Only" survived for five centuries in the dog-eat-dog world of early history. In contrast, Mesopotamia and Egypt both lasted multiple millennia.

The real kicker is that the next technological change didn't make human cultures more durable by insulating them, but instead *less* durable by ratcheting up the competition.

THE WIND REVOLUTION

In the seventh century CE, humanity's milling technologies finally ground through a series of technical barriers and married the milling wheel to a new power source. Instead of using paddle wheels to reach below a structure to tap the power of moving water, we used fins and sails to reach above and tap the power of moving air. The rest of the apparatus—a crankshaft and a pair of grinding surfaces—stayed more or less the same, but shifting the power source shifted the geography of where human development was possible.

In the water era, the only places that enjoyed surplus labor and labor specialization were those anchored into river systems. Everyone else had to reserve a chunk of their labor force for the grueling work of grinding. By tapping the wind, however, almost anyone could use a windmill to mill flour. Labor specialization—and from it, urbanization—could occur anywhere with rainfall and the occasional stiff breeze. It wasn't so much that these newer cultures were more stable or secure. They weren't. On the whole they suffered from far *less* strategic insulation than their pre-wind peers. But wind power expanded the zones where farming could generate surplus labor by a factor of one hundred.

This widespread spamming of new cultures had a rapid-fire series of consequences.

First, civilized life may have become far more common as the strait-jacket terms for the Geographies of Success loosened somewhat, but life became far *less* secure. With cities popping up anywhere the rain fell and the wind blew, cultures found themselves in each other's faces all the time. Wars involved players with better food supplies and increasingly capable technologies, meaning that war didn't simply become more common, it also became more destructive. For the first time, the existence of a human population was linked to specific pieces of *infrastructure*. Destroy the windmills and you could starve an opposing population.

Second, just as how in the jump to sedentary agriculture the geography of what generated success shifted from varied elevations to low-lying desert river valleys, the shift from water power to wind power favored different sorts of lands. The trick was to have as big an internal frontier as possible with easy distribution. Rivers were still great, of course, but any sort of large, open flatlands would work. Balancing that would be good, crunchy external barriers. Deserts would still work, but anything that did *not* allow agriculture would suffice. Armies had to walk, and walkers could only carry so much food. In this era most armies tended to loot their way through their invasions, so if your borderlands didn't have anything to loot you tended to get invaded less often and less . . . thoroughly.

Too open a frontier and groups like the Mongols tended to ruin your life. The Chinas and Russias of the world tended to do pretty badly. Too rugged an interior and you could never achieve enough cultural unification to put everyone on the same side. No one wanted to be Persia or Ireland, constantly struggling with internal discord. The goldilocks geographies were those with solid, crunchy outsides and gooey centers: England, Japan, the Ottoman Empire, Sweden.

Third, these new wind-dependent cultures didn't necessarily last any longer—in fact, most of them were just pan flashes—but there were so many *more* of them that the absolute supply of skilled labor that humanity could generate exploded, kicking the pace of technological advancement into a higher gear.

The first phase of sedentary agriculture kicked in with people more or less parking around 11,000 BCE. Another roughly three millennia and we figured out how to domesticate both animals and wheat. The jump to watermilling finally happened in the last couple of centuries BCE (and was popularized thanks to the Greeks and Romans). The grinding windmill took several additional centuries, not becoming common until the seventh and eighth centuries CE.

But now history sped up. Tens of thousands of proto-engineers found themselves constantly tinkering with dozens of windmill designs for the benefit of thousands of populated areas. All that nerdwork naturally had spin-off effects on a host of related wind-dependent technologies.

One of the oldest wind technologies is the simple, square-rigged sail. Sure, it will generate a bit of forward motion, but you can only sail in the direction the wind is going—a big limitation if you don't want to go in the direction the wind is blowing, or if there are ever, well, waves. A bigger sail doesn't really help (in fact, a bigger square of fabric tends to just make you almost certain to capsize).

All this new experimentation with windmills, however, meant bit by bit improvements in our understanding of air dynamics. Single-masted, single-square sailing vessels gave way to multi-masted vessels with a dizzying array of unique sail shapes designed for different water and wind conditions. The improved locomotion, maneuverability, and stability capacities sparked innovation in everything from ship construction methods (out with pegs, in with nails) to navigation techniques (out with staring at the sun, in with the compass) to weaponization (out with bows and arrows, in with gun ports and *cannons*).

In a "mere" eight centuries humanity's experience on the sea transformed utterly. The quantity of cargo that a single vessel could ship increased from a few hundred pounds to a few hundred *tons*—not counting weapons or supplies for the crew. Trips north to south across the Mediterranean—once so dangerous as to be considered borderline suicidal—simply became the first, small hop on multi-month, transoceanic and circumcontinental voyages.

The result was its own flotilla of consequences for the human condition.

Political entities that could leverage the new technologies gained an Olympic track of legs up over the competition. They could generate massive income flows, which were in turn used to fortify defenses, educate their populations, and pay for expanded civil services and military forces. The city-states of northern Italy became full-fledged independent regional powers on par with the empires of the era.

And the advances sailed on.

Until deepwater navigation, tyrannies of distance proved so consistently overwhelming that trade was exceedingly rare. Roads only existed within a culture and within most cultures there wasn't a wide enough variety of goods to justify much trade in the first place. (Places lucky enough to have navigable rivers were the exceptions, and as such tended to be the richest cultures.) Items ripe for trading tended to be limited to the exotic: spices, gold, porcelain—items that had to compete with foodstuffs in the would-be trader's cargo.

High-value goods generated their own problems. Someone showing up from out of town with a loaded wagon asking to buy some food was the equivalent of that idiot in contemporary times who puts a sterling silver luggage tag on his checked bag at the airport.* Because of the food restriction, no single trader could make the whole trip. Instead, trade took the form of hundreds of middlemen laced along rough routes like a string of pearls, with each adding their own price hikes to the goods' cost. Transcontinental trade via routes like the Silk Roads by necessity generated 10,000 percent markups as a matter of course. That kept trade goods firmly in the categories of lightweight, low bulk, and nonperishable.

---

*   Rob me, please!

Deepwater navigation sailed around the entire problem.

The new ships could not just sail out of sight of land for months at a time, reducing exposure to threats; their cavernous holds limited their need to stop for supplies. Their fearsome arsenals meant that when they *did* need to stop, the locals tended to *not* wander by and see what they could steal. The lack of middlemen reduced the cost of luxury goods by an excess of 90 percent—and that was before the powers backing the new deepwater traders started dispatching troops to directly take over the sources of the spices and silks and porcelain that the world found so valuable.

Smarter powers* didn't content themselves with sourcing and distribution, but also nabbed ports all along the sailing route so that their cargo and military vessels had places to shelter and resupply. Profits surged. If a ship could safely pick up supplies along the way, it wouldn't need to pack a year's worth of supplies. That freed up more cargo room for the valuable stuff. Or simply more dudes with guns so they could better protect themselves . . . or take other people's stuff.†

The income from such goods, goods access, and savings empowered the more successful geographies even more. The requirement of having large high-quality chunks of arable land didn't go away, but the importance of being able to secure yourself from land attack became far *more* important. As much money as there was to be made in maritime trade, the support infrastructure of docks and ships represented fundamentally new technologies that could only be exploited with great expense. Any cash dished out to float a merchant fleet would by definition not be available to maintain an army.

The new Geographies of Success weren't places that excelled at building ships or training sailors, but instead were those that weren't overworried about land invasions and had the strategic space to think over the horizon. The first deepwater cultures sat on peninsulas—Portugal and

---

* I'm looking at you, Portugal!
† Still looking at you, Portugal!

Spain to be specific. When armies can only approach you from one direction, it is easier to focus your efforts on floating a navy. But countries based on *islands* are even more defensible. In time, the English surpassed the Iberians.

There were plenty of also-rans—cultures that could harness deepwater techs but who couldn't necessarily keep up with the Spanish or English. A near-peer group that included everyone from the French to the Swedes to the Italians to the Dutch demonstrated that as revolutionary as deepwater technology was in everything from diet to wealth to warfare, it didn't necessarily shatter the balance of power if *everyone* had the new technologies. What it *did* do is open a yawning gap between those cultures that could pull it off and those who could *not* master the new technologies. France and England couldn't conquer one another, but they could—and did—sail to lands far removed and conquer the shit out of people who couldn't match their technical acumen. The world's dominant political unit rapidly evolved from sequestered agricultural communities to globe-spanning, trade-based deepwater empires.

With trade routes now measured not in tens of miles but thousands, the value and volume of the trade exploded even as the cost of that transport plummeted. The change hit the urbanization trend at both ends. Between the new naval industries and the dizzying array of traded products, the empires needed hubs to develop and process and craft and distribute everything under the sun. Demand for urbanization and labor specialization had never been higher. The collapse in per-unit shipping costs also opened up opportunities to ship far less exotic goods such as lumber, textiles, sugar, tea, or . . . wheat. Foodstuffs from a continent away could now supply Imperial Centers.

This did more than give rise to the world's first megacities. It created urban centers where *no one* was involved in agriculture. Where *everyone* was engaged in value-added labor. The resultant explosion in urbanization and skilled labor supplies accelerated the technological curve even more. Less than two centuries into its deepwater era, London—a city as far away from the trade hubs of the Silk Roads as is possible in Eurasia—became the world's largest, richest, and best-educated city.

Such a massive concentration of wealth and technical skills in one place quickly reached critical mass. All by themselves, the English generated sufficient new technologies to launch their own civilizational transformation.

THE INDUSTRIAL REVOLUTION

Despite the ever-building technological reach and depth of the deepwater era, humanity retained many of the limitations that had hobbled advancement since the beginning. As "recently" as 1700, all energy used by humans fell into one of three buckets: muscle, water, or wind. The previous thirteen millennia can be summed up as humanity's effort to capture the three forces in larger volumes and with better efficiencies, but in the end if the wind didn't blow or the water didn't flow or the meat wasn't fed and rested, nothing was going to get done.

The harnessing of fossil fuels upended it all. The ability to burn first coal (and later oil) to generate steam enabled humans to generate energy when and where and in the quantities desired. Ships no longer needed to sail around the world based on the seasons; they could carry their own power with them. Increasing the strength and precision of energy application by two orders of magnitude redefined industries as broadly arrayed as mining and metallurgy, construction and medicine, education and warfare, manufacturing and agriculture—each generating its own technological suite, which in turn transformed the human experience.

Advances in medicine didn't just improve health, they doubled life spans. Concrete didn't just allow for *real* roads, it gave us high-rises.* The development of dyes didn't just spawn a chemicals industry, it directly led to fertilizers that increased agricultural output by a factor of *four*. Steel—stronger, lighter, less brittle, and more corrosion-resistant than iron—

---

*   That's buildings with more than three floors.

provided every industry that used metal with a quantum leap in capacity, whether that industry be transport or manufacturing or war. Anything that made muscle power less necessary helped build a coffin for institutionalized slavery. Similarly, electricity didn't just expand worker productivity, it generated *light*, which manufactured *time*. In pushing back the night, people had more hours to (learn to) read, expanding literacy to the masses. It granted women the possibility of a life not utterly committed to garden-, house-, and child-care. No electricity, no women's rights movements.

The biggest restriction of this new industrial era was no longer muscle, water, or wind—or even energy in general—but instead capital. Everything about this new era—whether it be railroads or highways or assembly lines or skyscrapers or battleships—was, well, *new*. It replaced the infrastructure of the previous millennia with something lighter, stronger, faster, better . . . and that had to be built up from scratch. That required money, and lots of it. The demands of industrialized infrastructure necessitated new methods of mobilizing capital: capitalism, communism, and fascism all emerged.

The "simple" economics of moving goods from places of high supply to high demand became infinitely more complex, with industrialized locations providing massive volumes of fundamentally unique products adjacent to other industrialized locations providing similarly massive volumes of similarly fundamentally unique products. There were only two limitations on expansion: the ability to fund the industrial buildout, and the ability to transport the products of that buildout to paying customers.

And so the logic of Geographies of Success . . . split. Stretching all the way back to the shift from hunter/gatherer economics to the age of the waterwheel, it had *always* been better to be by a river. That had not changed. But it was no longer enough, and no one really had it all. Dense webs of navigable rivers could amp up local trade and generate scads of capital, but never enough to both fund local development *and* purchase the outcomes of that development. Trade became more important, both as a source of capital and as a source of customers. Germany proved the most successful at the former, with the Rhine, Elbe, Oder, and Danube decisively proving to be the industrial world's densest capital-generation zone and elevating the German Empire to the era's most powerful player. But it was Britain who ruled the waves, and therefore access to the trade routes and customers required to make Germany a global hegemon.

The pattern of favored geographies locked in by the rules of the deepwater era held solid in the industrial era. The empires of navigable waterways with far-flung dominions got bigger, tougher, and more lethal as they industrialized. Deepwater navigation made these empires global in reach, while the industrialization of warfare made that reach deadlier with the addition of machine guns, aircraft, and mustard gas. Even more importantly, the combination of deepwater navigation and industrialization enabled these deepwater empires to visit their new military capacities upon each other in a matter not of months and weeks, but days and hours. And to do so at any location on the planet.

From the first real industrial conflicts—the Crimean War of 1853–56, the American Civil War of 1861–65, and the Austro-Prussian War of 1866—it didn't take but two generations for the Industrial Age to generate the most horrific carnage in history, resulting in some 100 million deaths in the two world wars. One of the many reasons why the wars were so catastrophic in human terms was that the technological builds of the Industrial Revolution didn't simply make the weapons of war more destructive, they made the cultural fabric, technical expertise, economic vitality, and military relevance of society far more dependent upon artificial infrastructure. Combatants would target opposing civilian infrastructure because it was that infrastructure that enabled warfighting. But that same infrastructure also enabled mass education, mass employment, mass health, and an end to mass hunger.

If anything, the world wars proved that geography still mattered. For while Britain and Germany and Japan and China and France and Russia were busy *destroying* each other's wind and water and industrial-related infrastructure, a relatively new people—in a new geography—not only were not a target of all this broad-scale destruction, they were instead using the war to massively apply the technologies of water and wind and deepwater and industrial capacity to their territory . . . in many cases for the first time.

Maybe you've heard of them. They're called Americans.

ENTER THE ACCIDENTAL SUPERPOWER

The Americans are an odd lot.

There are a great many things about the Americans that generate a great deal of interest and offense, discussion and argument, gratitude and jealousy, respect and anger. Many point to the dynamism of the American economy as the quintessential manifestation of the United States' individualistic, polyglot culture. Others emphasize its military acumen as a global determinant. Still more see the flexibility of its constitution as being the secret to its two-going-on-three centuries of success. It isn't that any of these are incorrect. All certainly contribute to America's perseverance. But I'm a bit more straightforward:

The American story is the story of the *perfect* Geography of Success. That geography determines not only American power, but also America's role in the world.

THE UNITED STATES IS THE MOST POWERFUL RIVER POWER AND LAND POWER IN HISTORY

Conforming to the technologies of the time, the American colonies were all agricultural in nature. None of them were what we would call breadbaskets in the contemporary sense. The New England colonies of Connecticut, Rhode Island, Massachusetts, and New Hampshire suffered from thin, rocky soils, often-cloudy weather, and short summers, limiting farming options. Wheat was a hard no. Corn was a meh. The core agricultural economy was a mix of whaling, fishing, forestry, and Fireball.*

Georgia and the Carolinas enjoyed more farm-friendly weather, broadening and bettering agricultural options, but the soil was poor in a different way. Piedmont soils' primary inputs are the decayed remnants of the Appalachians—clay high in minerals, but not necessarily bursting with organic nutrients. The natural result was roving production, with farmers clearing land, growing crops on it for a few seasons until the nutrient profile was exhausted, and then moving on to a new patch. Staying in one place necessitated hand-applied fertilization, which is backbreaking work in any era. Non-standard employment models such as indentured servitude and slavery took root in the South because of the need to improve soil chemistry as much as anything else.

The best farmland of the Original Thirteen resided in the Middle Atlantic colonies of Maryland, Pennsylvania, Virginia, New York, and New Jersey. But we aren't talking about Iowa (midwestern) or Pampas (Argentinian) or Beauce (French) levels of quality.† They were only considered "good" due to a lack of competition. In addition to these colonies having the least-bad mix of land and weather, they also sported the bulk of the colonies' useful maritime frontage: the Chesapeake and Delaware Bays, Long Island Sound, and the Hudson and Delaware Rivers. The dense waterway network encouraged concentrations of populations (aka towns), and townies don't farm.

Less than ideal setups for farming, combined with geographic nudges in the general direction of urbanization, pushed the hardscrabble colonists in decidedly nonagricultural directions, leading to value-added products like crafts and textiles . . . something that put them into de facto economic conflict with Britain, who saw that par-

---

*   Or whatever nasty brown liquor they could distill back then.
†   Calling New Jersey the "Garden State" has pretty much always elicited eye rolls.

ticular part of the imperial economy as something the Imperial Center was supposed to dominate.*

The patchwork and shifting nature of agriculture in the colonies required some serious logistical ballet. Most local food distribution occurred via coastal maritime traffic; it was the cheapest and most effective means of moving goods among largely coastal colonial population centers. When the revolution arrived in 1775, things got decidedly animated, as the Americans' colonial overlord controlled the world's most powerful navy. Many colonial Americans went hungry for six long years. The American Revolution may have been successful in the end, but the economics of the new nation was, in a word, questionable.

Expansion solved most everything.

The Greater Midwest by itself boasts 200,000 square miles of the world's most fertile farmland—larger than the total land area of Spain. Midwestern soils are thick, deep prairie soils, laden with nutrients. The Midwest is squarely in the temperate zone. Winter brings insect kills, which keep pests under control, limiting pesticide costs as well as forcing an annual soil regeneration and decomposition process that limits fertilizer needs. The full four-season experience all but guarantees ample precipitation—including snow in the winter—which typically supplies adequate soil moisture and relegates supplemental irrigation to the region's western fringes.

The initial American cross-Appalachian migration wave funneled through the Cumberland Gap, leaving the most concentrated footprint in the Ohio territory. Ohio had access to the Great Lakes, so it behooved the New Yorkers to construct the Erie Canal in order to ship in Ohioan

---

*   It's a pattern we will see over and over and over right up to the naked now. Who gets to do the high value-added work is still something we fight about today. Such employments generate not simply the highest wages, but the fastest technological and capital builds and the largest tax bases.

agricultural bounty via the Hudson. The next big migration wave fanned out from Ohio into what is today Indiana, Illinois, Iowa, Wisconsin, and Missouri. It was far easier—and cheaper—for the new midwesterners to send their grain west and south via the Ohio and Mississippi Rivers to New Orleans. From there it was a cheap, easy (albeit long) sail via America's barrier islands' intercoastal route to Mobile and Savannah and Charleston and Richmond and Baltimore and New York and Boston.

Between the Great Lakes and the Greater Mississippi, everyone in those first two big settlement waves landed within 150 miles of the world's greatest navigable waterway system on some of the world's best farmland. The math was pretty easy. For the equivalent cost of a contemporary low-end hatchback—about $12,500 in 2020 money—a family could obtain a land grant from the government, Conestoga themselves out to the new territories, break ground, farm, and within several months be exporting high-quality grain.

The midwestern settlement proved utterly transformative—both for the new territories and the Original Thirteen—in a host of ways:

- With the twin exceptions of shortages related to British blockades during the War of 1812 and Confederate governmental collapse in the Civil War aftermath, famine is something continental Americans have zero experience with as an independent country. Food production is simply too reliable, too omnipresent, and America's internal transport system too efficient and effective for famine to be a meaningful concern.
- With the North able to access foodstuffs from the Midwest, most of the Middle Atlantic and nearly all the New England fields returned to forest, with what agriculture that remained tending to be in midwestern-inappropriate specialty crops like grapes, apples, potatoes, sweet corn, blueberries, and cranberries. This de-agriculturalization process freed up labor to throw at other projects. Projects like industrialization.
- Midwestern growth also nudged the South into cash crops. Growing indigo, cotton, or tobacco is far more labor intensive than growing wheat or corn. The Midwest didn't have the labor to pull it off, but courtesy of slavery, the South did. Each region of the country specialized in

outputs based on its local economic geography, with water transport enabling cheap and omnipresent intrastate trade, generating economies of scale heretofore unheard-of in the human experience.

- *All* the land in the new Midwest was high quality, so there were no massive gaps between settled areas like there were in the Appalachians. This relatively dense settlement pattern, combined with the region's high productivity and low transport costs, naturally led to the formation of the heartland's small-town culture. Small banks popped up throughout the Mississippi system to manage the capital generated from product sales to the East Coast and Europe. Financial depth soon became a defining American characteristic. This not only enabled steady expansions in midwestern agriculture in terms of territory and productivity, but it also provided Middle America with the capital required to bootstrap early regional development in terms of infrastructure and education.
- The easy movement of people and goods throughout the river network forced Americans to interact with one another regularly, contributing to the unification of American culture despite a wide variety of ethnic backgrounds.
- The Civil War obviously interrupted this process. The Midwest lost access to the Mississippi-intercoastal shipping route until the war's end. But by the beginning of Reconstruction in the late 1860s, farmer density in the Midwest had reached a critical mass and the steady stream of agricultural products reaching the East Coast became a flood. What had always been the most densely populated and industrialized portion of the country no longer had to worry about producing its own food at all. And all that midwestern grain generated massive capital inflows to the United States, amping up industrialization and urbanization processes that were already lumbering forward.

Beyond economics and culture and finance and trade and structure, there are security issues to consider as well.

America's territory is the very definition of "safe." To the north, deep, rugged forests and giant lakes separate most American and Canadian population centers. Only once, in the War of 1812, have the Americans fought their northern neighbors. Even that should be more accurately considered as a war with the Canadians' then-current colonial master—who at the time was the world's military superpower—than one between the Yanks and Mounties themselves. In the two centuries since the war, American-Canadian hostility has gradually given way to not simply neutrality or friendship, but an evolution into alliance and brotherhood.* The American-Canadian border today is the least-patrolled and longest undefended border in the world.

America's southern frontier is actually *more* secure against conventional military attack. The fact that illegal immigration across America's southern border is an issue in American politics underlines just how hostile that border is to formal state power. Rugged, high-altitude barrens like the American-Mexican border region are among the most difficult topographies in which to maintain meaningful populations, provide government services, or even to build basic infrastructure.†

Military action in such an unforgiving, remote area has never been anything other than borderline suicidal. The single large-scale invasion across the border—that of Santa Anna in 1835–36 in his attempt to crush the Texican rebellion—so enervated the Mexican army that it was roundly defeated by an irregular force half its size, guaranteeing success to the Texican secessionists.

No wonder that a decade later, during the Mexican-American War of 1846–48, the Americans simply waited until the bulk of the Mexican army was past the point of no return in its second attempt at crossing the border deserts before using naval forces to drop troops at Veracruz. One bloody, 250-mile march later and the Mexican capital was in American hands.

---

*   Complete with all the familiar spats for which brothers are famous.

†   Fun fact: the Trump administration's efforts to build a meaningful border wall first required the establishment of a web of roads for the wall's construction and maintenance. That new infrastructure made drug smuggling and illegal immigration *easier*, not more difficult.

THE UNITED STATES IS THE MOST POWERFUL DEEPWATER POWER IN HISTORY

Most of the world's ocean coasts are somewhat problematic. Flat coast-lines and extreme tidal variations expose would-be port locations to such unrelenting oceanic battering that truly epic port cities are a relative rarity. Except, that is, in the United States. The middle third of the North American continent's Atlantic coast isn't simply blessed by an egregious number of indentations that make siting port cities child's play; most of *those* port locations are then positioned *behind* peninsulas or barrier islands that shield America's coasts even more. From Brownsville on the Texas–Mexico border to Miami at Florida's tip to Chesapeake Bay, the barrier islands alone give the United States more natural port potential than all the world's other continents combined. Even without the barrier islands, America's beyond-world-class coastal indentations provide almost omnipresent shielded maritime access from Boston Harbor to the Long Island and Puget Sounds to the Delaware and San Francisco Bays. And don't forget those omnipresent rivers: of America's top 100 ports, fully half are *upriver*—some by as much as 2,000 *miles*.

Then there's the not-so-little issue that, unique among the world's major powers, only the United States has major populations on the coasts of two oceans. From economic and cultural angles, this enables the Americans to access trade and expansion opportunities in the bulk of the world as a matter of course. But the key word there is "opportunities." The vast distances between America's Pacific and Atlantic shores on one hand and the Asian and European continents on the other means that there is no *requirement* for interaction. Should the lands across the ocean be racked by recession or war—or should the Americans just be feeling antisocial—the Americans can quite simply stay home. No harm, no foul.

Those vast distances also mean the United States is at the very top of a very short list of countries that face no near- or mid-range threats from other oceanic powers. What islands that exist in the Pacific or Atlantic basins that theoretically could be used to launch an attack on North

America—Guam, Hawaii, or the Aleutians in the Pacific, or Bermuda, Newfoundland, or Iceland in the Atlantic—are held either by close allies or the Americans themselves.

The Americans—and the Americans alone—have the capacity to interact with any power on either ocean on their own terms, whether those terms be economic or military.

THE UNITED STATES IS THE STRONGEST AND MOST STABLE INDUSTRIAL POWER IN HISTORY

Industrializing isn't cheap or easy. It requires a wholesale tearing up of what occurred before and replacing wood and stone with more productive—and more expensive—steel and concrete. Replacing old one-at-a-time craftsmen laboring under lantern light with assembly lines, electricity, forged steel, and interchangeable parts. Overturning and discarding economic, social, and political traditions that stretch back not decades, but centuries, and replacing them with new systems that in many cases are as foreign to a culture as the new technologies that suddenly appear omnipresent. Anywhere industrialization occurs it is massively disruptive, as everything about how a country functions is tossed to the side, with entirely new systems then imposed—typically from above. The financial and social costs are typically the greatest disruptions a culture ever experiences.

In Europe, centuries of simple habitation had long ago gobbled up all available land, raising its cost. European workers were engaged in activities over every inch of that land, raising *their* cost. Any changes to the system demanded capital in large volume, raising *its* cost. Anything that made even a small change to the availability of land (like a flood or fire) or the supply of labor (like a strike or military skirmish) or the stock of capital (like someone important emigrating or a recession) would throw off the balance, raise costs dramatically for everyone, and trigger massive social upheaval. Ergo, European history for much of the preindustrial era has the feeling of a world living on a knife edge . . .

. . . and then the arrival of industrial technologies to this world tore the delicate balance apart at every level. The result was an avalanche of social upheaval, revolutions, riots, political collapses, and wars even as the countries of the Continent competed to apply the new technologies to their systems and in doing so transform themselves into massive industrial powers.

- The British experience led to product dumping, global in scale, that brought the British Empire into sharp military conflict with every major power.
- Russia's industrialization in the early twentieth century broke both the landlord and serf classes simultaneously, while failing to replace them with anything better. The resulting turmoil led directly to the mass oppressions of the Soviet Union (which generated its own flavor of not-anything-better).
- Germany's breakneck industrialization transformed the power of the country's military princes and gave rise to an industrial oligarchic class while shattering the middle class, generating a series of revolutions and civil wars that set the stage for the world wars.
- Japan's early industrialization efforts created a schism between the rising industrial-nationalists and the old feudal landlords, resulting in the eradication of the samurai class and the radicalization of the political system—taking Japan straight as an arrow to the oppression of Korea and China and the bombing of Pearl Harbor.
- China's process centralized power so firmly in so few hands that it unleashed the bleak horrors of the Great Leap Forward and the Cultural Revolution.

No country that has ever industrialized has ever managed the process without crippling social and political mayhem. Industrialization is necessary and unavoidable, but it is *hard*.

Unless you're American. Understanding the *why* of that begins with the understanding that the United States truly is a land of plenty:

The Americans were only starting to hit their stride when the industrial wave crashed upon American shores at the end of the 1800s. America's vast size kept land costs low. Its river network kept capital costs low. An open immigration system kept labor costs low. The low cost of preindustrial inputs changed the economics of industrialization in America, even as the lack of local geopolitical competition meant there was never a national security impulse to accelerate industrialization.*

Instead of hitting everywhere all at once, the new technologies first went where they could get the biggest bang for the buck: places where inputs of land and labor were already more expensive, typically in the line of cities from Washington, D.C., north to Boston. Then industrialization linked these cities together in a webwork of infrastructure. Only then does that infrastructure begin spreading out to generate suburbs, or linking in smaller cities and towns, or plunging deep into the countryside.

Germany industrialized and urbanized in barely more than a generation. In comparison, the United States didn't even finish electrifying the countryside until the 1960s. By many measures, the United States still isn't even close to finished. If one eliminates lands unsuitable for habitation like mountains, tundra, and deserts, the United States remains among the least densely populated countries even today. Of those in a similar population density category, most have recently hollowed out (post-Soviet republics) and so kind of cheated, or, like the United States, are also part of the New World (Canada, Argentina, and Australia).

Simply to achieve the degree of population density that Germany had in 1900, the United States would have to nearly *triple* its 2022 population (and that doesn't even count the half of American territories—such as the Rocky Mountains—that are not well suited to settling). Industrialization could and did happen in the United States, but the transformation was slower and less jarring, giving Americans generations to adapt to change.

America's industrial splash also didn't have a huge impact globally. Unique among the major powers, the American population was both expanding and wealthy. Industrial output—particularly in the Northeast

---

* The first such impulse didn't occur until World War II, 150 years after Germany and 200 after Britain.

and the Steel Belt—could be easily absorbed by America's own population. There was no need to export to maintain local balances, and so no need for the economic warfare for which the British Empire had become well known (and hated). The ability of local community banks to finance local developments prevented the sort of centralized authorities that so devastated the Russians and Chinese, or that so radicalized the Japanese and Germans.

Throughout America's early industrial period, the country's primary interface with the global economy remained via its agricultural exports. While the Industrial Revolution's introduction of chemical fertilizers in the late 1800s certainly increased output, it did so just as the Industrial Revolution's introduction of modern medicine was lengthening life spans. Supply increased hand in hand with demand. Americans' relative participation in the international economy simply wasn't altered to a huge degree.*

The Americans certainly had (and have) regional disparities and their own oligarchic issues, but America's oligarchs—most infamously their robber barons—had such massive opportunities in the private sector in large part because there were still so many resources to be metabolized, they had little need to enter government for business reasons. Economic stress did not automatically translate into political stress--or vice versa.

---

* Incidentally, we've seen this delayed and staged upgrading time and time again in the United States, whether it be for roads or rail lines or power lines or telephones or cell phones or broadband. Such staged development might seem to make the United States somewhat less advanced than countries like Germany or Japan or the Netherlands or Korea, where such processes occur at a breakneck pace, but it also means the American modernization process is (far) cheaper and less of a strain on the country's financial capacity. It isn't a bug. It's a feature.

AND NOW FOR SOMETHING COMPLETELY DIFFERENT

The Americans were only truly hitting their stride when World War II began. After three years of frenetic mobilization they emerged not simply as the most powerful expeditionary power in history—carrying out major integrated military actions in multiple theaters of operation simultaneously—but also as the only belligerent that at war's end occupied all the defeated powers.

And that wasn't all. On the roads to Rome, Berlin, and Tokyo, the Americans found themselves in control of key economic, population, and logistic nodes on three continents and two ocean basins. Between lend-lease deals and direct amphibious assaults, they now held all meaningful launching pads for attacks between the Western and Eastern Hemispheres. Combined with their massive wartime navy, the Americans had quite inadvertently become *the* determining factor in issues European and Asian, financial and agricultural, industrial and trade based, cultural and military.

If there was a moment in history that a power could have made a bid for global domination—for a new Rome to arise—this was it. And if there was ever a good reason to make such a bid, it was the nuclear-tinged competition that was arising with the Soviets the day after the guns fell silent in Germany.

It didn't happen.

Instead, the Americans offered their wartime allies a deal. The Americans would use their navy—the only navy of size to survive the war—to patrol the global ocean and protect the commerce of all. The Americans would open their market—the only market of size to survive the war—to allied exports so that all could export their way back to wealth. The

Americans would extend a strategic blanket over all, so that no friend of America need ever fear invasion again.

There was just one catch. You had to pick sides in the Americans' brewing Cold War. You could be safe and rich and develop your economy and culture however you wanted, but you had to stand with (technically, stand in *front* of) the Americans versus the Soviets. Instead of forging an empire global in scope, the Americans bribed up an alliance to contain the Soviet Union. The catch-all phrase for the pact is Bretton Woods, named after the New Hampshire ski resort where the Americans first made the pitch shortly after the Normandy invasion. It is perhaps more commonly known as the free-trade era of the post–World War II period, or simply as globalization.

Seems a bit like a copout, doesn't it? Why, at the very edge of victory, did the Americans give away a worldful of imperial opportunities?

Partly it was a numbers game. In 1945 the American population was roughly equal to that of the combined Western European population, which was roughly equal to that of the Soviet population. Even leaving teeming East and South Asia aside, not only did the Americans lack the forces at war's end to keep the territory it held, but simple math meant that they *could not* muster sufficient occupation forces to make a global empire work.

Partly it was a distance contest. Even with the strength of the U.S. Navy, the Atlantic and Pacific Oceans are some serious moats—and moats work both ways. The logistical costs and overreach of maintaining permanent forward-positioned garrison systems several thousand miles over the horizon simply wasn't practical. As the Americans discovered in the decades that followed, it is difficult to occupy a country on the other side of the world if the locals don't want you there. Korea, Vietnam, Lebanon, Iraq, and Afghanistan were often more than the Americans could handle when they were managed one at a time. Imagine what it would have been like to occupy Germany and France and Italy and Turkey and Arabia and Iran and Pakistan and India and Indonesia and Malaysia and Japan and China (and Korea and Vietnam and Lebanon and Iraq and Afghanistan) all at *once*.

Partly it was a map thing. The Soviet Union was a massive land-based empire that fought with huge, slow-moving armies. America's military may have been the largest of the Allies, but the United States was primarily a naval power. Duking it out with the Soviets soldier-to-soldier simply wasn't an option when the bulk of the American military capacity required, well, *water*, and wasn't designed to fight a thousand miles from the nearest friendly port.

Partly it was a culture clash. The United States was the modern world's first democracy. Democracies are pretty good at defending their own and tearing down dictatorships and fighting for truth and justice and all that. Long-term occupations expressly designed to bleed the locals dry? That's a harder sell.

Partly it was an organizational mismatch. The United States is a federation—where the states wield as much power as the national government—for good reason. The country's safe security geography combined with its rich economic geography meant the federal government didn't need to do much. For the first three generations of U.S. history, all the federal government was perennially responsible for was building a few roads, regulating immigration, and collecting tariffs. The Americans have never had a tradition of governing excellence* because for much of their history they didn't really need a government. Managing foreign territories twice the size of the United States would have been, like, really hard. And the Americans are, like, really bad at government.

If the United States couldn't—or wouldn't—forge an empire to fight the Soviets, then the Americans needed allies that were sufficiently numerous to make a difference, sufficiently proximate to the Soviet border to mitigate America's distance, sufficiently skilled in land-based warfare to compensate for America's naval and amphibious nature, sufficiently wealthy to pay for their own defense, and sufficiently motivated by their own independence to bleed for it should fighting be required. None of

---

*   A nontradition that proudly continues to the modern day.

that would have been possible with American occupation armies on their soils and American customs officials in their boardrooms.

But most of all, the Americans didn't *want* an empire because they *already had* an empire. The useful lands of the United States' portion of North America were greater in potential than that of any empire that had come before. And at war's end the Americans not only were not yet done metabolizing them; they wouldn't be for *decades*. Based on population density, one could (easily) argue that the Americans in 2022 are *still* not done. Why send your sons and daughters abroad to bleed in a day-to-day fight against dozens of peoples to maintain a global empire when you could just build some new roads around Detroit and Denver and get the same payout?

The American break with the traditions of international relations went beyond its abandonment of the to-the-winner-go-the-spoils style of postbellum realignments. It also extended to the nature of human existence itself, resulting in a fundamental rewiring of the human condition.

At war's end the Americans used Bretton Woods to create the globalized Order and fundamentally change the rules of the game. Instead of subjugating their allies and enemies, they offered peace and protection. They transformed regional geopolitics by putting nearly all the warring empires of the previous age—in many cases countries that had been in a shifting, cutthroat competition with one another for centuries—on the same team. Inter-imperial rivalry gave way to inter-state cooperation. Military competition was banned among the Bretton Woods participants, enabling the former empires (and in many cases, their former colonies) to focus their efforts not on armies or navies or borders, but instead on infrastructure and education and development.

Instead of having to fight for food or oil, everyone gained trade access global in scope. Instead of having to fight off empires, everyone gained local autonomy and safety. Compared to the thirteen millennia of history to this point, it was a pretty good deal. And it worked. Really well. In a "mere" forty-five years the Bretton Woods system succeeded in not just containing the Soviet Union, but in choking it to death. The Bretton Woods system generated the longest and deepest period of economic growth and stability in human history.

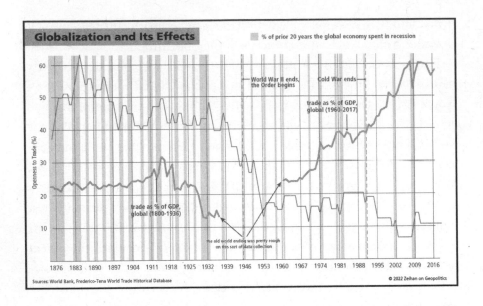

Or at least it did until disaster struck.

Until the Americans won.

On November 9, 1989, the Berlin Wall fell. Over the course of the next few years the Soviet Union lost control of its Central European satellites, Russia lost control of the Soviet Union, and Moscow even briefly lost control of the Russian Federation. Across the American alliance network, there were celebrations. Parties. Parades.* But there was also a new problem.

Bretton Woods was not a traditional military alliance. In order to combat the Soviets, the Americans had used their dominance of the oceans and superior economic geography to *purchase* an alliance. The United States enabled global trade and provided a bottomless market for alliance members' exports. Without a foe, the Bretton Woods alliance lost its reason to be. Why expect the Americans to continue paying for an alliance

---

*   Good ones!

when the war was over? It would be like continuing to make mortgage payments even after your house is paid for.

As the 1990s unfolded, the Americans somewhat lazily segued into an amorphous middle area. They would continue to uphold the Order so long as the Europeans and Japanese granted them deference in regional defense planning. Given that the Soviet Union was gone, the Russians were in disarray, and the Islamic world was more or less quiet, the costs to the Europeans seemed low and the benefits high. The biggest issue the NATO alliance faced was the disintegration of Yugoslavia, a rather esoteric event whose spillover didn't threaten the security of a single NATO country. The hottest event in the Middle East was the occasional pop of the Palestinian-Israeli conflict. In Asia, China may have been rising with the unwinding of the Mao cult, but to think of China as a serious military power was borderline laughable. In such a benign environment, no one thought much about rocking the proverbial boat.

The 1990s were a nice decade for most. Strong American-provided security. No serious international conflicts. Global trade penetrated deep into the former Soviet space as well as into countries that had done their best to sit out the Cold War. The cost of the American overwatch and market access steadily expanded, but in an environment of peace and prosperity it all seemed manageable. Germany reunified. *Europe* reunified. The Asian tigers roared. China came into its own, driving down the price of consumer products. Resource producers, whether in Africa, Latin America, or Down Under, made scads of money helping more parts of the world industrialize. Globe-spanning supply chains made the Digital Revolution not simply possible, but inevitable. Good times. We all came to think of it as normal.

It is not.

The post–Cold War era is possible only because of a lingering American commitment to a security paradigm that suspends geopolitical competition and subsidizes the global Order. With the Cold War security environment changed, it is a policy that no longer matches needs. What we all think of as normal is actually the most distorted moment in human history. That makes it incredibly fragile.

And it is over.

THE STORY OF . . . US

Different people behave differently. I'm not talking about the cultural differences geography causes among groups as diverse as Romanians and Russians and Rwandans and Roswellians. Instead I'm thinking about the horizontal layers within a society: differences based on age.

Kids act different than the postcollege crowd than middle-aged parents than empty-nesters than retirees. Stack them up and you get a modern economy. Hive them apart and you can identify many of the contemporary trends racking the global system. Modern population structures—the technical term is "demographics"—are a direct outcome of the Industrial Revolution.

DITCHING THE FARM

It matters *where* we live. One of the defining traits of the post–World War II era is mass urbanization. This urbanization process occurred in diverse ways at distinct rates in various eras. In large part the differentiator is time. Not everything in the Industrial Revolution happened at once.

The generally accepted first step of the Industrial Revolution occurred in the sleepy world of textiles. Preindustrial textile work was typically a cottage industry. A variety of different plant and animal inputs required a variety of different processing methods, ranging from cutting to breaking to scutching to heckling to boiling to retting to shearing to carding. Once the raw material had been somewhat processed, it could be spun or thrown into yarn or thread, plied into thicker yarn, and finally either woven into cloth with a loom or knitted or crocheted. It was all kind of tedious, the very definition of labor intensive, and few ever really enjoyed it.*

---

* Except perhaps contemporary hipsters, who only enjoy it ironically.

That hardly means there wasn't money to be made, with the British the first to become interested at scale. It began by using ultracheap Indian labor (that's South Asian "Indian," not North American "Indian") to do all the tedious, annoying work. The East India Company, founded in 1600 to bring in spices to make English food less soul-crushing, transitioned by the century's end to more heavily focus on distributing Indian cloth throughout the empire. Imperial citizens all became aware of the accessible glory of cotton, muslin, calico—even silk. Having tasted the profits of someone else's labor, and having discovered that pretty much everything out of India was better than the wool that was used in Britain's home-grown textile industry, the race began to do everything *better*.

As the 1700s rolled on, the British began importing cotton—at first from the Indian subcontinent and later the American colonies–turned–United States—and started building a larger-scale cottage-cum-guild industry for textiles. As the years ticked by and profits from cotton processing and textile manufacture grew, workers and bosses developed newfangled ways of increasing productivity, complexity, and durability. Flying shuttles, spinning wheels, water frames, spinning jennies, spinning mules, steam power, cotton gins, Jacquard looms, variable-speed battons, synthetic dyes. One by one the new inventions increased what was possible in terms of speed, volume, and value. By 1800 all these inventions (and more) were widespread throughout Britain.

Inventions built upon inventions to the point that in the early 1800s, cotton goods accounted for 40 percent of the value of British exports. Nor were they the end of the story. At the same time the British were experimenting with a million variations of how to spin, weave, and sew, they were making the transition from charcoal to coke to coal, from pig iron to wrought iron to cast iron to steel, from waterwheels to steam engines. Hand-made tools gave way to lathes and milling machines that could make the instruments that enabled the fabrication of chemicals.

Bit by bit, people found employment in the development and operationalization and refinement of these new techniques. Nearly all the new technologies required mass colocation at specific work sites with installed equipment. The old cottage textile system was farm- or ranch-based and wind- (or more likely, human-) powered. The new industrial conditions were urban-based and coal-driven. The countryside drained as people chased the money. Towns became cities. The new concentrations of people generated their own challenges, necessitating demand for and innovations in the fields of medicine, sanitation, transport, and logistics. And each of these hundreds of technological improvements altered the relationship of humans to economics and resources and place.

Governments started facilitating or providing mass services—everything from electricity to health care—and those services are easier to provide in dense urban footprints than across the scattered countryside. People moved en masse off the farm to the cities, seeking what they perceived as higher standards of living for less of an outlay of personal effort.

A second aspect of the Industrial Revolution proved equality adept at changing people-versus-geography relationships: the development of chemical fertilizers, pesticides, and herbicides. Once they were introduced in the mid-1800s it was fairly common to see agricultural output per acre triple (or more) while simultaneously *reducing* labor inputs. The economics of agriculture shifted irrevocably. It was no longer the towns pulling people from the farms, but now the farms were *pushing* people into the cities.

The net effect of the new urban industries and the newly hyperproductive countryside started all of us down the road to city living, spawning a host of issues the human race is still grappling with today. By far the most dramatic impact has been on birth rates. On the farm, having children was often more an economic decision than it was about love. Children were free labor that were de facto chained to their parents' economic needs. There was an understanding—rooted in millennia of cultural and economic norms—that children would either take over the farm as their parents aged, or at least not move all that far away. The extended family formed a tribe that consistently supported one another. This cultural-economic dynamic has held true since the dawn of recorded history, even to and through the consolidation of the world into empires and nation-states.

Much to my mom's chagrin, urbanization tossed those norms out the window. Move from a sprawling farm into a quarter-acre plot in a small town—much less a high-rise condo in a dense metropolis—and the economics of children collapse. There is no longer all that much work for the kids to do. Yet the kids still need to be clothed and fed. With the farm's output no longer at the parents' fingertips, food must be *paid* for. Even with summer jobs and paper routes, the best parents can hope for as regards their mini-me's is a net-zero financial position.

Move from the small town to the city, and children quickly (d)evolved (in economic terms) into being little more than really pricy conversation pieces. And while more than one parent cries tears of sad joy when the kids finally move out, there tends to be little of the panic that would have occurred had such vacating happened on a preindustrial, near-subsistence-level farm. When much of the economic rationale for having children evaporates, people do what comes naturally: they have fewer of them.

And yet, populations grew throughout the industrialization process. Part of the reason for this is obvious: vastly improved distribution systems, combined with the development and application of synthetic pesticides and herbicides and especially fertilizers, generated more and more reliable food production, removing the famine cap.

Part of this is less so: Sewers disposed of waste, reducing incidence of disease. Town living reduced accidents and improved access to medical care, reducing mortality—especially *infant* mortality. Better medicines reduced deaths from already-less-common disease and injury. All expanded life spans. Double the average life span and in a generation you have doubled the population, *independent of* people having more kids, because they have more child-bearing years to live through.

But it isn't like this all happened all at once. Take the power loom, which is generally credited as being the most significant of the early breakthroughs, increasing output per worker hour by a factor of *fifty*. The first prototype was built in 1785, but it ultimately went through five *decades* of refinement in seventeen distinct phases. Even then it took nearly another century of tinkering to make the loom fully automatic so that the whole operation didn't need to be shut down when the shuttle ran out of material.

The "Revolution" part of the Industrial Revolution is a bit of a misnomer. The new techs weren't magically developed or applied at once, but instead designed, prototyped, perfected, mass produced, and mass applied, and in turn they gave birth to daughter and granddaughter technologies over the course of *two hundred* years. The shift from the farm to the town took time. The growing of London into the world's largest, richest, most educated city took time. The transformation of cultural and economic norms of huge families flush with backup children, where the average adult died in his thirties, to tiny families where kids were considered obnoxiously loud and annoyingly mobile safety hazards and where sixty-year-olds were common took time. The tripling of the British home population took time.

For the British, the entire transformation took seven generations.

But *only* for the British.

HISTORY SPEEDS UP

Nothing about the industrial technologies the British developed was destined to remain purely British. Just as the previous technologies of the sedentary agriculture, water, wind, and deepwater eras diffused outward, so too did the industrial techs of textiles, steam, steel, electricity, and fertilizer. Because much of the work on developing and operationalizing these new techs had already been done, their application in new lands was much faster, which also means their impacts upon demographic structures were faster.

The second major country to experience the mass transformation of industrialization was Germany. In the century leading up to World War I in 1914, Germany rapidly evolved from a shattered, preindustrial, guild-based economic system, which was often preyed upon by its neighbors, to a united industrial, economic, technological, and military powerhouse that had in shockingly short order defeated Denmark, Austria, and France. The German population, like the British population before it, nearly tripled due to the industrialization and urbanization process. The German population, like the British population before it, aged due to lower mortality rates. The German population, like the British population before it, saw its birth rates plummet. But because the German population, *unlike* the British population before it, could follow a path blazed by others, the entire process from tip to tail occurred in just *four* generations.*

---

* The sheer speed of the German industrialization process combined with the German geography contributed to the traumatic horrors of the world wars. Germans lacked an overseas empire to absorb their surplus populations. Even at its pre–World War I peak, Germany just wasn't that big—a bit smaller than Montana plus Idaho—and half the territory is too rugged to be easily developed. Once industrial

Throughout the British and German experiences, three additional—and completely unrelated—issues intensified the urbanization trends that industrialization launched.

First was the rise of the women's rights movement.

At its core, the women's rights movement didn't really gain traction until the European revolutions of 1848. The technologies of the industrial era spawned massive economic and political upheaval across Europe, culminating in a series of intense civil wars as old political and social structures within and across countries struggled to contain unfamiliar pressures. The new technologies all had one thing in common: they required people, and lots of them. Some of the new techs, like the new assembly lines, required largely unskilled labor. Others, such as petrochemicals, demanded people who *really* knew what they were doing, because, you know, explosions. But for all classes of labor the new demand drove labor costs up. Culture and ethics and morality aside, whether it was women looking after the farm as the men took factory jobs in town, or the women themselves taking positions at the new industrial textile factories where they could easily earn more than double the income of a strapping lad back on the farm, there was now an *economic* case for women to be mistresses of their own lives.

In traditional societies women tend to be wed to a very specific physical location: farm and home. If there is a famine or war, it is the men who venture forth to scrounge or battle, while the women remain behind to care for the household. Such restrictions ensured women were typically . . . available. As such, in preindustrial societies it was very common for a woman to bear more than six children during the course of her life. But break the link to the household and agriculture. Enable mass female education. Allow women to earn their own income. Even women desiring large families quickly discovered that careers tend to crowd out

---

techs enabled the German population to expand, Germans quickly discovered they had nowhere to expand *into*, part and parcel of why Hitler was so obsessed with munching on the horizon.

other items on their to-do lists, in part because—regardless of intent—spending a few dozen hours a week at factory job reduces the opportunities for pregnancy.

The second factor encouraging a collapsing birth rate sits at the intersection of women's rights and industrial technologies: birth control. In the days before the Industrial Revolution, the most reliable method of birth control was good timing. Industrialization expanded the options list. In 1845 the U.S. government awarded a patent for rubber vulcanization to Charles Goodyear,* which set industry on the path to making cheap, reliable condoms. Combine such advances with the early women's rights movements, and the political and economic stars of the fairer sex began their long rise—but at the cost of overall fertility rates.

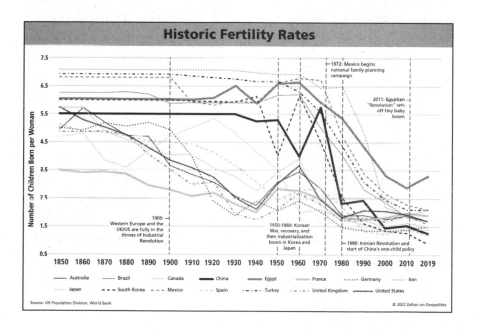

Historic Fertility Rates

Source: UN Population Division, World Bank   © 2022 Zeihan on Geopolitics

---

*   Yes, *that* Goodyear.

The third incidental factor depressing birth rates can be laid at the feet of the Americans' grand plan for their post–World War II international Order. The urbanization trend was already going full steam before the world wars blasted the old system apart, but with the onset of the free trade Order, the world's most advanced economies—most notably Western Europe and Japan—were no longer burdened with a world of constant, high-velocity war. Countries could focus on what they did best (or at least, what they wanted to do best), and the security placidity of the Order enabled them to import food from half a world away.

The very nature of the Bretton Woods globalization process depressed birth rates by squeezing the agricultural sector across the industrialized world. In the pre–free trade world, importing food en masse was rarely a viable, large-scale option. That drove government calculations both economic and strategic.

Cloudy, short-summer Germany is hardly known for its rich agricultural system, but in the general melee that was pre-1945 Europe, the Germans had no choice but to wring out as much crappy food from their crappy land as was required for the survival of the state.* Great Britain—known for its food only because the food is *so* bad—was able to take a different road only because the place is an island. By the late nineteenth century, the imperial system enabled the Brits to source their food from colonies far removed from Europe. Depending on the decade, that meant Egypt,† South Africa,‡ India,§ or Australia and New Zealand.¶ Such sourcing options enabled the Brits to not only focus their energies on the manufacturing side of the Industrial Revolution, but also gain the benefits from a globe-spanning empire to boot.

The Order turned this system inside out. By enforcing global security,

---

*   Ugh. Sauerkraut. So gross.
†   Mmmmm, kebabs.
‡   Mmmmm, pap.
§   Mmmmm, vindaloo.
¶   Mmmmm, pavlova.

shattering the empires, opening the world to trade, and enabling the spread of the agricultural technologies of the Industrial Revolution, the Americans inadvertently introduced the world to "global" agriculture. No longer did a country need to conquer some distant bit of farmland in order to guarantee food security. Parts of the old imperial networks could now maximize output with an eye toward servicing global demand rather than the narrow needs of their imperial masters.

Not only did opportunities increase in a globalized world; so too did scale. More capital flowing to more places triggered transformations in agriculture.

Larger farms could be more mechanized, achieving greater efficiencies and output with less and less labor. Such optimization granted them the economic heft to demand better pricing for inputs. Instead of getting a few dozen bags of fertilizer and the odd hoe and such from the local store, large farms would contract directly with petrochemical firms and manufacturers for their needs. The very rationale for small towns eroded.

Globalization didn't simply empty the countryside; it also gutted the world's smaller communities, forcing *everyone* into the major cities. And as true as this was in Nebraska or New South Wales, it was wildly *more* true in places like the Brazilian Cerrado or Russia's Black Earth region or China's rice belt. Every change results in the same change: more food grown and more food distributed, but done so with less labor.

The initial phases of the Industrial Revolution may have *pulled* people off the farms by providing industrial employment, and the development of synthetic agricultural inputs may have *pushed* them into the cities, but the global competition provided by the Order *hurled* farmers off their lands. And even *that* assumes the rising local agricultural behemoth firms don't muscle smallholders out, or that the government doesn't forcibly consolidate small plots into larger, more efficient factory farms.*

---

* The former is more common in places where centralized control is weak, such as Argentina, Brazil, and Ukraine, while the latter is the norm in countries with a reputation for national development plans, such as India, China, and South Africa.

And so it spread. Territories that had lacked regional security or sufficient capital since the dawn of recorded history could suddenly tap global
flows to become significant producers—and even exporters—for the first
time. Foodstuffs both increased in quality and decreased in cost. That
put pressure on legacy producers in the developed world, forcing them to
either up their game with tech to increase yields, or give up the ghost and
instead focus on things they did better. Tastes diversified. For the most
part countries gave up attempting to grow foods they couldn't grow well,
drastically increasing their output for the crops they *could* grow well. The
Americans' prohibition of military conflict among their allies eliminated
the heartburn of worrying where one might get their next meal. Global
agricultural trade exploded, and the need for national and imperial au-
tarky went out the window.

Americans' transformation of the global security and economic architecture—or more accurately, the Americans' *creation* of the world's *first*
truly global security and economic architecture—enabled the industrialization and urbanization experiences that had defined Europe for the
previous quarter millennia to go global.

The first wave of globalization impacted the early incarnations of the
Order alliance: Western Europe, the defeated Axis, the ward states of
South Korea, Taiwan, and Singapore, and the other Anglo settler states:
Australia, Canada, and New Zealand.* As with the British and Germans
before them, the peoples of all these nations experienced mass development,
mass urbanization, mass reductions in mortality, mass extensions of life
spans, mass expansions in population, and mass reductions in birth rates,
in that order. In fact, nearly all the population gains in the developed
world since 1965—overall a greater than 50 percent increase—are from
longer life spans. And just as the Germans had followed the British path

---

* Technically, many Western Hemisphere nations were also part of the first round
of the Order, as they were Bretton Woods signatories, but most of them chose to
embrace the security aspects of the system (no empires) without meaningfully participating in the economic aspects.

and so experienced a faster, more compressed version of the entire demographic transition, so too did the first big batch of post–World War II states.

After all, the path had gotten easier to follow. Water, not electricity, powered the first factories; there were as many limitations on where they could be built as there were on the cities of ancient times, which similarly limited the need for workers to staff them. Likewise, the rise of interchangeable parts and assembly lines predated electricity. Such early industrial efforts may have surpassed the output of previous manufacturing norms by an order of magnitude, but they still required either wind, water, or muscle to energize them. That limited the speed and scope and location of their adoption to very specific Geographies of Success, retarding the urbanization impact. But by 1945 the Germans had demonstrated that electricity was the *only* way to go. Suddenly a factory could be put *anywhere*. History sped up. The British may have blazed the path to development, but it was the Germans who paved it for the rest of us.

Instead of the seven generations it took to transform Britain or the four for Germany, the Canadians, Japanese, Koreans, Italians, and Argentines did it in two and a half, while a group of advanced nation latecomers—Spain, Portugal, and Greece—did it in two.

Nor did the story end there.

After the Cold War's end, the Americans threw open Order membership to the former neutrals as well as the former Soviet world. The result was the same assault of capital access, resource access, and technological access that generated the European and Japanese booms of the 1950s and 1960s, but across a *much* wider swath of the world and a *much* larger slice of humanity.

Now the vast bulk of the developing world could join in the industrializing, urbanizing, demographics-changing fun, with the largest new players being China, India, Indonesia, Pakistan, Brazil, Nigeria, Bangladesh, Russia, Mexico, Philippines, Vietnam, Egypt, Ethiopia, and Turkey. Just as the addition of electricity to the industrial tool kit sped up the process, so did the Digital Revolution. With information no longer locked within individual brains but instead flowing freely on a river of electrons, expertise could be shared with the click of a button. Prototyping sped up from a years-long process to mere weeks. What was known could be disseminated within seconds, while research collaboration could cross continents and oceans alike.

Just as the Germans were able to walk down the path faster than the British, and just as the Japanese were able to jog down the path faster than the Germans, and just as the Spanish were able to run down the path faster than the Japanese, now the more advanced nations of the developing world—specifically the Chinese, Brazilians, and Vietnamese—could sprint down that same road faster than the Spanish.

And yet, despite all the wildly unplanned changes, somehow it all not simply worked, but worked beautifully. What was truly spectacular, even magical, about the post–Cold War moment wasn't simply that war and famine had largely vanished from the world, but instead that all these countries' populations, aging and expanding at different rates, created the perfect foundation for breakneck, historically unprecedented economic growth.

Between roughly 1980 and 2015, *all* the world's internationally wired systems fell into one of two broad buckets.

In bucket #1 were those countries relatively early in their demographic transitions. Mortality was rapidly falling and life spans were rapidly expanding, but the drop in birth rates had not yet led to catastrophic reductions in the number of young workers. These countries were ravenous, and not just for food. Most of the spending a person does occurs between the ages of fifteen and forty-five—that's the life window when people are buying cars and homes and raising children and seeking higher education. Such consumption-led activity is what drives an economy forward, and this bucket of countries had consumption to spare.

The countries in bucket #2 were further along. Mortality was still falling, and life spans were still expanding, but the pace had slowed. After all, these countries had generally begun their industrialization a few decades earlier. But the drops in their birth rates had *also* begun earlier and the dearth of children in their demographic profiles was becoming obvious. Priorities changed. Fewer children meant fewer resources needed to be expended upon child rearing and education, while more could be splashed out on cars and condos. Older populations had accrued more capital, enabling more money to be saved and invested. These aging societies did *not* become less dynamic, but instead *more* so because they were able to develop and implement technologies at a more rapid pace. Productivity surged while the products produced became more sophisticated. What these countries lacked was enough young people to consume what they produced.

In this the Americans accidentally provided the solution. Not only was a central tenet of the Order that the American market would be open to all, but also the Americans' security commitment to holding up the world's collective civilizational ceiling meant that these older demographics—these export-led economies—could access consumer markets the world over. Consumption-led and export-led systems were not simply in approximate balance. The Americans seeing to the world's security concerns enabled a truly globalized world to not only emerge, but thrive.

But there is nothing about it that was normal. Globalization was *always* dependent upon the Americans' commitment to the global Order and that Order hasn't served Americans' strategic interests since the Berlin Wall fell in 1989. Without the Americans riding herd on *everyone*, it is only a matter of time before something in East Asia or the Middle East or the Russian periphery (like, I don't know, say, a *war*) breaks the global system beyond repair . . . assuming that the Americans don't do it themselves.

But even if the Americans choose to continue holding up the world's collective civilizational ceiling, there was nothing about the heyday of globalization that is sustainable. The halcyon days of 1980–2015 are over. The collapse in birth rates that began across the developed world in the 1960s and across the developing world in the 1990s now has decades of steam behind it.

The pipe bomb in the ointment is that what proved true for accelerated industrialization proved equally true for accelerated demographics. In 1700 the average British woman bore 4.6 children. That's almost identical to that of the average German woman in 1800 or the average Italian woman in 1900 or the average Korean woman in 1960 or the average

Chinese woman in the early 1970s. Now, in *all* these countries, the new average is below 1.8 and in many cases *well* below.* This is a position the average *Bangladeshi* woman will likely find herself in by 2030.

Now comes the other side of the hill.

A central factor in *every* growth story that accompanies industrialization is that much of the economic growth comes from a swelling population. What most people miss is that there's another step in the industrialization-cum-urbanization process: lower mortality increases the population to such a degree that it overwhelms any impact from a decline in birth rates . . . but only for a few decades. Eventually gains in longevity max out, leaving a country a greater population, but *with few children*. Yesterday's few children leads to today's few young workers leads to tomorrow's few mature workers. And now, at long last, tomorrow has arrived.

In the 2020s, birth rates are no longer simply dropping; they have been *so* low for *so* long that even the countries with the younger age structures are now running low of young *adults*—the demographic that *produces the children*. As the already smaller twenty-something and thirty-something cadres age into their thirties and forties, birth rates will not simply continue their long decline, they will collapse. And once a country has more older folks than children, the next, horrible step is utterly unavoidable: a population *crash*. And because any country that begins this process is one that has already run out of young adults, these countries will *never* recover.†

Even worse, just as the entire transformation from rural to urban has proceeded ever-faster since the British started us all down this road, so too does the *demographic transformation* from lots of children to lots of retirees. The faster the transformation and growth on the front end, the faster the population collapse on the back end.

By far the most unfortunate tsunami of consequence of this compression

---

*   As of early 2022 the most recent data out of Korea and China indicate the new normal is 1.2.

†   Barring a breakthrough in low-cost mass cloning technologies.

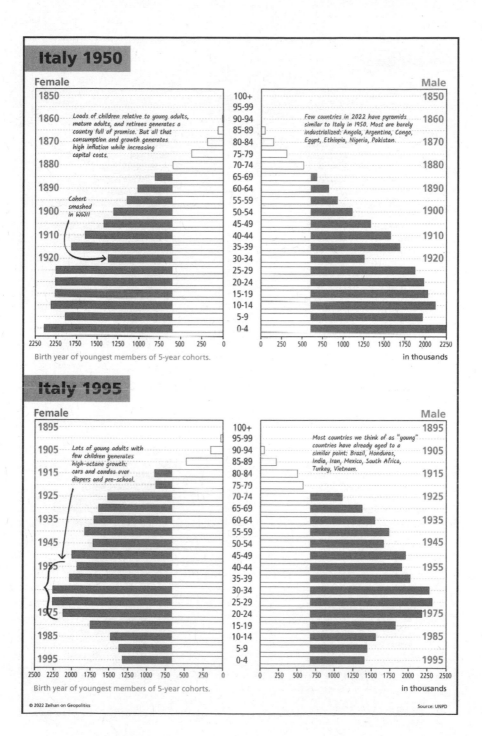

Italy 1950

Female | **Male**

Loads of children relative to young adults, mature adults, and retirees generates a country full of promise. But all that consumption and growth generates high inflation while increasing capital costs.

Few countries in 2022 have pyramids similar to Italy in 1950. Most are barely industrialized: Angola, Argentina, Congo, Egypt, Ethiopia, Nigeria, Pakistan.

Cohort smashed in WWII

Birth year of youngest members of 5-year cohorts.

in thousands

Italy 1995

Female | **Male**

Lots of young adults with few children generates high-octane growth: cars and condos over diapers and pre-school.

Most countries we think of as "young" countries have already aged to a similar point: Brazil, Honduras, India, Iran, Mexico, South Africa, Turkey, Vietnam.

Birth year of youngest members of 5-year cohorts.

in thousands

© 2022 Zeihan on Geopolitics

Source: UNPD

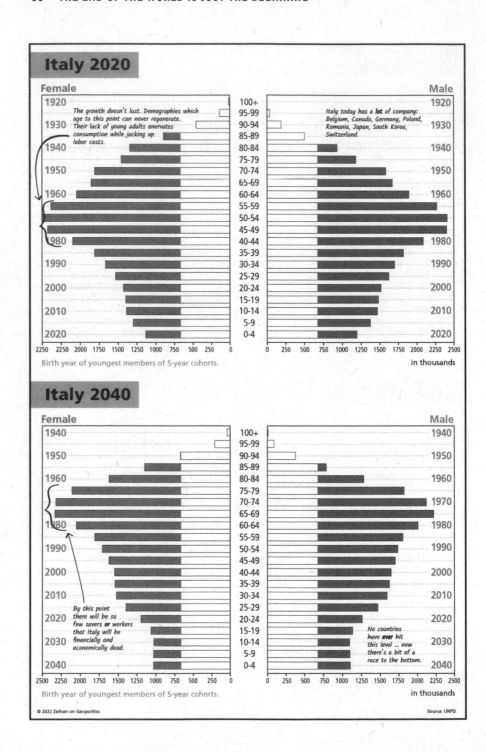

Italy 2020

Female   **Male**

The growth doesn't last. Demographics which age to this point can never regenerate. Their lack of young adults enervates consumption while jacking up labor costs.

*Italy today has a **lot** of company: Belgium, Canada, Germany, Poland, Romania, Japan, South Korea, Switzerland.*

Birth year of youngest members of 5-year cohorts.

in thousands

Italy 2040

Female   **Male**

By this point there will be so few savers or workers that Italy will be financially and economically dead.

*No countries have **ever** hit this level ... now there's a bit of a race to the bottom.*

Birth year of youngest members of 5-year cohorts.

in thousands

© 2022 Zeihan on Geopolitics

Source: UNPD

phenomenon at work is China. The long stretch of Chinese history was comparatively preindustrial until one Richard Milhous Nixon's 1972 visit to one Mao Zedong, in what would prove a successful effort to turn Red China against the Soviet Union. The price for Chinese realignment was pretty straightforward: admittance into the American-led global Order. Some 800 million Chinese started down the route to industrialization, a route that was now less a newly blazed path, and more a fourteen-lane superhighway with double HOV lanes. Following the patterns established by much of the rest of humanity, Chinese mortality plummeted by three-quarters and the Chinese population expanded to match. China, like everyone before, saw its population surge from under 800 million in 1970 to over 1.4 billion in 2021.[*]

What many in the world see as a threat—the rapid rise of China in economic, military, and demographic terms—is nothing more than two hundred years of economic and demographic transformation squeezed into a searing four decades, utterly transforming Chinese society and global patterns of trade . . .

. . . as well as the Chinese demography. No matter how you crunch the

---

[*]   If some of these data and timelines seem a bit squishy, it is because they are. Geographically, China is remarkably complex, generating a similarly complex—and disunited—political history. Between geographic variety and political scramble, there is no singular Chinese development path. Places like Shanghai had started industrializing (unevenly) as early as 1900, while most of northern China didn't even begin experimenting with the general process until the disasters of the Great Leap Forward of 1958–62. The result in population growth was similarly uneven: some of the coastal regions experienced the boom far earlier than others. Overall, between 1950 and 1970, China's population expanded from 540 million to 810 million. Ish. Countering that, the Great Leap Forward generated one of humanity's greatest man-made famines, resulting in between 15 million and 55 million deaths, depending on who is writing the history. So was "China" fully *un*industrialized when Nixon visited? No. China at that time was *already* responsible for 5 percent of global carbon emissions. But China is still *huge,* so even those emissions came from a very small percentage of the population living in the most advanced coastal/ southern cities.

numbers, China in 2022 is *the* fastest-aging society *in human history*. In China the population growth story is over and *has* been over since China's birth rate slipped below replacement levels in the 1990s. A full replacement birth rate is 2.1 children per woman. As of early-2022, China's only partly released 2011–2020 census indicates China's rate is at most 1.3, among the lowest of any people throughout human history. The country's demographic contraction is now occurring just as quickly as its expansion, with complete demographic collapse certain to occur *within a single generation*. China *is* amazing, just not for the reasons most opine. The country will soon have traveled from preindustrial levels of wealth and health to postindustrial demographic collapse *in a single human lifetime*. With a few years to spare.

Nor will China die alone. The time-staggered nature of the industrialization process—from Britain to Germany to Russia and northwestern Europe and Japan to Korea to Canada and Spain—combined with the steadily accelerating nature of that process, means that much of the world's population faces mass retirements followed by population crashes *at roughly the same time*. The world's demographic structure passed the point of no return twenty to forty years ago. The 2020s are the decade when it all breaks apart.

For countries as varied as China, Russia, Japan, Germany, Italy, South Korea, Ukraine, Canada, Malaysia, Taiwan, Romania, the Netherlands, Belgium, and Austria, the question isn't when these countries will age into demographic obsolescence. *All* will see their worker cadres pass into mass retirement in the 2020s. *None* have sufficient young people to even pretend to regenerate their populations. *All* suffer from terminal demographics. The real questions are how and how soon do their societies crack apart? And do they deflate in silence or lash out against the dying of the light?

Coming up behind them—*rapidly*—is another cadre of countries whose birth rates have dropped even faster, and so who will face a similar demographic disintegration in the 2030s and 2040s: Brazil, Spain, Thailand, Poland, Australia, Cuba, Greece, Portugal, Hungary, and Switzerland.

Even further forward, in the 2050s, are countries who started their birth rate collapse a bit later, and so who still *may* have a chance to avoid demographic disillusion if they can get today's twenty- and thirty-somethings to have a whole mess of kids, but honestly, these late arrivals' birth rate collapses have been so severe it doesn't look great: Bangladesh, India, Indonesia, Mexico, Vietnam, Iran, Turkey, Morocco, Uzbekistan, Saudi Arabia, Chile, the Czech Republic.

The next batch of countries—mostly in the poorer parts of Latin America or sub-Saharan Africa or the Middle East—are even more concerning. Their demographic structures are younger—*far* younger—but that doesn't mean they are in a better position, because there is more to economic and demographic health than just numbers and ages.

In most cases these countries are extractive economies that ship out this or that raw commodity, using the proceeds to supply their population with imported food and/or consumer goods. In many ways they've managed to access portions of the industrialization process—most notably lower mortality, more reliable food supplies, increased urbanization, and population booms—without experiencing the bits that make advancement stick: increased educational levels, a modernized state, a value-added economic system, social progress, industrial development, or technological achievement.

In a safe, globalized world such a hybridization model can limp along so long as the commodities flow out and the money flows in. But in an unsafe, fractured world where trade is sharply circumscribed, outright national collapse will by far *not* be the biggest problem these peoples face. In these countries the very population is vulnerable to changes farther abroad. The industrial technologies that reduce mortality and raise standards of living cannot be uninvented, but if trade collapses, *these technologies can be denied*. Should anything impact these countries' commodity outflows or the income or product inflows, the entire place will break down while experiencing deep-rooted famine on a biblical scale. Economic development, quality of life, longevity, health, and demographic expansion are all subject to the whims of globalization. Or rather, in this case, *de*globalization.

LEARNING A SCARY WORD

Let's make this a bit less theoretical:

I live at 7,500 feet above sea level in rural, mountainous Colorado. Snow is less a seasonal occurrence and more a way of life. When I first moved here I thought to myself, "Self? New start? New home? New 'you'? Let's get the *body* to go with it!" I started hiking nearly every day, and when the snow came I attacked with gusto! And a shovel.

Only a shovel.

It was . . . the stupidest thing I've ever done.

A month later I was ready with a Toro gasoline-powered snowblower. What had been a twenty-plus-hour ordeal that nearly put me in traction was now a slightly less than two-hour inconvenience.

That twenty-something hours was *just* for my drive- and walkways. Just my *home*. It's a two-mile hoof from my driveway to the base of my mountain, and another seven-and-a-half-mile canyon-threading ruck down to the highland plains which host the city of Denver. That's a *lot* of shoveling. Without gasoline-powered snow clearing gear, my house at 7,500 feet not only would have never been built, it could not even theoretically be maintained.[*]

And now we are in Denver, which sits in what used to be very appropriately known as the Great American Desert. As one moves west from the humid lowlands of the Midwest, the land steadily rises and dries. Denver

---

[*] For you greenies out there who think I should have gone for an electric model instead of gasoline, I tried. It was quicker than using a shovel, but electric motors simply lack the power to clear snow quickly. With about four inches of snow I could clear my spaces in about five hours. Any more than that and the electric engine threatened to burn itself out. The damn thing made good on its threat in very short order.

sits at on the eastern flank of the Rockies' Front Range, permanently and firmly in rain shadow, getting less than seven and a half inches of precipitation annually. Higher altitudes mean that whatever rain does fall tends to evaporate quickly. In "mile-high" Denver, the humidity is so low, light snows don't so much melt as sublimate directly into vapor. Roughly three-quarters of Colorado's population lives in similar conditions east of the continental divide, but roughly three-quarters of the precipitation that falls in Colorado lands to the divide's *west*.

Denver—*Colorado*—addresses this problem in two ways. The first is to put dams *everywhere*. Look at any map of any metro that, like Denver, lies on eastern edge of the Front Range. You'll notice lakes. Lots and lots of lakes. But they are not lakes. They are *reservoirs* designed to capture as much of the spring snowmelt rage as possible. Urban Colorado has modified its immediate terrain in order to store every drop of water it can for as long as it can.

It isn't nearly enough. The second action is to drill tunnels through the Rockies in order to connect the state's western watersheds to its eastern populations. At present there are two dozen of these transbasin diversion monsters. Collectively, storing every drop and relocating some 25 *billion* gallons annually enables Fort Collins, Estes Park, Greeley, Boulder, Colorado Springs, Pueblo, and Greater Denver to exist. Not to mention the near entirety of the state's agricultural sector.

Remove the technologies required to construct and maintain this water management system, and the maximum sustainable population of the Front Range cities would plummet from the roughly four and a half million it is today to something roughly one-tenth that.

Some version of this story exists for most of the world's populated places. Maybe it is an infrastructure issue. Maybe it's climatic. Maybe it's about resources or food or security. But the bottom line is always the same: If for whatever reason global flows of products and services and energy and foodstuffs are interrupted, the population and political and economic maps will change.

In a post-globalized world, large, diversely resource-rich countries like the United States can shuffle products around internally to make everything work. I live in zero fear that I won't be able to source gasoline (refined in Colorado from crude oil produced in Colorado) for my snowblower (manufactured in Minnesota) to keep clear the driveway (the asphalt is from Oklahoma) to my house (wood framing from Montana) that I often telecommute from (using a comms network composed of steel from Ohio, aluminum from Kentucky, and plastics from Texas).

Precious few places have this sort of diversity, reach, access, and redundancy. Most are dependent—often wholly—on globalization to do their locality's equivalent of something as "simple" as clearing the snow. It begs the question of what Shanghai would look like without oil? Or Berlin without steel? Riyadh without . . . food? Deglobalization doesn't simply mean a darker, poorer world, it means something far worse.

An unraveling.

The world currently has two reasonably disturbing and disturbingly reasonable examples as to what this unraveling might look like: Zimbabwe and Venezuela. In both cases mismanagement par excellence destroyed the ability of both countries to produce their for-export goods—foodstuffs in the case of Zimbabwe, oil and oil products in the case of Venezuela—resulting in funds shortages so extreme, the ability of the countries to import largely collapsed. In Zimbabwe, the end result was more than a decade of negative economic growth, generating outcomes far worse than those of the Great Depression, with the bulk of the population reduced to subsistence farming. Venezuela wasn't so . . . fortunate. It imported more than two-thirds of its foodstuffs *before* its economic collapse. Venezuelan oil production dropped so much, the country even lacks sufficient fuel to sow crops, contributing to the worst famine in the history of the Western Hemisphere.

I don't use these examples lightly. The word you are looking for to describe this outcome isn't "deglobalize" or even "deindustrialize," but instead "decivilize."

Everything we know about human civilization is based on the simple idea of organization. Once a government lays down some basic ground rules like "don't kill your neighbor," people start doing what people do:

raising families, growing food, hammering out widgets. People start trading, so that the farmer doesn't also have to make flour and the blacksmith doesn't have to grow his own food. This specialization makes us more productive in our chosen fields—be it farming or milling or blacksmithing. This society gets richer and expands. More land, more people, more specialization, more interaction, more internal trade, greater economies of scale.

This pattern developed bit by bit since the dawn of civilization, but there were often not merely setbacks but collapses. Empires rose and fell, and when they fell, much of their progress fell with them. The American-led Order (big *O*) did more than change the rules of the game; it institutionalized *order* (little *o*), which in turn allowed industrialization and urbanization to spread everywhere. That shifted the global demographic from one of lots of children to lots of young and mature workers, generating a sustained consumption and investment boom the likes of which humanity had no previous experience with. With security guaranteed and supplies of capital and energy and foodstuffs ample, six thousand years of ups and downs were replaced by an unstoppable freight train of progress.

Under the Order and this magical demographic moment, we have become so specialized and our technology has advanced so much that we have become totally incompetent at tasks that used to be essential. Try producing your own electricity or enough food to live on while keeping up your full-time job. What makes it all possible is the idea of continuity: the idea that the safety and security we enjoy today will still be here tomorrow and we can put our lives in the hands of these systems. After all, if you were pretty sure the government was going to collapse tomorrow, you'd probably worry less about whatever work-related color-coded minutiae your manager insists is so important and instead focus your time on learning how to can vegetables.

Labor hyperspecialization is now the norm, and trade has become so complex that entire economic subsectors (loan officers, aluminum extruders, warehouse planning consultancies, sand polishers) now exist to facilitate it. Nor is this specialization limited to individuals. With global peace, *countries* are able to specialize. Taiwan in semiconductors. Brazil in soy. Kuwait in oil. Germany in machinery. The civilizational process has been reaching for its ultimate, optimal peak.

But "optimal" is not the same thing as "natural." Everything about this moment—from the American rewiring of the security architecture to the historically unprecedented demographic structure—is artificial. And it is failing.

There are a number of ways down for countries looking down the maw of demographic oblivion and globalization's collapse, but they all share something in common: reduced interaction means reduced access means reduced income means fewer economies of scale means less labor specialization means reduced interaction. Shortage forces people—forces *countries*—to look after their own needs. The value-added advantages of continuity and labor specialization wither. Everyone becomes less efficient. Less productive. And that means less of everything: not just electronics but electricity, not just automobiles but gasoline, not just fertilizer but food. The parts are less than the sum. And it compounds. Electricity shortages gut manufacturing. Food shortages gut the population. Fewer people means less chance of keeping anything that requires specialized labor working. Say, things like road construction or the electrical grid or food production.

That is what "decivilization" means: a cascade of reinforcing breakdowns that do not simply damage, but destroy, the bedrock of what makes the modern world function. Not every location had the right geography to make a go of civilization before the Order. Not every location will be able to maintain civilization after Order's end.

It is one thing for a country like Mexico, which is wired into the United States, to struggle through an industrial buildout and get by without parts imported from Asia. It is quite another for a country like Korea to muddle through when it loses access to imported oil *and* iron ore *and* foodstuffs *and* export markets.

Worst of all, many less advanced countries are wholly dependent upon civilization holding together *in other places*. Zimbabwe and Venezuela are examples of countries that *chose* the path to a sort of decivilization. For most, it will be foisted upon them due to events a continent or more away in places they cannot hope to influence much less control. Even moderate struggles in places like Brazil or Germany or China will so disrupt demand for materials from Bolivia or Kazakhstan or the Democratic Republic of the Congo that the weaker states will lose the income required to enable import for the products that allow for basic modernity. And the world's Brazils and Germanys and Chinas face far more than mere moderate struggles.

There *are* a few bright spots in this deepening gloom, but only a few.

A precious few countries have managed a high degree of development while simultaneously *avoiding a collapse in birth rates*. It is . . . a painfully short list: the United States, France, Argentina, Sweden, and New Zealand. And . . . that's it. Even if politics aligned, even if everyone's hearts were in the right place, even if all the Americans and French and Argentines and Swedes and Kiwis wanted to put the rest of the world's needs in front of their own, the sheer scale of humanity's demographic turning means all of them combined would not comprise nearly enough of a foundation to support a new global system.

By most measures—most notably in education, wealth, and health—globalization has been great, but it was never going to last. What you and your parents (and in some cases, grandparents) assumed as the normal, good, and right way of living—that is, the past seven decades or so—is a historic anomaly for the human condition both in strategic and demographic terms. The period of 1980–2015 in particular has simply been a unique, isolated, blessed moment in time. A moment that has ended. A moment that will certainly not come again in our lifetimes.

And *that* isn't even the bad news.

THE END OF MORE

In the bad ol' days before deepwater navigation, the height of the human experience wasn't very high at all. Most governing systems were a mix of imperial and feudal.

The issue was one of reach.

The few places with rich geographies would establish themselves as Imperial Centers and use their wealth to reach out militarily and economically to control other territorial swaths. Sometimes these Centers would innovate or adapt a technology that would alter the regional balance of power, enabling more successful land grabs. The Romans used roads to dispatch troops here and there more quickly. The Mongols developed the iron stirrup, which enabled their mounted warriors to wipe the floor with, well, pretty much everyone.

But there was nothing about these techs that couldn't disseminate out to the competition, eliminating this or that power's momentary advantage. And of course, as few wanted to be another's occupied subjects, everyone would attempt to develop or adapt rival techs. Hannibal famously tamed a few critters—elephants—which enabled him to attack Rome's core territories in ways unexpected. The Poles erected a raft of horse-resistant castles, allowing them to wave their private parts in the general direction of Mongol raiders.

That's the big picture, but it isn't very accurate. Or at least, not very complete. Organizationally speaking, the imperial expansions were hardly the norm. Sure, we know these technological and countertechnological struggles as, well, history. But for every successful imperial *expansion* there was an imperial *collapse* as well as ten thousand territories that *never* managed to eke out a moment in the sun.

The smaller picture was very small indeed.

At the local level, life wasn't nearly so dramatic. Most people were serfs, a fancy term for grueling, near-subsistence farming. What security the serfs had was wholly due to their relationship to their local lords. These lords controlled a fortified town or keep, and when raiders or small armies came a-lootin', the serfs would rush in panic into the fortification, and hunker down until the threat passed. In "exchange" for this security, the feudal lords collected taxes and food and labor from the serfs.* Since the most common way to pay taxes was with some surplus food, the various lords didn't have much goods differentiation to trade among themselves. It wasn't a system that encouraged broad-scale interaction or education or advancement or development. Not a lot changed. Ever.

The economics of these two systems were depressingly similar. Feudalism was simply a trade of securities: the lords provide protection to the serfs, while the serfs pledge their lives to their lords. *Finis.* Imperial systems weren't much different: any large-scale "trade" had to exist within the borders of the empire. The only way to secure access to new goods was to venture out and conquer. And since any advantage would be temporary, it all came down to the security-for-loyalty trade of the Imperial Center to its provinces, as guaranteed by imperial armies.

The pie wasn't very big. It could get bigger only slowly. It often got smaller. No one had access to the whole thing, and the tyranny of geography kept trade sharply circumscribed. Humanity did battle with itself over who controlled what slices of a stagnant and fractured pie.

Then, all at once—historically speaking—everything changed.

The Columbus expeditions around the turn of the fifteenth century set off a runaway chain reaction of interconnectivity. Deepwater navigation enabled first the Spanish and Portuguese and later the British and, well, everybody to reach out and interact with every piece of land that touched ocean. Empires still existed, but their economic bases had changed because they could reach nearly any product nearly anywhere. With the now-broader economic bases of the larger systems, the economics of the

---

* "Exchange" implies a relationship of choice. Serfs were in essence slaves locked to the land. If a noble sold his land, the serfs typically went with the sale.

local, feudal systems collapsed. Imperial wars required more people. Imperial economic expansion required more workers. Imperial trade generated new industries. In all cases the unabashed losers were the feudal lords, who could offer nothing but a near-subsistence existence.

As the decades ticked into centuries, expectations changed because the economics changed. No longer was the pie singular and stagnant. It was growing. It would never *stop* growing. And that, above all else, is the world we know.

More products. More players. Bigger markets. More markets. Easier transport. More interconnectivity. More trade. More capital. More technology. More integration. More financial penetration. More and bigger and bigger and more.

A *world* of more.

Ever since Columbus sailed the ocean blue, human economics have been defined by this concept of *more*. The world's evolution within the idea of more, this *reasonable expectation* of more, is ultimately what destroyed the old economies of the pre-deepwater imperial and feudal systems. New products and markets and players and wealth and interactions and interdependencies and expansions required new methods of managing the new relationships. Humanity developed new economic models, with the most successful and durable ones proving to be fascist corporatism, command-driven communism, socialism, and capitalism. Competition among such systems—among these -isms—has defined the past few centuries of human history.

At their core, all economic models are systems of distribution: deciding who gets what, when, and how.

- Capitalism is what most Americans are most familiar with. The idea is that government should have a light touch and leave most decisions— especially as regards consumption and production, supply and demand, technology and communication—to private citizens and firms. Capitalism is America's economic baseline, but the Americans are hardly the world's only capitalists: Japan, Australia, Switzerland, Mexico,

Taiwan, Lebanon, and the Baltic states all have their own iterations of capitalist systems.

- Socialism is either the norm (if you're in Europe) or the enemy (if you're on the American political Right). In modern socialist systems, firms and government and the population exist in a shifting kaleidoscope of cooperation and struggle. The core idea to all truly socialist structures, however, is that government *belongs* as an inseparable part of the economic system. The debate is over *how* central the governmental role should be and *how* the government should use its power and reach to shape or maintain society. Canada and Germany are probably the best contemporary examples of well-run socialist systems. The Italian, Brazilian, and South African versions of socialism could . . . use some work.*

- Command-driven communism is socialism carried to its absurd extreme. The idea is that the government is the *sole* decider of all the things capitalism would outsource to the private sector and population. Eliminating private choice—and the private sector altogether— enables the government to direct the full power of society to achieve whatever goal needs tackling. The Soviet Union is the biggest and most successful country to use command-driven communism, but versions of it have popped up in many places where the political elite

---

* It's worth noting that many systems that claim to be socialist in reality are anything but. The version that most haunts the American Right, for example, is the "social- ism" of Venezuela. In Venezuela, socialism is the brand name used by the elite for political cover while they loot everything up to and including things that are liter- ally nailed down, all for their own personal gain. We *should* be afraid of it. But that's not socialism. That's kleptocracy. Definitely not a functional -ism.

And I'm sure there are some classic political scientists and/or ideologues who associate "socialism" with "workers owning the means of production." That has hap- pened exactly never, and I tend to ignore things that have never happened. Con- temporary economists equate the term "socialism" with the generous social welfare states popular in Europe, and I see no need to argue with them.

is particularly . . . bossy. Early Cold War–era South Korea was an exceedingly well-run, fairly closed, command-driven system, despite politically being vigorously "anti-communist."*

- Fascist corporatism is one we don't often think about; it fuses business leadership with state leadership. The government ultimately calls the shots and it obviously coordinates firms to work toward government goals, but the key word is "coordinate." Firms are government-linked and government-directed, but not as a rule government-operated. In a well-run fascist economy, the government can co-opt the private sector to achieve broad government-derived goals, like, say, building an autobahn or wiping out the Jews. But for the most part, day-to-day management is left up to the firms themselves. Hitlerite Germany is obviously the leading example of a modern fascist-corporatist system, while late Cold War–era South Korea put in a couple of fascist decades before segueing in a more capitalist/socialist direction. Contemporary "Communist" China far more closely resembles fascism than socialism, much less communism. The same goes for post–Arab Spring Egypt.

Each model has its own pros and cons. Capitalism trades away equality to maximize growth, both economic and technological. Socialism sacrifices growth at the altar of inclusivity and social placidity. Command-driven communism writes off dynamism, instead aiming for stability and focused achievements. Fascist corporatism attempts to achieve state goals without sacrificing growth or dynamism, but at the cost of popular will, a massively violent state, epically awe-inspiring levels of corruption, and the gnawing terror of knowing that state-sponsored genocide is but a

---

* I'm sure there are a few ideologues and/or economists reading this wondering what I think about "true" or "pure" communism: the idea that the state exists to be an impartial mechanism for distributing goods and services from those with ability to those with need. Since the time of Karl Marx, no one has tried it . . . and no one ever will, simply because people are people and under such a system those with the ability will either turn into sloths or defect. Disagree? Grow up. Or go off to your own planet and populate it with something that isn't human.

few pen strokes away. Capitalism and socialism are broadly compatible with democracy and all the political noise and chaos that comes with it. Command-driven communism and fascist corporatism are far more politically . . . quiet.

But what *all* these -isms we have developed in recent centuries and fine-tuned in recent decades have in common is something our world is about to lack: *more.*

Geopolitics tells us the post–World War II and especially the post–Cold War economic booms were artificial and transitory. Going back to something more "normal" by definition requires . . . shrinkage. Demographics tells us that the number and collective volume of mass-consumption-driven economies has already peaked. In 2019 the Earth for the first time in history had more people aged sixty-five and over than five and under. By 2030 there will be *twice* as many retirees, in relative terms.

Nearly all countries that boast sufficiently friendly geographies to enable development without American security sponsorship *have already developed*. Nearly all have been in terminal demographic decline *for decades*. Nearly all are now aging into mass obsolescence.

On the other side, those countries *without* good geographies who *need* that American sponsorship have now missed their window. In the middle, those countries that managed to develop under American sponsorship in recent decades are having the demographic and geopolitical rug pulled out from under them.

Combine geopolitics and demographics and we know there will be *no* new mass consumption systems. Even worse, the pie that is the global economy isn't going to simply shrink; it is being fractured into some very nonintegrated pieces, courtesy of American inaction.

Think of your hometown. What if everything it needed for manufactured goods and food and energy, it had to provide itself? Even if your hometown were Shanghai or Tokyo or London or Chicago, it would be impossible for you to live your current life. What the Order has done is encapsulate the bulk of the world into a single "town" in which we all specialize in whatever we are good at—whether it be picking avocados or cutting metal or purifying butadiene or assembling flash drives or wiring wind turbines or instructing yoga. We then use the income from the sales of what we're good at to pay for the items and services we aren't good at. It isn't perfect, but it *has* promoted the greatest technological advancement in human history, brought most of us into the Digital Age, and created ever-greater demand for ever-greater levels of education.

But none of this is a natural outcome of the "normal" world; rather, it is instead an artificial outcome of the American-created security and trade Order. Without global peace, the world gets smaller. Or, put more accurately, the one big world breaks up into several smaller worlds (and oftentimes, mutually antagonistic worlds).

To be blunt, our existing -isms are woefully unable to manage coming challenges.

- Capitalism without growth generates massive inequality, as those who already have political connections and wealth manipulate the system to control ever-bigger pieces of an ever-shrinking pie. The result tends in the direction of social explosions. Three, of many, examples of how it can go to pot are the anarchist movements within the United States during the Great Depression, the rise of Donald Trump in the Rust Belt as a reaction to the region's deindustrialization, and the general societal collapse of the Lebanese Civil War.
- The future of socialism is, if anything, darker. Socialism cannot generate capitalist levels of growth even when the pie is expanding, much less when it is shrinking. Socialism *might* be able to preserve economic equality, but that's unlikely to save the model. Unlike capitalism, where at least the elites might be able to struggle through, in socialism *everyone* will become noticeably worse off every year. Mass uprisings and state fracture are pretty much baked into that particular dessert product.
- Fascist corporatism *might* provide an option by outsourcing much of the clinical management of the economy to large corporations. But ultimately it will face the same problems as capitalism *and* socialism— inequality from concentrating power with firms, degrading stagnation from a shrinking pie—and since the government is *clearly* in charge

it wouldn't take long for finger-pointing to transition into pitchfork-marching.

- That just leaves command-driven communism. Sadly, it just might be the most viable of the four. But *only* if it crushes the population's souls to the degree that having an opinion is suppressed by an overarching, *1984*-style propagandaesque dictatorship. And of course, it will retain all the normal shortcomings of the model as we know it: it really only works if those running the command economy guess correctly on which techs will win out *and* which goods will be needed *and* how to access the relevant inputs to make them. Every. Single. Time.

We aren't simply looking at a demographically induced economic breakdown; we are looking at the end of a half millennium of economic history.

At present, I see only two preexisting economic models that *might* work for the world we're (d)evolving into. Both are *very* old-school:

The first is plain ol' imperialism. For this to work, the country in question must have a military, especially one with a powerful navy capable of large-scale amphibious assault. That military ventures forth to conquer territories and peoples, and then exploits said territories and peoples in whatever way it wishes: forcing conquered labor to craft products, stripping conquered territories of resources, treating conquered people as a captive market for its own products, etc. The British Empire at its height excelled at this, but to be honest, so did any other post-Columbus political entity that used the word "empire" in its name. If this sounds like mass slavery with some geographic and legal displacement between master and slave, you're thinking in the right general direction.

The second is something called mercantilism, an economic system in which you heavily restrict the ability of anyone to export anything to your consumer base, but in which you also ram whatever of your production you can down the throats of anyone else. Such ramming is often done with a secondary goal of wrecking local production capacity so the target market is dependent upon you in the long term. The imperial-era French engaged in mercantilism as a matter of course, but so too did any up-and-coming industrial power. The British famously product-dumped on the Germans in the early 1800s, while the Germans did the same to anyone they could reach in the late 1800s. One could argue (fairly easily) that mercantilism was more or less the standard national economic operating policy for China in the 2000s and 2010s (under American strategic cover, no less).

In essence, both possible models would be implemented with an eye toward sucking other peoples dry, and transferring the pain of general economic dislocation from the invaders to the invaded. Getting a larger slice of a smaller pie, as it were. Both models might theoretically work in a poorer, more violent, more fractured world—particularly if they are married. But even together, some version of imperialist mercantilism faces a singular, overarching, likely condemning problem:

Too many guns, not enough boots.

In the old imperial (and mercantile) days, when the Brits (or Germans, or French, or Dutch, or Belgians, or Japanese, or Portuguese, or Spanish, or Argentines, etc.) showed up, they'd bring guns and artillery to regions whose peak military technologies were decidedly spear- and knife-driven. The newcomers didn't typically have to make too many examples of the locals before the locals decided it would be best if they did what they were told (assuming they survived long enough to have a decision to make). Possessing such a sharp and obvious technological edge meant the occupiers could maintain control with tiny overseas forces. The best example is probably the British Raj in India. The British typically had (far) fewer than 50,000 soldiers in their South Asian colony—sometimes fewer than 10,000—to a local population of over 200 *million*. At the typical *high* ratio of one occupier per 4,000 occupied, it would be as if the population of my hometown of Marshalltown, Iowa, tried to occupy the entirety of the United States west of the Mississippi.

In an era when one side was industrialized and the other was not, such a numerical imbalance could work. But as the Indians became more technologically sophisticated, the idea that the Brits could maintain control went from eyebrow-raising to inordinately hysterical in short order. It was only a matter of time and political will before the Indians sent the Brits packing.*

Today there are certainly parts of the world that are more industrialized (and better armed) than others, but there no longer is a nineteenth-century-style yawning chasm between an industrialized world and a preindustrial world. Consider how much fun the United States (a country near the head of the pack) had attempting to reshape Afghanistan (a country near the bottom). It doesn't take excellence in guns and railroads and asphalt and electricity and computers and phones to still *have* guns and railroads and asphalt and electricity and computers and phones.

The only countries in a post-2022 world that might be able to maintain an overseas empire are those that can have three things going for them: a serious cultural superiority complex, a military capable of reliably projecting power onto locations that cannot effectively resist, and lots and lots and *lots* and *LOTS* of disposable young people.

The last country that boasted that combination of factors was the United States in the World War II aftermath. America's rise in the 1800s and early 1900s was technological, geographic, demographic, and economic, but when the guns fell silent in 1945, the Yanks enjoyed technological, geographic, demographic, economic *and* military *and* strategic *and numerical* advantages. But even then, the Americans chose *not* to occupy the territory they had conquered—even when their potential subjects had welcomed them as liberators. Today we live in a world of accelerating demographic collapse. There are *no* countries who boast the mix of youth and reach necessary to project power out of their own neighborhood on a cost-effective, sustained basis.

The best that might be managed is a pre-deepwater era, regional empire set up with local superpowers dominating their neighborhoods in the rudest sort of way: via direct intimidation and/or conquering. And

---

*   #GandhiIsBadass.

even then, I have a hard time seeing this working for any countries aside from France or Turkey, countries who have stable demographic structures, strong industrial bases, and a very large tech edge over their possible future neo-colonies.* Anything more would be a numbers game that few countries in few places could even theoretically play, much less play well enough that the effort could pay for itself. The point of this discussion into possible economic models isn't to depress you (although in my opinion that's a perfectly reasonable takeaway), or even to put a finger on what outcome is most plausible.

Instead, it is to underline two outcomes:

First, *everything* is going to change. Whatever new economic system or systems the world develops will be something we're unlikely to recognize as being viable today. We will probably need far higher volumes of capital (retirees absorb it like sponges), but we'll have far less of it (fewer workers means fewer taxpayers). That suggests economic growth and technological progress (both of which require capital as an input) will stall out. And that's just one facet. Everything that capitalism and fascism and the rest were designed to balance or manage—supply, demand, production, capital, labor, debt, scarcity, logistics—isn't so much contorting as evolving into forms we have literally never experienced as a species. We are entering a period of extreme transformation, with our strategic, political, economic, technological, demographic, and cultural norms all in flux at the same time. *Of course* we will shift to a different management system.

Second, the process will be the very definition of traumatic. The concept of more has been our guiding light as a species for centuries. From a certain point of view, the past seventy years of globalization have simply been "more" on steroids, a sharp uptake on our long-cherished economic understandings. Between the demographic inversion and the end of globalization, we are not simply ending our long experience with more, or even beginning a terrifying new world of less; we face economic free fall

---

*   There are loads on the whys and the hows of these two countries' pasts, presents, and futures in my previous book, *Disunited Nations*.

as everything that has underpinned humanity's economic existence since the Renaissance unwinds all at once.

Between the collapse of the global Order and the inversion of global demographics, the old rules clearly don't work, and it will take us decades to figure out what *might*. Different countries will feel the old system breaking down at different speeds in different ways, and they will react to such stimuli using approaches shaped by their own strengths and weaknesses and cultures and geographic positions. Nor will developing a new -ism be done under controlled circumstances over a leisurely period. It will happen in the here and now of demographic and geopolitical collapse.

We are *not* going to get this right on our first try. We will *not* follow the same paths forward. We will *not* arrive at the same destination. It took our world *centuries* to suss out our current quartet of economic models. It is a process, and not one that proceeds in a predictable, sedate, straight line. The last time humanity struggled with changing factors that necessitated new economic models, the causes were the Industrial Revolution paired with the first globalization wave. We argued—vigorously—over which system might be best. We had fights. We had wars. We had *big* wars. Most were *not* Cold.

Living through history is messy.

MESSY, MESSY MODELS

Now that we all need a fleet of drinks, let's look at a couple of examples of what success *might* . . . resemble. For while our world has never experienced anything like what we're about to go through, some countries' demographic and geopolitical realities have forced them to deal with this transformation's leading edge sooner than the rest of us. There are a couple of places we can look to for inspiration. Or for goalposts. Or at least for land mines.

I have two for you to consider.

RUSSIA . . . AS A SUCCESS STORY

While everything in Russia is and always has been done in its own . . . peculiar way, it is undeniable that Russia was part of the first big batch of countries to industrialize: after the Brits and on a similar time frame to the Germans. The intertwined demographic and industrialization stories of the Russians and Germans, in fact, have been *the* story of Europe from the early 1800s right up to the current day.[*]

But whereas the Germans used the American-led Order to take a quantum leap up the value-added scale and turn their economy from an industrialized one to a more export-oriented, technocratic structure, the Soviet Union was the Order's *target* and so could do none of that. Instead, the Soviets went down the road of command-driven communism. Outside of the military realm, Russia simply could not keep up with the

---

[*]   *Disunited Nations* has an equally fat section on this intertwined pair as well.

technological dynamism of the American-led world. As the years stacked up into decades, the Soviet economy plateaued in terms of sophistication, and nearly all economic growth in the 1960s and 1970s wasn't from technology or productivity, but instead from an expansion of the working-age population. More inputs, more outputs.

To believe the Soviet Union would continue to function over the long haul, you had to believe that the Soviet population would continue growing, and *that* just wasn't in the cards. Between devastation in the world wars, Stalin's tender urbanization and collectivization efforts, broad-scale mismanagement under Khrushchev, and organizational stagnation under Brezhnev, the Soviet Union stopped generating sufficient numbers of new workers. By 1980 the demographic pipeline was already running dry . . . and then the bottom fell out. The trauma of the Soviet collapse was economic, cultural, political, strategic—and *demographic*. Between 1986 and 1994, the birth rate halved while the death rate nearly doubled. Russia today is deindustrializing at the same time its population is collapsing.

Dark? Yes, but Russia is probably one of the *best-case* scenarios for much of the industrialized world. Russia, after all, at least has ample capacity at home to feed and fuel itself in addition to sufficient nuclear weapons to make any would-be aggressor stop and think (a few dozen times) before launching an assault. In a world of constrained trade and capital, one could be in significantly more dire straits than still having strategic depth plus reasonably reliable food, fuel, and electricity.

But the gold standard in terms of preparing for a postgrowth life is elsewhere.

JAPAN: GROWING OLD GRACEFULLY

Japan has been on the path to demographic oblivion for more than five *decades*. Extreme urbanization has been the norm since World War II and there simply isn't enough space in Tokyo's omnipresent condos to easily raise families, much less families of size. The aging process is so deeply entrenched that some thirty *thousand* Japanese die in their apartments every year without anyone noticing until there's a . . . smell. Necessitating fumigation. Japan passed the point of no return in its demographic structure back in the 1990s, but rather than crawl into a hole and die, the Japanese government and corporate world have long since branched out in ways that reflect the country's underlying demographic weaknesses—*and* strengths.

Japanese firms realize their local demographics are wretched, but they also realize that building products en masse at home requires young workers that they no longer have, and that dumping said products on other markets is often construed as somewhat rude. So the Japanese have opted for something new: *de*sourcing.

Japanese firms have relocated much of their industrial productive capacity to *other countries*, where they use more abundant *local* workers to produce the goods that are then sold into those same *local* markets. Then some of the income from those sales flows back to Japan to sustain the (ever-aging) Japanese population. Design and technical and very high-end manufacturing work—the sort of work done by high-skilled, *older* workers—is kept in Japan, but almost the entirety of the rest of the manufacturing supply chain is located on the other side of national borders. In essence, the Japanese read the writing on the wall in the 1980s. They saw how their American security guarantor resented product dumping and started a multi-decade effort to instead manufacture goods within their target markets. In particular, this concept of "build where you sell" has become Toyota's new corporate mantra.

This new industrial model has enabled Japan to age with a degree of grace. But there are a couple of glaring problems.

First, Japan's economy has stalled. In inflation-adjusted terms, the Japanese economy was smaller in 2019 than it was in 1995. Part and parcel of not being able to build and sell with and to your own population is that you need to move some goalposts. Even outsized economic success in a postgrowth world just doesn't have much, well, growth.

Second, it is exceedingly unlikely that Japan's path is replicable. After all, the Japanese experience of 1980–2019 is in many ways unique.

- Japan's transformation to a postgrowth system occurred under ironclad American security cover. Tokyo never had to fear for its own physical protection *at home*. Contemporary America's disinterest indicates such cover will not be available for most countries.

- Corporate Japan faced no serious security threats *abroad*, in part because of the we're-all-friends-now nature of the post–Cold War environment, and in part because the Americans prevented any security threats from arising. The American departure from the world means that most countries—most *trade routes*—will be bereft of the sort of ironclad protection the Japanese evolved under.

- Japan's transformation occurred when its firms had access to global consumer markets, most notably the American market. Aging demographics aside, the American political system has turned sharply insular and America simply is *not* going to be keeping the world open for trade. America certainly won't keep the world open for dumping products on the American consumer market.

- Japan was wildly *wealthy* at the beginning of its transition. In per capita terms Japan became as wealthy as America in the late 1980s. All that industrial plant the Japanese built abroad had to be paid for, and the Japanese had to pay for it themselves, but they *could* pay for it themselves because while their demographics were turning, *they had not turned yet*. When the Japanese started desourcing in the 1990s, they still had roughly twenty years of a functional workforce to draw upon. Today there are precious few countries who can lay claim to such a positive starting point in terms of wealth, and none have a tax base or worker capacity that will last more than a decade.

- Japan's population is the world's most homogeneous, with more than 98 percent of the population being purely ethnically Japanese. That unity enabled social and economic transformations that would have triggered mass upheaval in more diverse populations.

- Japan is eminently defensible. Japan is an archipelago that has never been successfully invaded. Even the Americans were so daunted by the task of conquering the Home Islands that they opted to nuke

Hiroshima and Nagasaki to force surrender, rather than sending the Marines into the grinder. Point being: Japan's defensive needs in a world without American overwatch are manageable, and the Japanese navy is right-sized to the task of home defense.

- Finally, as with everything demographic, Japan had in spades the most critical asset: time. Economic transformation doesn't happen overnight. From the point that the old Japanese economic model broke in the 1989 stock and property market crashes, Japan had three *decades* to transition to what has become its new normal.

There are precious few countries who boast the skilled labor and capital to attempt desourcing like the Japanese model. Denmark, the Netherlands, the United Kingdom, Singapore, South Korea, and Taiwan come to mind. The European states on the list *might* be able to look after their own security with limited American help or perhaps a partnership with a more demographically stable France. As to the Asian states, they *might* be able to throw themselves at none other than Japan's mercy for their security overwatch.

But for all of them it would be a crapshoot as to where they'd desource *to*.

To a degree, the Western Europeans who form the original core of the European Union have tried this strategy with the Central Europeans whom they admitted to the Union in the 2000s. But on average the Central Europeans are aging even faster than the Western Europeans, so this strategy will collapse under its own weight in the 2020s. The Asian Tigers have the possibility of desourcing to the Southeast Asian nations, and indeed some of that has already occurred. But *none* of them have the military capacity to sustain such a relationship without extensive external assistance. With the notable exception of the United States, any country with a reasonably healthy demographic is more likely to be an economic and/or security *competitor* and therefore an unwise destination for their investment funds.

Shifting to a new system was always going to be painful, and most countries simply were never going to make the cut. When I started tinkering with the core ideas for this book back in 2016, I figured we'd have about fifteen years to figure things out. That's a laughably short amount of time to upend a half millennium of history, but it was better than nothing. But then, suddenly, tragically, horribly, in the opening weeks of 2020, all hope fled.

SCREW YOU, CORONAVIRUS

The coronavirus pandemic didn't simply rob us of lives. It robbed us of what we needed more than anything else to prepare for the coming demographic devastation. It robbed us of the one thing no one on Earth can make more of.

It robbed us of time.

In November 2019, the pathogen the world would come to know as the novel coronavirus-2019—COVID-19, or simply COVID, for short—began circulating in the Chinese province of Hubei. Hyper face-conscious local authorities suppressed reporting of rising infection rates. Even to their superiors. Even to *medical personnel*. While many governments at many levels have shown staggering levels of creativity in mismanaging the crisis in a staggering variety of ways a staggering number of times, it was this first decision to suppress information that transformed a local health concern into a global pandemic. COVID is the most infectious disease to break into the general population since measles, and COVID's fatality rate is five times higher. At the time of this writing (February 2022), over 300 million people globally have been diagnosed with COVID, with 6 million of them perishing.*

COVID spreads almost exclusively via respiratory exhalation, which, from an economic point of view, is as bad as it gets. HIV can be stopped

---

* National, to say nothing of global, statistics on COVID are muddled. It isn't (just) policy incompetence. Upwards of 40 percent of COVID cases are asymptomatic, so the true numbers of infections and deaths are undoubtedly much higher than these figures.

with condoms. Cancer isn't communicable. Heart disease is largely a life-style issue. Getting tetanus requires a wrestling match with barbed wire. But if you can spread or catch a health destroyer by *breathing*? We have a problem. People live indoors. Most business is done indoors. Most food is eaten indoors. Most transport modes are operated with closed windows. COVID reached into and threatened every aspect of our existence.

The only effective means of dealing with a respiratory disease is to limit contact. Masks help, but isolation helps more. COVID mitigation efforts didn't shut *everything* down, but *wow*, did it sucker-punch most econo-mies over and over and over again.

The outcomes of such an easily spread pathogen are legion, but for our purposes four stand out:

First, decreased and inhibited contact among people translates directly into decreased and inhibited economic activity, or, as it is known by its technical name: a recession. By August 2020 it was clear the downturn wasn't going to be a one-off, but instead would persist until such time as the general population achieved herd immunity. By the time we reached October 2021 we learned that the immune response generated from suf-fering through COVID's then-dominant delta variant varied wildly in the protection it generated, but more important, for some such protection lasted only a handful of weeks. We learned that vaccination was the only reasonable way to go.* Luckily, a series of vaccines started hitting the market in December 2020, but between vaccine hesitancy and manufac-turing limitations, the bulk of the advanced world wasn't able to reach the 90 percent vaccination threshold necessary to prevent community trans-mission in 2021, and new variants kept moving the goal posts for what "success" meant.

Second, the very nature of our economic "normal" cavitated. Every one of the top thirty economies experienced lockdown and disruption. Direct recessions were bad enough, but the disruption to lifestyle changed

---

*   Or at least, most of us came to that conclusion.

the portfolio of goods everyone consumed: fewer services, more goods, and more of very specific sorts of goods like electronics and computing products. With every lockdown and/or opening, our consumption portfolio shifted, and with every lockdown and/or opening, manufacturers the world over attempted to shift their efforts to meet the altered demand. Each such effort required more workers, more investment, and more time. Put technically, each effort was wildly inflationary . . . at a time when more and more Baby Boomers were taking retirement and moving on to fixed incomes. At the time of this writing, in early 2022, the world's industrialists are on their *ninth* COVID-related retooling.

Third, if the goal was economic stability, the parts of the world that somehow escaped COVID were . . . the wrong parts. Sub-Saharan Africa did reasonably well, but to be blunt, in most of the region life expectancy is simply too low to have many people aged over seventy. (More than half of all coronavirus deaths are in those aged seventy-five or over, so the demographic that most suffers from the disease simply doesn't exist en masse.) The second region was East Asia, where quick and competent government responses crushed caseloads. Unfortunately for the global system, sub-Saharan Africa is a minor player, collectively generating only 1.9 percent of global gross domestic product (GDP), while *all* East Asian economies are export-led. It didn't matter much to global consumption if they weren't infected. They had lost markets to sell to.

Fourth, unrelated issues intensified during the coronavirus crisis to further fracture global connections. Specifically, the Trump administration was prosecuting a trade war with China, while China was descending into narcissistic nationalism. Both nudged all consumption-led systems—the United States included—to bring as much of their manufacturing needs in-house as possible. Whether for reasons of nationalistic fear, populism, health, national security, politics, or jobs, the complex supply chains that had increasingly dominated the manufacturing sector for decades aggressively unwound.

At the time of this writing, COVID already has disrupted the consumption-led part of the world for over two *years*. The export-led part of the world was going to slide from export-led to postgrowth in the 2020s regardless, with most of said sliding occurring in the decade's first half. COVID weakened the connections between export-led and consumption-led economies; this hived most consumption-led economies off into their own partially sequestered worlds, while simultaneously denying the export-led economies of the export sales they needed to fuel their systems *and* the transition time they needed to adapt their systems to whatever comes after globalization.

The globalization game is not simply ending. It is already over. Most countries will *never* return to the degree of stability or growth they experienced in 2019. And now most have lost the chance to even *try* to shift onto a newer, more appropriate footing.

The key word in that last sentence, of course, is "most."

THE LAST BITS OF MORE

There are precious few countries who against all odds have kept the demographic torch burning. Life for them will change, too, but not nearly as quickly or drastically or negatively. The one that matters more than all others combined is the United States.

THE AMERICAN MORE, PART 1: GEOGRAPHY

Let's start with all the rote geographic and strategic stuff.

- The United States has more high-quality, temperate-zone, arable farmland than any other country and its entire agricultural supply chain is contained within North America. This makes the United States the world's largest agricultural producer and exporter. Food security is a complete nonissue.
- America has more land suitable for habitation—reasonable climate, relatively flat, good water access, lack of pests, etc.—than any country in the world. In terms of usable land per person, the United States could probably support a population *double* its current 330 million before feeling crowded.
- Moving things around on water costs roughly one-twelfth that of moving them around on land. Courtesy of omnipresent internal waterways—more than the combined total of the rest of the world—the United States has lower internal transport costs than anyone else.[*]

---

[*] It would be even better if the Americans could get their internal regulatory structure untangled.

- Courtesy of the shale revolution, not only is the United States the world's largest oil producer, enabling it to be net oil-independent, but by-products of its shale oil production have granted it the lowest unsubsidized electricity costs in the world.
- The United States is the first-world country closest to the equator, granting it more solar power potential than any other country, while the positioning of its mountains compared to its coasts gives it more wind power potential than any other country. Green- or fossil-driven, electricity supply will never be an American problem.
- Cheaper inputs—whether in the form of land or energy—helped trigger a massive reindustrialization process in America as early as 2010. That's given the United States a head start on the broad-scale industrial reshufflings that will dominate the global breakdowns of the 2020s.
- The United States has not faced a security threat from within the North American continent since the 1840s. Deserts and mountains make an invasion from the south simply impossible, while lakes and forests (and a 10-to-1 demographic imbalance) limit the very concept of an invasion from the north to the realm of low-animation-quality, expletive-heavy film.*
- Instead of hostility, the Americans have worked with the Canadians and Mexicans to form an integrated manufacturing space and trade zone. The expanded economies of scale allow for a regional manufacturing footprint that is world-class in terms of both quality and cost.
- The Atlantic and Pacific Oceans make the United States all but immune to extra-hemispheric invasion. Very few countries have *any* vessels that can even cross an ocean unaided. Should anyone want to take a crack at America, they'd have to first get past the U.S. Navy, which is ten times as powerful as the *combined* navies of the rest of the world.†

---

*   They killed Kenny! You bastards!
†   And the world's second- and third-most powerful long-range navies—those of Japan and the United Kingdom—are allied.

- America has nukes. Thousands of them. In a rock-paper-scissors-lizard-Spock-nuke contest, nukes win every single time.

Bottom line: in a world without more, the United States not only still has plenty, it has *the capacity to keep it.*

But even better than that, to this point the Americans largely have managed to escape much of the global development and demographic trap.

THE AMERICAN MORE, PART 2: THE BOOMERS AND THE MILLENNIALS

Of the 17 million American men—more than 20 percent of the American male population—who fought overseas in World War II, all but 400,000 came home. And they came home ready to get on with their lives. The GI Bill helped them get educations. The Eisenhower Interstate Act of 1956 enabled the national road systems that enabled the former soldiers to settle anywhere. New programs for home loans enabled the young veterans to purchase or build their first homes and in doing so, combined with the new Interstate Highway System, launched what we now know as the suburbs.

All these new government programs were in many ways the first of their kind for Americans. Most were launched for fear of a repeat of the economic disaster that followed the last time several million American soldiers returned from war. After World War I the soldiers' sudden return had flooded the labor market, generating such massive oversupply that it triggered a deflationary spiral, which contributed to the Great Depression.

A core rationale for the new programs was to use government spending to alternatively mop up all that labor, or ship the now-former soldiers off to university for a few years to defer the pain. Many debated (and still debate) the pros and cons of so permanently expanding the government's footprint, but it is undeniable that with all these pieces in place, America experienced the greatest baby boom of its history. Between war's end and 1965, more than 70 million births occurred in a country that before the war had under 135 million souls. The horror of the Baby Boomers was unleashed upon us all.

There is no end of stories to tell about America's Boomer generation. They are the ones who came of age during the 1970s, creating what passes for American culture. Disco? Their fault. They are the ones who crafted the American welfare state, and from it their in-progress retirement has broken the federal budget. They are the ones who grew up in the shadow of the new manufacturing complexes that sprouted up after World War II, when the rest of the world was wrecked, and then watched bitterly as those same facilities relocated as the rest of the world recovered under the Order. From Vietnam to Afghanistan, from Johnson to Trump, from civil rights to long commutes, from the sexual revolution to technological invalidity, their collective decisions and foibles have determined precisely *what* America *is*.

Most of the rest of the world had a Boomer generation as well, and for similar formulative reasons. War's end plus the dawning of the new (mostly war-free) age under American sponsorship enabled most governments to busy themselves with their people's lives without needing to burden themselves with the task of national defense. European governments in particular spent a lot more time and energy trying to make their people's lives comfortable, and a lot less trying to kill all their neighbors. Many countries the world over developed—and experienced the same reductions in mortality of the more advanced states—for the first time. Populations expanded everywhere.

But relative to prewar populations, the American Boomers were a far larger cadre than their global peers. Even 170 years after independence and with a thirty-fold expansion in population, the Americans *still* enjoyed a *lot* of open land. The Americans were still growing into the territories made vacant by the eradication of the natives. Lots of useful land meant the Boomers enjoyed lots of low-cost, high-payout opportunities. In contrast, Europe had reached its lands' carrying capacity decades previous and there just wasn't much in the way of internal frontiers. Even in the newly developing countries, the countryside wasn't exactly teeming with unused territories.

But that was then, and this is now. As we enter the 2020s, the Boomers are a largely spent demographic force. Calendar years 2022 and 2023 are when the majority of the world's Boomers will have turned sixty-five and so shifted into retirement.

This generates a double hit to labor markets. The Baby Boomers are the largest-ever generation, so their absence is hugely impactful in numerical terms. They are also the oldest economically active generation, meaning that their numbers comprise the bulk of all available skilled labor. Remove so many high-skilled workers in a short period of time and labor shortages and labor inflation are a foregone conclusion for years to come.

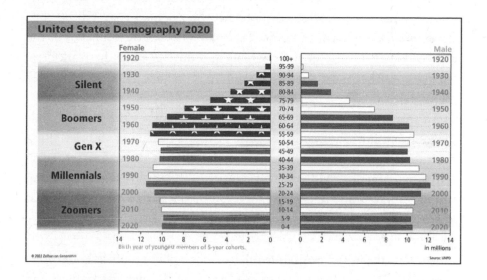

The next generation down is Generation X, a group that watched the trials and travails of their predecessors and . . . did not like what they saw. There were so many Baby Boomers that when they entered the market they outcompeted each other for wages, suppressing labor costs. This forced many Boomers to decide that two-income households were the only way to scrape by. That not only depressed labor costs more, but introduced considerable stress into interpersonal relationships, resulting in the Baby Boomers' high divorce rate. Gen X has attempted to avoid this outcome, to a degree. Gen X is far more likely to have single-income households compared to their elders, as they value their time at least as much as their money.

Generation X was already a smaller generation, and was never going to be able to fill the cavernous hole caused by the Boomers' departure, but with lower labor rate participation, the result will be a far larger labor shortage. That's *great* for Gen X—those who choose to work will have the best pricing power of any workforce to date!—but it is a bit of a disaster for the labor market writ large.

At the bottom of the scale are the Zoomers. They are eager workers, but very few exist. The Zoomers are the children of Gen X. A small generation generates a small generation. All the Zoomers that will be born have *already* been born, and even if they *all* follow in the footsteps of the Baby Boomers instead of their parents and they *all* enter the workforce, there are nowhere near enough of them to round out the labor force. *For the next two decades.*

To this point—Boomers, Gen Xers, and Zoomers—the picture holds globally, but now it diverges, because America's Boomers did one thing their global peers did not. They had kids. A *lot* of them. Say what you will about America's Millennial generation—and yes, there is a *lot* we can say—they have something going for them that nearly no other Millennial cadre globally does.

They *exist.*

Overall, the American Millennial demographic group falls into two categories. The first match the stereotype of entitlement and laziness and taking an extended adolescence between college and entering the workforce. The second . . . got screwed: they attempted to be adults, but got sideswiped by the combination of Boomers squeezing them out of the workforce, and the mass unemployment triggered by the 2007–09 financial crisis. Regardless of bucket, the Millennials lost *years* of meaningful work experience, and today are the *least* skilled of *any* equivalent age cohort in modern American history.

But they are *many.* The American Millennials are already the largest demographic in the workforce by number. That's great. That's *essential.*

But the real hope is with their *children*. The American Millennials' numbers raise the possibility that they will have enough children to someday fill the labor gap. But the soonest that will happen is when those children enter the labor force . . . a process that will not begin until the mid-*2040s*. And there is still risk here: there's the not-so-minor issue that the Millennials must first *have* those children. At present, birth rates for Millennials are the lowest in American history.

So for the United States, the Millennials for all their imperfections are rounding out the labor force to a degree. An insufficient degree by many measures, but the Millennials' very existence is both a plus now and a source of hope for later.

Beyond the United States, the picture is *much* darker, for the simple reason that most of the world's Boomer cohort didn't have kids. The reasons for this lack of reproduction vary greatly from place to place. East Asia was already densely populated; mass urbanization didn't help. Most of Europe spent its money on technical upgrades rather than making it easier to raise families. Canada is so cold everyone flocked to cities for warmth as soon it was an option, and apartments are the ultimate downsizing factor for family size no matter where they are located or why people live in them.

So, yes, American Boomers aging into mass retirement *will* break the bank. But between their smaller relative size as compared to global norms and their offspring's increasing contribution to the government's bottom line, their financial hammer blows are nothing compared to the meteor swarm of challenges that will utterly destroy the governing systems of countries as diverse as China, Korea, Japan, Thailand, Brazil, Germany, Italy, Poland, Russia, and Iran. Meanwhile, American Millennials' very existence means the United States will at least in part recover from its financial crunch in the 2030s, and probably its labor crunch in the 2040s. But for the rest of the world, it will never get better than it was in the 2010s. Never.

The Americans will have a small amount of company:

France, in a conscious, sustained effort to outpopulate West Germany, became one of the world's most family-friendly nations. Sweden's version of social democracy entails cradle-to-grave family support. New Zealand brims with elbow room, and in a (faint) shadow of Australian and American policy in eras past, deliberately reduced options for its own indigenous population in order to increase options for whites. But these three countries, plus the United States, are the exceptions that define the rule. Everyone else's Boomers failed to procreate to anything close to replacement levels. Six decades later, the global Millennial cadre of the advanced world is simply too small to even theoretically keep their nationalities in existence over the long haul.

Back-of-the-envelope math done by folks who live in the intersection of demographics and statistics (which looks a lot like calculus to me) suggests that places with fair-to-crappy demographics, like Spain, the United Kingdom, or Australia, will suffer a drag on their annual growth of about 2 percent of GDP annually. The truly terminal demographics of Germany, Italy, Japan, Korea, and China are looking at at least 4 percent, while the youngish populations of America and France will only suffer about a 1 percent reduction. Add that up for just a single decade and it is difficult to imagine how the "inevitable rise" of places like Germany and China can even *survive*, much less function, much less dominate.

Best yet, there is more to the Americans' more.

THE AMERICAN MORE, PART 3: CULTURE

The United States is one of the world's four settler states, which is a pseudo-technical term indicating that most Americans can trace their lineage to folks who aren't from what is currently American territory. On the front end in the 1700s and 1800s, these would-be Americans arrived *young*. Fogies and biddies couldn't (and wouldn't) put up with the sort of cramped conditions required for a multi-week sail across an ocean. That meant that upon arrival they were (a) less likely to die of old age, (b) more likely to immediately start having a lot of kids, (c) able to expand into all kinds of open land, and (d) reinforced by *more* young settlers in the next ship in the queue at Ellis Island. It added up to a very young, very rapidly growing demographic. Sure, this was all well over a century ago, but the echoes of demographic trends last a long time. (Contemporary Russia is only now reaping the poor demographic harvest of World War I and Stalin's pre–World War II purges.)

As a settler state, the United States tends to be far more confident in its political identity as well as friendly to immigration than other countries. To the point that the United States is one of only a very few countries that even publicly publishes data on how many of its citizens were born in another country. Everywhere else, even the process of collecting (much less reporting) such data falls somewhere between politically destabilizing and treasonous. This shouldn't come as a shock; with the exception of the indigenous population, no Americans are actually from America. Inward migration has ebbed and flowed over the decades based on U.S. and global economic conditions and gyrations within American political culture, but as a rule it is significantly higher than nearly every country in the world as a percentage of the overall citizenry.

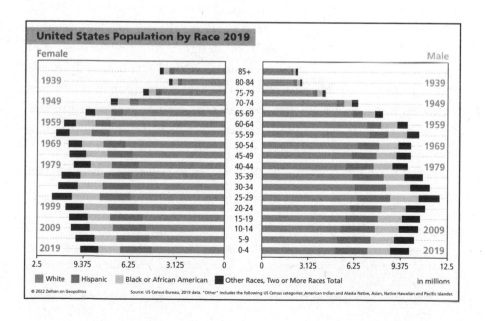

United States Population by Race 2019

In large part it has to do with the nature of national identities. Most countries are nation-states: their governments exist to serve the interests of a specific ethnicity (the nation) in a specific territory (the state). France for the French, Japan for the Japanese, China for the Chinese, and so on. In nation-states the central government tends to be the first and last word as to policy, because it *knows* whose interests it exists to serve. The technical term for such governments is *unitary*.

But not all governments are nation-states. Some are composed of different peoples residing in different geographies who each have their own local authorities, yet, due to the vicissitudes of history, war, necessity, and luck, have cobbled together a common administration. The result is a hybridized system with different, tiered levels of government—typically local, regional, and national—each with different rights, authorities, and responsibilities. Some, like Canada, Brazil, Switzerland, or Bosnia, are such loose associations that their national governments are really barely even governments in name: they are *confederal*. In others—like the United States, India, or Australia—the balances among the various levels is roughly equal: they are *federal.*

The takeaway from all this political blah-blah-blah is that in the United States the federal government—that's the one headquartered in Washington, D.C.—was expressly *not* designed to serve the interest of any specific ethnicity. Even adherents of critical race theory fully admit that the politically and economically dominant group in the United States—white Caucasians—are themselves a blend of peoples of English, German, Irish, Italian, French, Polish, Scottish, Dutch, Norwegian, Swedish, and Russian descent (in that order).

This relatively loose definition of what being "American" means makes

---

* Germany is a federal system as well, although not by choice. After World War II ended the Allies *wrote Germany's constitution for it*. The result was a constitutional structure purposely designed to hobble quick national decision making and in specific to prevent the Germans from going all Highlander on their neighbors. So far, so good.

it far easier for the United States in specific, the settler states in general, and in the broadest definition any federal or confederal system, to absorb rafts of new immigrants. In unitary systems, new migrants need to be *invited* to join the dominant culture. Failing that, they become an underclass. But in the United States, new migrants are often allowed to *define themselves* as members of the broader community.

In the world to come that'll be a helluva handy characteristic. With the world's consumption-led economies taking responsibility for more and more of their own production and becoming more and more insular, there simply won't be many economic opportunities for working-age adults living in export-led systems, much less postgrowth systems. Even if such weakening countries survive, their workers will have a choice between steadily higher tax rates to support their aging populations, or leaving. Expect a lot of the world's remaining labor—especially its high-skilled labor—to soon be knocking on America's door. With every such relocation, America's position vis-à-vis everyone else improves.

And even beyond the mechanics of immigration, the Americans have one final trump card.

THE AMERICAN MORE, PART 4: MEXICO

Part of the Mexico factor is obvious: in 2021 the average Mexican was nearly ten years younger than the average American. As a direct source of migrants, the Mexicans scratch several American itches. Mexican in-migration has held down the average age of Americans, kept semi- and unskilled labor costs under control, and filled out the broader demographic—especially in regions like the Deep South, which without Mexican inflows would suffer a demographic structure similar to that of rapidly aging Italy.

Part of the Mexico factor is a less-than-obvious reason: manufacturing integration. The Mexican system isn't as capable at providing electricity, education, and infrastructure to its people. This pushes down not only

Mexican wages, but Mexican skill sets and Mexican worker productivity. Any multi-stage manufacturing system will have steps that are highly technical as well as those that are highly *un*technical. Melting bauxite is easier than extruding aluminum. Snapping together the pieces of a computer is easier than coding software. Trenching ground is easier than manufacturing the cable laid in the aforementioned trench. Matching tasks to skill sets—aka division of labor—enables maximum production at a minimum of costs. Globalized supply chains are all about tapping different skill sets and labor cost structures to generate the most economically efficient outcomes. Few places are as lucky as the United States and Mexico in having the perfect *technical* complement *right next door.*

Part of the Mexico factor is downright counterintuitive. The dominant ethnic group in Mexico originates from Spain, while the dominant "ethnic" group in the United States is white Caucasian. In *Mexican* eyes, that isn't all that different. Mexicans of Spanish descent somewhat look down on Mexicans of indigenous descent, and they feel more or less the same way about Central American migrants as Americans do. Once Mexicans migrate to the United States, they assimilate quickly. It's fairly common for second-generation Mexican-Americans—and nearly reflexive for fourth-generation Mexican-Americans—to define themselves as *white*. Within their own social strata, Mexican-Americans have redefined "white" from an exclusive term that refers to "them" and especially "those gringos" to an inclusive term meaning not simply "us" but "*all* of us."

America's assimilative capacity has proven to work on Mexicans even better than it has on previous waves of migrants. In *all* cases, American English tends to rub out the migrants' language within two to three generations. In the case of Mexican-Americans, however, it rarely takes more than one. In contemporary times, Mexican-Americans are the most enthusiastic seekers of the American Dream, not just economically, but *culturally*.

Of course, it isn't all sunshine and tacos.

For all the economic and financial and demographic advantages of in-migration, cultures can only absorb so many so quickly and in the 2010s and early 2020s sometimes it feels as if America has hit its limit. It is more than simply a gut feeling. A peek at the data suggests why:

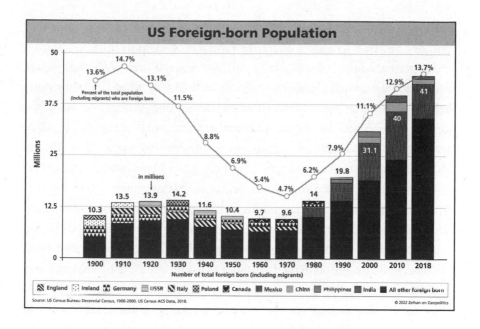

US Foreign-born Population

Percent of the total population (including migrants) who are foreign born

in millions

Number of total foreign born (including migrants)

England | Ireland | Germany | USSR | Italy | Poland | Canada | Mexico | China | Philippines | India | All other foreign born

Source: US Census Bureau Decennial Census, 1900-2000. US Census ACS Data, 2018.

© 2022 Zeihan on Geopolitics

In-migration to the United States hit a relative historical low in the 1970s—the decade in which America's Boomers came of age. For Boomers—an overwhelmingly white demographic—their primary experience with interracial politics was the civil rights movement, a movement that involved people who *were already here* at a time when the Boomers were young and politically liberal.

In-migration then rose steadily until reaching a near-historical high (again, in relative terms) in the 2010s, at which point the Boomers were nearing retirement and in doing so becoming politically . . . stodgy. In each and every decade as the Boomers aged, the largest single immigrant group was *always* Mexican. In the minds of many Boomers, Mexicans have long been not simply the "other," but the "other" that has arrived *in ever-larger numbers.* A big reason why so many Boomers have been so supportive of nativist politicians such as Donald Trump is that their feelings of shock at the pace of change in American society is not a collective hallucination. It is firmly backed up by reality.

This is one piece of the kaleidoscope of why American politics has turned so sharply insular in the 2010s and early 2020s. But regardless of what you think about Boomers or Mexicans or race or trade or assimilation or borders, there are a couple of thoughts to keep in mind:

First, the Mexicans *are already in the United States.* Whether you're concerned with what American culture feels like or what the labor market looks like, the great Mexican wave has not only come, it is *over.* Net migration of Mexicans to the United States peaked in the early 2000s and it has been *negative for twelve of the thirteen years since 2008.* Just as industrialization and urbanization pushed down birth rates in the developed world, the same process has begun in Mexico, just a few decades later. Today's Mexican demographic structure suggests it will never again be a net large-scale contributor to American migration. Most of the big migrant flows into the United States since 2014 have instead been from the near-failed Central American states of Honduras, El Salvador, and Guatemala.*

Second, even among the most nativist strains of American political thinking, room has been found for Mexicans. In just two years, none other than Donald Trump went from openly condemning Mexican migrants as rapists and "bad hombres" to embracing Mexico in trade and security deals that took bilateral relations to their friendliest and most productive in the history of both republics. Part and parcel of Trump's renegotiation of the NAFTA accords were clauses that expressly aim to bring manufacturing back to North America. Not to the United States specifically, but to *any* signatory of the accords. Team Trump added those clauses with Mexico expressly in mind.

On the other side of the equation, Mexican-Americans are turning *nativist.* The demographic in the United States that consistently polls the most anti-migration is not white Americans, but instead (non-first-generation) Mexican-Americans. They want family reunification, but

---

*   The collective demographics of this trio is going through the same birth rate collapse as Mexico, just a few years behind. One way or another, there aren't going to be large numbers of would-be immigrants walking to the United States much longer.

only for their own families. Never forget that anti-migrant, build-the-wall Donald Trump carried nearly every county on the southern border when running for *re*election in 2020.

Third, America and Mexico still have something most others don't: more. And they certainly have more more together.

There *are* some clouds on the horizon. While it is aging slowly, the American population is still aging. And while Mexicans are young, they are aging faster than Americans. At some point in the mid-2050s, the average Mexican is highly likely to be older than the average American.

But even in the worst-case scenario—demographically speaking—the United States has something hardly anyone else has in the world of Disorder we're all falling into: time.

While others must figure out how to unwind and rewire their systems, to design and implement a new -ism in just a few years, the Americans and Mexicans have *decades*. At least until the 2050s. There is something to be said for being a late bloomer: Americans and their Mexican partners will be able to look across the world and learn from what everyone else tried.

But perhaps the most notable takeaway isn't that the Americans (in league with the Mexicans) face the least traumatic adjustment to the world-which-soon-will-be, but instead that the future of the world is American.

The math is pretty simple: America's population is more than young enough that even without Mexico or inward migration, its population can keep growing for at least a few decades.

IT'S THE END OF THE WORLD AS WE KNOW IT . . .

Compare that to China. China's population path turned terminal two decades ago. Based on whose statistics you're using, the average Chinese citizen aged past the average American citizen sometime between 2017 and 2020. China's labor force and *overall population peaked* in the 2010s. In the best-case scenario, the Chinese population in the year 2070 will be less than half of what it was in 2020. More recent data that's leaked out of the Chinese census authority suggests that date may need to be pulled forward to 2050. China's collapse has *already* begun.

That particular bit of arithmetic doesn't even begin to take into account what will happen to global (and Chinese) mortality levels once globalization is firmly in the rearview mirror. Most of the world (China included) imports the vast majority of its energy as well as the inputs used to grow its food. Most of the world (China included) is dependent upon trade to keep its population not simply wealthy and healthy, but *alive*. Remove that and global (and Chinese) mortality levels *will* rise even as baked-in demographic trends mean birth rates will *continue* to fall.

Between demographic collapse in much of the world and demographic stability in the United States, America's share of the total global population is certain to increase within just the next couple of generations— probably by more than half. *And* America will retain control of the global oceans. *And* the Americans will have time to adapt their system. *And* the rest of the world is likely to brawl over the shattered remnants of a collapsed economic system.

At the time of this writing in 2022, I am forty-eight. I don't expect to be fully functional in the 2050s when this new world fully shakes out. What the world looks like over the horizon, what the world looks like when the Americans fully and finally reengage, is going to have to be a project for another time. Instead, the purpose of this book is to lay out what our transition looks like. What the world we are all going to live through is going to *feel* like. How do the things we know and understand about food and money and fuel and movement and widgets and the stuff we dig out of the ground change? Grow, rearrange.

Fail.

So, with that in mind, let's talk about life after the end of the world.

A QUICK NOTE FROM THE AUTHOR . . . AND MOSCOW

Publishing schedules are a bit weird. Let's assume you either recently assassinated a couple major world leaders or are Oprah. *Everyone* wants to hear what you have to say. Even then, from the point you finish jotting down your thoughts, the necessities of editing, copyediting, proofing, printing, and distribution mean it'll be at least five months before your book hits the stands.

I'm no Oprah (or assassin), so there is a necessary lag between my writing of this book and your reading (or listening to me read) these words. Our production and editorial teams have been racing nothing less than the return of history to get this book out as soon as possible, but as I'm sure you are aware, in some respects we've failed. We submitted the final final *final* version of this manuscript on February 16, 2022. Russia launched a full invasion of Ukraine less than two weeks later, and this book will not be released until June 14.

It is entirely possible there will be additional major disruptions between the writing of this note on February 28, 2022, and when you ingest these words. I'm eyeing the potential collapse of Chinese Communist Party Chairman Xi Jinping's cult of personality *very* closely. But such ongoing disruptions are less a bug and more a feature of the world we are already devolving into. The delaying actions that have kept history stuck are gone, and we are all advancing—rapidly—into the next age.

Best of luck to us all.

SECTION II:
TRANSPORT

THE LONG, LONG ROAD

Let's start with kimchi quesadillas.

I'm a big fan of fusion food. Hot-and-sour bacon. Breakfast pizza. Enchilasagna. Caramel cheesecake wontons. Pineapple burgers. Crème brûlée pavlova. Butter duck poutine. Bring. It. *On!*

Now, this may come as a surprise, but you can't just go to a grocery store and purchase a ready-made sushi corndog dish from the freezer section. (Very sad.) What you *can* do is purchase ground polenta, flour, Himalayan salt, green peppercorns, turbinado sugar, cholesterol-free eggs in a carton, sushi-grade tuna, rice vinegar, hothouse cucumbers, smoked salmon, wasabi, mayo, nori sheets, multicolor carrots, ginger, miso paste, soy sauce, sesame seeds, and safflower oil.

The average grocery store today has about forty *thousand* individual items, up from about two hundred at the dawn of the twentieth century. The humble grocery is a technological miracle that enables me to source nearly anything I need from anywhere, anytime I feel the need to experiment with some new wild-ass crazy cuisine combo.[*] Swedish? Thai? Moroccan? Out of season? No problem. The inputs are hardly ever out of stock, and are almost always available at prices that are not prohibitive. It isn't simply availability and low cost; it's *reliable* availability and *reliably* low cost.

Take this concept of utter availability, apply it to *absolutely everything*, and you now have a glimmer of the absolute connectivity that underpins the modern, globalized economy. The ingredients of today's industrial and consumer goods are only available because they can be moved from—

---

[*]   Fun fact: my Thanksgiving spread is *legendary*.

literally—halfway around the world at low costs and high speeds and in perfect security. Phones, fertilizers, oil, cherries, propylene, single-malt whiskey . . . you name it, it is in motion. All. The. Time. Transportation is the *ultimate* enabler.

Most technologies do not fundamentally change us. Consider the contemporary smartphone. It's a flashlight, a music player, a camera, a game console, a fare card, a remote control, a library, a television, a cookbook, a computer—all in one. It hasn't enabled us to do much that's fundamentally new, but it has combined more than a dozen preexisting devices into one, increasing efficiency and access. Important? Ridiculously. But such improvement-based techs do not fundamentally change *who we are*.

Transport technologies, on the other hand, profoundly alter our relationship with our geography. Today you can jump continents in a few hours. It wasn't always this way. In fact, it was almost *never* this way. Until a couple hundred years ago, it was rare for any of us to venture more than a few miles from home. The six millennia of human history has quite literally been a slow, agonizing crawl along a long, long road.

Understand the evolutions and revolutions in how we've traveled from A to B, understand the connectivity that has made our modern grocery stores and smartphones possible, and you can understand why our world is shaped the way it is.

And what wonders and terrors the coming decades will hold for us all.

THE AGONY OF THE PHYSICS OF TRANSPORT

The human body is a frail and ridiculously inefficient form of transporting goods.

Imagine you are any random human from the time of our first emergence as *Homo sapiens* to about the mid-1700s. Unfortunately for you, your legs are likely your only means of transportation. Wheelbarrows did not become a big deal until about 100 CE. Carts were too expensive for the average peasant until centuries later, even if there were roads to drag them upon. Even waiting around for something as old-school as a bicycle would have kept you twiddling your thumbs until the late eighteenth century (mid-nineteenth if you wanted pedals). There are good reasons traders still use camels even *today*.

For most people, your life, your town, and your livelihood were circumscribed by how far you were willing to walk in a day with a crushing load on your back.

That kept towns small. Before industrial techs remade the world, "urban" areas required nearly a half an acre of farmland per resident to prevent starvation—over seven times the land we use today, plus another *one hundred* times as much area in forestland to produce charcoal to cook and see the population through the winter. It made cities *stay* small. Grow too big and either a) food must come from too far away (in other words, you starve), or b) you cut down your forests to grow more food locally and the cutting-edge technology of the day—fire—is denied you (you starve while also freezing to death).

Wheels helped, but not as much as you might think. I'm sure you've all heard about Rome's famous roads being one of the greatest achievements of the premodern age. A few points of perspective:

Rome's roads stretched from Glasgow to Marrakech to Baghdad to Odessa, and were roughly equivalent in total length to the roads of modern-day . . . Maine. The Roman road network took six *centuries*—one *billion* labor-days—to construct, to say nothing of maintenance.

The very concept of "trade" was dubious. You couldn't call ahead to see if the next town over actually *needed* what you had to sell . . . and then there's the problem of spoilage. You simply couldn't carry enough *food* to make long-distance trade viable for anything but the most valuable items.

Concrete and asphalt, chemical preservatives and refrigeration are only a few of those pesky industrial-era technologies that didn't come around until the 1800s. Efficient, regular *overland* transport for bulk goods, even over relatively short distances, was not just difficult but also economically impossible for just about all of human history.

Even *breadbaskets* could not reliably feed themselves. Between 1500 and 1778, France suffered several national famines (and dozens of regional famines). Yes, *that* France—the country that has been Europe's largest and most reliable food producer stretching back a millennium, the country that has *three SEPARATE* agricultural regions, the country that had, bar none, *the* best internal transport system of the preindustrial world.

Moving things overland *sucks*.

So we figured out how to move stuff a different way. We figured out how to float.

While a camel could move a quarter ton and ox-drawn carts around a ton, even the earliest bulk ships could move several *hundred* tons at a fraction of the price per ton. The Romans famously imported most of their capital's food from Egypt. Remember those better-than-world-class Roman roads? In 300 CE it cost more to move grain 70 miles on those roads than it did to sail it some 1,400 miles from Egypt to Rome. The economics of water transport were so lopsided that some cultures (see: government; Dutch, Aztec, Chinese) would rearrange their entire governing systems around the capacity to mobilize labor to dig canals stretching hundreds of miles through rocky, undulating landscapes with little more than stone picks. All to float what was the pinnacle of human transport technology well into the second millennium CE: the lowly barge.

By the fourteenth century, history *finally* started picking up speed: Sails and nails, oars and rudders, holds and decks, guns and artillery, compasses and astrolabes. And crazy. Don't neglect a liberal infusion of crazy. The fabled Western discovery of the great monsoon winds was made by some Greek maniac willing to sail to the middle of the ocean with no idea what would happen next. Take it all together, and newer, larger, sturdier, faster, better-armed ships brought us into the deepwater age at the end of the fifteenth century.

Of course, that's the comfortable way to look at it from the far side of the Industrial Revolution.

TRANSPORT IN THE DEEPWATER AGE:
BETTER, FASTER, CHEAPER, SAFER . . .
BUT NOT GOOD, FAST, CHEAP, OR SAFE ENOUGH

Just because humanity now *could* ship goods long distances didn't mean we did so very *often*.

Post-deepwater but preindustrial shipments of grain from the Baltic region to continental Western Europe were hardly a regular affair. Even if Anglo-Dutch disputes didn't cut into deliveries, even if the Swedes didn't go all Viking on your ships, even if the Polish-Lithuanian Commonwealth was having a rare good day, half of the end-product cost typically still came from transport, with another quarter being racked up as storage fees. Grains produced in the interior, no matter how productive the land, tended to stay there. By the late 1700s the American colonists–cum–independent Americans *did* ship *some* grains across the Atlantic, but it was hardly a steady flow. Few things sucked more than making the grueling, six-week trip only to discover that England had had a bumper harvest.

Yet even as ships became more efficient, the intersection of technology and geopolitics left the world divided.

Geopolitics demanded that no empire buy food from any other. Even in the rare cases when shipping was thought reliable, the moods and appetites of opposing monarchs were most assuredly not. Geopolitics demanded that food shipments were rarely worth either the cost or the risk. But jade, pepper, cinnamon, porcelain, silk, and tobacco? Totes! It helped (a lot) that most luxury goods were not perishable. Tea was about as lowbrow a product there was to reliably make the cut.*

The luxuries "trade" was only considered "global" because of the distances

---

*   And even that was only because Europeans are weird.

involved. In reality, there was little trade among the empires. It was more accurately a series of closed systems sharing very few points of contact, and erratic contact at that. Cargoes were limited to the truly valuable, and to the sort of things you could ultimately do without. When you *did* see a transoceanic cargo vessel, it was a solid bet that disrupting its day would make yours. The Spanish called such disruptors "English." The British called such disruptors "French." Today we call such disruptors "pirates."*

As a result of this deliberate disconnectedness, neighbors were less for trading *with* and more for launching artillery shells *into*. The "civilized" world† existed in a state of near-permanent competition. Bringing order to such chaos was simply impossible. The superior naval power of the day—the Spanish in the seventeenth and early eighteenth centuries or the English in the late eighteenth and nineteenth centuries—would attempt to convince everyone they were large and in charge, but this was before the age of radar and cruise missiles. There was a lot of ocean to patrol. Rivals had compelling strategic and economic reasons to muck things up. Any "order" would only hold within sight of their military vessels.

The new technologies of the early industrial era—post-textiles, pre–steel ships—somewhat widened the range of goods that could be transported economically, which in turn carved out room for a new tier of country: the middlemen who brokered or ferried goods among opposing empires. It was risky business. The deals an empire categorized as "brokering" on Monday were often reclassified as "double dealing" by Thursday. The Dutch—every European's favorite middleman—became notorious for their massive booms when they carried European trade, and massive busts when the British or French or Germans decided they had had enough of the Dutch trading with the other side.

The Americans learned this lesson early and often. Many of the early geopolitical nightmares for the young country centered on trade of the decidedly Dutch variety.

---

*   ARRRRGH!!!
†   To use the European lingo of the era.

- America's first major strategic row, the Quasi War of 1798–1800, centered on French seizures of "neutral" American shipping to Britain. The Brits made some popcorn for the coming fight and had the nerve to talk shit about France to the recently independent Americans, but they were ultimately disappointed when both sides backed down.
- Just twelve years later, the Americans found themselves again in the middle of a French-British war (their third if you include the American Revolution*). This time around, France was run by Napoleon. The British were particularly aggressive in interdicting American ships they deemed blockade breakers, even impressing crews on American flagged ships into the Royal Navy.[†] Yadda yadda, stuff happened, things were said, triggers were pulled, torches were thrown, before you knew it the Brits were roasting marshmallows over the coals of the former White House, and the Canadians became forever unsure just how much they could trust the Yanks.

And yet and yet and *yet*, it was stunning—shocking—how much did *not* change.

At the close of the preindustrial era, most economies were still either self-contained or subjugated in one way or another, with the cities that enjoyed navigable rivers or safe coasts largely dominating. For while the economics and mechanics of over*seas* travel had improved remarkably over the centuries, over*land* travel had only seen occasional improvements.

It wasn't that nothing had gotten better. There *had* been steady advances in horse breeding, nutrient-rich-feeding, harnessing, and so on. Every bit of reach meant more access to resources to power industry, or access to new towns that could trade with the outside world. But unlike

---

* And you should.
† The Brits were total tools in this period. They didn't recognize naturalized American citizenship. So anyone who was born in the "colonies" was fair game for impressment. (Born in 1775? In Philadelphia? Yo, you're still a British subject! Get in muh navy!)

the thousandfold improvements in movement by water, movement by land in 1820 looked an awful lot like it did for the Romans, just with, in many cases, *worse* roads. Even as "recently" as the time of the Oregon Trail, you would not be happy, but instead *thrilled* should your ox-drawn cart manage to clock fifteen miles a *day*. While the technological advances in things like horseshoes and steel axles did lay important groundwork for what would come, these technologies didn't fundamentally change how we moved either ourselves or our stuff.

And they couldn't. And they wouldn't. That is, until such time that a completely new technological suite boiled forth and changed *everything*.

BREAKING FREE
INDUSTRIALIZING TRANSPORT

In the early industrial era, London, like most major early industrial cities, had grown beyond its ability to harvest timber for charcoal. Deforestation drove up the price of wood, improving the economics of the alternative: coal. Ever-higher coal demand led to ever-deeper coal mines.

Those deeper mines punched below the water table, necessitating pumps to force out water. Muscle didn't work at all to clear out *the freakin' water table*, so steam engines came into being to address the problem. It worked for a bit, but the new steam engines required power and that power came from coal and that coal came from ever-deeper shafts that filled with ever-more water, so miners hadn't really solved their problem, but instead industrialized its scale.

Faced with the cost of ever-deeper shafts and ever-more-expensive steam engines, some suppliers ventured farther afield to source coal from seams that were not directly adjacent to London. *That* fix required its own buildout: canals and boats to transport the black stuff back to Merry Ol' London. Soon half of Britain's private boats were used to move coal, generating its own inflationary price issue.

Nudged to consider other options, some enterprising coal suppliers combined the newer, more powerful steam engines with the rails used for cart transport within the mines, with a metal that only coal could smelt: steel. Bam! Railways.

Railroads were energy made animate. Getting man to the moon was cool and all, but humanity's greatest trick to date is building machines to get grain from more than fifty miles inland to the water. And to do so while still making a profit! Moving stuff on water remained cheaper, but a rail line could be built to anywhere that was flat and transporting stuff via rail was "only" twice the cost to operate of a ship. Compared to the >20 times the cost for pre-rail land transport, only having to pay double was a true revolution. The most prolific agricultural lands in the world, the ones that we rely on to this day not simply to keep modern society in motion but to quite literally keep everybody *alive*, could now be opened for business. In Europe, the shift from carriage to rail reduced the cost of internal transport by a factor of eight, enabling the rapid massing of nouns of all kinds at economically sustainable prices, whether the nouns in question be foodstuffs, coal, iron ore, or soldiers.

Russia provides an excellent example of how transformative this can be.

Much of southern Russian territory is a climate zone known as steppe: hot summers, cold winters, and so very demoralizingly flat and boring. Precipitation is fickle, but in a wet year agricultural growth can be explosive. The problem is getting the grain *out*. What navigable rivers Russia has don't flow through or to useful places, with most terminating in the Arctic.

Horses and carriages dragging thousands of tons of grain over the great Russian wide-open is far too taxing to be profitable in any era. What little trade occurred fit the normal bill: high value relative to weight; think pricy cloths and precious metals. Between the steppe's openness and the boom-bust economic cycle that followed the rain, it should come as no surprise that the horse-mounted Mongolians had no problem conquering the whole region and holding it for three centuries . . . while making a bang-up living taxing the northern branches of the Silk Roads.

In any case, high internal transport costs meant that any products that post-Mongol, Imperial Russia wished to export had to be sourced close to ports. As of the eighteenth century, some 70 percent of Russian grain exports were *not* grown in the empire's more fertile regions, but instead in Russia's Baltic provinces of Estonia and Livonia* by virtue of their proximity to the port of Riga. Inland Russian farmland, no matter how productive, was essentially cut off from the *Russian* market, never mind the world market.

---

* That's contemporary Latvia.

Changing this required two things:

First, in the mid-nineteenth century, Catherine the Great expanded Russian territory to the Black Sea, granting Russia warm-water port access for the first time. Not only was much of this land in the fertile zones of what is today Ukraine, but the Black Sea is also proximate to Russia's own Black Earth region north of the Caucasus (a zone in that infamous steppe).

Second, in the 1853–56 Crimean War, several industrializing European countries did not simply defeat but in fact thoroughly humiliated the largely unindustrialized Russian army. In an effort to prevent such a catastrophe from reoccurring, Russia under Alexander II made its first real efforts to industrialize. Considering how physically *huge* Russia is and how difficult it was to transport goods even within the empire's more populous territories, building a railroad network was at the top of the to-do list.

Suddenly Russian grain *could* reach international markets. And boy, did it! The Russian rail program began in earnest in 1866. In just fifteen years the Russian network roughly quadrupled to nearly 15,000 miles, adding more track than *all* of Europe had during the previous half century. During the same window, Russia's grain exports increased at nearly the same rate, to 4,200 metric tons. In this case, correlation *is* causation.

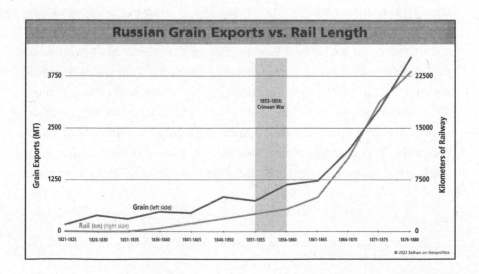

The Industrial Revolution came for water transport as well. It just took a bit longer, for a couple of semi-obvious technical reasons.

First, the steam engine was invented well before steel became available in large quantities. The early steamships were still made of wood. Steam engines ran on coal. Coal burns at over 3,000 degrees. It doesn't take a doctorate in chemistry to understand the complication.

Second, coal burns and then it is *gone*, while the wind is forever (if you plan your journey correctly). Steaming by coal too far from home turns a ship into an expensive raft. Much of the early Industrial Age logistical needs of the British Empire revolved around the establishment and protection of far-flung coaling stations like Aden and Perim on the Bab el-Mandeb, Hong Kong and Singapore in Southeast Asia, Fanning Island and Fiji in the central Pacific, Australia and New Zealand in the southwest Pacific, Diego Garcia in the Indian Ocean, Halifax in Canada, Bermuda in the central Atlantic, and Gibraltar and Malta in the Mediterranean. The Brits were pretty fly on the waves, but building an empire still takes time and effort. Technological requirements shaped the empire as much as the other way around.

Still, the saying about necessity and mothers held true, and everyone and their female forebears felt the need for speed.

Early steamships could move about 1,000 tons at 5–8 miles per hour, a reasonable speed for a lazy bicycle ride.* The 1840s brought us turn-screw motors (think propellers instead of paddle wheels) and faster speeds. Steel hulls debuted in the 1860s, largely solving the whole don't-burn-your-ship problem, along with a host of other speed-limiting issues, like hull fouling. By the 1890s these technologies and more had several generations of kink workouts behind them, setting the stage for bigger, faster vessels. By 1914, some all-steel merchant ships were sailing forth at an impressive and impressively reliable 12–15 miles per hour. Add in the Suez and Panama Canals (1869 and 1914, respectively) and goods could

---

* As slow as that sounds, it is still on average *five times* the average speed of preindustrial sailing vessels.

reach more locations without having to fully circumnavigate continents. More bang, less buck.

By 1940, oil-powered internal combustion engines started replacing coal-powered steam, increasing ranges, decreasing fuel-cargo requirements, and breaking the link between merchant marines and imperial-managed coal stations. Just as coal-fueled steam power trickled from the railways to the sea-lanes, now oil-powered internal combustion trickled back. Each advance helped make both transoceanic and inland transportation more regular and predictable. Costs plummeted, cargoes soared, reliability improved, and goods were moving on a scale hitherto undreamt of.

For the first time, *true* international trade in bulk goods was possible. Between 1825 and 1910, inflation-adjusted prices for freighting cotton and wheat fell by 94 percent. Between 1880 and 1910, the cost component of transport for wheat being shipped from the United States to Europe fell from 18 percent to 8 percent. Now that transport issues had gone from straitjacket to springboard, no one in Britain who had the option would keep eating local foodstuffs. Between 1850 and 1880, the proportion of British cereals in the average British diet fell from three-fifths to one-fifth.

It wasn't just stuff, but people, too. Just as the preindustrial tech of deep-sea transport provided new opportunities for many workers, railways and steamships allowed the average person to consider a new life. The journey—now easier, faster, cheaper, and above all, *safer*—opened up the world. Or at least, it opened up the world's temperate zones that white Europeans found comfortable. Thirty million Europeans—mostly British and Irish—relocated to the settler states.

For those who stayed behind, the cities fundamentally transformed. Limitations of local food and forest evaporated, with even *farmers*[*] discovering it was often easier to import food from elsewhere. Easier food

---

[*]   Especially *British* farmers.

supplies, combined with more steel, enabled cities to not simply expand *out*, but also *up*. Population density increased hand in hand with urban size, city planning, and new health-related technologies, compounding population growth. Whereas preindustrial cities often relied on a constant influx of people to replace those who died of starvation or disease, industrialized cities were not synonymous with death. They could sustain their populations, and so grew rapidly.

By the 1920s, the internal combustion engines that so revolutionized first water and then rail transport had been sufficiently miniaturized to lead to yet another transport-related overhaul: trucks. Unlike water transport, which required a port, or rail transport, which is largely limited to areas with slopes less than 1 percent, trucks could go anywhere that any road could reach. Demand for energy production entered an entirely new era. Trains retained dominance for trips over 500 miles, but trucks took over most of everything less, especially the all-important final mile of delivery. Concrete and asphalt started to replace dirt and brick as the primary road construction materials. Fifteen centuries after the fall of Rome, we *finally* got better roads. Horse poo finally, miraculously, suddenly—*thankfully*—vanished from urban streets.

By 1945, railways, barges, and trucks were all stuffed full of manufactured goods, agricultural products, and bulks like coal and wheat that were all ever-easier to produce. The transport and logistical logjams that had held humanity back since we fell out of trees on edges of the African savanna finally dissolved into the misty memories of yesteryear. History didn't so much speed up as launch forward. We went from the earliest days of steam, dying of dysentery and *Dr. Quinn, Medicine Woman*, to *get-off-my-side*-car-vacation-culture on the outside edge of a single human life span.

So much for walking everywhere with a load on your back.

THE AMERICANIZATION OF TRADE

Global trade before the modern era was a trickling dribble, barely a rounding error by the standards of the early twenty-first century. The East India Company traded about 50 tons of tea a year at the start of the nineteenth century and 15,000 toward the end of it. Today that same 15,000 tons is loaded or unloaded somewhere in the world every forty-five seconds or so. Don't let the small size fool you. Colonization, great power wars, the Industrial Revolution, and the slave trade are all among the consequences of that "rounding error." But the fact remains that in recent decades, we have ventured greatly from what once was. At the maximum extent of the imperial era in 1919, combined trade both within empires and among countries reached only 10 percent of GDP. As of the late Order era, that figure had tripled. Without empires.

Blame the Americans.

The Americans emerged from World War II financially strong and with the only remaining navy of any substance. Western Europe was weak and shaken, with Europeans feeling failed by capitalism during the Great Depression and failed by their leadership during the Great Wars. The United States agreed to rebuild the European states on the condition that trade would no longer be isolated within their imperial systems. Conversely, intercepting rivals' ships became the ultimate no-no. Oh, and one more thing: there would no longer be empires at all.

What was granted in exchange was truly transformational. The Americans would ensure that all countries on all continents would enjoy full access to the global ocean. What had once been a highly contested strategic environment transformed into a single, global, safe, functionally internal waterway filled and supplied by diesel-powered steel behemoths. The technologies developed during the previous couple of centuries would finally be allowed to function without the specter of war (or, more to the point, the Americans would handle said specter). No privateering. No piracy. No imperial confiscations. "Global" transport shifted from the jealous province of the empires to the unfettered circulatory system of the global economy.

While the Industrial Revolution made it much *cheaper* to ship products from A to B, it took the Americans' global Order to make transport much *safer*. Between the changed technological base and the changed geopolitical circumstances, what constitutes a Geography of Success expanded to . . . almost everywhere. And *that* marched us all in some unexpected directions.

IMPLICATION 1:
SHIPS: BIGGER, BETTER . . . SLOWER

In the age of globalization, *everyone* could get in on global access, manufacturing, and mass consumption. No longer was value-added work sequestered to the Imperial Centers. Manufacturing elsewhere required fuel and raw materials. Expanding industrial bases and infrastructure elsewhere required the same. Expanding middle classes elsewhere demanded even more.

The world needed more ships to transport more products, but in a world where competition among the Imperial Centers was no longer the global environment's defining feature, *security* was no longer the overriding concern. Competition was no longer about guns and sea-lane control, but instead about *cost*. This shift from security to efficiency as the predominant corporate concern meant the world didn't simply need *more* ships; it also needed different kinds of ships.

Economies of scale in transport come from four factors: size, crew, fuel, and packaging. The first three are pretty straightforward.

While the capital costs to build a vessel all increase with size, it is not a linear increase. Double the size of a vessel and it probably "only" costs about 80 percent more to build.* Double the size of that ship from 75 containers to 150 to 300 to 600 to 1,200 to 2,500 to 5,000 to 10,000 to today's maximum of 20,000 containers and you've racked up a per-container savings in excess of 80 percent. Similarly, the number of crew required to babysit 10,000 immobile containers or 5,000 tons of ore is not appreciably bigger than what is required to babysit 1,000 containers or 500 tons of ore. Fuel usage rates follow the same general trend as ship size: double the ship's size to reduce its fuel use by about 25 percent.

Then there's speed. Fuel costs writ large account for 60 percent of the cost of a voyage, with faster trips consuming *much* more than slower trips. The solution? If security isn't an issue, ships sail more slowly. It's rare for any modern vessel to get clocked at something faster than 18 miles per hour,† with most bulk cargo ships barely touching 14.

And of course, if *all* ships are moving more slowly, then there is far more cargo on the float at any given moment. The solution isn't simply more ships or bigger ships, but more ships *and* bigger ships.

Consequently, contemporary cargo vessels aren't simply bigger, but supersized. The ships that move soy from the American sector of the Gulf of Mexico to China are about eight times the size of the *Liberty*- and *Victory*-class cargo ships from World War II. By modern standards that's not even very accomplished. Relative to 1945 standards, modern container ships are sixteen times the size while modern crude carriers are over forty times. The numbers vary greatly by ship and cargo type, but as a rule,

---

*   The specifics vary wildly based on the type of vessel and what cargo it is designed to carry, but an 80 percent increase is a good rule of thumb.

†   Or 15 knots for those of you who like to sail.

War Risk Insurance Cost Estimates in a High Risk Environment

Ship Type	Maximum Carrying Capacity (Units)	Appx Secondhand Value*	Typical Cargo Value**	2.5% Normal Annual Hull Insurance Cost	5% Hull War Risk Premium for Seven Days	0.375% Additional Cargo Risk Premium for Duration at 80% Insured	Additional insurance cost per unit per seven days in high risk zone (USD)	Approximate Ship Dimensions - Length, Beam, Depth in Meters
				million USD				
Maersk Triple E	18,000 TEU	$180	$630	$4.50	$9.00	$1.89	$605 / container	400x59x15
Panamax Container (post-expansion)	12,500 TEU	$130	$438	$3.25	$6.50	$1.31	$625 / container	365x49x15
Panamax Container (pre-expansion)	5,000 TEU	$7.0	$175	$0.18	$0.35	$0.53	$175 / container	292x32x13
Very Large Crude Carrier	2,000,000 barrels	$62	$200	$1.55	$3.10	$0.60	$1.85 / barrel	333x58x31
Aframax Tanker	800,000 barrels	$18	$80	$0.45	$0.90	$0.24	$1.43 / barrel	245x34x20
Capesize Bulk Ship	196,000 metric tons	$33	$16	$0.83	$1.65	$0.05	$8.66 / metric ton	280x45x24
Panamax Bulk Ship (pre-expansion)	83,000 metric tons	$20	$7	$0.50	$1.00	$0.02	$12.29 / metric ton	225x32x14
Handymax Bulk Ship (feeder)	59,000 metric tons	$12	$5	$0.30	$0.60	$0.01	$10.41 / metric ton	190x32x11

© 2022 Zeihan on Geopolitics

* Values are based 5-year-old ships except for Handymax and Aframax where data was only available for 10-year-old ships and the Triple E class which are newbuilds. Prices are approximate based on reports from March 2017.
** With oil priced $100/barrel, coal $80/metric ton, clothing $35,000/TEU

Sources: Athenian, Clarkson, Maersk, ZoG Research

the all-in costs—crew, fuel, ship size, everything—for today's vessels run about one-quarter per unit of cargo compared to World War II–era vessels.*

I'm sure you noticed that I've only discussed the first three features on the list: size, crew, and fuel. The fourth—packaging—takes us in an entirely new direction.

IMPLICATION 2:
CONTAINERIZATION: BUILDING A BETTER BOX

Bretton Woods with the backdrop of the Cold War created the conditions necessary for free trade and the next round of globalization, but the reality on the ground was nothing like what we know today. Transport costs may have come down dramatically, but jagged, wild frictions existed across the entire system.

It took effort to pack goods into a truck, out of said truck into a warehouse, out of said warehouse onto a dock, packaged on said dock by a group of teamsters onto a pallet, said pallet shifted by another group of teamsters via a series of pulleys into a ship's hold, where another another another group of teamsters would secure said pallet for sailing. Said ship would then sail the ocean blue. Upon arrival at the receiving port, another another another group of teamsters would unload the previously mentioned pallet for inspection, another another another another group of teamsters would then load said pallet onto another truck, which would take it to a railyard where *another* another another another another set of teamsters would load it onto a railcar, and said railcar would then ship it to an unloading facility, where said pallet would be unloaded onto *another*

---

* Considering that today's megavessels are so mega—the world's largest container ship, the Korean-built Evergreen-A class, is bigger than the world's largest contemporary buildings—we have *probably* reached maximum size. After all, these behemoths still need to be able to enter ports, and the big boys require draft depths more than all but the largest bays can provide.

another truck. Only then—finally—would that truck be driven to the place that actually bought the thing.

One. Piece. At. A. Time.

By far the worst part—from a logistical and cost point of view—was the ports themselves. Each item needed to be separated from thousands of other items, unloaded onto the dock, physically inspected, often *re*loaded back onto the vessel (because it was in the way), then re-*un*loaded, and re-*re*-located to a local warehouse, before it could start making its way to the consumer. More and bigger ships required more and bigger warehouses farther and farther from the port, initiating an ever-longer, ever-more-congested slug trail of ever-more-relentless cargo reshuffling, with bottlenecks stretching back onto the vessels themselves. The typical port experience consumed five days, and multiple swarms of longshoremen on each end, not including the large and swarthy ship crew of large and swarthy deckhands. All in all it was a major pain in the ass that generated breathless opportunities for breathless levels of theft and corruption. No wonder that around the turn of the twentieth century, ports often accounted for half of total shipping costs.

Until, that is, we figured out how to . . . put things in . . . boxes.

By the 1960s, the ever-rising volumes of trade demanded an end to this packaging/repackaging agony. The solution was to debut a couple of models of shipping boxes—specifically the twenty-foot equivalent unit (or TEU) and the forty-foot equivalent unit (FEU). You probably know them by their colloquial name of "containers" and have undoubtedly seen scads of them being carted about by trains, trucks, and semis.

The containerization process transformed transport in general, and the world's ships and ports processes in specific.

Now a manufacturer fills a standardized container with their product and seals it. The container is mated to a truck, which drives the goods to a port, where the container is de-mated and stacked with others of its kind. When a ship is ready, the container is craned directly onto the ship (in the proper order for weight balance), moved across the ocean by a small crew that's better with keyboards than free weights, and lowered onto a container stack portside. Since unpackaging and repackaging no longer occurs in the ports at all, ports no longer *need* warehouses, save for equipment and personnel purposes. All they now need is a flat parking lot to host endless container stacks. When the time comes, the container might be railed a bit before being craned directly onto a truck, and then it is simply driven off to its final destination for unpacking and processing.

In theory, and largely in practice, the container is not opened once.

Let's make this more personally accessible. If you've ever moved, you know that most people can fit everything they own into the back of an eighteen-wheeler. One of those eighteen-wheeler units (that's a FEU) is 40 feet long and about 8 feet wide and tall, equaling about 2,700 cubic feet on the inside. Imagine a move where you have to stuff your things in storage for a few days. Would you rather unpack and stack everything into a storage facility and then repack and restack everything into another container when you're ready, or just keep everything in the original FEU in a parking lot until you get your new keys?

Now add in an ocean crossing and replay *that* sequence 200 *million* times per year and you begin to see the scale of change for the global economy. It doesn't matter what's in the container. Kias or kumquats. Bauxite or bar tools. So long as the container's total weight remains under upper limits, all containers can be handled identically.

What did it take for this standardization to occur? The Order. Global security, global commerce, global capital, global *scale*, and an overpowering willingness to provide reliability so the world could build its entire . . . world around a unified standard for size, weight, shape, and locks, enabling the ubiquitous container to move seamlessly through the supply chain. As early as 1966, the impact was obvious. Total port turnaround times on both ends shrank from three to five weeks to less than twenty-four hours. Port costs dipped from half the total cost of shipping to less than one-fifth. By 2019, containerships carried approximately 50 percent of total global trade by value, up from functionally zero in the early 1960s.

It isn't just ships and cargo methodology that have been redesigned. Ports have changed, too.

IMPLICATION 3:
PORTS: BIGGER, FEWER . . . ELSEWHERE

Ports have always required easy inland access, whether to access inputs or to distribute outputs. Before the Industrial Revolution, that typically meant a river. Think Hamburg, New Orleans, or Shanghai. At worst, ports required a big chunk of ocean-adjacent flat. Think St. Petersburg, Los Angeles, or Bangkok. In the modern day, however, containers' flexibility means all a port needs is road (and, preferably, rail) access. Instead of needing a rare—and therefore expensive—geographic alignment, ports can now be located *outside* cities, wherever the mix of land, labor, and electricity costs allow. Think Tianjin, Savannah, or St. John.

But while lower costs, combined with the container's flexibility, enabled port siting to be less finicky, the ports themselves had to become more so. Now that anything and everything could be containerized and shipped, the ports had to be able to serve as way stations for absolutely *colossal* through-volumes. And as ships became ever larger, not every port could play host.

First to go were the medium-sized regional ports that simply couldn't handle the new transoceanic behemoths. Cargo either went to the newer, gargantuan megacontainer ports or to the very small ports that managed local distribution. As the megaports drew more and more cargo and became more and more . . . mega, even small distribution hubs faded away. After all, rail lines could connect to the bigger ports and simply rail cargo to the small ports' own distribution network. Ports upriver, especially smaller ones that could not handle oceangoing vessels, became redundant.

These kinds of economic rearrangements happened all over the world, setting off concurrent races to become *the* regional hub. Ports designed to serve a single metro region—think the ports of Paris, London, Brooklyn, St. Louis, or Chicago—all but evaporated. Instead, locations that could contort themselves into a shape that facilitated broad-scale container distribution—think the ports of Rotterdam, Felixstowe, New Jersey, Houston, or Tacoma—exploded into being.

Larger and larger ships were sailing among fewer and fewer ports, which themselves became progressively larger and larger.

Collectively, these first three implications have made maritime shipping king.

Between 2000 and 2020, moving a container across the Atlantic or Pacific averaged out to about $700 per container. Or put another way, 11 cents per pair of shoes. Even traditional choke points aren't very . . . chokey. One of the world's largest container ship classes in reasonably large-scale production—the Maersk Triple-E class—pays about $1 million to transit the Suez Canal, but that duty gets split among 18,000-odd containers. That comes out to about $55 each, or less than a cent per shoe pair. Transport has become so rote that in 2019 the Chinese recycling industry had to place restrictions on the import of low-quality recycled *trash*.

Combined with bigger, slower ships, containerization has reduced the total cost of transporting goods to less than 1 percent of said goods' overall cost. Before industrialization, the figure was typically more than three-quarters. Pre-deepwater, the figure was often north of 99 percent.

Leaving aside the quiet little detail that you can't truck or rail cargo among London and Tokyo and Shanghai and Sydney and New York and Rio, even if the infrastructure were in place, cost comparisons would be utterly ridiculous. If you wanted a train that could compete in capacity with ships designed to just barely squeeze through the recently expanded Panama Canal, you'd need one more than forty *miles* long. Alternatively, you could go for a fleet of sixty-five *hundred* trucks.

With transport costs now rounding to zero, the math of everything else has changed to match.

IMPLICATION 4:
CITIES: THE URBAN EXPLOSION

Before the Industrial Revolution, wind, water, and muscle were the only power sources enabling a city to gather inputs. That put a hard cap on city size.

The technologies of the Industrial Age expanded a city's reach by orders of magnitude and enabled concentrations of resources in ways previously unheard-of. But this very expansion made cities ravenous. Bigger cities with more economic activity require more inputs to fuel that activity. It is a bit like the old adage where cities needed 100 times their land area for charcoal, but now they needed wheat for food, iron ore for steel, oil for fuel, limestone for concrete, copper for wiring, and on and on.

Cities expanded their reach to broader regions out of necessity. Regions expanded their reach to empires for the same. The Americans conquered the West and funneled its agricultural bounty and material resources to the cities of the East Coast. The Japanese did the same to Manchuria. The Europeans harvested their empires. The very nature of the new technologies ensured both imperial expansion and the conflicts over access that would contribute to the competition and mutual loathing that culminated in the world wars.

Fast-forward to after World War II and the Americans' Order removed even theoretical limits on just how far a city could reach. Coal, food, even people could now be brought in from somewhere else. Anywhere else. *Everywhere* else. Establishing control of the areas a city wanted to harvest—*needed* to harvest—was no longer necessary. With the *world* now the harvesting ground, *all* cities could increase in size.

IMPLICATION 5:
SUPPLY CHAINS: PRODUCING LOCALLY, SELLING GLOBALLY

A central feature of the preindustrial world was the Imperial Centers. All enjoyed some magic mix of mild climate and flattish terrain and maritime and/or riverine access, which granted not simply a leg up on the local competition, but enough strength and stability to reach out and conquer lands beyond. As the Industrial Age dawned, all were able to leverage centuries of accrued wealth and knowledge to engage in mass manufacturing.

But all faced common restrictions. Not all steps of a manufacturing process require the same access to the same inputs. Some need more iron, some more labor, some more coal, some more people with *doctorates*. But because none of the empires would ever trust one another, it was up to each individual Imperial Center to muddle through, attempting to host all steps of the production process within their own jealously independent system.

The dawn of the American-led Order changed all that. The Americans didn't simply outlaw conflict among their allies; the Americans guarded *all* global shipping as if it were their own *internal* commerce, ushering transport into an age of utterly *in*expensive sanctity.

In a world "safe" for all, the world's "successful" geographies could no longer lord over and/or exploit the rest. A somewhat unintended side effect of this was to demote geography from its fairly deterministic role in gauging the success or failure of a country, to something that became little more than background noise. Those geographies once left behind could now bloom in safety.

Nor did most old Imperial Centers overly mind. A process that the old Imperial Centers did not excel at, such as the relatively low-value-added process of pulling aluminum metal into wires or the cobbling of shoes, could be outsourced to another location—a *newer*, rising player in the now-globalized system—that could do it more efficiently and competitively. The ever-collapsing cost of transport, combined with the American-caused sanctity of said transport, enabled work that used to be done all in one city to be hived apart into a hundred different locations across the globe.

Shipping, once restricted to "only" raw inputs and finished outputs, now serviced a seemingly endless array of intermediate products. The modern multistep manufacturing supply chain system was born. By the 1960s such supply chains had become common, in automotive and electronics in particular.

South Korea, Brazil, India, and China were simply the four biggest of several dozen powers who suddenly held real roles. Many of the "core" areas that had done so well in the decades and centuries before Bretton Woods—the American Steel Belt and canalled Britain come to mind—

rusted into memory under the onslaught of these heretofore unheard-of competitors.

The Cold War and post–Cold War eras of extended global stability enabled more and more countries to join the fun. The new players didn't only join the game in different decades: they advanced at different rates, populating the world with more and more countries at wildly different levels of technical sophistication.

As of 2022, there are advanced technocracies in Western Europe, Japan, and Anglo-America; advanced industrialized economies in Northeast Asia and Central Europe; rapidly industrializing economies in southeastern Europe, Latin America, Anatolia, and Southeast Asia; and mixed economies in China, South Asia, Latin America, and the former Soviet Union. Ever-more-complex supply chains link them together. All were made possible by more and cheaper transport, which generated greater economic development and integration, which in turn demanded more and cheaper transport.

Add in bigger ships, containerization, and a new style of port, and not only did the many, many frictions that inhibited countries trading with their neighbors get sanded down; they melted away to the point that transoceanic, truly *global* multistep trade could not only become possible, but the everyday norm. As of 2022, some 80 percent of global trade by volume and 70 percent by value is transported by oceangoing vessels.

COMES APART

As the techs matured and the transport system thickened and diversified, two contrasting thoughts wove together to define our modern system:

First, industrial techs became ever *easier* to apply. Forging steel is more difficult than fashioning it into rail lines, which is more difficult than laying the rail lines, which is more difficult than operating a train, which is more difficult than filling a railcar. When the imperial system ended, it wasn't like the Dutch and Japanese could take the rail systems they had built home with them. It was pretty easy for their former colonies to appropriate and operate the assets. Unlike preindustrial technologies, which required master craftspeople, much of the Industrial Age—and especially the Digital Age—has proven to be plug-and-play.

Second, industrial techs have become ever *more difficult* to maintain. The ability to diversify supply systems over *any* distance means it is economically advantageous to break up manufacturing into dozens, even *thousands* of individual steps. Workers building this or that tiny piece of widget become *very* good at it, but they are clueless as to the rest of the process. The workforce that purifies silicon dioxide does not and cannot create silicon wafers, does not and cannot build motherboards, and does not and cannot code.

This combination of reach and specialization takes us to a very clear, and foreboding, conclusion: no longer do the goods *consumed* in a place by a people reflect the goods *produced* in a place by a people. The geographies of consumption and production are unmoored. We no longer only need safe transport at scale to link production and consumption together; we now need safe transport at scale to support production and consumption themselves.

In many ways this is all *great*. Industrialization plus globalization has not only generated the fastest economic growth in history; collectively they have dramatically increased the standard of living of billions of people the world over. Unlike the shockingly *un*equal preindustrial world, the industrialization/globalization combo has achieved the seemingly impossible duology of enabling the utterly unskilled to live at something above an abused subsistence level while pushing the frontiers of human knowledge and education further and faster and more broadly than ever before.

But in far more ways, this is utterly awful.

THE GREAT *UNMAKING*

Let's focus the mind with a little cheat-sheet set of bullets.

- Modern vessels are fat beasts. Container ships running full tilt max out at just under twenty-nine miles per hour. Bulkers at half that. The fastest civilian ships we have are . . . passenger cruise liners, mostly because they are mostly empty space. No joy in refitting them to ship corn.
- Modern transoceanic container ships hold *thousands* of containers, more than half of which are packed to the gills with intermediate goods essential to the fabrication of pretty much *all* manufactured products.
- Those intermediate products are built by a workforce who *only* know how to produce one specific piece of each product, particularly at the lower-quality end of the scale.
- Smart countries *can* do less-smart work. A semiconductor fabrication facility that makes chips for server farms can also make them for automobiles or toys. The reverse is *not* true.
- Modern ports are few, far between, absolutely massive, and typically *not* colocated with the populations they serve.
- Modern cities are so large and their economies so specialized that they require regular access not just to a huge swath of territory, but to the entire globe.

The central defining trait in all this work is safe, cheap transport. Inhibit that and the rest of . . . everything simply falls apart.

While industrial technologies' ease of adoption enabled them to spread easily, the reverse is also true. After all, there is very little skill capacity within the population that might enable it to *maintain* the contemporary world's flavor of industrialization should today's omnipresent transport links break apart for any reason. The workforce is alternatively hyper-specialized, nearly unskilled, or, testament to the fact that the world is nearly always stranger than you think, a combination of the two. Even worse, modern city life requires ever-present access to so many peoples and places scattered around the world and over which a city has no influence. Put simply, regions can *de*industrialize far more quickly than they *in*dustrialized, and the critical factor is what happens to transport.

Deindustrialization could happen far more quickly than you think.

Consider those big, fat, slow ships.

Quick war story, in this case, the Iran-Iraq War of the 1980s: By 1983 the conflict had reached a stalemate, inducing both countries to fling missiles at one another's shipping in attempts to strangle their opponent economically. Altogether some three hundred vessels were struck. About fifty were disabled, and a dozen sunk. Compared to the size of global shipping at the time, it was barely a footnote.

But that handful of events nearly destroyed the global . . . *insurance* sector.

The American security guarantee for shipping was considered ironclad. After all, there had been less than a handful of incidents globally for decades. There was even a period from roughly 1950 to 1975 with *zero* attacks on shipping. Loss provisions on maritime insurance, therefore, were, at most, minimal. Preparing for such incidents with large sums of cash would have been like setting aside billions to address earthquake claims in Illinois. But when the claims from the Iran-Iraq War rolled in, insurance firms quickly ran out of operating capital. So *they* filed claims with their reinsurance firms, who quickly ran dry as well. Suddenly *all* insurance companies discovered that their entire industry teetered on the precipice. Fire insurance, car insurance, mortgage insurance, health insurance—it didn't matter. And with most insurance firms being linked to most bond markets via large financial houses, catastrophe loomed.

The only thing that prevented a broad-scale, global financial breakdown was the Reagan administration's three-part decision to (a) physically escort non-Iranian shipping in the Persian Gulf, (b) reflag all such shipping as American vessels, and (c) provide a blanket sovereign indemnity to all such shipping. A local military spat between a pair of nonmerchant powers that didn't even *have* financial sectors quickly spiraled up to the point that only a superpower had the military, financial, and legal strength to prevent a *global* financial meltdown.

Imagine if a similar event were to occur today. From 1970 through 2008, the Americans nearly always had a carrier group in the Persian Gulf (and since the 1991 Desert Storm conflict, typically two). Escorting commercial shipping in 1983 merely required a few changes to patrol patterns. But since 2015 it has become normal for the Americans to go months at a time without ships of size in-region *at all*. By the end of 2021, the Americans had removed *all regular* ground troops from the region as a whole. Absent the United States, there are only a handful of powers— France, the United Kingdom, Japan, and China—who could even *reach* the Persian Gulf with military assets. Of them only Japan has the technical capacity to act in force, and none have the vessels required to establish meaningful convoys.

Imagine if the ships in question were container ships instead of bulkers. One ship would hold thousands of containers containing tens of thousands (hundreds of thousands?) of products. In the 1980s event, even those ships sunk were in time refloated and continued on with their lives. There is no way that would happen to modern containerized cargo (besides, would you buy a computer if a piece of the motherboard had sat on the bottom of the Gulf for a few days?).

Imagine if such an event occurred in a different location. Iran and Iraq in the 1980s were the ultimate no-value-added economies. Starkly limited local consumption. No participation in manufacturing supply systems. What if shipping was struck in the Baltic Sea or the East China Sea, places central to European and Asian manufacturing. Modern container ships do not take single products from one port to another, but instead run circuits. They travel to multiple ports, picking up and dropping off containers filled with a dizzying variety of products as they go. If any single ship is unable to transport or disgorge its cargo, impacts cascade throughout hundreds to thousands of supply chains across multiple industries and multiple regions. Even brief delays at only a handful of ports would be sufficient to force a rationalization of entire industries, to say nothing of *actually losing ships*. As the saying goes, it takes 30,000 pieces to make a car. If you only have 29,999 pieces you've got an ambitiously sized paperweight.

Imagine if such an event were not a one-off. The scale of 1983 versus 2022 is radically different. Between more differentiated supply chains, more wealth, and more countries, the total value of today's global seaborne cargo is now *six* times larger. Back-of-the-envelope math using data from throughout the past quarter millennia suggests that reducing transport costs by 1 percent results in an increase of trade volumes by about 5 percent. One doesn't need to run that in reverse for long before the trade-empowered modern world fades into a treasured memory.

Bottom line: the world we know is eminently fragile. And that's when it is working *to design*. Today's economic landscape isn't so much dependent upon as it is eminently addicted to American strategic and tactical overwatch. Remove the Americans, and long-haul shipping degrades from being the norm to being the exception. Remove mass consumption due to demographic collapses and the entire economic argument for mass integration collapses. One way or another, our "normal" is going to end, and end soon.

THE WORLD TO COME: COURTING—AND AVOIDING—DANGER

The most miraculous and, to a degree, unexpected outcome of the American-led Order is the extent to which it transformed areas that had rarely—if ever—been participants in any large-scale, multistate trading system. Most of the world does not enjoy a geographic setup that naturally encourages economic activity, like the temperate climates or the dense river networks common to Western Europe or North America.

The Order made geography matter less. The Americans would now protect your borders as well as your external commerce. Such a structure enabled geographies that had never developed before, or that had been crushed under the boot of this or that empire, to rise up as independent players. The greatest economic growth humanity has seen in the time since 1945 has been base-effect growth within these until-recently-neglected and until-recently-economically-defunct geographies. That means as the Americans descend into a mindset of not-my-pig, not-my-farmism, the greatest propensity for disruption *and* the greatest impacts of those disruptions will not only be in the same locations, they will be in the same *new* locations.

The first of these soon-to-be-crazy geographies are the territories on and coastward of Asia's First Island Chain, a region that includes Japan, China, Korea, and Taiwan, and to a lesser degree the Philippines, Vietnam, Indonesia, Malaysia, Thailand, and Singapore. What resources exist gradually peter out as one travels from south to north, while the value and volume of manufacturing tend to follow the opposite gradient. It is a natural area of intense competition characterized by concentrated resource demand, the longest supply lines on Earth, and massive export dependency. The result? Intermediate goods *everywhere*, with *all of them* being shipped by water.

This combination of vulnerability and integration could have only occurred in a security environment in which an external power forced everyone to play nice. Yet even with American overwatch, East Asia never developed a regional system of cooperation, or even diplomatic pressure release valves that fall short of military exchange. China hates Japan, Japan (perhaps now subconsciously) wants to colonize Korea and parts of China, Taiwan wants a nuclear deterrent, and the South Koreans trust no bitch.

Even worse, with the notable exception of Japan, *none* of the local powers has the ability to secure its own supply or trade lines. It is difficult to evaluate who is in a worse position: South Korea and Taiwan, who suffer a near-complete dependence upon American strategic naval overwatch, or China, who would have to punch through the waters of multiple hostile combatants (including *all* the countries of the Chain) as well as a half dozen more choke points to reach any market or resource access that matters . . . using a navy that is largely only capable of coastal operations.*

Chinese fascism has worked to this point, but between a collapse of domestic consumption due to demographic aging, a loss of export markets due to deglobalization, and an inability to protect the imports of energy and raw materials required to make it all work, China's embracing of narcissistic nationalism risks spawning internal unrest that will consume the Communist Party. Or at least that's what happened before (repeatedly) in Chinese history, when the government could no longer provide its people with the goods.

Japan would seem set to inherit the region, but the future isn't going to be nearly that tidy. Sure, Japan's superior naval reach means it can strangle China in a few weeks and choose the time and place of any blue-water conflicts, but even in weakness China has the ability to strike targets within a few hundred miles of its coast. That doesn't simply include portions of the Japanese Home Islands, but also most of South Korea and *all* of Taiwan. Anything short of a complete governance collapse in China (which admittedly *has* occurred several times throughout Chinese history) will turn the entire region into a danger zone for any sort of shipping on the water.

No region has benefited more from the Order, no region will suffer more from its end, and everything we know about modern manufacturing ends the first time anyone shoots at a single commercial ship.

The second region of concern is the Persian Gulf. Explaining why isn't particularly difficult. Local climates range from arid to . . . desert. Normally this would keep populations not so much small, but minute. But there's oil and that has changed everything.

Under globalization, the Americans had no choice but to patrol the Gulf in force, and involve themselves in the painful minutiae of the region's politics. Oil powered global trade, global trade powered the American

---

*   Okay. Never mind. I take it back. It's totally worse for China.

alliance, and the American alliance powered American security. Without the Gulf being relatively peaceable—and by historical standards, the Gulf since 1950 *has* been relatively peaceable—America's global strategy would have been dead on arrival.

That oil, combined with the Americans' presence, has transformed the region's possibilities. Instead of wandering Bedouin, a cluster of coastal pearling villages, and lands long ago salt-poisoned from millennia of irrigation, the region instead boasts an erratic mix of futuristic cities, over-populated megaplexes, war-torn cityscapes and hinterlands, and in many areas, a near-slave underclass.

The region exports oil and natural gas and . . . almost nothing else. It imports food. Technology. Electronics. White goods. Clothing. Cellular goods. Computer goods. Machinery. Planes. Automobiles. Building materials. Pretty much everything. Including labor—both skilled and unskilled. Even *camels*. Nearly every molecule of hydrocarbons is shipped out by water, while nearly every packet of imports travels the same way. In a world of collapsed internationalized shipping, Strait of Hormuz workarounds are ultimately of limited value. They were designed to bypass the threat of Iran, not the collapse of the Order.

This does *not* mean the region will vanish from humanity's collective radar. What the Gulf has—oil—is what South Asia, East Asia, and Europe will all desperately need. But *all* the local powers suffer from navies that cannot effectively patrol their own coastlines, much less escort local traffic, much less see ships safely in or out of Hormuz, much less guard tankers bound for end-consumers or bulk and container ships inbound from distant suppliers.

Nor can *any* foreign power smother the region with an American-style security blanket. In perhaps the preeminent demonstration of the undisputed fact that the U.S. military feels that overkill is underrated, the combined navies of the wider world have less than one-tenth the power projection capacity of the U.S. Navy. A global inability to impose norms on the region will guarantee a decades-long global depression as well as ensure a succession of woefully inadequate efforts by a half-dozen

powers—Japan, the United Kingdom, France, India, Turkey, and China—
to salvage . . . something from the bloody chaos. It's going to be a mess.

The third region to watch out for is Europe. We think of modern Europe as a region of culture, democracy, and peace. As having escaped
history. But that escape is largely due to the Americans' restructuring
of all things European. What lies under the historical veneer of calm is
the most war-torn and strategically unstable patch of land on the planet.
Modern Europe is the purest distillation of the heights and complete ar-
tifice of the Bretton Woods system.

Future Europe's problems are many, but four stand out.

- The first is energy: The Europeans are *more* dependent upon energy
  imports than the Asians, and no two major European countries think
  that problem can be solved the same way. The Germans fear that *not*
  having a deal with the Russians means war. The Poles want a deal
  with anyone *but* Russia. The Spanish *know* the only solution is in the
  Western Hemisphere. The Italians fear they must occupy Libya. The
  French want to force a deal on Algeria. The Brits are eyeing West Africa.
  Everyone is right. Everyone is wrong.
- The second is demographic: The European countries long ago aged past
  the point of even theoretical repopulation, meaning that the European
  Union is now functionally an export union. Without the American-
  led Order, the Europeans lose any possibility of exporting goods,
  which eliminates the possibility of maintaining European society in
  its current form.
- The third is economic preference: Perhaps it is mostly subconscious
  these days, but the Europeans *are* aware of their bloody history. A
  large number of conscious decisions were made by European leaders to
  remodel their systems with a socialist bent so their populations would
  be vested within their collective systems. This worked. This worked
  well. But only in the context of the Order with the Americans paying
  for the bulk of defense costs and enabling growth that the Europeans
  could have never fostered themselves. Deglobalize and Europe's

demographics and lack of global reach suggest that permanent recession is among the *better* interpretations of the geopolitical tea leaves. I do not see a path forward in which the core of the European socialist-democratic model can survive.

- The fourth and final problem: Not all European states are created equal. For every British heavyweight, there is a Greek basket case. For every insulated France, there is a vulnerable Latvia. Some countries are secure or rich or have a tradition of power projection. Others are vulnerable or poor or are little more than historical doormats. Perhaps worst of all, the biggest economic player (Germany) is the one with no options but to be the center weight of everything, while the two countries with the greatest capacity to go solo (France and the United Kingdom) hedged their bets and never really integrated with the rest of Europe. There's little reason to expect the French to use their reach to benefit Europe, and there's *no* reason to expect assistance from the British, who formally seceded from the European Union in 2020.

History, unfortunately, offers us some fairly clear paths forward. As the reliability of long-haul maritime transport evaporates and the United States—by far Europe's largest market—goes its own way, the Europeans will put a premium on protecting what they have and know: their own supply chains and their own markets. That Europe is *starting* as the most protectionist set of economies of the Order era doesn't help.

The end result will be the creation of several mini-Europes as various major powers attempt to throw economic, cultural, and (in some cases) military nets over wider regions. The United Kingdom, France, Germany, Sweden, and Turkey will all go their own way and attempt to attract and/ or coerce select neighbors to come along for the ride. Integration will suffer appropriately. For those of you who know your Persian, Greek, Roman, Byzantine, Ottoman, German, British, French, medieval, or early industrial histories, this will feel disturbingly familiar. After all, history has no endgame.

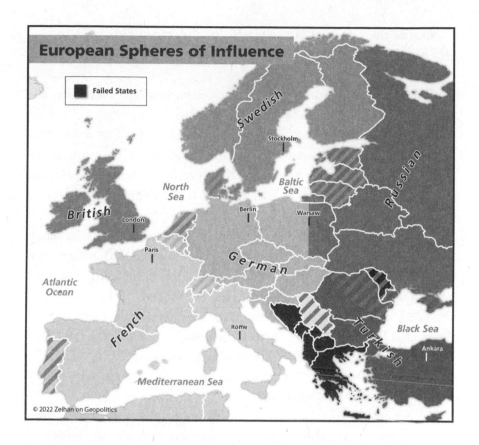

It will be worth the Europeans' while to obsess particularly about the Mediterranean. Under the Order it has been a bit of a lovely internal channel for the Continent, but looking forward it is far more likely to return to its historical norm of being the world's most contested waterway. Via the Suez Canal, the Mediterranean is Europe's connection to Persian Gulf oil and East Asian manufactures. Egypt cannot protect the canal zone, but neither can any individual European country dominate Egypt. Via the Turkish Straits, the Med is Europe's connection to the energy and agricultural surpluses of the former Soviet states. Turkey is absolutely certain to take over the Straits and *no one* has the capacity to challenge the Turks in their own front yard.

None of these competitions are new to students of history. What *has been* new is that the Americans have smothered them. *All* of them. For *decades*.

To believe that globalization will continue without an overarching enforcer and referee, you must believe three things:

First, that all powers in a given region will agree to do what the most potent regional power demands. That the Japanese and Taiwanese will accede to Chinese efforts to redefine the structural, economic, political, and military arrangements of East Asia. That the French, Poles, Danes, Dutch, and Hungarians (among others) will actively transfer wealth and control to Germany as the Germans age into obsolescence. That Saudi Arabia, Iraq, Kuwait, Qatar, Bahrain, and the United Arab Emirates will defer to Iran on issues of regional control and oil policy. That Ukraine, Estonia, Latvia, Lithuania, Sweden, Finland, Poland, Moldovia, Romania, and Uzbekistan will not resist Russia reasserting control over all of them. That Pakistan will accede to India being large and in charge. That Iran, Iraq, Syria, Russia, and Germany will not resist Turkey muscling itself up to the big table. That the various African nations will quietly accede to a renewed colonial wave.

The Americans have held all these reckonings in abeyance since 1945. Now remove the American security environment. Look at the map with fresh eyes. Look at *any* map with fresh eyes.

Second, you must believe that certain tools of statecraft will remain firmly off the table, most notably military tools. That the Germans, Russians, Iranians, and Chinese will not use military force to impress their wills upon their neighborhoods. That powers with military reach—France, the United Kingdom, Turkey, and Japan come to mind—will not use their capacity to short-circuit the actions of their less mobile competitors. History isn't simply littered with examples to the contrary. Most of history *is* the contrary. Except history from 1945 to the present, of course.

Third, you must believe that the dominant regional powers will not come into conflict. That the Russians and Germans, the Chinese and Indians, the Russians and Chinese, the Turks and the Russians, the Turks and the Iranians, will always see eye to eye. Offhand I can think of ten examples of this not working out in just the single century before 1945. The world's supply of grievances is inexhaustible. For the most part, those grievances have not been acted upon for seventy-five *years*. . . . but only because the Americans changed the rules of the game.

Regardless of what goes wrong, long-haul transport is an instant casualty, because long-haul transport doesn't simply require absolute peace in this or that region; it requires absolute peace in *all* regions. Such long-haul disruption describes three-quarters of *all* shipments in energy, manufacturing, and agriculture.

HARBORS IN THE STORM

Messy stuff, yes, but it won't *quite* be a world of all-against-all. What "safe zones" there are for commercial shipping will fall into one of two general categories.

First, a regional superpower establishes a regional pax to impose its preferred definition of security upon its desired geography. Japan will do this in Northeast Asia, with the probably not very hidden goal of keeping the Chinese broken. France will predominate in far Western Europe, much to the Brits' and Germans' disdain. Turkey will run roughshod over the Eastern Mediterranean, likely in league with the Israelis. The United States will update the Monroe Doctrine and turn the Western Hemisphere into an invitation-only American playground. Whether such zones of control are informal or ironclad, enable regional trade or block it, or are benevolent or otherwise, will be determined by a mix of cultural norms, economic demands, strategic diktats, and local needs and opportunities. No one size fits all.

Second, some clusters of countries will be able to jointly patrol their own. The United Kingdom is likely to partner with the Scandinavians to craft a regional order. Germany will do the same with the Central European states. The Southeast Asians will pool economic strength and military forces with the Australians and New Zealanders.

Conflict among the regional superpowers and blocs is a foregone conclusion, but that isn't the same as saying such conflicts will be chronic or kinetic. The French and the Turks will surely glare at one another from opposite ends of the Mediterranean, just as the French and Germans will surely find topics to cooperate on that reach beyond Belgium. The Dutch and Danes will seek a sort of dual membership in the British- and German-led blocs, while those two blocs themselves are likely to cooperate against Russian power. Everybody loves the Australians . . . but the Australians will merrily act as a spotter for the American hammer.

The defining characteristic of the new era is that *we will no longer all be on the same side.* And while many might reasonably argue such has always been the case, what made the Order work is that we all collectively agreed that there were limits as to what form intrastate competition could take. No one uses military force to confront an economic competitor. But most important, no one shoots at or hijacks commercial shipping. Period.

The end of this norm takes us down a lot of dark paths.

The days of *long*-haul transport are largely over. With the notable exceptions of Japan and the United States, *no* country can consistently project naval forces a continent away, and even for the world's top two naval powers, patrolling sufficiently wide swaths of ocean to enable escort-free cargo trade is beyond them. The Order worked because *only* the United States had a global navy and *everyone* agreed to not target ships. That world is gone.

Long-haul transport is what brings everything from areas of high supply to high demand, regardless of participant. For any product that is concentrated in terms of supply *or* demand, expect market collapse. Products particularly concentrated in terms of supply include oil, soy, lithium, and mid- and low-end microprocessors. Products particularly concentrated in terms of demand include liquefied natural gas, bauxite, high-speed train cars, and squid. Products facing a double squeeze include iron ore, helium, cocoa beans, and printer toner.

Breaking the economies of scale and supply lines that an interlinked world makes possible will impact everyone, but the unravelling will also impact everyone differently. The Western Hemisphere is fine for food-stuffs and energy but will need to build out its manufacturing capacity for products as wildly varied as laptops and shoes. The German bloc's manufacturing capacity is largely in-house, but the raw inputs that enable it to operate are wholly absent. The Japanese and Chinese are going to have to head out to secure food *and* energy *and* raw materials *and* markets. It's a good thing that Japan likes to manufacture products where it sells them, and fields a potent long-reach navy. It's a bad thing that most of China's navy can't make it past Vietnam, even in an era of peace.

And it *really* matters what each regional bloc decides is priority shipping and so deserves priority protection on any given day. Complex manufacturing systems are most efficient when they have more players, both for a larger consumer pool and a more differentiated—and from that, more efficient—supply chain system. The bigger the bloc, the more successful and sustainable regional manufacturing is likely to be. The Russians are certain to leverage a fractured world against their oil and natural gas customers, a feature that will prompt the Germans *and* Turks *and* Brits *and* Japanese *and* Chinese to source energy from elsewhere and so initiate and inflame competition all around. Somewhat ironically, in a fractured world the slowest ships—those boring bulkers—are likely to end up being the most important. After all, should containerized shipping break down, much of the world will be economically decimated from the collapse in manufacturing. But should bulk shipping—which transports food and fuel—break down, many of the world's people will starve. Alone. In the dark.

Inter-bloc conflict over and against shipping will be the new norm, but keep in mind that most countries lack long-arm navies. That suggests the real excitement in shipping will occur in the no-man's-lands where no bloc holds reliable sway—and where no vessel can reliably call for assistance.

In that sort of environment, shippers will face a trifecta of security problems.

First and most obvious are the pirates.[*] Any zone without a reasonably potent local naval force is one that is all but certain to host Somalia-style pirate harassment. Second and less obvious are the privateers, in essence pirates sponsored by an actual country to harass their competitors, and who have been granted rights to seek succor, fuel, and crew (and sell their

---

[*]   ARRRRGH!

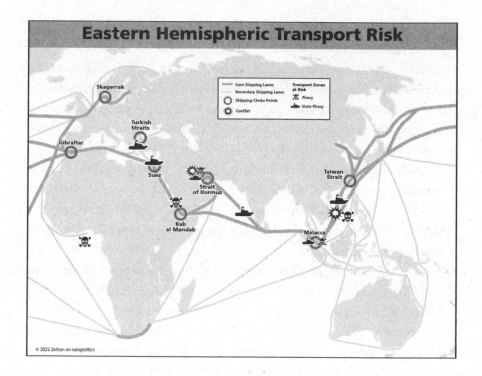

Eastern Hemispheric Transport Risk

ahem booty) in allied ports. Because sponsoring privateers allows at least a veneer of deniability, and so is a step down from full-on war, expect pretty much *everyone* to get in on that particular game.

The third security concern isn't likely to be constrained to the no-man's-lands: *state* piracy. We're moving into a world where the ability to import *anything*—whether it be iron ore or diesel fuel or fertilizer or wire or mufflers—will be sharply circumscribed. Simply sending out your navy to *take* what you need from others is an age-old solution that long predates the relatively recent saga of Columbus sailing the ocean blue.

- Expect state piracy to come back into vogue with particular verve in the Turkish bloc, with the Turks (and Israelis) gleefully (and relentlessly) raiding anyone desperate enough to attempt to ship crude oil through the Suez Canal and Eastern Mediterranean without first paying whatever level of protection money that Ankara and Jerusalem deem appropriate.

- India is another power to watch out for, but in a slightly different way. The Indian Navy may be, well, below awful, but within the Indian Ocean it faces no regional peer. The subcontinent is also the first stop for any shipments out of the Persian Gulf. Would-be shippers will have little choice but to pay whatever "passage" fees New Delhi insists upon. Luckily for those shippers, India is likely to be very flexible when it comes to payment. India is eminently likely to accept payment in direct crude transfers, while the country's large and sophisticated refining operations means it could even absorb *all* of a shipper's cargo while sending on refined fuels.

- In a world of circumscribed shipping, the inputs needed to maintain modern manufacturing systems—a long list of materials that range from high-grade silicon to cobalt to nickel to rare earths to bauxite—are going to be top-tier targets. It's far easier to nab those slow-moving bulk ships than to occupy a country for its mining capacity. The coasts of Africa and Southeast Asia are likely to be particularly nuts not just because many of the requisite materials are sourced in or pass through these areas, but because there are no powers indigenous to either region with the naval capacity to keep piracy—especially *state* piracy—at bay.

- The Eastern Hemisphere as a whole is a net food importer, with the imbalance being most extreme on Asia's eastern and southwestern fringes. Expect the Japanese to discover that the "regulation" of food shipments from the Western Hemisphere to the Asian mainland is both big business *and* excellent strategic leverage.

- Do *not* forget the Americans. America's post-Order foreign policy will be erratic, but just because the Americans have precious few global *interests* does not mean they have any intention of giving up their global *reach*. Expect the Navy and Marines both to be assigned a set of secondary tasks that include aggressive sanctions enforcement. Perhaps the most jarring issue *all* countries and companies must adapt to is the Americans not simply giving up their role as the global guarantor of *order*, but transforming into active agents of *dis*order.

Everything we've come to expect about transport since 1946 dies in this world. Bigger, slower, more specialized vessels are little more than tasty floating buffets for whatever privateer or pirate (state or otherwise) happens to be in the area. Larger vessels might maximize efficiency in a unified, low-threat world, but in a fractured, high-threat environment they also concentrate risk.

The next generation of vessels will have far more in common with their far smaller, pre-1945 ancestors. Such ships by necessity will be shorter range and be able to carry less cargo, not simply because they are smaller, but because they will need more fuel per unit of cargo in order to sail *faster*. They will also need to be designed so that cargo need not be stored on their decks. After all, if a pirate or privateer can identify ship type from a distance, the whole hijacking process can be more targeted. That feature alone shrinks the cargo capacity of container ships by two-thirds. Say goodbye to sea-dependent integrated manufacturing supply chains.

This transformation, even independent of the changes to the security environment, unravels the economic norms of the age now ending.

Modern ports—and especially modern megaports—can only function as transit and distribution hubs for megaships that will no longer be sailing. That will decrease the popularity of containerization and necessitate a return to the structure of more, smaller ports closer to consumption points. More secure? Certainly. But also more costly. Between the changes to ships and ports, expect what transport remains to cost at least quadruple what we've become used to. And that's *within* the future blocs where security is more or less guaranteed. The biggest winners? Those locations that entered the Industrial Age in force because they had *internal* geographies brimming with navigable waterways *as well as* a degree of stand-off distance from threats: the United States, the United Kingdom, Japan, France, Turkey, and Argentina, in that order.

Even worse, as transport costs rise, low-margin non-energy and non-food goods are less likely to be shipped in the first place. Not only does this further weaken what economic ties still bind; it also means that anything that *is* shipped is more likely to be oil or edible or otherwise *valuable*. The bad ol' days of if-it's-in-a-ship-then-it's-worth-taking are returning. The biggest losers? Those countries at the very end of very exposed shipping routes, which lack the naval capacity to convoy their own merchant vessels: Korea, Poland, China, Germany, Taiwan, Iran, and Iraq, also in that order.

If shippers cannot count on a benign security environment, and if shippers have convinced themselves that a cargo must make it to a destination, then the only reasonable decision is to ensure that the ship has the capacity to look after itself . . . by arming it. Such decision making generated an unhealthy amount of sketch when it was the norm in the seventeenth and eighteenth centuries, when the height of ship-mobile military tech was muskets and cannon. Now add in missiles. And drones. And missiles fired from drones. A return to the days of militarized merchant marines is not far off. You think folks the world over are nervous about some countries having no restrictions on their military exports *now*? Just imagine what happens when the Koreans or Israelis or French start selling idiot-proof anti-ship weaponry designed to be mounted on bulkers operated by India or Saudi Arabia or Egypt.

Modern manufacturing—and especially modern *tech* manufacturing—can only function in a world in which gajillions of intermediate products can frictionlessly scuttle about. Only blocs in which manufacturing supply can be colocated with manufacturing demand won't suffer from catastrophic disruption. That's a massive problem for German manufacturing, as many of its suppliers are from beyond the horizon and roughly half of its customers aren't even in Europe.

It's a much bigger problem for Asian manufacturing, where *all* intermediate products travel by sea (Germany can at least rail intermediate products among its supply chain partners), and most all of the raw materials and end markets are a multi-thousand-mile sail away. China, in particular, is dependent upon countries either a continent away or with which it nurses heavy historical or geopolitical grudges, for nearly all of the high-value-added components in its manufacturing system. With transport costs rising sharply, the portion of the manufacturing supply system that will face the greatest disruption is those low-margin pieces that rely upon low costs . . . such as cheap transport.

The sheer fluidity of the future security environment won't help. The industrial plant required to support multi-step supply chains exists in multiple locations by definition, and takes years to build. Every time there's a tweak to a demand profile—either for intermediate or finished goods—it typically takes a year of retooling efforts to work its way forward and back through the system. We have learned that little lesson the hard way with COVID. Every ship diverted, every shot fired disrupts some part of the supply and forces that same year-long reset. In such an environment, multi-step supply chains in any region without rock-solid local security *and* rock-solid local consumption just don't make much sense. Those supply chains must be concentrated into tighter and tighter geographies, with most needing to become fully internal to specific countries. Anything else spells persistent mismatches, and no end products.

Modern cities—and especially East Asia's modern megacities—are particularly screwed. All *only* exist because the Order has made it easy for them both to source the building blocks of industrialized systems as well as to access end markets for their exports. Remove the global system, remove global *transport*, and cities will be responsible for their own food and energy and industrial inputs.

That is, in a word, impossible. Only cities that are part of a bloc with sufficient reach can hope to keep populations employed, fed, and warm. For most of the global urban population, this leads to the same place: massive *de*industrialization *and de*population as people are forced to return to the countryside. The bigger the urban conglomerate, the greater the risk of catastrophic failure. At least half the global population faces the unwinding of decades of urbanization.

So, one final question for this chapter: where are the areas where cities can still tap the lands required to enable modern functionality?

The Americas are broadly okay. In part it is geographic. The two American continents have more food and energy than they have people to consume them. So, you know, solid start.

It is also economic. The Western Hemisphere's (the *world's*) most demographically stable developing country—Mexico—is already heavily integrated with the hemisphere's (the *world's*) largest economy and most demographically stable developed power—the United States. The two buttress one another in ways unparalleled in the modern world.

It is also geopolitical. The Americans have the interest and the ability to prevent Eastern Hemispheric chicanery from bleeding into the Western Hemisphere. For all intents and purposes, the Americans may be abandoning the *global* Order (big *O*), but they will still uphold a *Western Hemispheric* order (little *o*).

Honestly, that's probably *more* than what the Americans actually *need* to do. The United States is a continental economy with robust *internal* commercial activity, as opposed to a global economy with robust external trade. Only half of America's international trade and less than 3 percent of its domestic trade—which collectively accounts for just 10 percent of GDP—floats at all. Most trade with Mexico and Canada is carried out via rail, truck, or pipeline. The Americans are not dependent upon international maritime trade for their food supply, their energy supply, or their internal or even the bulk of their internationally dependent supply chains.

Even America's single globally busy port, at Los Angeles/Long Beach, California, is unique. Unlike the Asian and European ports, which are first and foremost transshipment centers, Los Angeles/Long Beach is a *destination* port. It does not process scads of *intermediate* products, but instead serves as the final port of call for largely *finished* goods that are built and assembled elsewhere. Such goods are loaded onto truck and rail for distribution throughout the United States. Supply interruption certainly still has consequences, but not the sort of system-shattering ones that will become the norm throughout the bulk of Eurasia.

The second-largest piece of the globe that can be "gathered" to help cities survive is the continent of Australia plus the islands of New Zealand. Like the Western Hemisphere, the pair of southwest Pacific nations have far more resources and foodstuffs than they could ever consume. And just as Mexico and the United States now boast a mutually reinforcing relationship, so too will the Aussies and Kiwis enjoy one with the countries of Southeast Asia.

The Southeast Asian nations run the gamut in terms of levels of wealth and technical sophistication, from hypertechnocratic Singapore, to nearly preindustrial Myanmar. From most points of view, such diversification is a feature, not a bug. It enables multi-step manufacturing systems to occur regionally, without overly needing to tap anything beyond. Add in reasonable levels of food and energy supply within the bloc, balanced out by Australian and New Zealander assistance, and this region should be able to squeak by.

The problem for this Southeast Asian bloc is that (a) no one is large and in charge, and (b) the group lacks the military capacity to look out for its varied interests. This need not end in disaster, nor is it likely to. Both the Americans and the Japanese will have reason to seek economic and strategic partnerships with the Southeast Asians (including the Aussies and Kiwis). The trick for all three sides of the relationship will be to keep Japanese and American views in rough alignment. A serious falling-out would be devastating to anyone west of the International Date Line.

After that, things get dicey pretty quick.

Russia has loads of stuff that countries need, but the Kremlin has long used its resource wealth to extract geopolitical concessions out of its customers. Russia's economic strategic policy can best be summed up as . . . failed. In the *pre*–Cold War eras, the strategy oscillated between Russian subjugation of said customers and said customers flat-out invading Russia. In the Cold War and post–Cold War eras of easy global access, competition from other suppliers made this strategy a dead letter. The Russians today think that their Trans-Siberian Railway (TSR), theoretically capable of transporting massive volumes of goods between East Asia and Europe, is an excellent way to break America's hold on the seas.

Reality disagrees: a single one of those large container ships transported more cargo than *total annual* TSR traffic in the entirety of calendar year 2019. Bottom line: I've personally long found Russian confusion amusing given their use of an 1800s playbook that has consistently failed them in the twenty-first century. Rather than the Russian strategies finally working, instead expect a reprise from the earlier periods of history, potentially with atomic complications.

The Middle East is packed with energy but imports more than two-thirds of its food needs. Expect massive and rapid-fire population . . .

adjustments as global commodities trade craters along with everything else. In the aftermath, France and Turkey will feast on the region's bounty to fuel their own needs and ambitions, perhaps with the Japanese making the odd guest appearance. Expect all three to enjoy their time in the region as much as the Americans did.

Sub-Saharan Africa remains the world's last frontier for trade. In many ways it faces similar constraints as the Middle East. It has partially industrialized—up to and including expansions in food production—and it cannot maintain its level of development without ongoing global engagement. In many ways it reflects the bounty of the Western Hemisphere—its low level of industrialization means it has far more industrial commodities than it could ever use . . . and that *will* attract outsiders.

Expect a new scramble for Africa as a result, but this is *not* the 1800s. Sub-Saharan Africa may not be *as* industrialized as Europe, but neither is it fully *un*industrialized. This time around the Europeans will not enjoy the sort of technological imbalances that enabled empires to enjoy massive advantages in weapons and troop numbers. This time the Africans can and will fight back to the degree that imperial-style conquerings or occupations are simply untenable. Instead, the Europeans (primarily the French and British) will need to *partner* with local authorities to access the inputs they need. How quickly the outsiders can get over themselves and come to that conclusion will determine the flavor and texture of African history for the next few decades.

By far the biggest loser in this new dis-structure is China.

Everything about modern China—from its industrial structure to its food sourcing to its income streams—is a direct outcome of the American-led Order. Remove the Americans and China loses energy access, income from manufactures sales, the ability to import the raw materials to make those manufactures in the first place, and the ability to either import or grow its own food. China absolutely faces deindustrialization and de-urbanization on a scale that is nothing less than mythic. It almost certainly faces political disintegration and even de-civilization. And it does so against a backdrop of an already disintegrating demography.

The outstanding question for all things Chinese is simple: Will it collapse completely? Or will portions of China be able to hold on by its fingernails so that outside powers might treat it in the same way that they will treat . . . sub-Saharan Africa? If the latter holds true, expect a few coastal cities such as Shanghai to collaborate. After all, the cities of China's southern coast have a far richer history of interaction—especially when it comes to little things like putting food on tables—with outsiders than they do with Beijing.

DEEP BREATH

Transportation is the connective tissue that holds the world together, and, if anything, what you've just absorbed is only the *beginning* of the transport story. For example, modern ships of all types require diesel fuel. Diesel requires oil. Supplying oil to the world requires the stability of the Order. Think oil shipments are going to happen with the same volume and reliability in a post-Order world? What sort of impact do you think oil and diesel shortages will have on transport? It's all very ouroboros. I have another *five* sections packed with minefields of surprises for you.

So take a break. Maybe a nap. Get a drink. And when you are ready, let's tackle the *other* half of the global connectivity question.

Money.

SECTION III:
FINANCE

SECTION IV

FINANCE

CURRENCIES

NAVIGATING THE ROAD LESS TRAVELED

At the time of this writing, in early 2022, every country in the *world* has experienced financial crises and market meltdowns multiple times in the post–Cold War era. If you think this is symptomatic of deep structural issues, you are right. If you think it's all wildly unsustainable, right again! If you cannot fathom why the Chinese are able to develop so quickly, you are once again on the right track. And if you're worrying about the collapse of the dollar . . . you're not thinking *nearly* big enough.

These gnawing questions are the story of modern finance.

Even what answers we believe we have to these questions are unsatisfactory. That feeling you have in the pit of your stomach that we're all making up finance as we go? Listen to that feeling. It is dead-on. The rules of finance changed drastically not at the beginning of the American-led Order, but in the years *after*. In the 2020s they will change *again* into something we have never seen before.

This is going to require a bit of unpacking.

Once again, let's start at the beginning.

THE LONG PATH TO MONEY

Long before the world of the American greenback or British pound or even Egyptian gold, there was no real medium of exchange. When it was time to trade, you had to hope against hope that your partners wanted whatever it was you had extra of, and vice versa. But even if desires matched, there was the nagging question of worth. How much is a large plank of cedar wood worth? Is your cargo worth one basket of copper ore or two? Is it the same this year as last? Can I interest you in a roll of papyrus? The barter "market," such as it was, moved, and there was no way to know which *way* it had moved until *after* you arrived to present your goods.

Considering the mutual isolation among the peoples of the ancient world, that was more than a major problem.

The Egyptians' desert buffers were the best natural barriers of the Ancient Age. The Egyptians' primary trade route was up the Nile Valley into Sudan (aka Nubia), but the Nile south of populated Egypt was cursed with rapids (no sailing) as well as canyons (no following the river). Traders had to cross the open desert . . . in an era before the domestication of camels. This all made the Egyptians secure, but it also meant they didn't get out much to shop.

We don't know nearly as much about the early Indus civilization as we do about our earliest forebears, but what we *do* know is *not* pretty. The best guess is that an earthquake or flood (or both) shifted the path of the Indus River a few dozen miles to the southeast at one point, leaving the mighty, independent city-states of the floodplain suddenly high and dry. Everyone contracting tuberculosis didn't help. Regardless of how residents of the early Indus civilizations died, while they were around they were the light in the darkness. Deserts drier than the Sahara exist to their west in what is today Pakistani and Iranian Baluchistan, while peoples of the semi-adjacent Ganges Valley or the foothills of the Hindu Kush were late to emerge from hunter/gatherer economics. The Indus may not have been *quite* as isolated as the Nile, but it probably didn't feel that way at the time.

This left the Mesopotamians as the men in the middle.

Unlike the Nile and Indus systems, Mesopotamia *needed* to trade because it *only* had food. Lumber, granite, and metals all required import. Luckily, Mesopotamia wasn't simply bracketed by the other two of the First Three founding civilizational peers, but also by its civilizational daughters: Anatolia (today's Turkey), the Zagros Mountains (today's Iran), the Levant (today's Israel, Lebanon, Syria, and Jordan), and the coastal communities of the Persian Gulf. Mesopotamia was at the center of it all. And since the Mesopotamians never got into building out the sorts of sprawling urban infrastructure of the Indus cities* or the omnipresent vanity projects of the Egyptians,† they could focus on generating ever-greater barley surpluses for use in trade.

Barley? Barley was *the* currency of exchange for more than two millennia. Why?

Simple. Place matters. To everything.

Early irrigation systems in all of the First Three civilizations were flood-driven. Workers would divert seasonal spring flows into fields and drown everything. As all of the First Three were in those low-altitude, low-latitude desert river valleys, evaporation effects concentrated the tiny amounts of salinity in the mountain runoff into the soil, resulting in incrementally higher soil-salt levels year on year. Barley could tolerate this salinity better than other plants.‡ It made barley a popular crop throughout the First Three.

Now that we have our basis for value, the problem becomes transport. A quart of barley weighs about a pound. Issues of bulk and weight limited its usefulness, especially if your plan was to schlep a few tons of it across the desert. As the people with the greatest need for and ability to trade, the Mesopotamians needed a way to square their barley circle.

The circa 2000 BCE solution was the shekel. Three one-hundredths of a shekel could be traded for one quart of barley. One shekel was equal to 11 grains of silver. Over time the shekel became synonymous with our modern concept of money. One shekel could pay a laborer for a month. Twenty shekels bought you a slave. By 1700 BCE and courtesy of Hammurabi, if someone injured you, you had the option of choosing restitution in the form of shekels rather than eyeballs. Bam! Finance was born!

Armed with a commonly agreed-upon medium of exchange, labor

---

* Indoor plumbing for the masses in 2000 BCE!
† Alllllll those pyramids!
‡ Also, beer.

specialization took a leap forward. There was now far less risk for a once-farmer to evolve into an anything-else. Income from anything-else could be swapped for barley at a known rate. After all, the shekel was literally redeemable for food.

So handy was the breakthrough, use of the shekel spread far and wide. Good data from a hundred human lifetimes in the past can be hard to come by, but so central—literally and figuratively—were all things Mesopotamian that even the Egyptians and the people of the Indus Valley Civilization adopted the Mesopotamian shekel standard on those rare occasions when they engaged in transregional trade.

It . . . took a while before things stuck. Not just currency. Civilization, too.

The First Three civilizations date back to some point in the fourth or third millennium BCE, but they were only the beginning of the story. Tribes in lands adjacent to the First Three would pick up some tricks of the civilizational trade and found their own echo civilizations. Mesopotamia inspired the Persians and Hittites. The Egyptian expansions encouraged the emergence of Nubia and Phoenicia. The Indus birthed Aryan offshoots.* None of them really lasted because none of them had that all-important crunch-coat desert shielding of their forebears. Invaders could reach them. Precipitation for the newbies was more important than irrigation, so bad harvests happened—and bad harvests often meant everyone died. Or at least enough people died or fled to wreck any sort of civilizational progress.

The period from roughly 1600 BCE to 800 BCE in particular was an era of civilizational chaos. It wasn't simply that these daughter civilizations rose and fell and rose and fell, but that at times all the daughter civilizations throughout an entire region would fall *together*. China expe-

---

*   Probably. The circa 1300 BCE collapse of the Indus Valley Civilization was so sudden and holistic, no one had time to jot down any easily deciphered notes about the apocalypse in progress.

rienced some truly epic collapses. Two of the mass civilizational falls in this time window were so severe they took Mesopotamia and the Indus with them, with Indus civilization never recovering. Even eternal Egypt teetered there for a bit. Archaeologists refer to a subset of this timeframe as the Late Bronze Age Collapse. Christians, Jews, and Muslims know it as the era of Exodus.

Roughly around the seventh century BCE, three things changed—for both civilization *and* for finance.

First, when a civilization falls, it's rare to follow the example of the Indus and have every person, product, and idea utterly vanish from the Earth. Citizens become survivors. Survivors become diasporas. Diasporas intermingle and form new communities. It isn't just people who mix but also ideas and products and techniques. People need a medium of exchange to lubricate the increased variation. Enter currency.

Second, this post-collapse merging naturally led both to technical booms from the skill mixing of the various overlapping diasporas and the desire to reconnect with others in their fallen cultures.* The combination of more technological advancement, greater product differentiation, and a bit more outwardly focused mentality not only granted us greater heft and stability and populations, they contributed to the shift from the Bronze Age to the Iron Age. Some outcomes of this accelerated technological track were any number of new agricultural tools and techniques, culminating in the emergence of classical Greece, with its all-important water wheels. Human civilization still had plenty of bumps and scrapes ahead of it—setbacks and horrors like the fall of Rome, the Dark Ages, twerking, the 2020 American presidential debate—but this post-collapse intermixing pushed the technical envelope sufficiently forward that humanity never again suffered a mass collapse event. And if the wolf of

---

*   In contemporary times, we have witnessed this trend in spades. America's 1990s and 2000s tech explosion would not have been nearly as massive without the talent imported in the aftermath of the Soviet collapse.

civilizational collapse is no longer at the door, you're more willing to accept payment in coin as opposed to barley.

Third, with both stability and economic dynamism steadily increasing, traders had more confidence that the city or country or empire they wanted to trade with or for would be there when they got back. For the first time in history there was a *geopolitical* rationale for developing a currency better than barley.

All at once in multiple locations, we developed metal coinage as a method of exchange: in China, in India, in the Eastern Mediterranean. The rest, as they say, is history. Instead of surpluses or shortages of a good triggering a flurry of confusingly haphazard barter, courtesy of metal coinage the value of one side of the trade was now always known. The whims of climate and season and culture and scarcity and plenty were no longer obstacles that discouraged economic activity, but instead were its fuel.

BUILDING TRUST

Yet, historically speaking, people have had a hard time taking this or that currency seriously. As a rule it is only valued within a very specific area, ruled by a very specific government. Leave that area and foreign coin is little more than a low-quality paperweight.

There are a couple of ways around this. The first is to make your coin out of something that people want. Gold, silver, electrum, and copper are all good choices, but really, anything a culture deems valuable can be used. Options through the ages have included barley, strips of iron, cocoa beans,* dolphin teeth, potato mashers, tulips, wheels of Parmesan, and, my personal favorite, beaver pelts.†

---

*   Nom nom nom.
†   O Canada!

Such systems have one far-from-minor drawback. A poor person might be able to get a few silver coins over the course of years of labor, but a wealthy person will have literally tons of the stuff. Carrying three hundred pounds of silver simply isn't practical, not to mention it makes you a robbery target.*

This brings us to the second option: make your publicly circulating currency *exchangeable* for something of value. Again, a metal of high worth is the obvious choice; you just keep the actual metal in a government vault instead of having the value reside in the coin itself. Wealthy merchants in the vicinity of the Sichuan Basin—home to the contemporary Chinese cities of Chengdu and Chongqing—started up a system like this in the seventh century, using a sort of promissory note that could be exchanged for silver.

So that's the setup. See the problem? You have to be able to convince people that you really *do* have the stuff of value squirreled away somewhere, and it really *can* be exchanged on demand.

Financial collapses triggered by countries doing things *un*well and *un*properly and *un*wisely are as common as the stars in the sky. In *un*successful systems, governments often find themselves beset with spending needs greater than their means. The temptation is to issue more currency without simultaneously securing more assets to back it. The technical term is "debasement." That works for while . . . until people stop believing the government line.

As soon as word leaks out that you are lying about how much gold (or Parmesan) you have in that government vault, folks stop accepting payment in the official currency, or refuse services altogether if crap cash is all on offer. Currency, after all, is about trust. Such lack of trust is part of the reason why Russians have long had a habit of trading in their rubles for German marks or British pounds or U.S. dollars and stuffing such better-respected currencies into furniture.

---

* While carrying three hundred beaver pelts just makes you look silly.

Once that trust is damaged, the volume of your currency in circulation soars as people dump it. Your currency's corresponding value then plummets due to oversupply. At that point, even really important people tend to lose trust. The Quebecois once infamously paid their troops with pieces of playing cards.[*] Imperial Japan issued cardboard currency due to wartime metal shortages.[†]

Folks shift to alternatives, whether it be a physical asset that is supposedly more solid, or even other countries' currencies. Barter—with all its limitations—comes back into fashion out of necessity. At that point, governmental and civil collapse is rarely far off, with leaders finding themselves holding tickets for admission to history's ash heap.

What most do not realize is that while *bad* economic management obviously culminates in currency collapses, so too does *good* economic management.

In a successful system, the stability a real currency provides generates economic specialization and growth. Economic specialization and growth require ever-larger volumes of currency to lubricate ever-growing volumes of economic activity. Ever-larger volumes of currency necessitate ever-larger volumes of the stuff needed to back the currency.

Getting such ever-larger volumes of said "stuff" is far easier said than done.

The Roman Empire is an excellent case in point.

The empire was by far the most stable political entity humanity had yet to invent. That stability encouraged development and technological evolution and trade within the Roman system. That required more currency, and more precious metals to back the currency. That need forced the Romans to expand beyond territories within easy reach and beyond territories that could generate wealth into ever-farther-removed lands simply in order to secure *mines*.

Some such locales, like the Iberian Peninsula, were within arm's reach

---

[*]   The Quebecois lost the war.

[†]   The Japanese lost as well.

and were pacified and integrated fairly easily. Others, like the Taurus Mountains of southern Anatolia, were much farther away and required centuries of sparring with distant and stubbornly hostile powers. Still others, such as the lands that comprise the contemporary Sahelian country of Mali, were trading hubs that could access gold sources that are part of contemporary Ghana and Nigeria (the once-famed "Gold Coast"). The Romans didn't cross the Sahara to get a tan, but because they *had* to if they were to maintain domestic financial stability. Ultimately Rome expanded beyond its ability to defend the realm. Once the Romans lost their marches (where the gold came from), the imperial economy seized up, taking short-term political stability and long-term military capacity with it.

Nor does "venturing forth" need to occur with legions assaulting geography. It can occur with bureaucrats assaulting economics. Rather than gobbling up someone else's resources, some governments choose to gobble up their own from an adjacent sector. The Tang Dynasty followed such a perpendicular course. Rather than expanding the empire physically to source more silver, they instead expanded the list of metals that "backed" their currency to include copper. The Tang's adoption of copper as currency succeeded at stabilizing the financial system, but at the cost of causing empire-wide metals shortages that enervated . . . everything else.

Such snatching of defeat from the jaws of victory, as it were, has been the ultimate fate of every ostensibly *successful* currency regime throughout human history. Including the biggest and most successful ones.

Especially the biggest and most successful ones.

RESERVE CURRENCIES: THE BIG BOYS

If you are looking for *the* place and *the* year the modern world began, that would be in the Viceroyalty of Peru in the Bolivian highlands in 1545, when one Diego Huallpa—a native doing the equivalent of contract work for a local Spanish conquistador—was literally blown over by a strong gust and tumbled down into a bit of loose soil. Huallpa stood up and brushed off dirt . . . that was quite literally sparkling with silver dust. In under a year this windfall took physical form as the mines of Potosi, the largest single deposit of silver ever discovered in the six-millennia history of humanity.

As long as I'm giving you the full treatment, let me give you the dirty first.

Silver is often co-produced with lead, making extraction toxic. Purification methods of the sixteenth and seventeenth centuries used mercury, so there's some more toxicity for you. Mining techniques of the time were not what we would call OSHA-approved. They included lugging a couple hundred pounds of ore on your back while climbing up out of the bowels of the earth via hundreds of feet of ladders with the only light being a candle *strapped to your forehead.*

No one was going to emigrate from Spain for *that* sort of work, so the Spanish regularly raided indigenous populations for labor. Spanish law of the time indicated that so long as you baptized your workforce, it really didn't matter if they lived. And one final schmear on the shit sandwich: Potosi is at thirteen thousand feet of elevation. In the preindustrial era, growing food in a place with double the elevation and half the rainfall of Park City, Utah, was, shall we say, challenging. Even if you survived everything else, you very well might starve.

The Imperial Spanish weren't very good accountants, but the best guess is that somewhere between four million and twelve million people died during the course of the Potosi silver operations. (For a point of reference, the entire population of Old Spain in 1600 was only 8.2 million.)

The Spanish didn't really care, because they were the big men. Launching the first truly global system required two things. The first was a single economic and military structure that could span multiple continents. The second was a large enough volume of precious metals to support a global currency. Potosi funded the first and provided the material to back the second. For several decades in the sixteenth and seventeenth centuries, Potosi produced more silver than the rest of the world combined.

Very soon the Spanish were not simply lubricating economic exchange in and around Iberia, but kicking names and taking ass the world over.

Allies, partners, neutrals, and even rivals started using the Spanish "pieces of eight" coins as their exclusive method of exchange. The Portuguese Empire—Spain's premier contemporary rival—had no choice but to use Spanish silver currency in *internal* commerce.* Even in the late Spanish period, well into the British rise, Spanish coin remained so large in volume, so far-reaching in circulation, and so reliable in purity that it was used more in British America than the British pound. Spanish currency was especially popular in the rum-sugar-slave triangle linking Britain's American, Caribbean, and African possessions.

But all things pass in time.

For anyone else who had a metals-backed currency, the perpetual flood of Spanish coin was de facto economic war. For anyone whom the Spanish found strategically problematic, the perpetual flood of Spanish coin was *actual* war. Just as bad: when the Spanish used all that Peruvian silver to hoover up resources and goods and man-hours, the result was always the same: runaway inflation not only in Spain, but in any territory that could supply the Spanish with what they wanted. Considering that Spain's empire of the time was *global*, that was pretty much everywhere. Holding Potosi meant the Spanish could muddle through. The rest of everywhere, less so.

After two centuries of expansion and war and inflation, a mix of truly creative strategic and economic mismanagement in Old Spain, combined with Napoleon Bonaparte's disturbing habit of invading his neighbors, resulted in both the fall of the Spanish Empire in general and of the Spanish currency in specific. The first half of the 1820s ushered in the independence of both Peru and Bolivia, ending Spanish access to Potosi and finishing off the Spanish Empire with brutal, uncaring finality.

But the possibility of global trade had been let out of the bottle, and nothing as minor as Bolivian independence was going to stuff *that* genie back in.

---

*   Unofficially, of course.

As the Spanish were falling, the British were rising. The early British "pound" was quite literally a pound-weight of silver, but the Brits didn't have a Potosi of their own, and no matter how hard they tried they couldn't capture anywhere near enough Spanish treasure galleons to back a sizable currency supply.

None other than Sir Isaac Newton found a workaround to this problem during his thirty years in charge of the Royal Mint. He initiated a century-plus effort to tap the totality of the British Empire for gold—most notably the territories that today comprise Australia, Canada, South Africa, and Africa's Gold Coast—to unofficially create a counterweight to Spain. By the mid-1800s the gold-backed pound we know had come into being.

By the late 1800s Britain's command of the seas often translated into trade chokeholds. The rise of the Germans in Central Europe generated alternating and overlapping regions and periods of inflationary growth and strategic collapse, leading many Europeans to seek the relative stability of the decidedly non-Continental pound. To the Germans this was one of many things worth fighting over . . . that ultimately didn't work out. By the time World War I had stretched into its third year, *all* the continental European countries were debasing their currencies to pay for the conflict, triggering currency collapses and runaway inflation . . . which only accelerated the pound's de facto adoption as Europe's only desirable currency.

It didn't last long. In the post–World War I chaos and economic collapse, even the British Empire proved insufficiently large to support the currency that everyone in Europe needed. As with the Romans and Spanish before them, demand for the pound generated currency-based inflation *on top of* the general economic dislocation of the war *on top of* the unwinding of a half-millennium of colonial/imperial economic systems *on top of* a global tariff war. Add it up and the Great Depression turned out to be perhaps a bit greater than it needed to be.

Which brings us to the Americans. By 1900 the United States had *already* displaced the entirety of the British Empire as the world's single-largest economy. Furthermore, the Americans didn't even *join* World

War I until three years in, and so were able to serve as *creditor* to the Europeans rather than needing to debase their currency to keep fighting. The British pound wasn't as debased as the franc or deutschmark or ruble, but the dollar wasn't debased at all.[*]

Even better, the Americans were perfectly willing to provide the World War II Allies with anything they needed—oil or fuel, steel or guns, wheat or flour—*so long as they were paid in gold*. By war's end the U.S. economy wasn't only far larger and that of Europe far smaller. The U.S. dollar wasn't just the only reasonable medium of exchange in the entire Western Hemisphere: it had sucked the very metal out of Europe that would have enabled a long-term currency competitor anywhere in the Eastern Hemisphere. If anything, this is truer than it sounds. After all, the metals-backed currencies of Europe were the culmination of *all* human civilizations of *all* eras stripping the *entire* planet of precious metals since *before* the dawn of recorded history.

Now it was in Fort Knox.

Between continental Europe's woes and insufficient supplies of the British pound, pretty much everyone in Europe abandoned their precious-metals pegs and shifted to a system where their own currencies were backed by none other than the U.S. dollar (which was in turn backed by gold . . . that had until recently been European).

FROM SUCCESS, FAILURE

When the guns finally fell silent that second full week of August in 1945, all the major powers of the previous five centuries were smashed, impoverished, enervated, isolated from the wider world, or some combination thereof. Only the United States had the precious metals required to back

---

[*]   It was also pretty new. The Americans didn't even form their Federal Reserve and formally launch the currency we know today as the "dollar" until 1914.

an extra-national, much less global, currency. Only the United States had the military capacity to take that currency far and wide. The only even *theoretical* candidate for a global medium of exchange was the U.S. dollar. It did not need to be formalized in the Bretton Woods treaties for that to happen.*

Gold-backed dollarization on a global scale was a certainty. It was similarly certain that gold-backed dollarization was doomed to failure.

The commencement of the Order meant that peoples who had been at each other's throats for the entirety of their histories were not only at peace but were *forced* to be on the same side. All at once, local economies once hardwired to support a distant imperial sovereign could reinvent themselves on the basis of local development and expansion. All at once, anyone and everyone—and I mean *any*one and *every*one—could *trade* for *any*thing and *every*thing. More countries, rapid rebuilding, rapid growth, rapid modernization, rapid industrialization, rapid urbanization, burgeoning trade. Places like Germany and Japan that had suffered infrastructure-targeting bombing raids for years proved once again that they could build *anything*. Well. And quickly.

All of it took money. Most of it took hard currency, and there was only one hard currency to choose from.

Lubricating such a rapidly growing system required a *lot* of dollars, particularly as the trade in intermediate goods shifted from an internal to a multinational phenomenon. The Americans expanded their money supply to meet the expanding global economy's needs, which also meant the Americans needed more and more gold to back the ever-expanding currency supply.

The numbers not only didn't add up, they *couldn't* add up. Throughout human history, humanity has probably produced no more than 6 billion

---

* The Brits had this supercute idea that the Americans would lend them a bottomless supply of gold at generous credit terms so the pound could once again reign supreme. The American response was to graciously allow the Brits to be in charge of the seating assignments at Bretton Woods. Not really. The Boy Scouts handled that.

troy ounces of gold (about 420 million pounds). Assuming every scrap of gold ever mined was available to the U.S. government, that would only be enough to "back" a total global currency supply of $210 billion.* From 1950 to 1971, global trade expanded by *quintuple* that figure, on top of the fact that the U.S. dollar was the currency of the United States itself, which already had a GDP larger than total global trade. The peace and economic growth that the Order encouraged also increased the global population from 2.5 billion to 3.8 billion, suggesting *much* stronger demand for U.S.-dollar-enabled trade to come.† Even if the politics had been perfect, the gold standard was doomed to fail.

The Americans awkwardly and painfully discovered for themselves not only the age-old issue that asset-backed currencies were incompatible with rapid growth, but the very age-new issue that asset-backed currencies were incompatible with global *peace*—the sort of peace that formed the backbone of America's anti-Soviet alliance.

The Americans found themselves hostage to their own master plan, and the politics were most assuredly *not* perfect.

One of the clauses of the original Bretton Woods agreements—designed to ensure confidence in the new system—was that any signatory could cash in their dollars for gold, in any volume, on demand. Throughout the 1960s the French did just that, with increasingly maniacal hwahwa-hwainess. Normally such rising demand for gold would jack up its price, but the price of gold was fixed via treaty at the rate of $35 per troy ounce in order to build that all-important trust. With the "normal" avenue for price discovery eliminated, the only possible outcome was to drive up demand for the dollar itself. The result? Increasing shortages in the exchange medium—the U.S. dollar—a process that threatened to

---

* At 1950 prices.

† If anything, I'm greatly understating the case. Even though the Americans via their war profits had accrued by far the largest gold reserves in history, something like 90 percent of the gold that humanity has produced is locked up in things like museum exhibits and wedding bands.

unwind all the economic achievements of the postwar Order. The French (and others) were betting that the entire system would fail and so were hoarding gold in preparation for the aftermath.

Faced with the possibility of a global economic depression that would leave America facing down a nuclear-armed Soviet Union alone, the Americans did the only thing they could. In a series of steps in the early 1970s, the Nixon administration cut the cord and put the U.S. dollar on a full, free float.

For the first time, a major government *didn't even pretend* to have anything in the vault. The only "asset" backing the dollar was the "full faith and credit" of the U.S. government. The very nature of America's post-1971 globalization-fueled alliance gambit was quite literally based upon none other than Tricky Dick Nixon saying, "Trust me."

We had zero idea what to expect as, hand in hand, we all gaily skipped down the road less traveled: the road of fiat currency.

ADVENTURES IN CAPITAL

If there was a singular rule of finance in the era before 1971, it was that there was *never* enough money. Currency value was directly linked to some sort of asset, while currency volume was determined by the capacity and reach of the sovereign power in question. Both characteristics generated extreme limitations, both for the governments issuing the currencies and for the people and firms (and other governments) who used them.

In this strange new world, that singular rule—that money exists in limited quantity—evaporated. Instead of money existing in a finite amount and so needing to be scrupulously managed, there was no longer any practical cap on capital availability. Limitations became a purely political question.

For the Americans that "limitation" was pretty straightforward: keep expanding the money supply until there is sufficient currency to support the overall globalized trading system. But for everyone else who used the U.S. dollar as their currency backer, the definition of "limitation" meant whateeeeever each individual government thought it needed to mean. That broad divergence allowed the development of tools and options that could have never existed in the world of asset-backed currencies. These tools and options in turn gave birth to entire governing systems that would have had zero chances of existing in the pre-fiat age.

MONEY FOR NOTHING: THE ASIAN FINANCIAL MODEL

It all begins with Japan.

Long before the world wars, even long before America's Admiral Perry forced Japan open to the world, the Japanese had a unique view of debt. In Japan capital exists not to serve economic needs, but instead to serve *political* needs. To that end, debt was allowed, even encouraged . . . so long as it didn't become inconvenient to the sovereign. Dating back to the seventh century, if widespread debt got in the way of the emperor or shogun's goals, it was simply dissolved under the debt forgiveness doctrine of *tokusei*. Drought? *Tokusei!* Floods? *Tokusei!* Famine? *Tokusei!* Government in the red? *Tokusei* . . . with a 10 percent processing fee!

As such, debt tended to boom, especially when debt was already widespread. After all, the worse the overall financial situation, the better the chance the emperor would emerge onto his balcony, wave his fabulous scepter, and declare this or that class of debts null and void. It happened so often that bankers went to extraordinary lengths to protect their economic and physical well-being: they had a tendency to write *tokusei* riders into their loans so borrowers couldn't count on the debt simply evaporating, and they similarly needed to live in walled compounds so when a *tokusei* was declared, mobs could not storm their homes, beat them to death, and burn the loan documentation to prevent such riders from being executed. Fun times.

Anyhow, the point here is that while economics and politics have always been intertwined, Japan was the trendsetter in making finance a *tool of the state*. Once that particular seal was broken, it became pretty common for the Japanese government to shove embarrassingly large amounts of cash at whatever project needed doing. In most cases such "cash" took the form of loans because—you guessed it—sometimes the government found it handy to simply dissolve its *own* debts and start from financial scratch. *Tokusei* always left *someone* holding the bag, but in rough-and-tumble pre–World War II Japan, it was typically some faction of society that happened to be on the outs with the central government, so . . . whatever.

The end of World War II triggered another debt reset, albeit less because of imperial decree and more because everything had been leveled. Considering the absolute devastation and humiliation the *gaijin* had visited upon the Japanese, it was paramount that postwar Japan move in cultural lockstep. That no one be left behind.

The solution was to apply the peculiar Japanese attitude to debt toward broad-scale rebuilding efforts, with massive volumes of capital poured into any possible development project. The specific focus was less on the repair and expansion of physical infrastructure and industrial plant than on maximizing market share and throughput as a means of achieving mass employment. Purchasing the loyalty and happiness of the population—who rightly felt betrayed by their wartime leadership—was more important than generating profits or building stuff. That a loyal and happy population was pretty good at building stuff didn't hurt.

From a Western economic point of view, such decision making would be called "poor capital allocation," the idea being that there were few prospects that the debt would ever be paid back in full. But that wasn't the point. The Japanese financial model wasn't about achieving *economic* stability, but instead about securing *political* stability.

That focus came at a cost. When the goals are market share and employment, cost management and profitability quietly fade into the background. In a debt-driven system that doesn't care about profitability, any shortfall could simply be covered with more debt. Debt to hire staff and purchase raw materials. Debt to develop new products. Debt to market those products to new customers. Debt to help the new customers finance those new purchases.

Debt to roll over the debt.

The Japanese were hardly alone. War's end saw a new crop of players take a page from the Japanese book. South Korea, Taiwan, Singapore, and Hong Kong had been Japanese protectorates for years (in some cases for decades) and enjoyed (or suffered) the greatest Japanese cultural imprint. That imprint extended into Japan's view that finance is as much about politics and state goals as it is about economics.

The four leveraged that belief, funneling scads of Western (and Japanese) capital to leapfrog entire phases of the development, industrialization, and urbanization processes. In the 1950s and 1960s they did so by borrowing massively from foreigners and applying the capital to root-and-branch overhauls of every aspect of their systems. The industrialization process that took Germans more than a century—and the Germans are no slouches when it comes to building and overhauling things quickly—

took the Taiwanese, Singaporeans, and Hong Kongers less than three *decades*. The Koreans did it in less than *two*.

Enter 1971. Suddenly foreign (gold-backed) capital became less critical to the equation. If profits could not cover debt payments, then export earnings would. If earnings could not, firms could simply take out more loans. If loans were not available, the government could always expand the money supply to push everything forward. (It didn't hurt that expanding the money supply also drove down the value of the Asians' currencies, making their exports more competitive and therefore driving up export income.)

In the first Asian wave, agriculture gave way to textiles and heavy industry. In the post-1971 wave, heavy industry gave way to ever-more-advanced manufacturing of every imaginable sort: white goods, toys, automotive, electronics, computers, cellular products. Capital-driven growth upon capital-driven growth meant that within two generations, all four countries had transformed themselves into modern industrialized systems on par with many of the world's most established cities. Considering that most were among the least developed and poorest patches of the planet at the onset, their collective makeover is among history's greatest economic success stories.

Three things helped:

First, the Americans steadily outsourced their own industry to the Asian states. That provided an excellent rationale for the Asians' debt-driven model, as well as ensuring ravenous American (and in time, global) demand for the Asians' products.

Second, that foreign demand proved robust and stable enough to make the Asians' exports profitable enough that all four managed to (for the most part) grow out of the debt.

Third, as the most enthusiastic of the fiat currency adopters, the Asians were willing to push the limits of what was possible to the point that Americans and Europeans got a bit skittish about the very nature of Asian finance. In addition to playing fast and loose with the math, the Asians used a mix of legal and cultural barriers to actively discourage foreign penetration into their financial world. For example, most Asian conglomerates developed banks *within* their own corporate structures—good luck investing in *that*. Such a combination of growth, profits, and control enabled the Asians to have occasional semi-planned debt crises to shake out the worst financial imbalances without risking their political or economic systems.

In time, the model spread to other Asian nations, with mixed results. Singapore evolved into a global financial hub, applying Western capital following (mostly) Western norms to projects that made sense to Westerners, while spamming Asian money at more questionable projects throughout Southeast Asia. Malaysia and Thailand used Asian financial strategies to move successfully into semiconductors and electronics, and to (far less successfully) try their hands at automotive. Indonesia focused more on the inherent opportunities for corruption that manifest when money is, in a sense, free. Many of the poor capital allocation decisions shook out from all four (and Korea and Japan and Taiwan) when the 1997–98 Asian financial crisis forced a reckoning.

The biggest of the adherents to the Asian financial model is, of course, China. It isn't so much that the Chinese applied the model in any fundamentally new ways, but instead that they carried the model to its absurd extremes by nearly every measure.

Part of the absurdity is simply size. When China started down its development path in 1980, it already had one billion people, more than the combined total of the rest of the East Asian nations, from Japan to Indonesia.

Part was timing. China's entrance into the global Order did not occur until after the Nixon-Mao summit, the death of Mao, and the initiation of broad-spectrum economic reforms in the late 1970s. By the time the Chinese were ready to get down to the business of business, the gold standard was nearly a decade gone. Modern Communist China has known nothing *but* the era of fiat currencies and cheap money. It had no good habits to break.

Part was the nature of Beijing's unification goals. Korea, Malaysia, and Indonesia have half their populations on a small footprint (Greater Seoul for the Koreans, the west coast of the middle Malay Peninsula for Malaysia, and the island of Java for Indonesia). Japan was the world's most ethnically pure state *before* it industrialized. Singapore is a *city*. These Asian states *began* with reasonably unified populations.

Not so with China. China is messy.

Even eliminating the un- and lightly populated portions, China spans more than 1.5 million square miles, about the same size as all of Western Europe. This populated 1.5 million square miles spans climate zones from near desert to near tundra to near tropics.* Even the "simple" part of China, the North China Plain, has witnessed more wars and ethnic cleansings than any other spot on the planet. The Yangtze Valley in China's center has ranked among the world's most sophisticated economies for most of recorded history. Southern China's rugged landscapes have hosted everything from the poorest and most technologically backward of Asia's many peoples to the hypertechnocracy of Hong Kong.

Every country puts a premium on political unification. *Every* country has fought internal wars to achieve it. China's own internal unification effort is one of the world's most heinous, stretching back across four millennia and dozens of discrete conflicts. The most recent major dustup—Mao's Cultural Revolution—killed at least 40 million people, twenty-five times the number of Americans killed in *all* wars. The Chinese belief in the necessity of internal political violence, repression, and propaganda didn't manifest out of nowhere, but is instead viewed as a necessary reality to avoid nightmarish civil wars. The solution?

Spend!

The Chinese government assigns capital to *everything*. Infrastructure development. Industrial plant buildout. Transport systems. Educational systems. Health systems. Everything and anything that puts people in jobs. Excruciatingly little of it would qualify as "wise capital allocation." The goal isn't efficiency or profitability, but instead achieving the singular political goal of overcoming regional, geographic, climatic, demographic,

---

* *Un*populated China has *actual* desert and *actual* tundra and *actual* tropics.

ethnic, and millennia of historical barriers to unity. No price is too high.

And so a price was indeed paid:

Fresh new lending in calendar year 2020 was about 34.9 trillion yuan (roughly US$5.4 trillion), which, even if you use the statistics for national economic size that even Chinese state economists say are bloated, comes to just shy of 40 percent of GDP. The best guess is that as of calendar year 2022, total outstanding corporate debt in China has reached 350 percent of GDP, or some 385 trillion yuan (US$58 trillion).

The Chinese have embraced the fiat currency era just as warmly as they embraced the Asian financial model. China regularly prints currency at more than double the rate of the United States, sometimes at *five* times the U.S. rate. And whereas the U.S. dollar is *the* store of value for the world and *the* global medium of exchange, the Chinese yuan wasn't even used in Hong Kong until the 2010s.*

Part and parcel of the Chinese financial model is that there is no top. Because the system throws a bottomless supply of money at issues, it is *hongry*. Nothing—and I mean *nothing*—is allowed to stand in the way of development. Price is no issue because the volume of credit is no issue. One result among many is insane bidding wars for any product that exists in limited quantity. If ravenous demand for cement or copper or oil drives product prices up, then the system simply deploys more capital to secure them.

Something similar occurred in Japan in the 1980s with real estate, when for a brief and bizarre moment a square mile of downtown Tokyo was supposedly worth more than the entire U.S. western seaboard. The

---

* One of the (many) reasons I've never had confidence in the Chinese system is that the Chinese . . . don't. A few years back, the Chinese government loosened restrictions on financial transfers in an effort to establish the Chinese yuan as a global reserve currency. It backfired. Within six months the Chinese citizenry had shuffled more than $1 trillion in assets beyond the reach of the Chinese government. Beijing quickly aborted the plans and slammed the transfer system shut.

Japanese immediately recognized that this was not a sign that things had gone radically right, but instead that something had gone radically *wrong*. The Chinese have yet to register such a dark eureka. In particular the Chinese boom stressed global commodities markets between 2003 and 2007, with oil prices reaching historical, inflation-adjusted highs in 2007 of approximately $150 a barrel.

Another result is massive overproduction. China is worried about idle hands, not bottom lines. China is by far the world's largest exporter of steel and aluminum and cement because it produces more of all three than even hyper-ravenous China can use. China's much-discussed One Belt One Road global infrastructure program—which many non-Chinese fear is part influence peddling, part strategic gambit—is in many ways little more than a means of disposing of the surpluses.

Perhaps the most significant result of the Chinese derivation of the Asian financial model is that there is no *end*. All the other Asian states ultimately came to terms with the massive-debt-eventually-leads-to-dumpster-fires nature of the model. Japan crashed in 1989 and took thirty *years* to emerge from under the debt. The recovery took so long that Japan lost the entirety of its demographic dividend and is unlikely to ever have meaningful economic growth again. Indonesia crashed in 1998, which destroyed its government. Twice. The country's political system remains a chaotic mess. Korea and Thailand also crashed in 1998 and used the pain to solidify transition to civilian rule (a process that bore more durable results in Korea than Thailand).

None of these options can be considered in Beijing. The Chinese Communist Party's *only* source of legitimacy is economic growth, and China's *only* economic growth comes from egregious volumes of financing. Every time the Chinese government attempts to dial back the credit and make the country's economy more healthy or sustainable, growth crashes, the natives start talking about making lengthy strolls in large groups, and the government turns the credit spigot back to full. In the CCP's mind, moving away from debt-as-all is synonymous with the end of modern China, unified China, and the CCP. In that, the Party is probably correct. It's no surprise then that the CCP's preferred method of storing their wealth is in U.S. currency . . . *outside* of China.

THE GREAT CONFLATION: THE EURO MODEL

The Europeans are far more reserved than the Asians when it comes to finance, but that's a bit like saying Joan Rivers didn't like plastic surgery as much as Cher.

The profit motive is alive and well in Europe, with everything from home ownership to industrial expansion constrained by capital availability. Yet Europeans demand higher levels of service, stability, and support from their governments, and most European governments secure that service, stability, and support by tinkering with financial systems, most notably via banks.

The most common tinkerings? Directing "private" banks to expend capital to support state financing, either via direct loans to state-approved projects or firms, or via bond purchases to support government budgets. This partial state capture of the financial world has a wide variety of sometimes-not-very-subtle outcomes. An obvious one is that European stock markets aren't nearly as large as America's, in part because there isn't as much free private cash available to fill out that particular method of capital generation. A less obvious one is the existence of the European common currency, the euro, itself.

According to traditional (and certainly non-Asian) financial norms, issues such as collateral requirements, credit access, and borrowing costs are based on a combination of factors ranging from personal or corporate history, preexisting debt loads, and straight-up believability. It isn't too complicated: if you want to borrow, it behooves you to prove that you have paid off your debts in the past, that you can afford the loan servicing that will come from new borrowing, and that you aren't planning to do anything stupid with the money. Add in some decision-making brackets based on the health of the broader economy, and color everything for current government policy as regards finance in general, and voila! Lending policy.

An obvious characteristic that comes from this is that no two economies are the same. Credit at the *national* level is also colored by a combination of size and diversity. Germans tend to enjoy easy access to credit not simply because they are frugal and borrow little and so are good credit bets, but also because the German economy is first-rate, highly diversified, macroeconomically stable, and highly productive, and German firms and governments tend to be run by . . . frugal Germans. Borrowing in Italy costs more because the Italian government and population are as laid-back about debt repayments as they are about everything else. The Greek economy is a one-horse tourism show manned by a people with relatively loose understanding of what makes places like Germany tick. Everyone's a bit different. Europe has thirty different countries with thirty different credit traditions.

Somewhere along the line, the Europeans misplaced this basic understanding. They conflated the idea that having a unified currency would deepen economic regional integration as well as push Europe along toward the goal of becoming globally powerful.

For reasons that only made sense at the time, in the 1990s and early 2000s it became Europe's conventional wisdom that everyone in Europe should be able to borrow at terms that previously had only been offered to the most scrupulous of Europeans. Furthermore, such borrowing should be green-lighted in *any* volume for *any* project by *any* government or corporation at *any* level. Austrian banks gorged on the near-free capital and lent it on to Hungary's own version of subprime. Spanish banks started up flat-out slush funds for their local political influencers. Italian banks started lending en masse not simply to their own mob, but to organized crime syndicates in the Balkans. The Greek government took out massive loans, which it disbursed to pretty much everyone. Construction of entire towns where no one wanted to live. Workers received thirteenth- and fourteenth-month salary bonuses. Citizens received direct payments *simply for being citizens*. Greece hosted an Olympics *entirely on credit*. Massive graft. Everyone could (and did) play.

Greece became the poster child of the ensuing financial calamity. Despite only adopting the euro in 2001, Greece by 2012 sported a national debt in excess of 175 percent of GDP, in addition to busted loans within its private banking system, which contributed another 20 percent of GDP to the stack. Greece was hardly alone. Before all was said and done, nine EU member states required bailouts. Nor did the Brits, who didn't even join the eurozone, escape unscathed. Between euro borrowing and a certain keeping-up-with-the-Joneses mindset when it came to lending, the European financial crisis ultimately pushed two of the United Kingdom's five biggest banks into outright receivership.

The truly scary thing is Europe never recovered from the popping of the euro bubble. It was not until 2018 that the Europeans finally managed to committee their banking sector into the same degree of crisis mitigation that the Americans pulled off in the first *week* of the financial crisis that started in 2007. At the dawn of the coronavirus crisis in 2019, debt as a percentage of GDP was higher across the board as compared to 2007. The bulk of the eurozone had been in and out of recession multiple times before the 2020–21 COVID pandemic pushed everyone underwater at the same time. The countries that experienced credit breakdowns—most notably Greece—remain in receivership in 2022.

The only way to recover from COVID required even more debt—to the tune of *another* 6.5 percent of GDP.* It is debt that will *never* be repaid, because not only is today's Europe long past the point of demographic no return, but also, most of the core European countries have *already* aged into obsolescence, absolutely precluding any of them returning to the economic status of 2006. Europe faces hordes of problems, but if they hadn't mucked up their financial world, the Europeans would have at least had some powerful tools to cope. No more. The entire European system is now doing little more than going through the motions until the common currency inevitably shatters.

---

* On average. COVID generated a bit of an every-country-for-itself scramble across the Continent, so the data, and results, vary wildly from place to place.

Before you get all judgy about the Asians or Europeans, please understand that they are hardly the only ones taking advantage of the cash-for-everyone world we currently live in. The Americans are *no* exception.

BOOM TO BUST AND BACK AGAIN: THE AMERICAN MODEL

In the pre-1971 world, the scarcity of capital meant most work in the energy sphere was managed top-down, with as few players as possible, in order to manage risk. Exxon produced the crude oil in foreign countries. Exxon shipped the crude home via tankers. Exxon refined the crude into fuel at refineries it owned. Exxon distributed that fuel to retail stations. Exxon's network of franchises sold the fuel to consumers.

Post-1971, however, the laws of capital were, if not repealed, then certainly loosened. The new structure of capital supported risk taking almost by default. New firms popped up to handle discrete tasks such as prospecting or transport or refining rather than the full well-to-customer chain. These new firms swam alongside—or even within—the internal systems of the major energy players.

Enter Enron. In the late 1980s, Enron began its expansion with an eye to becoming the quintessential middleman throughout the American energy complex. It created natural gas "banks" that enabled it to be the connective tissue between producer and consumer. In a pre-1971 world, the cost of inventorying a product as squirrelly as natural gas anywhere but at the point of consumption would have been silly.* But post-1971, the capital was available to try out all kinds of new ideas. Enron's original business in natural gas expanded into oil expanded into electricity expanded into pulp and paper expanded into telecommunications expanded into data transfer.†

---

*   Since natural gas is, well, a *gas*, it is difficult to contain. It's also somewhat . . . explosive if managed badly.

†   If you fail to see the natural connections among these industries, you are . . . not even remotely alone.

But Enron owned practically nothing, not even the means of transmission in most cases. Instead, Enron earned its income by buying and selling promises for the future taking and delivering of various products. The futures market is a real thing—it provides reliability to both producers and consumers by linking them with partners before the instant delivery is required—but playing in the middle space requires some pretty sacrosanct bookkeeping.

Enron was great at bookkeeping. The sacrosanct part? Not so much. It turns out that when you don't actually own anything or move anything or add value to anything, your *sole* income comes from what is in your ledger. Enron got really good at moving things on paper, "adding value" on paper to simulate income. They were so good that many believed Enron was the wave of the future, and so bought in. At its peak, Enron was the United States' seventh most valuable publicly traded company.

The word for what Enron did is "fraud."

When Enron introduced *weather* futures and changed its motto to "the world's best company," even the firm's biggest cheerleaders picked up on the Danish stench. Within five months of the first leaks, Enron's high-flying stock plunged to the single digits of cents and the firm was undeniably in bankruptcy. Since the firm held so few assets, its creditors didn't have many bones to gnaw on.

A more scaring example:

As the United States' 2000–01, Enron-tinged recession gave way to a long, robust, low-inflation expansion, the American housing market grew in leaps and bounds.

Part and parcel of the American Dream is that you will enjoy a better economic life than the preceding generation. From the 1950s through the 1980s, middle-class white Americans codefined "American Dream" with "home ownership." Via a mix of evolving cultural norms and government prodding, this aspect of the dream threw a wider net in the 1990s and 2000s. Banks played a bigger role in housing markets. Home-building firms expanded in number and reach. Government institutions more directly intervened to reduce transaction and interest costs for home purchasers.

Backed by broad-scale government, financial, and cultural forces, an entirely new sort of firm manifested. These new "mortgage origination companies" identified would-be homebuyers, provided the financing to get them into homes, and then sold the resulting mortgages on to investors. Those investors bundled the mortgages together into packages and then sliced them into pieces for circulation on bond markets. The idea was that mortgages were the safest of investments (people will do whatever they can to not lose their home and the money they've sunk into it). By turning mortgages into bonds (specifically "mortgage-backed securities"), more investors of more types could put more money into the market, driving financing costs down for everyone.

With capital no longer being the restrictive factor it once was, credit terms gradually got easier. Long gone were the days when a would-be homebuyer would have to put half down. Half became a quarter. A quarter became a fifth. A fifth became a tenth. A tenth became a twentieth. A twentieth became nothing. Nothing became . . . 5 percent *cash back*. Credit checks became less strict. Eventually they disappeared altogether. Now issuing mortgages to clients they *knew* could not service payments on their new homes, the mortgage origination companies started selling their mortgages within days, even hours, of arranging home sales, for fear someone would discover the jig was up. The mortgage-backed securities quickly degraded from the safest of all investments to something even Enron would have balked at. New homeowners started defaulting on their mortgages *before they had even made a single payment*. It all went belly-up. We know the subsequent economic carnage as the 2007–09 financial crisis.

An example with longer reach:

The United States in the 2000s was far and away the world's largest oil consumer and importer, making it sensitive to the ebb and flow of global oil markets. Starting in 2004, oil markets got a serious flow on. Prices quadrupled in under four years. Such a crushing increase was more than enough motivation to drive a spate of new innovations in America to generate higher levels of domestic energy supplies.

Some of these new innovations you've undoubtedly heard of: horizontal

drilling provided access to new sources of crude that conventional production techniques could not, pressurized water injection fractured the
source rock, enabling trillions of packets of crude oil to flow to the well
shaft, better recycling techniques reduced the volume of water required
by more than 90 percent, better fluid management removed toxicity from
the system, and improved data management enabled drillers to fine-tune
their operations to strike only the very specific spots that held hydrocarbons. The world knows these collective advances as either "fracking" or
the "shale revolution" and collectively they made the United States the
world's largest oil and natural gas producer.

But there's an aspect to shale most have overlooked: finance.

Developing new technologies isn't cheap. Drilling down a vertical mile
isn't cheap. Turning that vertical drill shaft and then drilling two *horizontal* miles isn't cheap. Pressurizing liquids on the surface to crack apart
rock three miles down the drill shaft isn't cheap. Getting server time to
interpret the seismic backscatter in order to optimize the fracking process
isn't cheap. Training crews to do work that has never been done before
isn't cheap. And then all the "normal" parts of the oil industry—most
notably building webworks of gathering and distribution pipe and rail
infrastructure—isn't exactly free, either. All in, as recently as 2012 producing a barrel of oil from shale formations cost around $90 a barrel.

As is normal in the United States, most technological innovations in
rapidly evolving industries—like shale—are made by the smaller players.
If there is one thing smaller companies have in common, it is that they
need help accessing capital. But combine the overwhelming American
strategic and economic need for more domestic oil production in a high-
price environment with the financial possibilities of the fiat currency era
and this issue simply melted away. Wall Street spammed the shale patch
with money: commercial loans, direct loans, bonds, stock purchases, direct
cash infusions from financial groups in the form of drilling joint ventures,
production hedging contracts. All these and more funneled capital into
the growing industry.

In retrospect, not all of it made a great deal of sense. Shale wells tend to
kick out the majority of their production in just the first several months of

their twentyish-year life cycle. That tends to suggest that the capital will either be repaid quickly . . . or never. In many cases, it definitely proved to be never. Yet for more than a decade, few firms were called to the carpet. Instead, those same small firms were able to go back to the market again and again to secure *more* financing to enable *more* drilling. The treadmill of production, production, production—but not necessarily profit—had an eerily familiar Chinese quality to it. Such repeatedly questionable financing decisions would have never been made in the world before 1971, but because they *could* be made in the world of fiat currencies, the United States experienced the greatest expansion in oil output in absolute terms of any oil patch, ever.

Don't think for a moment that such profligacy in the United States is limited to finance, real estate, and energy. The last American president to even pretend to care about fiscal prudence was Bill Clinton, a dude not known for . . . prudence. On his watch, the U.S. government did indeed balance the federal budget. Then along came George W. Bush, who ran some of the largest budget deficits since World War II. His successor, Barack Obama, doubled those deficits. The next guy, Donald Trump, doubled them again. At the time of this writing, in early 2022, the next dude in line, Joe Biden, has bet his political life on multiple spending plans that if enacted would double those deficits *again*.

None of this—Enron, subprime, shale, or the federal fiscal deficit, to say nothing of the European common currency or modern China *as a country*—would have been possible without the near-limitless capital of the fiat age.

DISASTER IS RELATIVE

The point of this not-so-little, historically heavy diatribe into the foibles of the fiat age is threefold:

First, the fiat age has enabled economies large and small, countries near and far, to paper over their problems with cash. The factors that enable this or that place to do well in any given age—the Geography of Success—pale in comparison to a bottomless supply of low-cost capital. Sure, we've seen plenty of financial bubbles under fiat, but the most important takeaway is that all that money has put economic history on hold. Under fiat, every*one* every*where* can be successful. So long as the money keeps coming.

Second, everyone—and I mean everyone—is doing it. The only systems in existence today that are *not* expanding their money supply are those that have consciously chosen to forgo economic growth in favor of price stability. Typically, these are locations that have experienced recent economic shocks and are attempting to find their footing. In the late-capitalism era, such exceptions are very few, very far between, and insignificant to the broader picture.

Third, no one—and I mean no one—is printing currency at the same rate.

Yes, the Americans have probably expanded their money supply more than is entirely reasonable, but try to maintain some perspective:

- America had a record number of homes available when the subprime bubble popped (roughly 3.5 million), but that was then. The United States still has positive population growth, so people *want* those homes. They are *not* stranded assets. The generation moving into single-family homes in the 2010s and early 2020s are the Millennials—the second-largest generation in U.S. history. And about 1 percent of the housing stock is destroyed every year simply due to obsolescence, fire, and tear-downs. By 2021 the number of homes available had plunged to below 700,000, a record *low*. I'm not attempting to wave away poor capital allocation decisions from the 2000s, but without the subprime pulse, America's housing issues in the 2020s would be far, far worse.

- A similar balancing occurred with the shale sector. Credit terms tightened in chunks, because banks wised up, because Wall Street turned dubious, because of price shocks in the energy market that no financially strapped firm could survive. By 2022 the number of shale operators had dropped by two-thirds compared to 2016. Yes, a lot of small companies lasted far too long on the cheap credit, but their collective efforts developed an entire new generation of technologies the Americans will coast on for decades.

- The American monetary expansion during the 2007–9 financial crisis was about preventing financial Armageddon. It was strictly necessary, and in part because of the crisis-related reforms, American banks are now by far the healthiest on the planet. Nor was the financial crisis expansion all that big, relatively speaking. Total monetary expansion for the entire period was "only" about $1 trillion—less than 15 percent of the money supply.

Compare that to Europe, where monetary expansion since 2006 has occurred as a matter of course in order to keep alive a banking sector that is among the world's least stable and healthy. In under two years, the European banking crisis expansion increased the euro money supply by 80 percent. And it isn't just about crisis mitigation. The Europeans and Japanese regularly expand their money supply whenever they have a polit-ical goal to meet, a decision-making process that encourages most people who are not European and Japanese from holding or transacting in their currencies at all. As such, their money supplies have often *surpassed* that of the United States, despite the fact that both the European euro and especially the Japanese yen are no longer true global currencies.

But it is China, where monetary expansion is the standard operating procedure for everything, that has truly broken the bank. Since 2007—the year everyone started talking about the Chinese taking over the planet—the supply of yuan has increased by more than eight *hundred* percent.

Outside the mainland, the Chinese yuan is *only* popular in Hong Kong, and *only* because Hong Kong serves as the financial intersection between China proper and the rest of the world. Anywhere else, the yuan is nearly nonexistent. The Chinese economy, even by the boasts of the most ultranationalist of Chinese, is still significantly smaller than the American economy, and yet the Chinese money supply has been larger than America's for a decade—often twice as big. So of course the yuan is a store of value for no one. Capital flight out of China to the U.S. dollar network regularly tops $1 trillion annually.

China's financial system, paired with its terminal demographics, condemns it to not being consumption-led, or even export-led, but lending-led. That makes China vulnerable to any development anywhere in the world that might impinge raw material supply, energy supply, or export routes—developments Beijing cannot influence, much less control. China has been on this path to destruction for nearly a half century. This is not the sort of iceberg-on-the-horizon disaster that any tightly controlled, forward-thinking, competently led government should fall prey to.

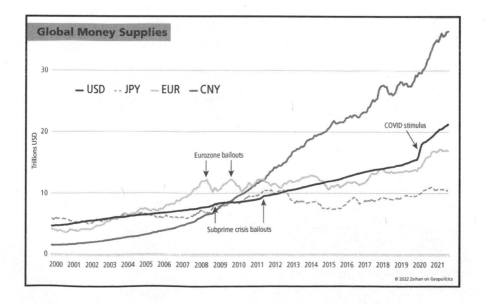

Global Money Supplies

— USD ·· JPY — EUR — CNY

Trillions USD

Eurozone bailouts

Subprime crisis bailouts

COVID stimulus

30
20
10
0

2000 2001 2002 2003 2004 2005 2006 2007 2008 2009 2010 2011 2012 2013 2014 2015 2016 2017 2018 2019 2020 2021

© 2022 Zeihan on Geopolitics

So, have the Americans played a bit fast and loose with their monetary policy? Perhaps. Will that have consequences down the line? Probably. Will those consequences be comfortable? Probably not. But it is the Europeans and Japanese who have gone off the deep end, while the Chinese have swum out to sea during a hurricane and dived headfirst into the Texas-sized whirlpool that serves as Godzilla's front door. Scale matters.

Particularly when the rules change.

At issue is that the general surge of capital availability of the fiat age is only *half* the problem. There is a second, more traditional factor that has amped up capital supplies and smothered capital costs in recent years. And it is in the process of imploding.

THE END OF MORE, REDUX
DEMOGRAPHICS AND CAPITAL

It is a simple issue of age.

From the dawn of civilization right up through the mid–Industrial Age, the various age groups—children, young workers, advanced workers, and retirees—existed in a rough balance that only changed at the margin. That made for a very stable, if very limited, capital supply. Young people borrow to fuel their spending, and there are a lot of them demanding that capital.

Mature workers tend to spend less, while simultaneously being the rich people of their societies. They have accrued wealth over their life spans, while simultaneously spending less than they did when they were young. Their financial output—whether in the form of investments made or taxes paid—forms the backbone of every society. But simple mortality means they don't exist in large numbers. Few savers, many spenders. Supply and demand. Borrowing costs stay high.

Industrialization changed the game. The early industrializers experienced longer life spans and lower child mortality, leading to a rough tripling of their populations. At the same time, industrialization triggered mass urbanization, which in time led to smaller families and aging populations. The key phrase there is "in time." Not everyone started at the same time or saw changes to population structures at the same rate. As a rule, the early industrializers proceeded the most slowly.

Then the Americans used the Order to extend globalization and stability to the entire human family, China included. *Every* country started down the path toward industrialization and urbanization. The latecomers were able to jump over entire phases of the industrialization process, progressing directly from iron to steel, from aluminum to fiberglass, from copper pipes to PVC to flexible tubing, from landlines to cell phones to smartphones. The later a country began the urbanization process, the faster that urbanization process unfolded and the *faster that birth rates crashed.*

Since the Cold War's end, nearly all peoples have gotten richer, but more important for the world of finance, the time-compressed nature of the modernization process means all peoples have gotten *older.* In the world of 1990 through 2020, this has been just peachy because it meant all the richest and most upwardly mobile countries of the world were in the capital-rich stage of their aging process more or less at the same time. Throughout that three-decade period there have been a *lot* of countries with a *lot* of late-forty- through early-sixty-somethings, the age group that generates the most capital. Their investment dollars and euros and yen and yuan have flooded out into the system, often ignoring international borders. Collectively, their savings has pushed the supply of capital up while pushing the cost of capital down. For *everything. Everywhere.* Between 1990 and 2020 this broad convergence of factors brought us the cheapest capital supplies and fastest economic growth in the history of our species. On top of the general craziness of the fiat age. On top of the hypergrowth of the Order era.

Mortgage rates have been the lowest in history and advanced governments have on occasion been able to borrow at negative rates, while the major stock markets continue to explore higher and higher ground. Omnipresent, historically cheap capital has also pushed down financing costs for anyone who wants to start a new production line or clear new agricultural land or write new software or build a new ship. The explosion in industrial output and technological advances of the past decade or so are largely due to the combination of the lingering Bretton Woods system and this demographic moment of a huge oversupply of mature workers. *And their money.*

The same capital is also responsible for recent explosions of stupid. In early 2021 a bunch of *gamers* hurled so much capital into the video game platform GameStop that it briefly became one of America's most valuable firms, despite being about to file for bankruptcy. Cyptocurrencies like Bitcoin are not backed by a government, are not readily exchangeable, are not useful in making payments, have no intrinsic value, and are primarily generated by Chinese magnates seeking an end run around sanctions, yet the combined value of all cryptos is in excess of $2 trillion. My personal favorite is something called Dogecoin, which was literally *formed as a joke to highlight how idiotic crypto investors could be.* At times the total value of dogecoins has topped $50 billion. All of this and more is textbook over-capitalization of a nearly Chinese scale. When capital is cheap enough, even pigs can fly.

Once.

Back to demographics. People don't stop aging just because times are good. The slowly aging demography of the United States and the moderately aging demographies of Japan and the Europeans and the quickly aging demographies of the advanced developing world all converge on mass retirement in the 2020s and 2030s. And when they retire—when *all of them retire at once*—they will stop providing the capital that has fueled our world. At about the same time the United States stops holding up the ceiling.

Two big things come from this.

First, much of this new development generates greater production and higher consumption regardless of the underpinning realities of an economy. This encourages government bingeing (think Obamacare or the Trump administration's federal budget or the Greek debt crisis). This encourages consumer bingeing (think Italian bank debt or American subprime real estate). This encourages overproduction of an endless variety of products that might have questionable economics (think Chinese manufacturing or the dot-com boom/bust). Cheap credit grants people and firms who normally couldn't be in the game the illusion of unde-featability. But what feels natural and heady and sustainable during good times does not—cannot—last forever. When the money stops flowing and financing costs increase, the whole thing comes crashing down.

Second, it is *so* coming crashing down. There's no geopolitical forecast here. It is basic math. The majority of the men and women in the world's mature worker bulge—those all-important Baby Boomers—will hit retirement in the first half of the 2020s. Retirees no longer have new income to invest.

That's worse than it sounds for the world of finance.

Not only is there nothing new to be invested, but what investments they do have tend to be reapportioned from high-earning stocks, corporate bonds, and foreign assets to investments that are inflation-proof, stock market crash-proof, and currency crash-proof. Out with the Chinese tech start-up fund, Rwandan infrastructure bonds, and Bolivian lithium projects, and in with T-bills, money markets, and cash. Otherwise a single market correction could wipe out decades of savings and the now-retiree could lose everything. This is smart and logical for the individual, but not so hot for the broader system, for two reasons.

The first is pretty obvious. Credit is the lifeblood of a modern economy. If you're a company, borrowing helps you meet payroll, fund expansions, purchase machinery, and build new facilities. Every Jane or Joe uses credit every day: college loans, car loans, mortgage loans, home equity loans, credit cards. It is the lubrication that makes pretty much everything possible. Without credit, one of the few methods of purchasing goods is with cash, up front and in full. How long would it take you to earn enough to pay for your car, your college education, or your house—up front and in full?

Raise the costs of that credit and everything slows down, assuming it doesn't simply grind to a stop. In the 2021 fiscal year, the United States government paid about $550 billion in interest. Raise government borrowing costs by a single percentage point and those payments *double*. The United States government can swing that sort of increase. But what about Brazil? Or Russia? Or India? Let's make this more personal. Raise the interest rate on a standard mortgage loan by 2.5 percent—which would make mortgage rates *still well below the half-century average*—and your monthly payment increases by *half*. That's more than enough to put home purchases out of reach of most people.

The second is less obvious, but equally as noticeable. Mature workers don't only generate a lot of income and capital; they pay a lot of *taxes*. The world in general and the advanced world in particular has had loads of mature workers in recent decades, making government coffers the flushest they have ever been. That's *great*! It pays for things like education and law enforcement and health care and infrastructure and disaster relief.

Or at least it's great until those mature workers retire. Instead of paying into the system, retirees *draw* from the system in the form of pensions and health care costs. Replace a tax-heavy, mature-worker-heavy demographic of the 2000s and 2010s with the tax-poor, retiree-heavy demographic of the 2020s and 2030s and the governing models of the post–World War II era do not simply go broke, they become societal suicide pacts.

Once again, recent decades have been *the* best time in human history, and we are *never* going back. Even worse, we're not looking down the maw of a return to 1950s-style government services—at that point there was relative balance between young workers, mature workers, and retirees. For much of the world, we're looking down the maw of *1850s*-style government services before most governments even offered services, but without the attendant economic growth that would allow populations a chance to take care of themselves.

A CREDIT COMPENDIUM

Add the extravagances and exaggerations of the fiat era to the excesses and eruptions of the demographic moment and we have experienced the largest credit surges in human history. In the United States we know the biggest chunk of those surges as the subprime era. From 2000, when the subprime industry was birthed, to 2007, when it ended, total credit in the United States roughly doubled. The ensuing crash from such irrational exuberance knocked roughly 5 percent off of U.S. GDP in the two years before the economy found its footing.

Doubling of credit. Five percent economic drop. That's a good baseline. Now let's look at everyone else . . .

- Everyone has heard about the mess that is **Greece**. The Greeks were admitted into the eurozone despite not meeting . . . well . . . *any* of the requirements in regard to debts and deficits. They then proceeded to act like a college dropout wielding a distant stepparent's platinum credit card. Total credit expanded by a factor of seven in just seven years. The bill eventually came due, the country crashed, and during the following three years the Greek economy proceeded to implode by twice as much in relative terms as the United States did during the Great Depression. By 2019 things were looking . . . if not better, then at least not quite as bad. Enter COVID. As a tourism-dependent economy, Greece once again dropped into free fall. If the country continues to exist at all, it will be as a ward of someone else.

- **Germany**, unsurprisingly, is the polar opposite. The Germans are remarkably conservative in their financial dealings, both as a people and a government. Qualifying for a mortgage first requires making regular mortgage-like payments into a sequestered bank account for several *years* to prove attitude and bona fides. As such, the Germans avoided the sort of catastrophic financial collapses that bedeviled much of Europe in the 2007–9 financial crisis. One result among many was that the German economy bounced back first and fastest, leading firms across the Continent to put their eggs in the German basket while the rest of Europe withered. Two cheers for the Germans! But only two. The establishment of all things German at Europe's center bred resentment throughout Europe.

- A far from insignificant amount of that resentment put down roots in the **United Kingdom**, where the 2007–9 financial crisis emboldened economic and ethnic nationalists to push for separating the kingdom from the European Union. As part of the ensuing struggle, Britain's political right and left both imploded. Populists ultimately took control of the British political right and led the kingdom through the haphazard process we know today as Brexit, while the left fell under the control of barely whitewashed neofascists for a time.

- The credit build in **Hungary** in the 2000s was among Europe's biggest, expanding by a factor of *eight*. Much of that capital flooded into the housing market in a way that would make American subprime financiers blush, putting people with minimal income or credit histories into homes they could not pretend to afford. Making matters worse, most of the loans were in foreign currencies, so when the inevitable currency swings occurred, even Hungarians who were able to afford their homes under normal circumstances suddenly saw their mortgage payments double. The ensuing economic and financial chaos hardened the political landscape against outsiders of all flavors, enabling Prime Minister Viktor Orban to seize control of the country's entire financial and political space. For all intents and purposes, as of 2022 Hungary is no longer a democracy.

- **Singapore** has a big credit signature, with a fivefold increase in credit since 2000. But Singapore is a financial center and so is constantly investing in places outside of itself. Much of its "private credit" is wrapped up in foreign economies. Additionally, Singapore has a government investment agency—Temasek—that is responsible for funneling a lot of the city-state's money into projects abroad. Factor those items out and the picture doesn't look all that bubbly. That said, Singapore sits on the Strait of Malacca—the world's busiest trade route—and serves as the world's largest transshipment center, to such a degree that its fuel tanks hold and manage the distribution of so much petroleum that they constitute a global price standard. Should anything happen to the velocity of global trade, Singapore's trade-centric economy could not help but suffer in the short term regardless of how well managed the city-state's finances happen to be.

- With the combination of a fairly diversified economy, government policies welcoming immigration, and a bevy of mineral reserves big enough to feed insatiable Chinese demand, **Australia** has avoided recession for a generation. Others noticed, and foreign money has spammed into the country to take advantage of the longest continuous period of economic growth in human history. That has turned the Great Down Under into the most overcredited of the Western countries to not yet experience a credit collapse. Credit has increased sixfold since 2000. Housing and household debt are of course the expected bugaboos, but the credit inflows have pushed the Australian dollar up to uncomfortably unsustainable highs, eroding the competitiveness of every economic sector outside of mining. Any effort the government has taken to decrease demand with regulatory hammers has been overwhelmed by a tax code that not only encourages property ownership, but in fact encourages those already owning residential property to purchase *more*. This would be a problem anywhere, but in Australia it is particularly acute. Oz might seem like a place with a lot of land, but the Outback is beyond useless to residential real estate. The vast bulk of the Aussie population lives in fewer than ten largely disconnected metro regions, sharply limiting availability and driving up the cost of building new housing inventory. This *will* blow. The question is when?

- In **Colombia** credit expanded by a factor of five in a single ten-year period beginning in 2003, but everything about Colombia is a special case. Enmeshed in the Western Hemisphere's worst civil war for the better part of the past century, a particularly violent period pushed the economy (credit availability included) off the cliff in the late 1990s. Much of the 2003–14 credit expansion went hand in hand with progress in the war: as the Colombians reformulated and consolidated their political space and military strategy, the government succeeded in boxing their military opponents into smaller and smaller enclaves, until securing an ultimate peace deal and de facto surrender in 2015. This political and military recovery was mirrored by an economic recovery. Colombia's credit "binge" was, if anything, about regaining lost ground. The challenge moving forward will be to win the peace by demonstrating to those on both sides of the war that not shooting at one another is good for business. The most likely path? Easy credit for all, to spark infrastructure development and consumer activity. Colombia's credit binge isn't in its past. It is in its future.

- **Indonesia** is a country I tend to be bullish about for a mix of reasons: a large, young, upwardly mobile population; a government that by design focuses on the densely (over)populated island of Java, enabling it to concentrate its efforts on a fairly specific and politically unified geography; broad-scale energy security; an excellent location astride the world's most prolific trade routes; and proximity to the massive mineral and agricultural exporters of Australia and New Zealand on one hand, and to the complementary industrial and financial partners of Singapore, Thailand, and Malaysia on the other. To this I add a surprisingly conservative credit profile. Yes, *overall* credit in the Southeast Asian country has risen by a factor of more than seven, but economic growth has outpaced it. Back in 2000 overall credit was equal to GDP—something that would normally be more than a little worrying for a poor, sprawling country like Indonesia. But despite year-on-year rises in absolute credit for the next seventeen years, the ratio of credit to the overall economy has actually fallen by a third. Indonesia still faces a bevy of significant challenges—insufficient skilled labor, rickety infrastructure, corruption (which sits either near the top or *at* the top of the list)—but the country's overcrediting is far less concerning than the headline figure would suggest.

- The credit picture of **Brazil** is a reasonable echo of Greece: a sixfold increase, peaking in 2014. In that year investor sentiment and the Brazilian political system broke at the same time, triggering a political crisis and deep recession that at the time of this writing shows no sign of abating. Making matters worse, Brazil's constitution and currency only date back to the 1990s. Not only is this modern Brazil's first true political and economic crisis, but it is a full-blown *constitutional* crisis that hits at the very bedrock of everything that makes Brazil Brazil. Assuming for the moment that the Brazilian political system regenerates in short order (and there is no sign of that) and that Brazil's governing institutions suffer no additional damage (and that seems sheer fantasy), Brazil faces *years* of severe recession simply to recover from their credit overexpansion. Brazil isn't looking down the maw of a lost decade, but instead at two. At least.

- Given that it has been the world's largest oil exporter for the past fifty straight years, the word "credit" isn't what normally comes to mind when one thinks of **Saudi Arabia**. Yet the Saudis have quite successfully leveraged their oil income stream to acquire rafts of credit for all portions of their system, generating a credit boom of 750 percent since 2000. As this credit is backed by unrelenting income, it *probably* is not as problematic as the situation in Brazil or Australia—and certainly not as bad as Greece. But most of the credit has gone either to vanity projects in the desert, or to subsidies for the population in order to purchase citizen loyalty. When the flow breaks—and it will—that loyalty will crumble. Luckily for the Saudi leadership, the country's internal security services are among the world's most effective . . . at quelling dissent.

- Credit in **India** is up by a cool factor of ten since 2000, with barely a dip along the way. The steady drumbeat of economic expansion has made India a far calmer place politically than its constant bouts of famine and religious and racial churn would suggest. When the correction inevitably arrives, it will be *epic*. I'm perfectly capable of being bullish on India for reasons geopolitical and demographic, while simultaneously warning of a helluva financial crisis.

- In **Turkey** the picture is getting complicated. Between 2000 and 2013, total credit increased by more than a factor of twelve—one of the sharpest and most sustained increases in the world. The boom granted Prime Minister (and now President) Recep Tayyip Erdogan the political capital required to consolidate control over an often-fractious system, ending decades of uncomfortable cohabitation between his own Anatolian religious conservatives, the pro-Western modernizers of the Greater Istanbul region, and a secularized military that saw itself as the guardian of the state. Now there is only Erdogan. But in 2013 the credit expansion stopped in its tracks. The loss of economic legitimacy, the pressure of 3 million refugees from the Syrian civil war, and rising geopolitical hostility from and toward Europe, Russia, Iraq, and the United States mean Erdogan's rule has become brittle, harsh, and increasingly authoritarian. And all that *before* Turkey suffers the inevitable credit correction.

- At the time of this paragraph's addition on February 28, 2022, Russia is being melon-scooped out of global finance as punishment for the Ukraine War, the Russian Central Bank included. By the time you read this, the world will have a fascinating, horrific case study of true financial disintegration. Nor is Russia done. Beset with a population aging into decrepitude and a system that has given up educating the next generation, Russia's credit collapse is but one of a phalanx of factors capable of ending the Russian state. The question isn't will the Russians go out swinging—Russia's invasion of Ukraine is testament to that—but instead, who *else* will they swing at? Over-credited countries beware. Credit collapses can be caused by any number of actions or inactions. They do *not* require a war. Or sanctions.

- Not to belabor the point, but the absolute financial blowout that is **China** has generated the largest and most unsustainable credit boom in human history both in absolute and relative measures. The Chinese will exit the modern world just as they entered it: with a *big* splash. The only question is when. If I had the answer to that you wouldn't be reading this book, because instead of struggling through edits I'd be idling away my days on the Peter Virgin Islands.

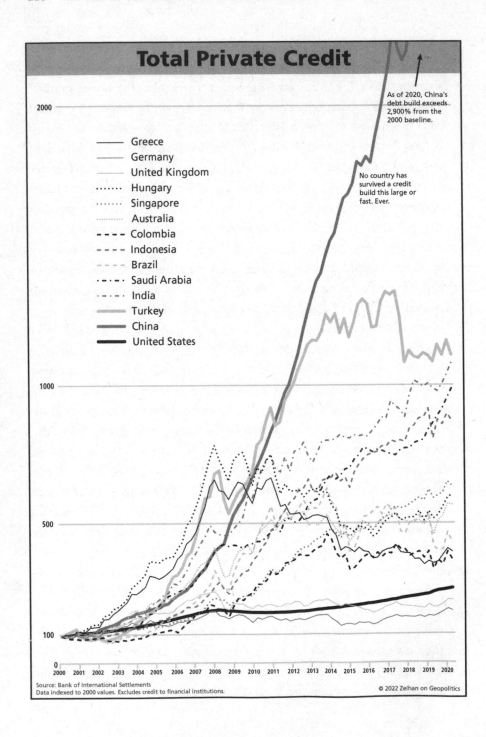

Total Private Credit

As of 2020, China's debt build exceeds 2,900% from the 2000 baseline.

No country has survived a credit build this large or fast. Ever.

Legend:
- Greece
- Germany
- United Kingdom
- Hungary
- Singapore
- Australia
- Colombia
- Indonesia
- Brazil
- Saudi Arabia
- India
- Turkey
- China
- United States

Source: Bank of International Settlements
Data indexed to 2000 values. Excludes credit to financial institutions.

© 2022 Zeihan on Geopolitics

FINAGLING FUTURE FINANCING FAILURES

Between fiat failures and the demographic crunch, the days of cheap, easy, omnipresent finance are ending. Impacts and outcomes will vary not only in nature, but also in application.

We of course need to begin with changed **Geographies of Success**. In any capital-constrained world, more money tends to be applied to locations and populations that have a lot of low-hanging fruit. Infrastructure is easier and cheaper to construct and maintain in flat, temperate zones than in mountains or tropics. Similarly, it is easier and cheaper to maintain skill sets for populations that are already educated than to boost low skill levels. Under the high-capital environment of the late Order, these sorts of simple rules blurred because there was just So. Much. Money! That is ending. In the 2020s and 2030s and beyond, the more familiar patterns we've seen throughout history will reassert themselves with a vengeance, with some regions better able to generate and apply capital than others. Northern Europe over southern Europe over India over Russia over Brazil over the Middle East over sub-Saharan Africa.

Technology is going to be a mess. Server farms, smartphones, and software don't just magically manifest. They are the end results of thousands of concurrent and often unrelated trends. Most broadly, a healthy and growing technology sector requires a massive market to generate revenues and fuel development, gobs of skilled labor to do the brain and implementation work, and a near-bottomless supply of financing to fuel research, operationalization, and mass application.

All three of these broad categories face evaporation. Deglobalization will shrink the global whole and shatter what remains into segregated markets. Global aging is collapsing the skilled labor supply. And financial shrinkage will make *everything* more expensive and more difficult.

Perhaps the worst aspect will be that as capital and labor supplies shrink, the projects that get funding will be those that can slim down their employment profile the most—particularly when it comes to the sort of manufacturing that would normally be outsourced to low-labor-cost locations.

We *are* going to reach a new e-quilibrium, but it is not going to be a techtopia that raises all boats. Countries that have not yet been able to get involved with the technology sector at all now can't even try. Others that had a foot in the door are going to lose their feet. It will be less a story of developed countries' richness and the developing world's poverty, and more a story of a handful of developed countries' richness and everyone else's nothing.

Expect to hear a *lot* about **capital flight** and **capital controls**. In the more or less unified world of the Order, capital can fly back and forth across borders with few limitations. Very few countries have meaningful restrictions, because of a general realization that any steps taken to slow the flow of capital in or out will starve the country of investment, and that has costs: in economic growth, employment, tourism, technological transfer, and opportunities to participate in the modern world in general. Historically, such openness is as abnormal as everything else in the world of the Order, and for the same reasons. "Normally" the world is a bit of a rat race, and capital is something to be hoarded.

The bad ol' days of such capital shortages are coming back. Add in a dozen or so fat dollops of insecurity and instability and you can expect people in much of the world to attempt to relocate their money—and in many cases, themselves—to greener and safer pastures.

Capital flight is already a feature of the late Order. The United States' mostly well-earned reputation for having a hands-off approach to private capital has made it the undeniable global financial hub. The Chinese hyperfinancialization model (and to a lesser degree, similar financial systems throughout East Asia) has sent irregular bursts of cash into the United States. European wobbles since 2000 provided even more. Data on this is extraordinarily hard to come by and even more difficult to vet, but a good guesstimate is that since 2000 somewhere between $1 trillion and $2.5 trillion of foreign money has flowed into the United States each and every year. As the gap between American growth and stability and global depression and instability widens, expect that figure to inflate. A *lot*.

That's great for the Americans, and promises to take a bit of the heat out of rising capital costs, but it is a potential disaster for the countries the money will be coming *from*. Rapidly retiring populations increase demands for state spending, while shrinking working-age populations simultaneously gut government capacity to raise funds. Anyone looking to ship their money out will be viewed as borderline traitorous. Restrictions on such flight—aka capital controls—are the solution.

Outcomes manifest quickly. When firms don't think they will be able to get their profits out of a foreign country, they are far less likely to have any interest in operations in that country in the first place. The biggest risks to capital will be in the places with the fastest-aging populations as well as those with the most rapidly retiring workforces: Russia, China, Korea, Japan, and Germany, in that order.

Inflation will be all over the place. A quick economics lesson:

*In*flation occurs when costs rise, and can be caused by any sort of disconnect in supply and demand: supply chain disruptions when someone hijacks a container ship, a young and/or hungry population that needs more housing and food, fads where everyone *must* have a Cabbage Patch doll, or when a monetary authority expands the money supply to deliberately increase demand. Inflation levels below 2 percent are generally considered okay, but anything above that becomes less and less enjoyable.

*Dis*inflation is a very specific sort of price drop. When your smartphone or computer gets an update that enables you to do something better and quicker, that's disinflationary. It's the same when a new oil field or car plant or copper smelter comes online and increases supply. Prices drop, but the relationships that make up the market are not unduly tweaked. Most folks love a bit of disinflation. I know I sure do.

Then there is *de*flation. Prices drop, but it's because something is very, very wrong. Perhaps your population has aged faster than your housing market or industrial plant can adjust. Cratering demand generates an oversupply in something basic, like electricity or condos or electronics. Markets cannot adjust without amputating part of the production side, which hurts workers, which reduces demand even more. Some version of deflation has been plaguing Japan ever since its economic crash in the 1990s, and the European Union ever since the 2007–09 financial crisis, and it is probably already endemic in China, where increasing-production-at-all-costs is the state mantra.

So, with that under your belt, let's talk about the future.

Monetary expansion is *in*flationary. Endemic capital shortages inject *in*flation directly into finance. The falling consumption of an aging population is *de*flationary, while breaking supply chains are *in*flationary. Building new industrial plant to replace international supply chains is *in*flationary while the process is under way, and *dis*inflationary once the work is completed. New digital technologies tend to be *dis*inflationary, unless international supply chains are needed to keep them running, in which case they are *in*flationary. Currency collapses are *in*flationary in the countries that suffer them as everyone shifts from cash to goods they can hoard, but such collapses are *dis*inflationary in the countries where fleeing capital seeks succor. Commodity shortages are pretty much always *in*flationary, but if the shortage is caused by a supply chain break, then they can be *de*flationary near the commodity's source, which means lower prices, which leads to lower production, which leads to higher prices, which are once again *in*flationary.[*]

My bottom line here is a total cop-out: the future of the . . . -flations[†] will be different in every region, every country, every sector, every *product*, and will change wildly, based on a wide variety of factors that can barely be influenced, much less predicted. I would *hate* to be a bond trader.

Expect a *lot* more **populism**. The global demographic is aging rapidly, and most older folks are rather . . . set in their ways. But more than that,

---

[*]   That was exhausting.

[†]   Yes, I just made up a word.

retirees are dependent upon their **pensions**. Most pension schemes are funded either by tax revenues or by dividends provided by large-scale bond holdings. Bond-related income tends to be low and stable. That means retirees need stable prices. Bond-related income streams tend to break down in prolonged recessions. For many (most?) countries, a depression lasting a decade or two is pretty much baked in at this point. Between de-globalization, demographic collapse, and the coronavirus, most countries will never recover to where they were in 2019. Most pensions are going to fly apart in a world of rising and variable inflation levels.

As a voting bloc, retirees don't so much fear change as endlessly bitch about it, resulting in cultures both reactionary and brittle. One outcome is governments that increasingly cater to populist demands, walling them-selves off from others economically and taking more aggressive stances on military matters. Did you wince at your parents' and grandparents' voting patterns before? Just imagine the sorts of loons they'll support should their pension income fail.

There will be **American exceptions**. The world's best geography will keep development costs low. The rich world's best demography will make America's capital cost increases less onerous. The rise of the American Millennials suggests that by the 2040s—when the Millennials finally age into that capital-rich age bracket—capital *supply* will once again rise, taking the heat out of capital *costs*. The relative conservatism of American monetary policy combined with the U.S. dollar's status as the sole reserve currency grants the Americans more wiggle room in compensating for capital loss and guarantees the Americans the largest proportion of capi-tal flight from a troubled world.

And, oddity of oddities, America's ongoing **inequality** issues might actually provide some help.

Remember how people's income increases with work experience, and how the proportion of income that is invested similarly increases? That happens with the rich just as it does with "normal" people. Where the two groups diverge is at retirement. "Normal" retirees have to shift their holdings into low-risk investments because they cannot tolerate volatility, but rich folks have *so* much stored up that they do two things differently.

First, the ultra-rich only need to preserve a fraction of their holdings to maintain their lifestyle. They can tolerate a much higher risk level and so keep much of their investment portfolio—typically well over *half*—fully engaged in stock and bond markets. Second, the rich are far more likely to realize they can't take it with them, and there's no reason to die with $100 million in the bank. They tend to start transferring assets to the next generation or charities long before they pass on.

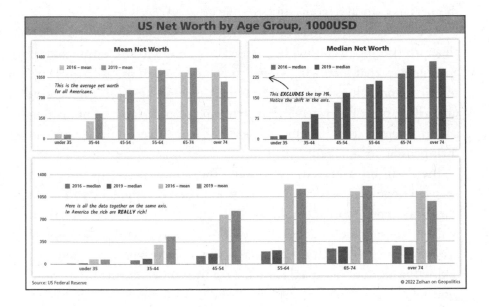

In most countries these differences do not move the needle very much, but in the United States the top 1 percent controls upwards of half of *all* financial assets. If just half of the 1 percent's capital in the American stock and bond markets is *not* liquidated and remains engaged (or is transferred to younger people, who will deploy the capital following more normal patterns), then the general shift to a capital-constrained environment won't be quite so jarring. But this only holds true in advanced countries with large capital markets and screaming inequality. That is a list of exactly one. A large volume of mobile capital cannot fix everything, but in a world of constrained capital? Solid start.

If none of this sounds particularly capitalistic, that's because it is not. The environment that allowed capitalism to exist is part of the "more" we've all become used to, and it is highly questionable whether capitalism can exist without ongoing economic growth.

My point isn't that capitalism is dead, but instead that even the Americans, the youngest and richest advanced population in the world—the people with the most "more" of all—are already eyeball-deep into the transition from a capitalist, globalized system to . . . whatever comes next.

On top of that, if what we know, or at least what we think we know, is *already* fading away in America in the here and now, then what hope does the rest of the world have for figuring out the future?

Now that everyone is cheered up, let's talk about what happens when the lights go out.

SECTION IV:
ENERGY

HARPOONING PROGRESS

Allow me to tell a crazy little story.

In the former Soviet republic of Kazakhstan, there is an oil deposit called Kashagan. It's located two miles *under* the floor of the Caspian Sea, in a zone regularly pummeled by sixty-mile-per-hour winds. In winter not only is there moving sea ice, but the winds carry sea spray, which often entombs the entire offshore production facility itself in *feet* of ice. Kashagan has, bar none, the world's worst operating conditions.

Atypical for oil fields, Kashagan is a vertical deposit, over two miles from top to bottom. It sports wildly variant pressure levels, leading to frequent—and impressively terrifying—blowouts. Its oil is so high in sulfur that the crude must be processed once it makes landfall, generating miles-wide sulfur beds. Kashagan boasts, bar none, the world's most difficult technical environment.

Tapping Kashagan required that the best minds in the industry develop fundamentally new technologies to deal with the field's unique challenges. The consortium of companies developing it spent over $150 *billion*—considerably more than the entire annual GDP of Kazakhstan at the time—and fourteen *years* before even getting to first commercial production. Start-up costs at Kashagan are—bar none—the world's highest. The running joke in energy circles is that "Kashagan" is really pronounced "cash-all-gone."

Once Kashagan's crude is pumped up, depressurized, and processed, it is piped more than one thousand miles to the Black Sea, where it is loaded onto small tankers for transit through the Turkish Straits to the Mediterranean, passing through downtown Istanbul, before sailing on through the Suez Canal to the Red Sea. It its then reloaded onto long-haul supertankers that transport the crude another eight *thousand* miles past Pakistan and India, through the Strait of Malacca, and by the entirety of the Vietnamese and Chinese coasts before reaching its final destination in Japan.

It's a dicey route. Kazakhstan is a former province of Russia and the two do not get along. Turkey has fought eleven (more?) major wars with Russia and they do not get along. Egypt is a former province of Turkey and they do not get along. Saudi Arabia considers Kazakhstan an economic competitor and they do not get along. The route passes by Pakistan and India, who do not get along, and Vietnam and China, who do not get along, and China and Japan, who do not get along. Oh, and there are pirates in the Red Sea and Malacca as well. Kashagan's export route is— bar none—the world's riskiest.

(There *are* iffy plans to ship Kashagan oil east through a series of patched-together and patched-up Soviet pipes to extreme western China, before it is sent on across the two-thousandish-mile trip to the population centers on the Chinese coast. Considering that that route exposes people and infrastructure to temperature swings from 40 degrees below zero every winter to 105 degrees above zero every summer, it is unclear if this would be a logistical improvement.)

Whenever I consider the history and mechanics and export routes of Kashagan, all I can think is, What. The. *Hell???*

The bewildering, Frankensteinian wonder that is Kashagan and its export route could only occur under the aegis of the Order. The Order has made everything so peaceable and stable and wealthy for so long that production and transport systems that would have been considered several steps beyond asinine in any other age are well within reach.

It. Will. Not. Last.

Kashagan's half a million barrels of daily output is obviously not long for this world. But it is hardly the only production zone that faces complete collapse in the years to come. That will be crushing. Modern energy in general and oil in specific is what separates our contemporary world from the preindustrial. It separates what we define as "civilization" from what came before.

Considering the transport conundrums that have held humanity back throughout the six-millennia-long stretch of recorded history, oil is a pretty magical substance. Oil-derived liquid transport fuels increased our capacity to move objects at distance by a factor of one *thousand*. On-demand electricity, directly or indirectly made possible by oil, had a similar impact upon our productivity. For the first time in history, we could do any*thing* and go any*where* at any*time*. Even better, for the first time "we" didn't mean the most powerful empire of the era, but instead *every individual person*. Once your home is wired, everyone can have electricity at low cost. Unlike wood or coal, oil-based liquid fuels such as gasoline and diesel are so energy-dense and so easily stored that we store them *within* our modes of transport.

Without oil, the American-led global Order would have never had a chance. Nor would have passenger cars. Or global food distribution. Or global manufacturing. Or modern health care. Or the shoes most of us are wearing. Oil's power is such that in many ways, it has almost enabled us to ignore nothing less than geography itself.

Almost. Oil is not quite *that* perfect. The restriction oil insists upon is not technological, but instead one of sourcing. Oil feels no obligation to exist in locations that are convenient. For the entirety of the Industrial Age, getting the oil from where it exists to where it is needed has been . . . gnarly. In *that*, Kashagan is no standout.

It is best to start at the beginning. With Captain Ahab.

THE PATH TO MODERN ENERGY: WARS, WORSHIP, WHALES, AND . . . KNITTING?

There are only so many ways to advance the human condition. One is to conquer a big chunk of land and make it your own. Another is to give as many people as you can within your society a stake in the system, so their collective actions support all aspects of the government and economy. A third idea is to drive back the night, and in doing so manufacture that rarest of commodities: time.

By the late 1700s the British were playing around with textiles ever more aggressively and at an ever-larger scale. The newer looms and spindles and spinning jennies had a couple of common characteristics. They were the newest and most expensive technologies of the age. It was important to protect such assets from the elements, and working them required a very keen eye both for quality output and to avoid losing fingers. If you've ever been to England, you'll recognize the problem. English weather is often wet and dark. London is far enough north that December averages less than eight hours of light a day . . . assuming it isn't raining.* That made the interior of the cotton mills *dark*. Traditional torches would have contaminated the yarn and cloth, candles don't generate enough light, and the long-distance backpacker in me can assure you that raw cotton is an excellent fire starter.

The solution was whale oil. Clean, bright, long burning, and easily contained within an appropriate lamp, whale oil protected the staff by limiting injuries while simultaneously boosting how many shifts a facility could run. The stuff quickly became the go-to for everything from church services to cocktail parties to middle-class apartments. And with the early Industrial Revolution providing Europe with food surpluses, humanity was quickly expanding to fill all available space, demanding more oil to light more church services and more cocktail parties and more middle-class apartments.

Nor was whale oil only used for light. The early Industrial Age produced lots of machinery with lots of parts that could get stuck very easily (including the aforementioned textile equipment). To prevent damage to both man and machine, lubrication was the solution. The whale became a panacea: light, lubrication, and some steaks on the side. Everybody won.

Except the whales.

Courtesy of Captain Ahab and men like him, creatures that once existed in the literal millions were reduced in short order to the tens of thousands. Fewer whales meant less whale oil, and the price of whale oil rose.

The solution took two forms:

---

* And it's *always* raining.

First, coal. One of the common dangers in coal mines is methane, a gaseous substance that we know alternatively as natural gas, cow farts, and coal gas. Managing coal gas is a constant challenge for coal miners, since every time a miner cracks into a seam, there's a chance of releasing some hidden pocket of the stuff. Common outcomes are asphyxiation and explosion.

Yet where there's a risk of something *exploding un*controllably, there is also a possibility of making it *burn con*trollably. Add in a bit of Industrial Age chemistry know-how and we figured out how to process coal to generate methane on demand. We'd then pipe it into streetlamps (or textile factories) for light. We saw a fair amount of this sort of thing in southern England, the American Northeast, and Germany.

The second and more widespread solution was something called kerosene. Unlike coal gas, dangers of explosion were nonexistent, *and* you didn't have to be proximate to a coal supply *and* you didn't need to install any infrastructure. You just needed a lamp.

Early kerosene was sourced from coal, but the distillation process was far more expensive and dangerous than getting on a wind-powered vessel and sailing halfway around the world do battle with colossal cetaceans before climbing into their corpses to hack away their insides and then boiling the bits on the same vessel and voyaging back, all while accompanied by a bunch of violently horny ex-cons. Near-simultaneous technological breakthroughs in America and Poland in the early 1850s proved it was far cheaper, faster, and safer to source kerosene from something that at the time was known as "rock oil." Today we call it "crude oil" or simply "oil."

We then turned to sourcing. Humanity had known about crude oil "seeps" since ancient times. The Byzantines used such oil sources to make a party favor known as "Greek fire" for their enemies, while the Zoroastrians preferred to light the seeps on fire to ensure the party never ended. The problem was volume. Such seeps rarely generated more than a few quarts of the stuff a day. Humanity needed a million times more. A billion times more.

The solution bubbled up out of America. In 1858 one Edwin Drake applied some railway engine parts to a vertical drill outside of Titusville, Pennsylvania. Within a few weeks the world's first-ever oil well was producing more crude oil in a couple of hours than most seeps would in a year. Within a few short years, kerosene proved so cheap and easy that whale oil all but vanished from the lighting and lubrication markets.

Then the real miracle arrived. We started applying material science expertise we had only recently gained from tinkering with coal to this new world of oil. It wasn't long before whale-oil-replacement kerosene showed us the way to wind-power-replacement fuel oil and horse-replacement gasoline.* Oil was no longer merely a product needed to push back the night and slick up gears. It was the material that allowed us to do . . . everything. Which meant we didn't simply need more, we needed _more_!

Where do you look for something you need? Well, the last place you saw it, of course. The empires of the day began a hunt, global in scope, for those famous seeps that had colored cultures throughout antiquity, so that they could drill the tar out of them. The northern seeps of Zoroastrian lands (contemporary Azerbaijan) were now in Russian hands. Their southern seeps lay in Persian territory, but that didn't stop the Brits from taking control. The Dutch asserted imperial power over the seeps of Java. The Americans had not only Pennsylvania and the Appalachian Basin, but also the wider Ohio River Valley and Texas. In the rough-and-tumble world of imperial competition up to and including World War II, control of such production sites was not simply an issue of critical importance, but often the difference between strategic strength and obsolescence.

The commonality of these early decades of the oil era were simple: either you had oil and so could field modern military gear, complete with the insane speed and range and striking power it granted, or you were . . . on horseback. Thus oil production sites were among the world's most jealously guarded locations. And *everyone* kept their oil in-house.

This last point was key. Each country had its own major oil company—

---

* "Wasn't long" in relative terms, that is. Whale oil had many uses and it took the better part of seven decades for petroleum to completely eclipse it.

Compagnie Française des Pétroles for France, the Anglo-Persian Oil Company for the United Kingdom, Standard Oil Company for the United States, and so on.* Their first and primary responsibility was to fuel the home front. To that end, exports were sharply limited, foreign production was shipped home, and each country had its own internal pricing structure. Prices among these sequestered systems regularly varied by in excess of a factor of three. The Americans, who produced everything they needed at home and so didn't need a globe-spanning merchant marine, were pretty much always on the low end of the pricing scale.

Between the newness of the oil-related technologies and the criticality of the oil supply, World War II showcased resource centrality in a way unprecedented in human history. Empires used to fight over pepper because of the money its sale could generate. Empires fought over oil because they *couldn't fight a war without it*. The Japanese successfully captured Java in 1942 to acquire Dutch oil resources, while America's unrestricted submarine warfare by the end of 1944 starved the Japanese of fuel. The Germans' desperate bid for those old Zoroastrian assets in Soviet Azerbaijan foundered at Stalingrad in the winter of 1942–43, while the Americans bombed Romanian oil fields in August 1943 to deny the Nazis their output.

On the flip side, America's crude oil came from the Lower 48, not some far-off land dangling at the end of a vulnerable supply line. Not only did the American war machine never face large-scale fuel shortages, but the Yanks were able to keep their British and even Soviet allies fueled up. Without Pennsylvania and Texas, the war would have ended very differently.

Of course, the way the Americans rewired the world at war's end changed everything. Oil was no exception.

---

*   We know them today as Total, BP, and ExxonMobil, respectively.

THE ORDER'S ORDER FOR OIL

When the Americans killed the Imperial Age, they also killed the imperial economic structures that had managed the Imperial Age's oil distribution system. In part this was done with an eye toward firmly condemning the old imperial system to history. After all, if the Brits no longer wholly owned Persian oil, then London would have less global heft.

But a bigger piece of it was the same economics-for-security trade that drove most of the American strategic calculus.

The American plan to contain the Soviets required allies, those allies had to be purchased with the promise of economic access and growth, that access and growth needed to be fueled, and the fuel could only be sourced from so many locations. All of a sudden, instead of British oil and Dutch oil and French oil there was only *global* oil . . . as guaranteed by the U.S. Navy. Any crude could now reach any buyer. All the varied sequestered pricing models collapsed into a single global price, modified only by distance and the specific chemical peculiarities of crude from this or that field.

Oil immediately became tangled up in the new strategic environment.

Known energy producers such as Persia and the Dutch East Indies gained a new lease on life, becoming the independent countries we now know as Iran and Indonesia. Budding energy producers that were technically independent but in reality were half foreign-managed (think: Iraq and Saudi Arabia) were allowed to come into their own. Somewhat unsurprisingly, some European countries resisted decolonialization, but the Americans proved uncharacteristically patient and would often wait until revolutionary movements within the colonies reached critical mass before pressuring their allies, or until the ebb and flow of bilateral relations provided an opening. Thus countries as diverse as Nigeria (1960) and the United Arab Emirates (1971) received independence from the United Kingdom, Algeria (1962) from France, and Angola from Portugal (1975). The end result was as intended: an increasingly diverse list of independent, significant oil suppliers to a globalized—and above all, American-managed—system.

But as much as the logic of the Bretton Woods Order demanded that the Americans build, safeguard, and expand a global oil market, it was the *outcomes* of Bretton Woods that made the process exhausting. The core tease of the Bretton Woods system—what made it so successful in attracting and keeping allies—was the idea of secure, steady, reliable economic growth via access to the American market and global systems. As those allied economies grew, they used more and more crude from places farther and farther away. As the United States drew more and more countries into the alliance, *the Americans* used more and more crude from places farther and farther away, too. By the early 1970s, economic growth back at home had reached the point that America's own energy demands outstripped its production capacity. Not only could the Americans no longer fuel their allies, but they couldn't even fuel themselves. In many ways it was the same problem that ultimately gutted the gold standard: success begot use begot more success begot more use begot failure. The Arab Oil Embargos of 1973 and 1979 turned what had until then been a hypothetical discussion in America into brass tacks.

When events transpired that threatened oil access, the Americans responded as if the end was nigh because, well, it was. Without sufficient volumes of affordable oil, the entire Order would collapse. American (and British!) actions included sponsoring a coup in Iran in 1953 to overthrow a semidemocratic system in favor of a pro-American monarchy. American actions included supporting of a borderline-genocidal purge in Indonesia of communist elements in 1965–66. American actions included the quiet backing of an authoritarian Mexican government against prodemocracy forces in 1968. American actions included the largest American expeditionary military action since World War II as part of the forcible ejection of Iraqi troops from Kuwait in 1992.

With the end of the Cold War, the interconnections of the Bretton Woods system were applied even more broadly, with the Americans deliberately, methodically, unrelentingly expanding the scope of oil availability. The Russian post-Soviet economic collapse hit Russian industry far harder than Russian oil production, with the surplus output reaching global markets. American firms entered former Soviet republics—most notably Kazakhstan and Azerbaijan—to bring ever-larger volumes of crude to the world. As always, the focus was on diversity and security of supply, leading the Clinton administration to push for circuitous pipeline routes to bring as much of the new flows to the global market as possible without utilizing Russian territory.

Throughout the entire period of 1945 on, the process earned the Americans no small amount of umbrage, from . . . nearly everyone. The Europeans resented losing their colonies. The newly freed colonies disliked American efforts to corral them into a bloc to contain a country, the Soviet Union, that few had had any previous contact with. The Arab world didn't appreciate the Americans forcing their energy cog into the Bretton Woods machine (much less attempting to make them bedfellows with the Israelis). The Mexicans begrudged Washington's heavy-handed approach. The (post-Soviet) Russians hated how the Americans expressly worked to undermine their influence in their own backyard. The Iranians *really* didn't appreciate the coup.

But the scale simply kept increasing. At the dawn of the Bretton Woods era, the entire alliance (sans the United States) used under 10 million barrels per day (mbpd), the majority of which was sourced from the United States itself. By 1990 just the advanced members of the coalition were using well over double that, 90 percent of which was imported—and with the Americans all by themselves importing another 8mbpd. With the Cold War's end and the rules of the Order going truly global, an entire new raft of countries joined the party—and added their own demands to the oil story. Prices hit their historical high of $150 a barrel in 2008, a fifteenfold increase from just a decade earlier, even as global demand topped 85mbpd.

What had begun as an effort to subsidize a military alliance with American crude had devolved into a bloated, unsustainable, and above all *expensive* mess that the Americans themselves were now economically dependent upon. With the Cold War's end, the Americans may have wanted to take a less active role in global affairs, they may have wanted to disengage, but a single global oil price meant that doing so would risk instability, supply shortages, and oil prices so high as to wreck the American economy. The Americans had become *economically* trapped in their own outdated *security* policy.

THE MAP OF OIL

CONTEMPORARY EDITION

The bulk of all internationally traded crude oil in 2022 comes from three regions:

The first is the most important, the most obvious, *and* the most problematic: **the Persian Gulf.**

Unlike the various major regions of the past half millennia, the Persian Gulf region has aggressively *not* mattered. True, before roughly 1500 the region was in the middle of everything, ergo why it is called the "Middle" East. What "global" trade existed was dependent upon the lands and waters surrounding the Persian Gulf as a means of connecting the vast territories between Europe and the Far East. But the Americans were hardly the first people to find the region aggravating. In large part the very existence of the deepwater technologies owes itself to European attempts to *avoid* the Middle East altogether. From the time the Portuguese were able to shoot their way into India in the early 1500s, the need to pass through or stop in the region more or less evaporated, and the entirety of the Middle East from Egypt to Persia more or less slid into strategic irrelevance.

Oil changed things. The monetization of the old Zoroastrian lands made Persia matter enough to trigger British imperial attention, with the status of Persia becoming integral to war efforts in 1939–45. The real explosion of activity happened later, with the discovery and exploitation of oil deposits throughout territory that now comprises not just southwestern Iran, but also Iraq, Kuwait, Saudi Arabia, Bahrain, Qatar, the United Arab Emirates, and Oman. While evolutions and manipulations both market and military have varied these players' individual output widely over the years, their collective output has been a fairly reliable 20mbpd for the past seven decades. As of 2021 that 20 million barrels is roughly one-fifth of global supplies and one-half of internationally traded crude.

These eight countries have two things in common. First, they are technologically incompetent or, at the very best, criminally lazy. Their educational systems are sad jokes, and local citizens lucky enough to gain technical degrees out-of-region tend not to return. The locals' incompetence is hardly limited to the energy sector. These countries as a matter of course import millions of foreign workers to handle everything from their power systems to building construction to civic infrastructure. All eight countries rely on outside workers—primarily from the United States, the United Kingdom, France, Russia, Turkey, Algeria, and Egypt—to keep the crude flowing. The region doesn't need *all* of these foreign players, but each in-region country at least needs *one* of them.

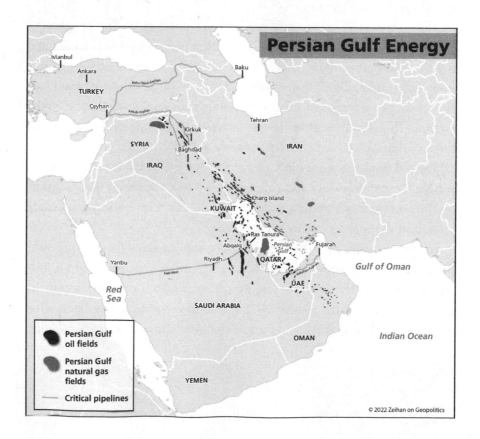

© 2022 Zeihan on Geopolitics

Second, as technically incompetent as these states are, they are even *less* competent when it comes to naval action. Few have ever domestically constructed anything more interesting than a speedboat, and in nearly all cases, not even that. Iran's navy in particular is mostly composed of inflatable Zodiacs.* None have the capacity to patrol their own coastlines, much less their trade approaches, much less the trade lanes upon which their income—their *existence*—depends. Every single one of them is utterly dependent upon outside powers to get every drop of their crude production to end consumers. For more than half of those exports, that means reaching the Northeast Asian states of Japan, Korea, Taiwan, and China. For half of the remainder, it means reaching Europe or North America. The Order may not have been possible without these countries' oil, but neither would these countries have been possible without the strategic overwatch of the Order.

The second major zone of oil production is the **former Soviet space**.

While this region's politics and geopolitics are, if anything, louder and messier and heftier than the Persian Gulf's, the calculus of the region's oil is far simpler. The Soviet Union was a massive producer of the black stuff, but the vast majority of that output was consumed within the Soviet empire. Things only started to get internationally interesting when the Soviet Union collapsed. Soviet industry collapsed along with it, while all the old Soviet satellites in Central Europe broke away. With Russian *internal* demand failing, and other former Soviet imperial demand now on the other side of international borders, the Russians had scads of spare oil output that needed to find new homes.

In the first wave of post-Soviet exports, the Russians focused not simply on what they knew, but on what their infrastructure would allow: piped exports to their former satellites, one of which was now a constituent part of a reunited Germany. The second wave expanded upon what the Russians knew, thickening and extending those pipe links through

---

* Imported, of course.

Central Europe into western Germany, Austria, the western Balkans, and Turkey.

In implementing wave two, the Russians discovered that ports like Gdansk in Poland, Ventspils in Latvia, and Constanta in Romania could serve as offloading facilities for Russian crude, enabling it to sail on to customers far and wide. Phase three was about linking up and building out Russia's own ports to serve the same purpose: Primorsk near St. Petersburg on the Baltic Sea, and Novorossiysk and Tuapse on the Black Sea.

During these first three phases, the other former Soviet states were hardly standing still. Now divorced from their former imperial master, all needed to establish their own income streams—preferably ones that were not beholden to Moscow. Azerbaijan and Kazakhstan both courted any and all foreign investors, with BP and Exxon proving the most interested. The foreigners executed some of the most complex seismic, drilling, processing, and infrastructure programs the energy world had ever seen and began shipping crude out via whatever route proved possible. Some routes tapped into legacy Soviet infrastructure, heading north and west to places like Venspils or Novorossiysk. But as time ticked by, the flows were increasingly concentrated into a single pipe corridor that began at Baku, Azerbaijan, and ended at a supertanker port in the Mediterranean city of Ceyhan, Turkey.

What all these options have in common is that they all flow in the general direction of Eurasia's European extremities. And since Europe was peaking demographically, there was little reason to expect European oil demand to increase ever again. Sure, the Russians were filling a larger and larger slice of that demand, but market saturation was decreasing their pricing power. The Russians *hated* that. So in the fourth phase, the Russians started the long, expensive process of routing fresh pipe infrastructure east to the Pacific. Problems relating to permafrost and mountains and distance abound, but if there is one thing that can be said for the Russians, they are never intimidated by *size*. As of 2021 there were two main lines in operation: a very long, very expensive, very economically questionable pipe that stretches from western Siberia to the Russian port of Nakhodka on the Sea of Japan, and a far shorter spur line that delivers crude direct to the old Chinese refining hub of Daqing.

Add it all up and you're talking about 15mbpd of former Soviet oil, fully 11mbpd of which originates within Russia's border, of which slightly over half is exported—easily the second-largest source of internationally traded crude flows on the planet.

There are problems.

Most of Russia's oil fields are both old and extraordinarily remote from Russia's customers. Fields in the North Caucasus are all but tapped out, those of Tatarstan and Bashkortostan are well past their peak, and even those in western Siberia have been showing signs of diminishing returns for more than a decade. With few exceptions, Russia's newer discoveries are deeper, smaller, more technically challenging, and even farther from population centers. Russian output isn't in danger of collapsing, but maintaining output will require more infrastructure, far higher up-front costs, and ongoing technical love and care to prevent steady output declines from becoming something far worse.

The Russians are no slouches when it comes to oil work, but they *were* out of circulation from 1940 through 2000. The techs involved came a long way in that time. Foreigners—most notably supermajor BP and services firms Halliburton and Schlumberger—are responsible for half(ish) of contemporary Russia's output. Any broad-scale removal of Western firms from the mix would have catastrophic impacts upon oil production throughout the entire former Soviet space. The Ukraine War is stress-testing that theory.

For their part, the Azerbaijani and Kazakh projects are far and away the world's most technically exacting (think: Kashagan!). Aside from the handful of folks in the world's supermajors who *designed* these projects, *no one on the planet* can maintain them.

Then there's the issue of export routes. All of the broader region's oil flows first travel by pipe—in some cases for literally thousands of miles—before they reach either a customer or a discharge port. Pipes can't . . . dodge. Anything that impedes a single inch of a pipe shuts the whole thing down. In the Order, that's fine and dandy. Post-Order, not so much.

About half the flows terminate in end users like Germany, while the other half must be loaded on tankers for sail. That's where things get extra dicey. In the Pacific, the Nakhodka port sits smack in the middle of Japanese, Chinese, and Korean spheres of influence. Any meaningful conflict involving any of the three and Nakhodka becomes either occupied or a crater.[*] Out to the west, exports via the Black Sea ports of Novorossiysk

---

[*]   Or, more likely, occupied and *then* a crater.

and Tuapse are fully dependent upon sails through downtown Istanbul, so any hiccup in relations with the Turks kills a couple million barrels of daily flows. Farther north, anything out of Primorsk has to sail the Baltic Sea and the Skagerrak strait, sailing by no fewer than seven navally overcapable-to-their-size countries that tend to nurse pathological fears and hatreds toward all things Russian. In addition to Germany. In addition to the United Kingdom.

Even if that were not enough, there's one more complicating factor. Siberia, despite getting cold enough to literally freeze your nose off in *October*, doesn't get cold enough.

Most Russian oil production is in the permafrost, and for most of the *summer* the permafrost is inaccessible because its top layer melts into a messy, horizon-spanning swamp. Tapping oil here requires waiting for the land to freeze, building dike roads across the wasteland, and drilling in the Siberian *winter*. Should something happen to consumption of Russian crude, flows back up through the literally thousands of miles of pipes right up to the drill site. Should exports fail—whether due to a war far away, a war on Russia, or a war *by* Russia—there is but one mitigation. Shut it all down. Turning production back on would require manually checking everything, all the way from the well to the border. The last time this happened was the Soviet collapse in 1989. Thirty-three years on at the time of this writing, Russia *still* hasn't gotten back to its Cold War production levels. Only during the oil-ravenous stability of the post–Cold War period of the American-led Order is the current iteration of Russia's internationalized oil complex even possible. And with the Ukraine War, it is already over.

The third and final major source of global crude is within **North America**.

A lot of oil output on the continent falls into the general category of legacy: in regions that have been producing for upwards of a century. The first Mexican production dates all the way back to the 1920s and has been supplying Mexico with everything it needs and more ever since. In recent years many of Mexico's large, old fields have been giving up the ghost. In part the reason is geology, but at least as important is Mexican state policy, which often bars foreign capital, expertise, and technology from playing much of a role at all.* Left to their own devices, the Mexicans are proving incapable at both keeping their old fields on life support and exploiting newer discoveries either on or offshore. Still, even with this glaring weakness, Mexico's oil needs are roughly in balance. It exports some crude to the United States, and then imports a similar volume of refined product. On balance Mexico produces—and uses—about 2mbpd.

Up north, the Canadian oil sector got its start in the 1950s, becoming globally significant in the 1970s. But it wasn't until the 1980s that the province of Alberta started cracking the code on some seriously unconventional output. Traditionally, oil migrates through rock formations until it reaches an impermeable rock layer. For example, the crude might migrate through sandstone, but granite would stop it cold. Pressure then builds behind the impermeable layer. When a drill punches through the cap, the pressure—and oil—are released.

Most of Alberta's oil is nothing like that.

Instead of big, pressurized liquid pools of crude locked behind tough rock, Alberta's oil is diffused through far softer rock, functionally integrated into the rock's matrix in *solid* form. Getting it out requires either injecting steam into the formation to melt the oil out or *mining* it and washing the oil out with hot water. From there this ultra-thick crude oil must be mixed with lighter crude grades to thin it so it can be pumped via conventional pipeline.

No matter how it is measured, Canada produces far more than it could ever use. It consumes a similar amount to Mexico, but exports that much again. Almost all of Alberta's "oil sands" production is shipped south to the United States, mostly for processing in Texas.

In the continent's middle latitudes, the Americans have . . . a lot going on. They have a legacy offshore sector in the Gulf of Mexico that didn't really get going until the 1970s. There's still conventional crude trickling

---

* For decades, even North Korea had less stringent investment laws on its energy sector.

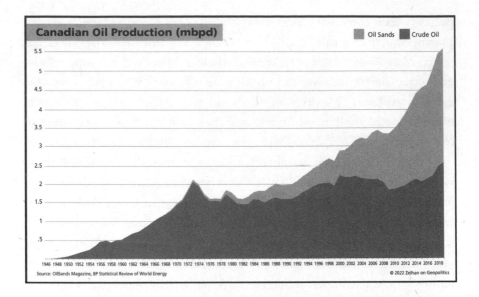

out of Pennsylvania and Texas in places that have been producing oil longer than any other spots on the planet. Even California was among the country's largest oil producers until quite recently, with one of the country's most prolific wells located in a *mall* on Wilshire Boulevard while another is cleverly disguised as a synagogue.

Taken together, the American conventional oil legacy remains substantial: still kicking out about 4mbpd, a volume that compares favorably to Iran at its 1970s height and is about the same as the total output from Canada today.

But the real story is the new stuff: America's shale oil sector.

Back in the early 2000s the world of oil got slammed by four simultaneous and unrelated events. First, the U.S. subprime build was already getting out of hand, generating unhealthy levels of demand for all the things that go into home construction: lumber, concrete, copper, steel . . . and oil. Second, the Chinese boom was getting a touch insane. Price-insensitive demand drove up the price of *all* globally available commodities, oil included. Third, in 2002 a very unsuccessful coup in Venezuela led to a very successful political purge of the country's state oil firm—a purge that focused on the technocrats who produced the oil. The country's energy sector never recovered. Fourth, in 2003 the Americans invaded Iraq, taking *all* its oil output offline. The country didn't return to prewar levels of output for sixteen years. Between higher demand and lower supplies, oil prices steadily climbed from below $10 a barrel in 1998 to nearly $150 a barrel in 2008.

When your work earns you $10, you tend to stick to the tried-and-true. When your work earns you $150, you can afford to try all kinds of things!

With a few years of experimentation, the collective American energy complex was able to crack the code on something we now call the "shale revolution." In essence, shale operators drill down as per normal, but when they reach a petroleum-rich rock strata they take a sharp turn, drilling horizontally along the entire layer. Then they pump water and sand at high pressure into the formation. Since liquids do not compress, the rock cracks apart from within, freeing untold trillions of tiny pockets of oil and natural gas that would otherwise be far too small to harvest with conventional drilling. The sand suspended in the frack fluid props the cracks open, while the now-freed oil provides reverse pressure that pushes the water back up the pipe. Once the water has cleared, the oil continues flowing. Voilà! A shale well is born.

At the dawn of the shale era in 2005, these horizontal wells were only 600 feet long per drilling platform and only produced a few dozen barrels of oil per day. As of 2022, many of the newer laterals are in excess of two *miles*, with many of the wells sporting a veritable tree of branches of sub-laterals in excess of a mile long each, all connecting to the same vertical pipe. With improvements in everything from water management to drilling apparatuses to data processing to seismic imaging to pump power, it is now common to have individual wells kick out in excess of 5,000 barrels of oil a day—a figure that puts individual American shale wells on par with some of the most prolific oil wells in Iraq and Saudi Arabia.

Collectively these changes have added some 10mbpd, making the United States the largest producer of oil in the world, while simultaneously enabling it to achieve net oil independence. Now there are a veritable forest of yes-buts in that statement, ranging from complications as regards crude quality, natural gas, infrastructure, and climate change—

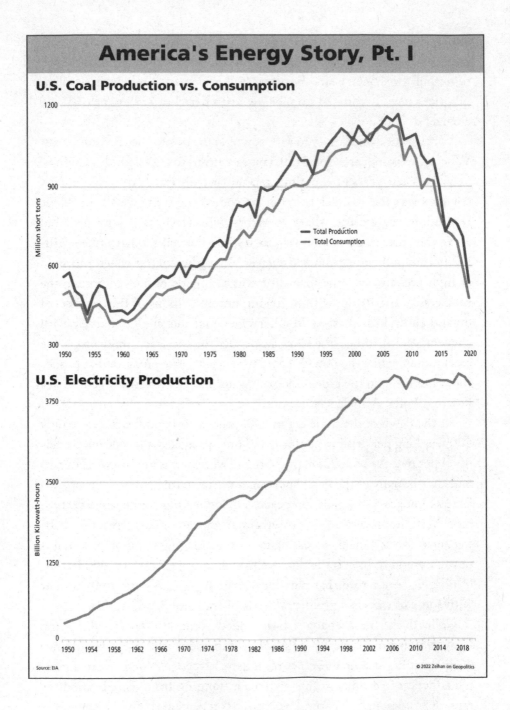

America's Energy Story, Pt. I

U.S. Coal Production vs. Consumption

Million short tons

— Total Production
— Total Consumption

U.S. Electricity Production

Billion Kilowatt-hours

Source: EIA

© 2022 Zeihan on Geopolitics

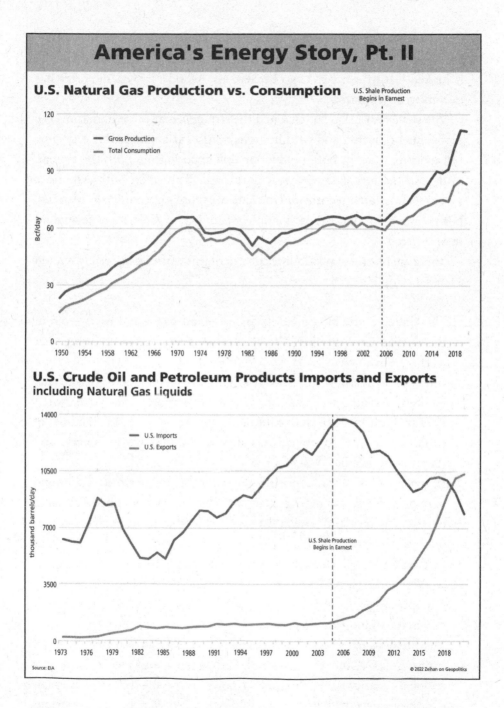

America's Energy Story, Pt. II

U.S. Natural Gas Production vs. Consumption

U.S. Shale Production Begins in Earnest

- Gross Production
- Total Consumption

Bcf/day

120

90

60

30

0

1950 1954 1958 1962 1966 1970 1974 1978 1982 1986 1990 1994 1998 2002 2006 2010 2014 2018

U.S. Crude Oil and Petroleum Products Imports and Exports
including Natural Gas Liquids

- U.S. Imports
- U.S. Exports

thousand barrels/day

14000

10500

7000

3500

0

U.S. Shale Production Begins in Earnest

1973 1976 1979 1982 1985 1988 1991 1994 1997 2000 2003 2006 2009 2012 2015 2018

Source: EIA

© 2022 Zeihan on Geopolitics

and we will get to them all—but the central takeaway is easily graspable: the world's energy map is radically different in 2022 compared to how it looked just fifteen years ago because the world's largest importer has become a net exporter.

The shale revolution has changed the strategic math that underpins the global energy sector, and with it, globalization as a whole. Put very simply and very directly, both production *and* exports from both the Persian Gulf *and* the former Soviet space are dependent upon both America's global security architecture *and* the ability of foreign technicians to access both regions. In contrast, production within North America is dependent upon *neither*.

There are no end of possibilities of where this can all go horribly wrong. Here's a sampling.

- The United States has pulled its forces—land-based and naval—out of the Persian Gulf, leaving it to the Iranians and Saudis to argue over who is really in charge. At risk: 26.5mbpd.
- India reacts to rising oil prices by seizing tankers bound for East Asia. No East Asian power has the capacity to project naval force to the Persian Gulf without active Indian complicity. At risk: 21mbpd of export flows from Hormuz, plus another 1.5mbpd from Nigeria and Angola that head to Asia.
- Egypt restricts cargo transiting the Suez. Again. At risk: 4.25mbpd of export flows, about 60 percent of which is transshipped via canal bypass pipelines and so could prove vulnerable to internal Egyptian political violence.
- In the absence of American naval power, piracy blooms off the coasts of West and East Africa. At risk: 3.5mbpd of West African oil exports, plus any longer-haul shipments from the Persian Gulf to Europe that unwisely sail too close to shore.
- The Russians have very different views from the Norwegians, Swedes, Finns, Poles, Estonians, Latvians, Lithuanians, and Danes as to how regional security issues should be resolved. At risk: 2mbpd of Russian export flows via the Baltic Sea and 2mbpd of Norwegian oil production.

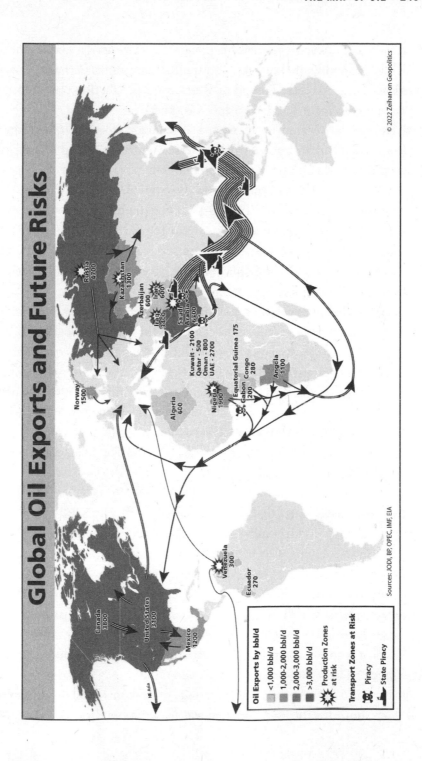

Global Oil Exports and Future Risks

Oil Exports by bbl/d
- <1,000 bbl/d
- 1,000–2,000 bbl/d
- 2,000–3,000 bbl/d
- >3,000 bbl/d

✹ Production Zones at risk

Transport Zones at Risk
- 🕱 Piracy
- State Piracy

Canada 3800
United States 3100
Mexico 1200
Venezuela 300
Ecuador 270
Norway 1500
Russia 4700
Kazakhstan 1300
Azerbaijan 600
Iran 600
Iraq 3400
Saudi Arabia 6700
Kuwait – 2100
Qatar – 500
Oman – 800
UAE – 2700
Algeria 600
Nigeria 1900
Equatorial Guinea 175
Gabon 200
Congo 280
Angola 1100
NE Asia

Sources: JODI, BP, OPEC, IMF, EIA

© 2022 Zeihan on Geopolitics

- Relations between the major suppliers of oil expertise—the United Kingdom and United States—and the Russians tank. Perhaps because *there's a war*. At risk: 5mbpd of Russian oil production, and another 1mbpd each from Azerbaijan and Kazakhstan.
- Islamist-related security concerns discourage foreign oil workers from remaining in Iraq and Saudi Arabia. At risk: 2mbpd of Iraqi oil production and 6mbpd of Saudi production.
- The internal politics of the West and central African nations are . . . exceedingly violent. From 1967 to 1970 Nigeria fought a civil war over who got to control the country's oil, resulting in the deaths of some two million people. Remove the American overwatch and things could get nasty fast. At risk: 2mbpd of flows from Nigeria plus another 1.5mbpd from the other regional producers.
- Without Russia and China bonding over their hatred of the United States, oil shipments from the former to the latter are hardly sacrosanct. The two nearly nuked each other in the late 1960s over a territorial dispute, both peoples are impressively racist toward one another, and if Russia never uses energy leverage over China, well then, China would be the only country the Russians haven't played that card with. At risk: roughly 1.8mbpd of direct Russian shipments, and another 200kbpd of Central Asian shipments that the Russians could easily interfere with.

Even this list assumes that the United States will take a fully hands-off approach to the world, instead of being perhaps a disruptor. Americans *love* levying sanctions. On technology. On transport. On finance. On insurance. Any of those sanctions can impact product flows anywhere, anytime, to anyone. And as the ongoing security guarantors of the Western Hemisphere, it will be up to the Americans to decide if any regional oil headed out of the hemisphere actually makes it.

While it is true that any of these restrictions could have happened under the Order, there are a few things to keep in mind:

First, the United States had a vested interest in maintaining global oil flows, both for its own economic well-being as well as for its broader

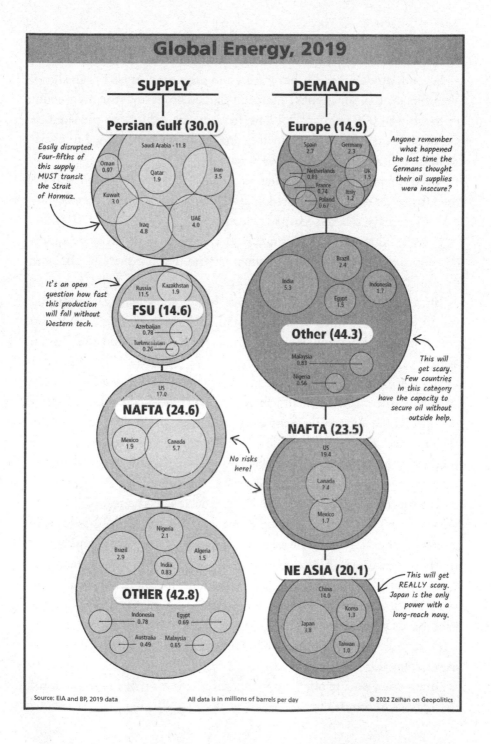

Global Energy, 2019

SUPPLY

Persian Gulf (30.0)

Easily disrupted. Four-fifths of this supply MUST transit the Strait of Hormuz.

- Saudi Arabia - 11.8
- Oman 0.97
- Qatar 1.9
- Iran 3.5
- Kuwait 3.0
- UAE 4.0
- Iraq 4.8

FSU (14.6)

It's an open question how fast this production will fall without Western tech.

- Russia 11.5
- Kazakhstan 1.9
- Azerbaijan 0.78
- Turkmenistan 0.26

NAFTA (24.6)

- US 17.0
- Mexico 1.9
- Canada 5.7

No risks here!

OTHER (42.8)

- Nigeria 2.1
- Brazil 2.9
- Algeria 1.5
- India 0.83
- Indonesia 0.78
- Egypt 0.69
- Australia 0.49
- Malaysia 0.65

DEMAND

Europe (14.9)

Anyone remember what happened the last time the Germans thought their oil supplies were insecure?

- Spain 2.7
- Germany 2.3
- Netherlands 0.83
- UK 1.5
- France 0.74
- Italy 1.2
- Poland 0.67

Other (44.3)

- Brazil 2.4
- India 5.3
- Indonesia 1.7
- Egypt 1.5
- Malaysia 0.83
- Nigeria 0.56

This will get scary. Few countries in this category have the capacity to secure oil without outside help.

NAFTA (23.5)

- US 19.4
- Canada 2.4
- Mexico 1.7

NE ASIA (20.1)

This will get REALLY scary. Japan is the only power with a long-reach navy.

- China 14.0
- Korea 1.3
- Japan 3.8
- Taiwan 1.0

Source: EIA and BP, 2019 data   All data is in millions of barrels per day   © 2022 Zeihan on Geopolitics

strategic goals. Those concerns no longer apply and no other country has America's technical energy acumen or military reach.

Second, producing oil is never free, and oftentimes it isn't even cheap. Venezuelan oil production is so difficult that up-front investments amount to roughly $4,000 per barrel of long-term oil production. In the late Order of cheap capital, that's eminently doable. In the constrained financial conditions of the Disorder, not so much.

Third, due to the concentration of supply, oil is *the* product that sails the farthest to reach its destination. The longer the sail, the more important it is to have a calm security environment.

Fourth, oil projects are not quick. A typical onshore project requires three to six years between first evaluation and first production. Offshore projects typically take a decade or more.

By far the best example of these four factors working together during the Order is none other than Kashagan. But the same logic applies to energy production throughout the former Soviet world and the Persian Gulf.

Recovering from any disruptions in the world to come will be difficult. Achieving the magic constellation of security factors, cost inputs, technical skill access, and a sufficiently long time frame to produce the crude in the first place simply won't be viable for large portions of the world. Once production goes offline, a bounceback simply won't be in the cards for the vast majority of locations. Certainly not a quick one.

The specifics will be as wild and unpredictable as the rest of the post-Order chaos, but a good starting point is to assume that 40 percent of global supplies fall into the Kashagan-style bucket: too-dangerous export routes to survive globalization's end, too-expensive projects to maintain without outside financing, too difficult technically to operate without an army of out-of-region workers. Such projects will go away and not come back for decades. If ever. And oil's absence for a few weeks, never mind a few decades, would be more than enough to crash modern civilization as we know it.

That's not even a remotely sufficient foreshadowing of the scope of the disruptions to come.

THERE'S MORE TO OIL THAN OIL

Oil is no "normal" product. Of the myriad ways in which it is unique, seven bear consideration for the utter change in circumstance the world is about to find itself in.

INELASTICITY

Quick Economics 101 lesson. Under normal circumstances, prices are the result of the relationship between supply and demand. Should supply rise while demand remains constant, prices will drop. Similarly, should demand rise while supplies remain constant, prices will rise. The inverse for both statements is true as well. This concept is called price elasticity and it holds true for everything from skateboards to bread to potted plants to construction workers.[*]

Oil is different. Because oil is central to everything from the shingles on your roof to the phone in your hand to the spatula in your kitchen to the pipes and hoses in your plumbing to the diapers on your kid to the paint on your walls to your daily commute to how products cross the ocean, a slight increase in demand for oil or a slight decrease in supply for oil results in wild price swings that are most assuredly *not* proportional. Perhaps even more important, oil is *the* transport fuel. No oil and your car doesn't work. Neither does that giant container ship bringing you that

---

[*] Congratulations! I just saved you three months of college.

shiny new washing machine from Korea. You. Must. Have. It. The details vary from place to place and time to time, but a good rule of thumb is that a change in demand of about 10 percent results in a price shift around 75 percent.

During the 2000s, when supply and demand were particularly out of whack, it didn't take long for prices to increase by 500 percent. Similarly, when the American subprime bubble burst in the context of a global financial crisis, the subsequent drop in demand quickly made oil give back some four-fifths of those price gains.

DISRUPTABILITY

All products travel the ocean, so all products face a degree of risk moving forward, but all products are not created equal. Whether you're evaluating the supply chain of cut lumber or mixing bowls, pretty much everything has different sources and supply routes that can become active as the market dictates.

Oil is different. Since everyone has to have it, and since only a few places produce it in exportable volumes, the transport routes are far more concentrated. Even more problematic, the thickest of these supply lines are very long. Flows out of the Persian Gulf must travel between 5,000 and 7,000 miles to East Asian destinations, between 3,000 to 6,000 miles to European destinations, and 5,000 to 9,000 miles to North American destinations. Other minor suppliers aren't any better. Venezuela, for example, has on occasion shipped crude around South America and across the Pacific to northern China—a 12,000-mile journey that is the world's longest supply run, literally *longer* than halfway around the planet.

This is obviously a problem. Oil tankers are pretty easy to identify, they travel slowly, and they have little choice but to stick to the shortest possible route, which is already pretty long. For most of those oil shipments, there are no good alternatives. Nearly all oil that originates in the Persian Gulf *must* use the Strait of Hormuz. Even bypass pipelines have limited use since they terminate either on the eastern side of Hormuz or in the

Red Sea, where shipments still need to go through either Suez or the Bab el-Mandeb. Bypassing the Strait of Malacca still requires punching through the Indonesian archipelago at a different location. And in the end, the terminus point for a lot of these shipments is an unavoidable location-of-difficulty, whether it be in the South China Sea, the East China Sea, the Sea of Japan, the Mediterranean, or the North Sea.

INSEPARABILITY

One of the many transformative impacts of the Order was the combining of the entire world into a single market. With few exceptions, products can flow from areas of high supply to high demand. For most products, this mellows any price shocks because there is typically extra stuff somewhere that can be used to pour fresh supply oil on troubled demand waters.

Oil, with its price inelasticity, does the opposite. Any sudden change in supply *or* demand rapidly ripples throughout the entire system. For example, the Asian financial crisis of 1997–98 may have only impacted oil demand on the margin and only on a regional basis, but those small changes crashed the price of crude by more than half. *Globally.* This locks much of the world into a bit of a suicide pact. Any disruptions that occur in any production zone or along any transport route will reverberate through the entire world.

There will be a few exceptions, which fall into two general categories:

First are those proto-empires that are able to militarily command shipments out of specific nearby production areas. Such interjections will not typically be clean, easy, or welcomed by the oil producers, but they will happen nonetheless. The second set of exceptions involves the major powers who produce the crude they need *internally* and so can block exports with a few pen flicks or switch flips.

In both types of regional systems, the economics of oil will echo models established in the pre-Order world. Each system will have its own supply and demand mechanics, its own security risk premiums, its own crude grade patterns, and above all its own pricing logic.

- The easiest of these pockets to predict is the United States. Most conventional oil wells take years of work to bring online, but shale wells only need a few weeks. Expect any price spikes in the soon-to-be-sequestered American market to be easily ameliorated, with a fairly even-keeled price structure topping out at roughly $70 a barrel. (Canada will be brought along for the ride since all meaningful Canadian export infrastructure terminates on U.S. territory.)
- A close second is Russia. While Russian civilian technological acumen has all but collapsed since the Cold War's end, so too has Russian industrial capacity. The end result has freed up five *million* barrels of oil and around 10 billion cubic feet of natural gas for daily export. The Russians have never been slaves to modern capitalistic norms, and the future will be no exception. I have exceedingly high confidence that in time, Russian shortages in capital, labor, and technical command will erode away *all* of those exports. The key words here, however, are "in time." Under any scenario that doesn't involve mushroom clouds or extreme civil breakdown, the Russians will have more than sufficient energy for their own needs at least until the early 2040s. And since Russia will in essence be a closed system, internal energy prices will be precisely what the Kremlin decrees them to be.
- Argentina is likely to experience an oil system not all that different from the United States. Despite some wildly . . . creative approaches to economic management, Argentina *already* has the world's second-most-advanced shale sector as well as all the infrastructure necessary to bring local shale output to its population centers.
- France and Turkey also look fairly good. Both are proximate to regional energy producers—Algeria and Libya for France, Azerbaijan and Iraq for Turkey—as well as sporting the local technical skills required to make those oil patches work. That said, *securing* said output will require a neocolonial approach to their regions, and that will generate . . . drama.
- The United Kingdom, India, and Japan are up next. All need to venture out, but all have naval forces more or less right-sized to reach potential sources. In this the Brits have the easiest jaunts to make; Norway

provides local supplies, while the British navy can easily reach West Africa for the balance. The Indians look good, too: the Persian Gulf is only a short hop away. Japan gets a bit dicey. Sure, Japan sports the world's second-most-powerful long-reach navy, but the Persian Gulf oil fields are a daunting seven *thousand* miles away. Of the countries that can secure their needs, it is Japan that will face the greatest risk of disruptions, shortages, and high prices.

Outside of this short list of states, the picture darkens in every conceivable way. Without the supply redundancy and variety that has dominated the post-1945 world, any single shipment interruption spells immediate price explosions. Even worse, many of the world's oil suppliers are not in what I'd call particularly stable areas.* Should a field become damaged—either by militancy, war, incompetency, or lack of maintenance—it doesn't simply go offline, it goes offline for *years*.

Expect prices to be wildly erratic, dropping below $150 a barrel only on painfully rare occasions. Assuming supplies can be sourced at all.

THE BACKUP ISN'T MUCH OF A BACKUP

There is far more to global oil than just the major production zones in the Persian Gulf, former Soviet Union, and North America. It feels like some of them should be able to help smooth out the problems of the future. There is a little truth to this, but only a little.

Consider the candidates:

Let's start with the good news: the Western Hemispheric countries of **Colombia, Peru,** and **Trinidad and Tobago.** None are huge producers but all are reasonably stable ones. In a post-Order world the Americans

---

* I'm looking at you, Iran. And Iraq. And Kuwait. And Saudi Arabia and Qatar and South Sudan and Sudan and Azerbaijan and Uzbekistan and Turkmenistan and Nigeria and Egypt.

will establish a security cordon around the entire hemisphere to keep the Eurasian powers from dabbling. Trade will be allowed. Even the export of Latin American oil products to the Eastern Hemisphere will be seen as harmless—so long as no Eastern Hemispheric power establishes a footprint that the Americans perceive as *strategic*. This trio might not be big players—collectively we're not talking about much more than one million barrels per day—but at minimum the Americans can and will ensure maritime security for any transport on their side of the planet.

Brazil is a bit more complicated. Most of Brazil's production is offshore and most of its truly promising fields are not simply under two miles of ocean, but under an additional two miles of seabed. Brazilian energy presents very difficult operating environments, very high production costs, and a very challenging political backdrop. The problem is nothing less than the future coherence of Brazil as a state. The Order has been perfect for Brazil: large global markets, bottomless Chinese demand, cheap global financing. As Brazil's tropical and rugged geography saddles it with among the world's highest development costs for . . . everything, that has been fantastic. It's all going away, and it just isn't clear if there will be sufficient technically capable, capital-flush foreign partners on the other side of the Order. Even if the answer proves to be an enthusiastic "yes," large-scale Brazilian output sufficient to generate large exports is a minimum of two decades and *hundreds* of billions of dollars of investment away.

Venezuela used to matter. It used to be among the world's most reliable producers and exporters. By many measures, decisions made in Caracas ultimately broke the Arab Oil Embargos of the 1970s. Those days are long past. Two-plus decades of horrific, deliberate, and increasingly creative and violent mismanagement all but destroyed the country's energy complex. Output is down by more than 90 percent from peak, extraction and transport infrastructure is crumbling, and internal government leaks suggest irreparable damage to the country's petroleum reservoirs.

Most of Venezuela's oil used to go to the United States, but American refiners have given up on Venezuela ever returning to the market, and so have retooled their equipment to operate using different input streams.

With the Americans no longer interested, Venezuela no longer even has dedicated buyers for its specific ultraheavy crude grades. Government finances have collapsed and taken down both food production and food *imports* within them. Famine is now among the country's better-case scenarios, with outright civilizational collapse more likely.

If Venezuela—and the correct word is "if"—is to contribute to global oil supplies, someone will need to deploy forces to the country to impose security, arrest the fall, and bring in billions of dollars of supplies to support the population and tens of billions to overhaul the energy infrastructure, all while convincing the Americans that they won't try anything cute. Impossible? No. But at a minimum it would be a three-*decade* reconstruction project. A slightly more likely outcome would be if one of Venezuela's oil regions—specifically the Maracaibo—were to *secede* from Venezuela and seek foreign protection, most likely either from the United States directly, or from neighboring Colombia. That could potentially bring a couple of million barrels of daily output back to markets with an investment of "only" a few years and $30 billion or so.

The western African states of **Nigeria, Equatorial Guinea**, and **Angola** have always been sketchy operating environments for foreign oil firms. It is largely a security issue. The African states have a poor track record of controlling their own territories, which often leaves foreigners prey to kidnapping, sabotage, or worse—and even that assumes oil production does not fall prey to internal political squabbles. Which it does. Constantly. In a post-Order world such internal security concerns are all but certain to intensify, which will force most foreign players to focus on very specific sorts of production: those in the deep offshore, dozens of miles from the coastline. Such offshore platforms will by necessity need to be militarized to prevent pirate assault. The Western countries most likely to play are those that have the most proximity to the West Africans as well as the technical and military capacity to reach them: the United Kingdom and France. There definitely are rough seas ahead, but it is this trio of African states that is likely to generate what little good news the oil markets of the Eastern Hemisphere will see in the next few decades.

In Southeast Asia, the countries of **Australia, Brunei, Indonesia**,

Malaysia, **Thailand**, and **Vietnam** are all reasonable producers. However, in recent decades these countries have experienced sufficient economic growth that rising regional oil demand has gobbled up nearly all available regional supply. Collectively, these countries are no longer significant net exporters of oil. And that's before geopolitical preferences are factored in. This region is tightly bound together with not only manufacturing integration, but a series of largely friendly and cooperative political and security pacts. They would *really* prefer that the rest of an increasingly chaotic world would just butt out. They'd dig a hole and pull it in after them if they could.

The **North Sea** is Europe's only significant remaining production zone, with the vast bulk of the output lying in the sea's Norwegian sector. The Norwegians enjoy excellent relations with their cultural cousins in Sweden, Finland, and Denmark, as well as their primary maritime neighbor, the United Kingdom. To be perfectly blunt, this entire roster of countries is likely to find themselves on opposite sides of the table from both the French and Germans moving forward, and they are already on the opposite sides of barbed wire from the Russians. In order to preserve themselves, this collective is all but certain to take joint action to prevent North Sea energy from going anywhere except to the members of their group. That's great if you're in the club. Less so if you're not.

Algeria has been a major producer for decades, and its output has helped mitigate some of the pricing chaos the Persian Gulf so reliably creates. That's not going to happen for much longer. In the post-Order world there will be exceedingly few countries that can look out for their own economic and security needs, and the country at the top of that very short list is France . . . which sits directly across the Mediterranean from Algeria. France was Algeria's former colonial master and the breakup was . . . rough. The best Algerian move will likely be to approach either Spain or Italy and offer them supplies so that Algiers won't have to deal with the French. It might even work. Barring that, the Algerians can look forward to the French gobbling up their entire energy export capacity. At least the French will pay for it. Probably.

Libya will get messier because it is, well, Libya. Home to at least three major insurrections, in the middle of an ongoing civil war, it is a place my gut tells me to simply write off completely. But then there's Italy. In a world in which former Soviet and Persian Gulf crude becomes constricted and France de facto takes over Algerian fields, Libya becomes Italy's *only* source of oil. Unless the Italians choose to give up on their country's existence, they will have no choice but to venture forth to secure Libya's major ports, Libya's production sites deep in the desert, and all the connecting infrastructure in between. Considering Italy's trademark disorganization, general out-of-practiceness when it comes to colonial occupations, and flat-out racism when it comes to Arabs, this little chapterette of history is certain to be entertaining. And horrifying.

So how much is left?

Factor out captive supplies in places like North America, the North Sea, North Africa, or Southeast Asia, and eminently disruptable supplies from the Persian Gulf and former Soviet space, then put supplies for local demand in places like North America and Russia into a different bucket, and *total* exportable, kinda-sorta-reliable supplies *globally* only amount to a paltry 6 million barrels per day . . . versus a global *demand* of 97 million.

THERE IS MORE TO OIL THAN OIL

No one simply puts raw oil in their tank. It must first be processed at a refinery. The supply chains of oil may not be nearly as complicated as they are for, say, computers, but the outcomes can be far more dramatic. No two crude oil streams have exactly the same chemical makeup. Some are gooey and laden with impurities, most commonly sulfur, which can make up to 3 percent of the crude oil by volume. Such crudes are called "heavy sours." Some, like Canada's oil sands, are *so* heavy that they are solid at room temperature. Others are so pure they have the color and consistency of nail polish remover and are called "light sweets."

Between these extremes lies an entire worldful of other possibilities, each with its own specific chemical makeup. Each of the world's hundreds of refineries has a preferred input blend, which in the case of many older refineries was *tailored to a specific oil field*. This too is an outcome of the Order. In a safe world, there was nothing stopping crude from any particular source from reaching any particular processor. But post-Order? Anything that scrambles upstream production patterns or midstream transport patterns also scrambles everything in the energy sector's refinery downstream.

Running the "wrong" crude in the worst case can cause major damage to multibillion-dollar facilities. Even in the best case it is certain to trigger something called run-loss, a not-so-fancy term that means exactly what it suggests: a certain percentage of the crude run through a refinery for processing is simply lost due to inappropriate input mixes. Run-loss increases quickly either when a refinery is asked to do something it was not designed to do or when it lacks access to the "correct" crude oil blend. The Europeans, for example, *love* diesel, and Russia's Urals blend (a medium/sour crude) is a pretty good feedstock for refining diesel. Interrupt Urals flows, replace Urals with a different crude grade, and the Europeans are going to face serious product bottlenecks even if they can somehow keep their refineries running at their designed capacity. Considering oil's price inelasticity issue, something as little as a 1 percent refinery loss can have massive impacts on customers.

We're looking at a lot more than 1 percent run-loss moving forward. Most of the world's refineries were designed to run on lighter, sweeter crudes because they have fewer contaminants and so are easier to process. Today most of the world's lighter, sweeter crudes come from American shale plays. Refurbishing refineries can be done, but it takes two things the new world will have in short supply: time and money. Besides, most retooling simply locks you into a new crude formula. In an unstable world, reliability of specific crude input streams can occur only if you are very close to the secure source. For most refineries, that's simply not a possibility.

THERE'S EVEN *MORE* TO OIL THAN OIL

There's also something called natural gas, which along with oil is one of the classic fossil fuels.

In many ways, the two are similar. Both have the same three concentrations of supply: the Persian Gulf, the former Soviet Union, and North America. Both have the same three concentrations of demand: Northeast Asia, Europe, and North America. Both can be used for similar things, ranging from a transport fuel to a petrochemical feedstock.

They do, however, have a critical difference that shapes their use, their prevalence, and their impact.

Oil is a liquid. It can be moved by pipe or barge or tanker or truck, and can be stored in a nonpressurized tank. Large oil tanks at major ports even have floating lids that rise and fall with the fill level.

There's no way you are doing that with natural gas. It is a . . . gas. Gases are difficult to contain and transport, and even if the gas itself is not flammable (and natural gas most assuredly *is* flammable), they tend to be explosive under pressure.

This difference has a few direct outcomes.

- Because gases burn far more thoroughly than liquids, natural gas is one of the world's premier electricity-generation fuels (while hardly anyone uses oil for direct power generation any longer*). When burned in a modern power facility, natural gas typically generates barely more than half the carbon dioxide emissions compared to coal. Most American reductions in CO_2 emissions since 2005 have taken place because natural gas has been displacing coal in the American electricity fuel

---

* Although, boy howdy, several of those Persian Gulf countries burn oil for electricity a *lot*!

mix. Somewhat similar displacements are in play in much of the rest of the world, most notably in Europe and China.

- Most natural gas that humans use is transported via pipe, which requires far tighter economic links between producer and consumer. As such, most piped natural gas is produced in the country from which it is sourced, making the geopolitics of natural gas far less sexy writ large than the geopolitics of oil. Of course, there are exceptions. Russia is the world's largest natural gas exporter, in large part due to legacy infrastructure left over from the Soviet era. But the Kremlin feels (not without merit) that piped natural gas generates geopolitical dependencies, and has extended its natural gas networks into Germany, Italy, Turkey, and China with an eye toward manipulating those countries' strategic policies. Results (from the Russian viewpoint) tended to be positive . . . until they started invading their customers' neighbors.

- Natural gas *can* be chilled and pressurized and transported by ship, but that is expensive and requires specialized infrastructure and so is only done with about 15 percent of the total. The supply-demand math for this "liquefied natural gas," or LNG, is reminiscent of that for oil. Most LNG comes from Qatar, Australia, Nigeria, or the United States and goes to Europe or, especially, Northeast Asia. That means when it comes to LNG shipments, producers and consumers alike should expect disruptions in natural gas supply as they will for oil.

Taken together, these three differences don't necessarily spell out a brighter future for this corner of the global energy system, but instead a different kind of dark. And dark *is* the word. Oil is primarily used for transport fuel, so shortages slow human interaction to a crawl. Natural gas is primarily used for electricity generation, so shortages mean the lights literally go out. The most vulnerable locations are those most dependent upon massive natural gas flows from or through the territories and waters of countries that are less than reliable: Korea, Taiwan, Turkey, China, Ukraine, Germany, Austria, Spain, Japan, France, Poland, and India, roughly in that order.

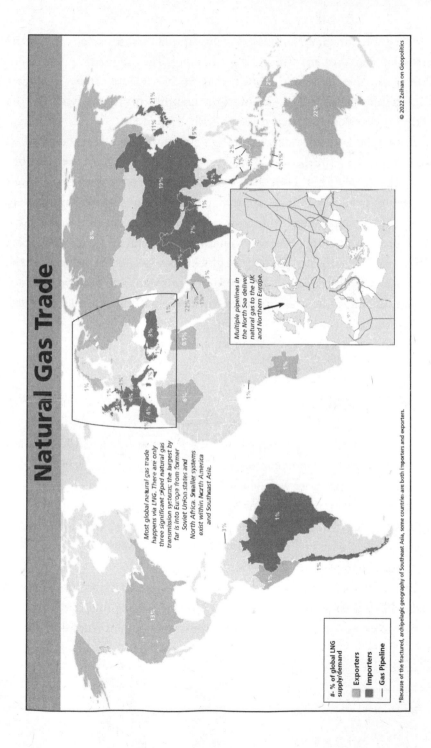

Natural Gas Trade

Most global natural gas trade happens via LNG. There are only three significant piped natural gas transmission systems; the largest by far is into Europe from former Soviet Union states and North Africa. Smaller systems exist within North America and Southeast Asia.

Multiple pipelines in the North Sea deliver natural gas to the UK and Northern Europe.

#- % of global LNG supply/demand

- Exporters
- Importers
- Gas Pipeline

© 2022 Zeihan on Geopolitics

*Because of the fractured, archipelagic geography of Southeast Asia, some countries are both importers and exporters.

One more fun fact. Natural gas is *vital* to places that . . . lack it: Northeast Asia and Western Europe most notably. They regularly pay $10 per thousand cubic feet for the stuff, and must navigate tetchy producers and tetchier transit states and outright hostility from neighbors. In the Ukraine War's opening act, prices quickly topped $40.

But in the United States, natural gas is frequently a by-product of its shale sector's *oil* efforts. The Americans often have to flare the stuff because they cannot build out their distribution infrastructure fast enough to capture it all. Once it *is* captured, it is typically sold into the system at or near zero, and even adding in processing and transport costs, most American end users get access at something less than one-quarter the cost of the rest of the world. Change the global system and the only tweak the Americans might make in their natural gas setup is to start to produce some more on purpose so that they can process it into finished products for sale abroad.

Finally, there's the fire on the horizon.

CLIMATE CHANGE

I'm sure many of you are wondering how I can go this far into a chapter on energy with barely an oblique mention of climate change. It's not that I don't buy the math. In a previous life I was in training to be an organic chemist. The idea that different gases sport different heat-trapping and light-reflecting* characteristics is pretty basic science, with well over a century of evidence behind it. No, that's not the problem.

The problem is more . . . involved.

First, I work in **geo**politics. Geo. Geography. Locations. The study of place. How dozens of geographic factors interconnect to shape how culture, economics, security, and populations emerge and interplay. If you

---

* The technical word is "albedo" if you want to sound smart.

tell me the whole world is going to heat up by four degrees I can tell you how that will play out. But that is *not* what is happening.

Just as different gases have different heat-trapping and light-reflecting characteristics, so too do different climates. And land covers. And latitudes. And altitudes. We're not looking at an even heating, but instead an extremely *un*even heating that has more of an impact on land versus water, on the Arctic versus the tropics, on cities versus forests. That affects not only local temperatures, but regional wind patterns and global ocean currents. Such inconsistency does far more than add one more variable to the mix of latitude, elevation, humidity, temperature, soil composition, surface angle, and so on that enables me to read the planet. The entire map of everything is changing. We've only started parsing out the *localities* of climate change within the past few years. For the purposes of this specific chapter, we'll "only" be dealing with the technicalities and applicability of greentech from the angle of energy production and substitution, as opposed to the specific economic and strategic outcomes of climate change.* Since everything is changing, it is critical to first establish a solid baseline. That's why I'm dealing with climate change last, rather than right out of the box.

Second, no matter what happens politically or technologically, **we are nowhere near being "done" with oil.** The dominant environmental concern with all things oil has been about carbon dioxide emissions, but technologies, like the internal combustion engine, that burn oil products to produce those emissions are hardly the only things that use oil. Oil is also the base material for the bulk of the world's petrochemical needs. That sector is *not* a rounding error.

Modern petrochemicals are responsible for the bulk of what we today consider "normal," comprising the majority of the inputs in food packaging, medical equipment, detergents, coolants, footwear, tires, adhesives, sports equipment, luggage, diapers, paints, inks, chewing gum, lubricants,

---

* I'll give my best shot on the region-by-region impacts in the Agriculture chapters.

insulation, fertilizers, pesticides, and herbicides, and the second-largest component of material inputs in paper, pharmaceuticals, clothes, furniture, construction, glass, consumer electronics, automotive, home appliances, and furnishings. Oil-derived transport fuels do constitute the majority of oil use—nearly three-fifths, to be specific—but petrochemicals account for a full one-fifth. That's about as much as the entire Persian Gulf exports in a typical year.

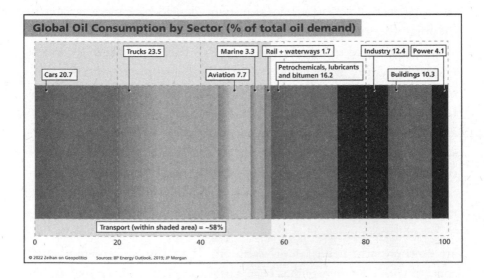

Global Oil Consumption by Sector (% of total oil demand)

Cars 20.7 | Trucks 23.5 | Aviation 7.7 | Marine 3.3 | Rail + waterways 1.7 | Petrochemicals, lubricants and bitumen 16.2 | Industry 12.4 | Power 4.1 | Buildings 10.3

Transport (within shaded area) = ~58%

© 2022 Zeihan on Geopolitics   Sources: BP Energy Outlook, 2019; JP Morgan

Many of these products *do* have potential substitute inputs, but in nearly all cases that substitute . . . is natural gas. Move beyond fossil fuel possibilities and either the cost of the substitute is in excess of ten times that of the original input, the carbon footprint is in excess of ten times that of the original input, or, more likely, both. Even that assumes a substitute exists at all.

Third, **greentech does not make a country immune to geopolitics.** It just shifts the view. Climate, temperature, land cover, resource location, distance, and maritime choke points are hardly the only geopolitical factors. So too are latitude, elevation, humidity, temperature, surface angle, windspeed, wind reliability, solar radiation, and seasonal weather variation. Just as different geographic features impact deepwater navigation and industrialization differently or manufacturing and finance differently, so too do they impact greentech and conventional power generation differently. And if the tech is of varying usefulness based on location, then there are relative winners and losers. Just as there are with deepwater transport or industrialization or oil.

Me personally? I used to live in Austin and now reside just outside Denver. I've put up solar systems on both homes. In hot, sunny Texas I recouped my investment in under eight years. It'll likely take *less* time living in Colorado. Denver is the United States' sunniest metro area, and at high altitude there is no humidity (and very little air) to block sunlight. I'm absolutely a believer in the technology *when it's matched to the correct geography*.

There isn't a lot of that "correct" geography.

Most parts of the world are neither very windy nor very sunny. Eastern Canada and northern and Central Europe are cloud-bound for more than nine months of the year on average, in addition to having painfully short winter days. No one goes to Florida or northern Brazil to kiteboard. The eastern two-thirds of China, the vast bulk of India, and nearly the entirety of Southeast Asia—home to fully *half* the world's population—have so little solar and wind potential that a large-scale greentech buildout would emit more carbon than it would ever save. Same for West Africa. And the northern Andes. And the more populated portions of the former Soviet Union. And Ontario.

Zones for which today's greentech makes both environmental and economic sense comprise less than one-fifth of the land area of the populated continents, most of which is far removed from our major population centers. Think Patagonia for wind, or the Outback for solar. The unfortunate fact is that greentech in its current form simply isn't useful for most people in most places—either to reduce carbon emissions *or* to provide a substitute for energy inputs in a more chaotic, post-Order world.

Fourth, is the issue of **density**. I live in a rural area and my home sprawls accordingly. I've got a ten-kilowatt solar system, which covers the majority of my south- and west-facing roof lines and generates sufficient power

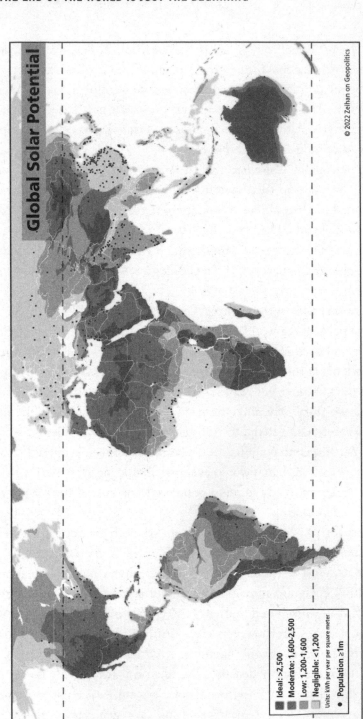

Global Solar Potential

Ideal: >2,500
Moderate: 1,600–2,500
Low: 1,200–1,600
Negligible: <1,200
Units: kWh per year per square meter
• Population ≥1m

© 2022 Zeihan on Geopolitics

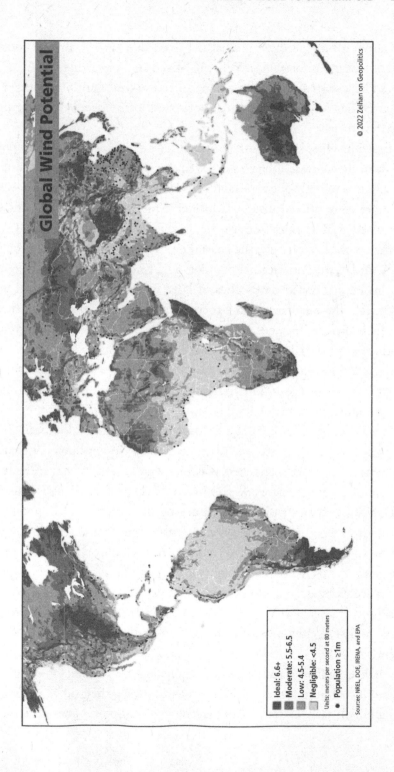

Global Wind Potential

Ideal: 6.6+
Moderate: 5.5-6.5
Low: 4.5-5.4
Negligible: <4.5
Units: meters per second at 80 meters
● Population ≥1m

Sources: NREL, DOE, IRENA, and EPA

© 2022 Zeihan on Geopolitics

for nearly all my needs. But what if I lived in a city? A smaller roofline means less room for panels. What if I lived in an apartment? My "roof" would be a shared space whose panels need to feed multiple units. What if I lived in a high-rise? Minimal roof space, lots of people drawing upon very few panels.

Fossil fuels are so concentrated that they are literally "energy" in physical form. In contrast, all greentechs require *space*. Solar is the worst of the bunch: it is roughly one thousand times less dense than systems powered by more conventional means. Consider America's Megalopolis, the line of densely packed cities from Boston in the north to the Greater DC area in the south. Collectively, the coastal cities of this line comprise roughly one-third of the American population on a tiny footprint. They also happen to be positioned on patches of land with very low solar and wind potential. The idea they could generate sufficient volumes of electricity locally is asinine. They need to import it. The closest zone with reasonably good solar potential (*not* "good," "*reasonably* good") is south-central Virginia. That's an inconvenient six hundred miles away from Boston, and Boston would be last in line for sips of electricity after D.C., Baltimore, Philadelphia, New York City, Hartford, and Providence.

It isn't simply an issue for cities located in cloudy, still locations. It is a problem for cities *everywhere*. Every technological development that has brought us to our industrialized, urbanized present must be reevaluated to make today's greentech work. But by far the biggest challenge is the very existence of cities themselves. All are by definition densely populated, while greentech by definition is *not* dense. Squaring that circle even in sunny and windy locations will require massive infrastructure to bridge the gap between dense population patterns and far more dispersed greentech electricity-generating systems. Such infrastructure would be on a scale and of a scope that humanity has not yet attempted. The alternative is to empty the cities and unwind six thousand years of history. Color me skeptical.

Fifth, even if solar and wind were equivalent technologies to oil, natural gas, and coal in terms of reliability, **decarbonizing the grid** would remain a mammoth task. Currently, 38 percent of global power generation is carbon free, suggesting we'd "only" need to roughly triple the good slice to displace the bad. Wrong. Hydropower has already used all available appropriate geographies globally. Nuclear would first need a helluva PR campaign to sufficiently improve its image. If only solar and wind are doing the lifting, they would need a ninefold buildout to fully displace fossil fuels.

Sixth, even in the geographies where greentech works well, it is at best only a partial patch. **Greentech *only* generates electricity.** Wind and solar might theoretically be able to replace coal in some specific locations, but electricity of any type is *not* compatible with existing infrastructure and vehicles that use oil-derived liquid fuels.

Such a restriction naturally leads to discussion of electric vehicles as a wholesale replacement for those powered by internal combustion engines. Such is far more difficult than it sounds.

The *entirety* of the *global* electricity sector generates roughly as much power as liquid transport fuels. Run the math: switching all transport from internal combustion to electric would necessitate a doubling of humanity's capacity to generate electricity. Again, hydro and nuclear couldn't help, so that ninefold increase in solar and wind is now a twenty-fold increase. Nor are you even remotely done. You now need absolutely *massive* transmission capacity to link the locations where wind and solar systems can generate power to where that power would ultimately be consumed. In the case of Europe and China, those power lines have to jump continents. You're also assuming minor little details break your way, such as the wind always blowing or the sun never setting or there never being hiccups in transmitting power from the Libyan desert to Berlin or the Outback to Beijing. More likely, EVs with today's technology will work only if we double down on the very energy sources that environmentalists say we're trying to cut out of the system.

In my not so humble opinion, we need to tackle first things first: we need to green the grid before we expand it. And unfortunately, the pace of that effort is painfully slow: From 2014, when the solar boom began, until 2020, solar has only increased to become 1.5 percent of total energy use.

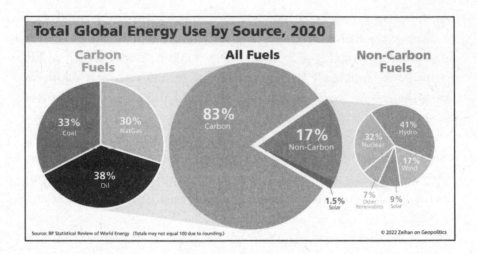

Total Global Energy Use by Source, 2020

Carbon Fuels

All Fuels

Non-Carbon Fuels

33% Coal

30% NatGas

38% Oil

83% Carbon

17% Non-Carbon

1.5% Solar

41% Hydro

32% Nuclear

17% Wind

9% Solar

7% Other Renewables

Source: BP Statistical Review of World Energy (Totals may not equal 100 due to rounding.)   © 2022 Zeihan on Geopolitics

Seventh, the **practical aspects** of a potential switchover are beyond Herculean, both in terms of technical challenges and cost, and I am *not* talking about the relatively simple task of installing enough solar panels and wind turbines to generate 43,000 terawatt-hours of electricity, roughly seventy times the total greentech buildout of 2010 through 2021.

- Part of what makes the modern world work is on-demand electricity. This requires something called dispatchability: the idea that a power plant can ramp its power output up and down to match demand. Not only can wind and solar not do this; they are also intermittent. Power levels vary based on that most mercurial of forces: the weather. Hardware upgrades can prevent such surges from alternatively shorting out or browning out industrial and residential customers, but that's not free.
- Part of what makes dispatchability so attractive is that there are peaks and troughs in normal electricity demand. Specifically, in most locations peak electricity *demand* is between 6 p.m. and 10 p.m., with higher demand rates in the *winter*. However, peak solar *supply* is between 11 a.m. and 3 p.m., with higher supply profiles in the *summer*. And that's before considering that the same panel will generate different amounts of power based on location. My panels in the highlands of

Colorado would spit out less than one-fifth the power in the doldrums of Toronto. No amount of money enables us to ignore this little geographic problem.

- Unlike coal or natural gas, which can be prepositioned, the wind blows where the wind blows and the sun shines where the sun shines. Any greentech-generated electricity must then be wired to where it can be used. This is also not free, and often results in the doubling (or more) of the cost of the delivered power (the details vary massively based on where the power is coming from, where it will be consumed, the nature of the connecting infrastructure, what sort of political borders must be crossed, etc.). It's no wonder fully 95 percent of humanity sources its electricity from power plants less than fifty miles away.

- Addressing such issues requires a parallel power system. With the status of greentech technology in 2022, in most cases that parallel system is a boring, conventional system that runs on either natural gas or coal. Let me underline that: greentech today is so unreliable in most locations that those localities that do attempt greentech have no choice but to maintain a full conventional system for their total peak demand—at full cost.

Greentech in its current form simply isn't able to shave more than a dozen or so percentage points off fossil fuel demand, and even this "achievement" is only possible within geographies fairly perfect for it. A few places with good greentech potential have attempted to replace *half* of their preexisting conventional power generation with greentech, but working around issues of grid capacity and intermittency and transmission results in a quadrupling of power prices.[*]

---

[*] In California, the price increase is closer to triple, but that's because Cali cheats. California doesn't maintain a full backup fossil fuel system but instead imports fossil-fuel-derived power from neighboring states. In an act of accounting chicanery, California calls such imports zero-carbon because the carbon was generated on the other side of the state line. Cue the eye rolls.

That said, there *is* a complementary technology out there that might—emphasis on the word "might"—be able to square these circles: batteries. The idea is that greentech-generated power can be stored in batteries until such time as it is needed. Intermittency? Dispatchability? Supply-demand mismatches? All solved! Even transmission distances can be shortened in some cases.

Unfortunately, what works beautifully in theory faces a couple of problems in practice. The first is supply chains. Just as oil's production is concentrated, so too is the primary input for the best battery chemistry of the day: lithium. And just as oil needs to be refined into usable products, raw lithium must be processed into concentrate, refined into metals, and then built into battery assemblies. Today's lithium supply chains require unimpeded access to Australia, Chile, China, and Japan. That's a bit simpler than oil, but not by all that much. Should anything happen to East Asia writ large—and all of East Asia is due for a great deal of happening—the bulk of the value-added system for batteries will need to be rebuilt elsewhere. That will take time. And money. A lot of it. Especially if the goal is to apply lithium battery tech at scale.

That scale is the second problem. Lithium batteries are expensive. They are the second- or third-most-expensive component in the average smartphone, and that's a battery that stores but a few watt-hours. They comprise in excess of three-quarters the cost and weight of most electric vehicles, and that's a battery that stores but a few kilowatt-hours.

City-grid batteries require *mega*watt-*days*. Achieving meaningful greentech power storage would require grid-level battery systems that could store a minimum of four hours of power to cover the bulk of that daily high-demand period. Assuming that the technological improvements in the world of batteries that have unfolded since 1990 continue into 2026, the cost of a four-hour lithium grid storage system will be about $240 per megawatt-hour of capacity, or *six* times that of the standard combined-cycle natural gas plant, which is currently the most common electricity-generating asset in the United States. Important note: that 6x figure does not include the cost of the electricity-generating asset that actually *charges* the battery, nor the transmission asset to get the electricity to the battery.

As of 2021, the United States had 1,100 gigawatts of installed electricity-generation capacity, but only 23.2 gigawatts of electricity storage. Roughly 70 percent of that 23.2 gigawatts is something called "pumped storage," in essence using excess generated power to pump water uphill, and then allowing that water to flow down a watercourse to power a generator as needed. Most of the other 30 percent is some sort of storage capacity located in people's *homes*. Only 0.73 gigawatts of storage is actually in the form of batteries. The American state that is most committed to the ideology of a green future is California. The state as a whole has but enough total storage—not battery storage, *total* storage—for one *minute* of power. Los Angeles, the American metropolitan area with the most aggressive plan for installing grid storage, doesn't anticipate reaching one hour of total storage capacity until 2045.

Remember, that's one hour of storage for LA's *current* electricity system—not the doubling that would be required to realize the dream of universal EV adoption for cars and light trucks.

Nor would that magical four hours be anything more than the first step on a long and tortuous road. A true shift to a carbon-neutral power system would require the capacity to camel not hours, but *months* of electricity for the seasons that are not as windy or sunny. We don't know everything about the world of energy, but we know for certain that there is not enough lithium ore on the entire planet to enable a rich country like the United States to achieve such a goal, much less the world writ large.*

Eighth, there is a little-discussed **financial issue** that might soon make this entire discussion moot.

---

*   Does this mean grid storage as a concept is stupid? Nah. Not what I'm saying. Right now, most power utilities maintain a secondary fleet of power generation assets that *only* get turned on for peak heating and/or cooling needs a few days a year. Those are some expensive paperweights. Not only does installing a single hour of grid storage enable the retirement of many of those peaker plants, but such storage capacity can be used *every day* to shave down the normal *daily* peak demand. Based on location and weather, that reduces fuel use by 4–8 percent. Apply that nationwide and, while you're definitely not within reach of net zero, you're still talking about a lot of apples.

In places with good solar or wind resources, most current price assessments suggest that the combined lifetime cost of fuel, maintenance, and installation for greentech versus conventional is more or less equal. From a financial point of view, the primary difference is *when* capital must be committed. About one-fifth of the total costs for the entire life span of a conventional power are spent up front on land acquisition and facility construction, with the rest dribbled out over decades for fuel purchase and facility maintenance. In contrast, for greentech nearly the entire cost is up front, two-thirds up front in the case of onshore wind turbines. After all, fuel costs are zero.

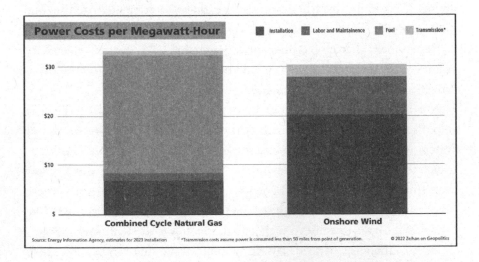

In the capital-rich world of the late Order, this is a footnote, and not a particularly important one at that. There is nothing wrong with financing twenty-five years of power bills up front when capital is cheap. But in the capital-*poor* world of the Disorder, this could well be everything. Should investment capital become harder to source or borrowing costs go up, all such up-front investments degrade from an easy carry to unsatisfactorily risky and expensive. In that world, the far lower installation costs of conventional systems make a great deal more sense.

Greentech in its current form simply isn't mature enough or cheap enough to move the needle for most peoples in most locations. It is largely limited to developed countries with rich capital supplies who just coincidentally happen to have large population centers fairly close to sunny or windy locations. The southwest quarter of the United States looks great, as do the American Great Plains, Australia, and the coasts of the North Sea.

Nearly all other locations will remain dependent upon more traditional fuels for the vast majority of their energy needs. This is far worse than it sounds from the point of view of greenhouse gas emissions because *the vast majority of these locations will not be able to retain access to internationally traded oil and natural gas, either.* If they cannot source oil or natural gas and their geographies do not enable sufficient use of solar and wind, they will have a simple decision to make. Option A is to do without the products that have enabled humanity to advance for the past two centuries, to suffer catastrophic reductions in product access and food production, triggering massive downward revisions in standards of living and population. To go without electricity. To deindustrialize. To *decivilize.*

Or—Option B—to use the one fuel source that nearly all countries have locally: coal. Many particularly unlucky people will be stuck with something called lignite, a barely-qualifies-as-coal fuel that is typically one-fifth water by weight and is by far the least efficient *and* dirtiest fuel in use today. Germany already today uses lignite as its primary power input fuel because greentech is so woefully unapplicable to the German geography, and yet the Germans—for environmental reasons—have shut down most of their other power-generation options.[*]

As a planet, we are perfectly capable of suffering broad-scale economic collapse *and* vastly increasing our carbon emissions at the same time.

---

[*]   Germans: not as smart as you might think.

FUELING THE FUTURE

We're slouching into a world where energy supplies out of both the Persian Gulf and the borderlands of the former Soviet Union will be subject to highly contested strategic environments. Even if none of the regions' issues erupt into formal wars, their instability and insecurity all but guarantees that oil and natural gas production and flows will be disrupted for years. Or more likely, decades. Even that assumes no strategic competition in East Asia, and no piracy—state or otherwise—along the coasts of Southeast Asia or Africa. The days of reliable, inexpensive oil shipments are coming to an inglorious end.

It will be worse than it sounds, and not just at the high-level, this-will-happen-to-that-country sort of way, but instead deeply personally.

Between the entrance of China into the global system and the end of the Cold War, total global oil demand has doubled since 1980—mostly due to new players starting their journeys down the roads of industrialization and urbanization. The modern, industrial, urban lifestyles of most of the human population require oil, and with the Americans having lost interest, that oil will *not be there*. Transport links will shrivel, which will impact everything from the coherence of manufacturing supply chains to food distribution. Many electricity systems will fail due to lack of fuel. The physical concentrations of urbanization—what enables us to live relatively low-carbon-impact, high-value-added lives—are simply not possible without ample energy. The end of globalization may herald the end of the world we know, but the end of global energy heralds the end of the *lives* we know.

The locations facing the greatest shortages are those major consumers at the very end of those vulnerable supply lines: Northeast Asia and Central Europe, with Germany, Korea, and China by far facing the greatest threats, as none have proximate oil or natural gas sourcing, nor the military capacity to venture out to secure someone else's. There will be electricity problems as well. All three use a mix of nuclear, natural gas, and coal for the vast bulk of their electricity needs, all based upon imported fuel. Of these, China is by far the most vulnerable. Three decades of growth has strained the country's electricity system; the country has *no* spare capacity—it runs *all* of its power generation flat-out regardless of the input fuel—so any input shortage would at a minimum lead to large-scale rotating blackouts. It's already happened. As China struggled in late 2021 with the dual impacts of COVID and the stricter environmental rules, regions responsible for one-third of the country's GDP faced rolling blackouts and electricity rationing.

For the countries with more means, the picture is brighter, but there are still loads of problems. Countries like the United Kingdom, France, Japan, and India do have the military wherewithal and geographic position that will enable them to go out and secure resources themselves, but all will face a price environment of terrifying proportions. Their solution is obvious: establish a degree of neo-imperial control over a supply system to keep all supplies in-house and divorce themselves from the vulgar vicissitudes of global pricing that is alternatively insultingly expensive and erratically insane. That's great for these new proto-empires, but such actions would remove even more oil from the rest of the system.

The ironic bottom line is that the United States is one of only a handful of countries that not only will not face a protracted energy crisis, but can also attempt oil and natural gas substitutes at scale. It is the developed country closest to the equator, granting it the world's second-best opportunities for mass solar installations (Australia is far away in the top spot). It has huge swaths of windswept lands in the Great Plains, granting it the world's best wind resources. The Americans even have an ace in the hole in terms of their oil demand: One of the by-products from most shale oil wells is a steady flow of natural gas. The Americans, and pretty much *only* the Americans, can use that natural gas in lieu of oil in their petrochemical systems. Add in a relatively stable and robust capital structure and secure access to lithium deposits in Australia and Chile, and the Americans can even attempt battery systems and EV rollouts with current technologies, should they so choose.

For all the topics we've addressed so far—transport, finance, and energy—the United States is the lucky country. That luck is deep, rooted in geography, which means it can be applied to other situations as well. For if you think the Americans have it made on these first three topics, just wait until you see the impact of the Americans' luck upon the next three.

SECTION V:
INDUSTRIAL MATERIALS

DISASSEMBLING HISTORY

I don't have a snazzy introduction to this chapter because the materials we rely upon to make our technology and our world work are kinda sorta embedded in the names of our eras: The Stone Age. The Bronze Age. The Iron Age. Many, reasonably, say the early twenty-first century is fully part of the Silicon Age.

Not to put too fine a point on it, but if you lack iron in the Iron Age, then history tends to forget about you. I think you see where I'm going with this. Whether oil or copper, either you have it, you can get it, or you don't. And if you don't, you do not get to play.

What might not be so obvious is just how multifaceted our trade in and dependency upon the various industrial materials have become in recent decades.

Again, it's best to dial back to the beginning.

Early conflicts over materials were not so much imperial or national, as there were no empires or nations to speak of. Instead, such struggles were about clan, tribe, and family. There also wasn't a lot to fight over. In the Stone Age it wasn't like you had to go that far to find . . . stone. Sure, there were certain rocks that were better for cutting or arrowheads—obsidian comes to mind—but the tyranny of transport limited everyone's reach. You used what you had access to and that shaped your culture. We were far more likely to fight over food (and lands that could grow it reliably) than rocks.

As the age of Stone gave way to the age of Bronze, the math subtly shifted. Egypt—(in)famously—had nothing but wheat, barley, stones, sand, reeds, some copper, and a near-bottomless supply of labor. Every trade delegation sent, every war fought, was about accessing resources not on that list. The top items the Egyptians needed were the arsenic and/or tin required to forge bronze. The Mesopotamian city-states were similarly wheat- and barley-rich and material-poor, and so regularly warred and traded with one another and their upstream and up-mountain neighbors to access the ancient equivalent of iPhones.[*]

Fast-forward to the next age—that of Iron—and the math tightened up again. Copper was nearly unique as a material in that it is one of the few materials that on occasion can be found lying about in its natural, metal form. That *never* happens with iron. Nor was iron nearly as common as copper. But still, it wasn't exactly unheard-of, particularly since we're now talking about the age of 800 BCE on. The Age of Empires was in full swing, so the governing systems of the day had the ability to reach a wide variety of source mines. Instead of facing materials shortages, the primary concern was *skill* shortages. Iron ore on its own is useless, and the art of turning the ore into actual iron required hundreds of someones who knew what they were doing. Most governments were more likely to launch attacks to abduct blacksmiths than to secure iron ore or copper mines.

From a technological point of view, things puttered on for another millennium before the slow, incremental progress witnessed under the technological Ages of Stone, Bronze, and Iron found itself rudely interrupted by the fall of the Roman Empire in 476 CE, the Islamic jihad of 622–750, and above all, the cultural and technological flameouts of the European Dark Ages during the sixth through eleventh centuries. The rough overlap among the three certainly was not conducive to technological preservation, much less advancement.

Salvation, of a sort, came in the most bizarre of forms: mass carnage. In 1345–46 the Mongols' Golden Horde was laying siege to several Crimean fortress-cities in one of their stereotypical do-things-our-way-or-we-will-kill-you-all-and-oh-yeah-we-want-to-trade-too-how-about-some-tea military campaigns. Once the Mongols started catapult-launching corpses into the city of Kaffa, a group of Genoese traders decided *not* to stick around and see how the fight would end. They fled—casually—by

---

[*]　The city-states of the ancient Indus River undoubtedly did the same thing, but they all died out without bothering to take notes during their civilization's collapse, so that's really just a semi-educated guess.

sea (although not before picking up one final shipment of slaves from a city where suddenly any pretense of morality had evaporated).

As has been common on all ships for the entirety of human history, the Genoese vessels had rats. Unknown to the Genoese, those rats were carrying bubonic plague. The Genoese's first stop was Constantinople, the Singapore of the day. Within five years, nearly all of the European, Russian, and North African world was battling the worst epidemic in regional history. Ultimately, one-third of the region's population was wiped out, with population densities not restored for 150 years.*

Anywho, without the Plague, we may well have remained *stuck in the Dark Ages.*

Funny thing about mass death events: For those who *don't* die, life . . . continues. Food still needs to be grown, horseshoes hammered out, barns erected, stone cut. Even if a plague is indiscriminate in whom it eliminates, in the aftermath there will be regional disparities for this or that skill set. Once the Black Death lifted, many locations lacked a sufficient number of weavers, or carpenters, or bricklayers. In every case of shortage, two things happened.

First, supply and demand: those in the relevant profession experienced an *increase* in take-home pay, setting the stage for our modern concept of skilled labor. Second, the need to expand the output of such skill sets led local workers, guilds, and rulers alike to increase productivity. Some did this by training new workers. Some by developing new techniques. Some by importing the long-forgotten knowledge preserved by the Arabs in the aftermath of Rome's fall.†

---

* Don't be too hard on the Italians. The Mongol-Crimea-Constantinople-Genoa route, while likely the first vector that brought the Black Death to Europe, certainly wasn't the only one.

† Thank Allah the Muslim empires preserved the technical knowledges they came across. If they hadn't, Europe's repeated disintegrations post-Rome would have led to a very different present. On the flip side, if the Muslim empires had *applied* en masse the knowledges they stewarded, we'd all probably be vacationing in other star systems by now. And be speaking Arabic or Turkish.

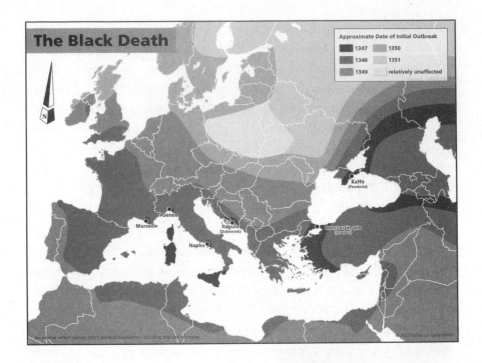

By the fifteenth century, such advances in process and learning had reached the critical mass we now recognize as the Renaissance. Reinforcing advances in social thought, culture, mathematics, and science culminated not simply in restarting technological development after a millennium of Dark, but also started us down the path to another technological age: the Industrial. Among the *many* outcomes of the broad-based expansions in knowledge and understanding of the natural world were steadily improving methods to detect, isolate, and purify this or that material from this or that ore.

Going back dozens of centuries, we had been limited to copper, lead, gold, silver, tin, arsenic, iron, and zinc. With the codification of the rules of chemistry and physics, we expanded that list to include cobalt, platinum, nickel, manganese, tungsten, uranium, titanium, chromium, tantalum, palladium, sodium, iodine, lithium, silicon, aluminum, thorium, helium, and neon. Once we knew of these materials, and knew how to separate them from rock, and knew how to purify them sufficiently for use, we developed the ability to put them back together and mix-and-match them under controlled circumstances. Consequently, now we have everything from flamethrowers to steel that won't melt if exposed to said flamethrowers, to meshes of copper and gold and silicon that can place more brainpower in one *hand* than the entire intelligentsia of the medieval world, to party balloons.

LESSONS FROM THE PAST, LESSONS FOR THE FUTURE

Every material has its own use. Every material combined with others has more uses. Some are discrete. Some allow substitution. But all share a simple characteristic. Whether used in construction or war or urbanization or manufacturing, *all* are children of the Industrial Age. They require Industrial Age technologies to be produced, shipped, refined, purified, alloyed, and rearranged into value-added products. Should anything happen to the sustainability or reach of the industrial technology set, *all* of them will simply fade away—and take all their benefits with them.

We have seen this before. Many times.

Many of the world's past empires launched specific military campaigns to secure this or that material, while others leveraged their control of this or that material to achieve breakthrough and become something more than their geographies would normally allow.

Poland became Europe's premier power due to the income from a single *salt* mine (salt being the only reliable method of the 1300s for preserving large amounts of meat or fish). Spain's experience with the Potosi silver mine easily extended its tenure as the global superpower for a century. In the late 1800s, Chile warred with Peru and Bolivia over the Atacama Desert and its rich deposits of copper, silver, and nitrates (a key component in early-industrial gunpowder). Britain made a bad habit of sailing anywhere at any *time* to attack any*one* who had any*thing* the Brits might fancy. The Brits were particularly fond of seizing access points like Manhattan or Singapore or Suez or the Gambia or the Irrawaddy, all locales which enabled them to take cuts of interesting regional trades in nonperishable goods.

Some of these competitions were a bit more recent.

World War II was in many ways a fight over inputs. Most of us have at least an inkling of the strategic competitions that took place for agricultural land and oil, but battles over industrial materials were just as front and center.

France had iron ore while Germany had coal. Both materials were necessary to forge steel. You can see the problem. Germany's May 1940 invasion of France resolved the issue. For Berlin at least. Postwar, the French spearheaded the formation of the European Coal and Steel Community in an attempt to resolve the same iron-ore-here, coal-there problem with diplomacy instead of bullets. We know the ECSC today as the European Union.

The German invasion of Russia in June 1941 obviously marked the end of the German-Russian alliance, but the first big wedge in the relationship had occurred nineteen months earlier, when the Russians invaded Finland, threatening German access to what had been the Nazi war machine's primary source of nickel, a critical input into high-grade steel.

Among the many reasons the Japanese conquered Korea in 1904–05 was for timber for use in construction. The subsequent Japanese expansion into Southeast Asia is often—and accurately—billed as an oil grab. But the Home Islands weren't simply energy-poor; they also lack other central industrial materials that could only be sourced by physical expansion, ranging from iron ore to tin to rubber to copper to bauxite.

In all cases, the dominant technologies of the age demanded that every country either have sufficient access to all these inputs and more, or be lorded over by others.

The list of such "required" materials has expanded exponentially since 1945 . . . just as the Americans have made the world sufficiently safe for every*one* to have access to every*thing*. That suggests the materials competition of the future will be far more wide-ranging and multifaceted, while the fallout from failure to access such materials will be far more damning.

Nor are any of these industrial materials evenly distributed across the globe. As with oil, each has its own geography of access.

It's easy to draw some dotted lines based on likely trading zones and envision an Africa that has access to the inputs for electronics but not steel, a Europe with nuclear power but no greentech, or a China with old-timey batteries but lacking the capacity to transmit electricity. These sorts of disconnects will *not* be allowed to stand.

This will be a struggle for everything that is required to maintain a modern system. As such, every tool will be on the table. Some will attempt this-for-that trades. Others will be more . . . energetic in their efforts.

Does my obsession with state piracy make more sense now? Does piracy *in general* make more sense? To think we are all going to just sit in our little bubbles and make do and not venture out to at least *try* to get what we don't have is to take a very creative read of human history. We're entering a world that Jack Sparrow would find very familiar. This is not a game for the weak.

The greatest of these challenges of access will layer atop the already insurmountable challenge of dealing with climate change. Looking back, the geopolitics of oil have proven to be surprisingly . . . straightforward. Oil exists in commercially accessible and viable volumes in only a few locations. The Persian Gulf obviously comes to mind. We might not like the challenges of such locations, and those challenges may have absorbed an outsized chunk of everyone's attention in the late-industrial and globalization eras, but at least we are familiar with them. Most important, oil is more or less a once-and-done.

That is absolutely not how it will work with greentech in a deglobalized world. In "moving on from oil" we would be walking away from a complex and often-violent and always critical supply and transport system, only to replace it with *at least ten more.*

Megawatt of electricity-generating capacity for megawatt of electricity-generating capacity, greentech requires two to five times the copper and chromium of more traditional methods of generating power, as well as

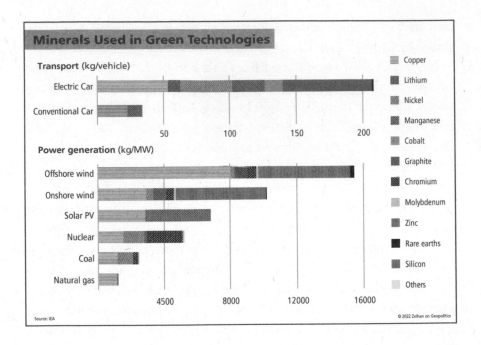

Minerals Used in Green Technologies

Transport (kg/vehicle)

Electric Car
Conventional Car

50   100   150   200

Power generation (kg/MW)

Offshore wind
Onshore wind
Solar PV
Nuclear
Coal
Natural gas

4500   8000   12000   16000

Copper
Lithium
Nickel
Manganese
Cobalt
Graphite
Chromium
Molybdenum
Zinc
Rare earths
Silicon
Others

Source: IEA   © 2022 Zeihan on Geopolitics

a host of other materials that do not feature at all in our current power plant inputs: most notably manganese, zinc, graphite, and silicon. And EVs? You think going to war for oil was bad? Materials inputs for just the drivetrain of an EV are six times what's required for an internal combustion engine. If we're truly serious about a green transition that will electrify *everything*, our consumption of all these materials and more must increase by more than an order of magnitude.

Even worse, the mixed supply chains for these inputs are not nearly as "simple" as what was required for oil. We won't "simply" be dealing with Russia and Saudi Arabia and Iran; we will all need to engage regularly with Chile and China and Bolivia and Brazil and Japan and Italy and Peru and Mexico and Germany and the Philippines and Mozambique and South Africa and Guinea and Gabon and Indonesia and Australia and Congo and, oh yeah, still Russia.

Not only does greentech fail to generate sufficient electricity in most locations to contribute meaningfully to addressing our climate concerns but also it's laughable to think that most locations could manufacture the necessary components in the first place, simply due to the lack of inputs. In truly unfortunate contrast, one product that *does* exist in most places is low-quality coal. The end of globalization doesn't just mean we are leaving behind the most positive economic environment in human history; we may soon look at our carbon emissions of the 2010s as the good ol' days.

THE CAVEATS BEFORE THE PLUNGE

The remainder of this chapter aims to explore just how central these materials are to our way of life. Where they come from. What they are used for. What's at stake in a degrading world.

To that end, please keep four things in mind:

First, I cannot *possibly* communicate the end-all and be-all of *all* industrial materials. There are literally hundreds of them in their base forms, which combine into thousands of intermediate alloys and mixtures to create millions of end products. We're going to focus on the top fifteen in terms of international exchange. Hopefully, that will sufficiently map out our present so we can glean some glimpses of our future.

Second, there *is* a more or less common thread to follow. The story of today's industrial materials is the story of mass industrialization, which braids up with the stories of the Order and China.

The Order largely removed the geographic constraints of materials access. Anyone could access anything at any time; as with so many other sectors, the Order transformed the concept of Geographies of Success into a good of the global commons. That simple fact has inextricably bound up many of these materials with the unsustainable present of the People's Republic. China has become the world's biggest importer, consumer, and processor of many of them.

The world will survive China's fall—the world of industrial materials will survive China's fall—but many of the bounces *will* hurt. A lot. And not all bounces are created equal. As the Industrial Age has matured, and as industrial materials have become more numerous, discrete, and specialized, the geography of their production and processing matters far more now than when you could simply scrape up some copper during a stroll through the woods.

Third, industrialization and the Order are *not* the end of the story. Beginning roughly in 1980, the human condition launched into its next technological era: the Digital Age. Just as Bronze could not have happened without Stone, and Iron without Bronze, and Industrial without Iron, mass digitization could not have happened without mass industrialization. It is industrialization that has enabled us to identify, locate, mine, refine, and purify the materials that drive modern society. Many parts of the world are on the verge of deindustrializing, which, among other things, means their access to the industrial materials is not long for this world. Perhaps more than anything else it is this looming inadequacy and incompleteness of access that will rive the world apart.

Fourth, it isn't all (horribly) bad news. History tells us we may—*may*—be on the verge of a series of massive breakthroughs in materials science. The in-progress demographic bust threatens to reduce the human population writ large over the next few decades by as much in relative terms as the Black Death effect. The impact upon working-age populations will be even bigger. No matter what specifics the future holds, we will all need to get by with fewer workers.

While we'll be discovering the edges of our new economic models as we go, our history strongly suggests that fewer workers by definition means more expensive labor. That in turn should prompt everyone to figure out how to make that scarce labor more productive. The Black Death's boost to labor productivity set us on the path to the materials science breakthroughs that enabled and enhanced both the Renaissance and the Industrial Revolution. Our demographic decline, holistic as it is, suggests that a possible silver (or platinum, or vanadium) lining might lurk off in the dark clouds pouring over the horizon.

This lining *is* dependent upon the parts of the planet that do not deindustrialize post-globalization, and we are unlikely to perceive that lining until it is far too late for me to play any personal role in a Second Renaissance, but you never know. This world surprises me. All the time.

So, with such clarifications and guidelines in place, let's dive in.

THE ESSENTIAL MATERIALS

The first material is arguably the most important since it is *the* base material that makes everything from buildings to roads to telecom towers possible: **iron ore**. Regardless of variety or quality, iron ore comprises at least the majority—and often more than 90 percent—of the material in every bit of steel humans use. This makes understanding the world of iron ore very simple: you just need to understand China.

China sits squarely in the intersection of two quintessential trends of the modern age: rapid industrialization and urbanization on one hand, and China's trademark hyperfinancing on the other. Any successful industrialization and urbanization requires new roads, new buildings, and new industrial plant, all of which require massive volumes of steel. Hyperfinancing can help make all that happen, but in doing so it overbuilds *everything*, not just the roads and buildings that mean yet more steel demand, but also the industrial plant that is used to make the steel in the first place.

China's industrialization push has proven so huge and so fast and so overfinanced that China isn't simply the world's largest producer of steel; it regularly ranks among the world's top four *importers* of steel, particularly the product sets on the higher end of the quality scale. But that overfinance also means China produces steel with zero regard for the reality of domestic needs, and so China is also the world's largest steel *exporter*—particularly steel product sets on the lower end of the quality scale.

All that requires a worldful of iron ore. China isn't just the world's largest importer of the stuff, it doesn't simply take in more than the rest of the world combined. China imports more than the rest of the world combined times *three*. China *is* the global iron ore market. As to production, Australia exports half of global iron ore volumes, with Brazil exporting half the remainder. Unsurprisingly, China gobbles up nearly all these Southern Hemispheric powers' exports, as well as additional big chunks from Russia, India, and South Africa.

Nor is China the only country that uses steel; it's just the only country where the economics of steel are so fundamentally out of whack. Most everyone else uses iron ore produced a bit closer to home (or in many cases, *at* home). Their balances are rounded out by the very big business of steel recycling. Roughly 1 percent of buildings in the advanced world are torn down every year, and every scrap of the steel used to reinforce them is melted down, reforged, and given a second life. Or third. Or eighteenth.

This duality between the ravenousness of China and the rather placid pace of steel work everywhere else makes the forecast rather straight-forward.

The vast bulk of the world's iron ore production comes from countries that face limited to no security threats as the world deglobalizes: in descending order, Australia, Brazil, India, South Africa, Canada, and the United States. However, the countries that export the vastness of global steel—in ascending order, Ukraine, Germany, Russia, Korea, Japan, and above all China—are somewhere on the sliding scale between "facing severe complications" and "utterly screwed." The world is going to have massive shortages of steel, at the same time that the supplies of the raw material to make that steel will overflow.

The solution is simple—the world will need more smelting capacity—but it is critical to understand that not all steel is created equal. Unlike most materials, all steel is 100 percent recyclable, but recycled steel is not the same as virgin steel.

Think of steel as if it were a sheet of aluminum foil. Then crumple it, and smooth it out. Hell, try ironing it. Then rinse and repeat. Recycled steel is just as strong as virgin steel, but it cannot be made as pretty. So recycled steel is used in rebar and I-beams and auto parts, but fresh steel is used in exposed applications you can see, such as appliance cladding and roofing.

First-round steel is made with coal-powered blast furnaces to up the carbon content, which makes the steel stronger. The process is extremely carbon intensive, because, you know, it uses *coal*. Also, steel forging demands not just any coal, but a coal derivative that's had its impurities burned out, called coking coal. In essence the coal has to be burned *twice*.

Somewhat similar blast furnaces *can* also handle the recycling, but a far more efficient process is to use something called an arc furnace to run a current through scrap steel and literally electrify it until it melts.[*] That means the best economics for recycled steel involve not simply physical security and proximity to the raw inputs, but also cheap-cheap-cheap electricity.

The winner on all three counts will be the United States, with America's Gulf Coast looking the most promising, for the triple reasons of having great electricity prices, plenty of greenfield industrial space—particularly at potential port locations—and proximity to both large local and regional markets (think Texas, the East Coast, and Mexico). Add in ample coal supplies and the Americans could get into virgin steel production, too.

Secondary locations that look very favorable for steel recycling include Sweden (hydropower) and France (nuclear power). Australia has a wonderful opportunity to surprise to the upside and move from the low-value business of digging up ore to the high-value business of forging virgin steel. "All" the Aussies need to do is bring their iron ore and coal together from where they are produced . . . on opposite sides of the continent. Put up an army of solar panels and wind turbines throughout the sunny, windy Outback and the Aussies could recycle steel on the cheap as well.

Outsized successes in these four countries might not sound like enough to maintain global steel supplies at their current level. You're right. They would not even come close. But we're not kicking around that option as feasible, or even necessary. A world without China needs less than half as much of the stuff, and that's before considering the likely far slower paces of building and industrializing that will define the future world.

Another material integral to all things in the modern world is **bauxite**, the raw material that gives us aluminum.

---

[*]   #ScienceIsCool.

The aluminum refining process is pretty straightforward. Strip mining produces bauxite ore, which is then boiled in sodium hydroxide to create an intermediate product called alumina. This cocaine-white powder has a variety of uses in ceramics, filters, body armor, insulation, and paint. Some 90 percent of alumin*a* is then in essence electrified *Jaws 2*–style until it becomes alumi*num*, which goes on to be molded, bent, and extruded into everything from airplane and car parts to soda cans to frames to tubings to casings to machinery to wires—pretty much anything where low weight and/or low-cost conductivity is a primary concern. The process is also pretty predictable, assuming you begin with decent-quality ore: four-to-five tons of bauxite becomes two tons of alumina becomes one ton of finished metal. As a rule, bauxite mines and the alumina processors are owned by the same firms, while aluminum smelters are completely different entities in different countries.

China has long since mined itself out of its high-quality bauxite reserves, and is now left with a dwindling supply of low-quality mines whose output requires much more filtering and much more power to produce much less end product per ton of ore. That has turned China into a voracious importer of bauxite from *everywhere*. As of 2021, China absorbs two-thirds of all internationally traded bauxite, while smelting about three-fifths of all aluminum. In true Chinese fashion, the majority of China's aluminum output is almost immediately dumped on international markets.

This is both great and awful. It's great in that it simplifies understanding of the supply chains: China's penchant for hyperfinancing and overbuilding makes it all China, all the time. It is awful in that the global supply chain for one of the world's most utilized metals is wrapped up in a failing system. When China cracks, the world will face global shortages of aluminum, as there simply are not sufficient smelting facilities elsewhere to cover more than a few percentage points of the pending shortfall.

The problem isn't so much access to bauxite. The stuff is sourced in countries that will be broadly okay in the post-globalized system: Australia produces more than one-quarter of the world's exports, with Brazil, Guinea, and India kicking in another tenth each. No, the problem is power. From shovel to final metal, electricity accounts for roughly 40 percent of the total cost—and that's a statistic that takes into account the fact that in most places that smelt, power is ridiculously cheap and/or heavily subsidized. Countries with ample hydropower—Norway, Canada, Russia—are big players.

Such a restriction limits the wheres for siting new smelters. The biggest new player will be an old player. Courtesy of the shale revolution, the United States already has the world's cheapest electricity. Add in some of the world's best greentech potential and power prices in large portions of the country are likely to go *down* in the years to come. The biggest competitive advantages will likely be felt in Texas, where the shale-related and greentech power generation trends overlap with plenty of port capacity to site a smelter or five.

Norway's ample hydro capacity combined with its location just above a mainland Europe that can produce but one-third of its needs argues for massive Norwegian expansions. Luckily—*for everyone*—aluminum recycles very easily. In Europe, capture programs are enough to supply one-third of demand.

For humanity, **copper** is where it all started. Easy to smelt in nothing more complicated than a clay pot, easy to shape with nothing more complicated than hands and rocks, copper was our very first metal. Sometimes we were even lucky enough to find it in nature as actual *metal*.

The love affair never ended. Dope copper a touch with either arsenic or tin and you get bronze, a firmer metal that's better for tools. Turn it into tubing or containers and copper's natural antiseptic and antimicrobial characteristics allow for longer-term food and drink storage, reduced disease, and extended life spans. Fast-forward our review of history to the Industrial Age and we discovered copper was also an excellent conductor of electricity, elevating *the* material of the ancient world to *the* material of the industrial world.

Today some three-quarters of copper mined ends up in some sort of electrical application, ranging from the wires in your lights to the generators in power plants to the semiconductors in your phone to the magnets in your microwave. Another quarter finds its way into construction, with plumbing and roofing materials the biggest slice. The bulk of the remainder finds its way into electric motors; with the world's EV craze surging we'll need a *lot* more copper in the decades to come.

But that's the future. For now, the story is all China. Large country, large population, rapidly industrializing. Everything about China demands copper in large volume, and so China hoovers up both metal and ore from the world over, and houses ten of the world's twenty largest copper smelters.

This means copper producers face a dark midterm future. Copper demand, and from it copper prices, are directly linked to very well-known demand in the sectors of electrification, construction, and transport. Melon-scoop out China, the world's largest and most rapidly expanding market in all three sectors, and most producers face years of operating in the red.

The key word, of course, is "most." Chile and Peru run the world's highest-quality mines along the Atacama Desert's many fault lines, mines that also have the lowest operating costs per unit of output. Collectively the two countries supply two-fifths of global needs. Chile also smelts most of its own ore into copper metal, making it the world's one-stop shop in a post-China world. It's a good thing Chile is both in a good neighborhood from a security point of view *and* the most politically stable country in Latin America. But mind those earthquakes.

THE FUTURE MATERIALS

Cobalt is going to be a tricky one.

Like all materials, cobalt has any number of minor industrial uses, particularly in metal alloys, but all of them combined pale when compared to their big demand source: batteries—specifically the sort of rechargeable batteries that lie at the heart of the energy transition. The larger iPhones have nearly half an ounce each, while the average Tesla has fifty *pounds*.

You think that electrifying everything and going green is the only way forward? As of 2022, cobalt is the *only* sufficiently energy-dense material that even hints that we might be able to use rechargeable batteries to tech our way out of our climate challenges. It simply cannot be done—even *attempted*—without cobalt, and a lot more cobalt than we currently have access to, at that. Assuming all else holds equal (which is, of course, a hilarious statement considering the topic of this book), annual cobalt metal demand between 2022 and 2025 alone needs to double to 220,000 tons simply to keep pace with Green aspirations.

That won't happen. That can't happen.

Like with the iron ore/steel nexus, the refining of cobalt ore into finished metal is utterly wrapped up in China's hyperfinance model. Eight of the world's fourteen largest cobalt sources are China-owned, and nearly all cobalt refining occurs in the PRC (with Canada a very distant second).

As if that weren't bad enough, there is no such thing as a "cobalt mine." Cobalt is one of those tricky things formed at similar times and under similar conditions as other materials. Some 98 percent of global cobalt production is generated as a by-product of nickel and copper output. The reality is even more complicated than that, because not all nickel and copper mines generate cobalt. More than half of commercially usable cobalt comes from a single country: the Democratic Republic of the Congo (a near-dictatorial place that is neither democratic nor a republic nor all that far from being outright failed). Much of *that* production is generated illegally, with artisanal miners (a fancy term to describe individuals who grab a shovel, climb over barbed wire, and evade shoot-on-sight guards in order to scrape out a few bits of ore) selling their output to Chinese middlemen for pennies.

In an increasingly decentralized world, Congo is most certainly *not* on the list of countries that will "make it," with its future likely to be a Hobbesian sort of famine-riddled anarchy. As goes Congo, so goes the world's cobalt access.

There are only four options for the future, and none of them are pretty.

Option 1: Mine the tar out of the third- and fourth-largest producers, Australia and the Philippines. Even with massive production expansions into remote and geographically difficult regions, the Aussies and Filipinos can produce at most one-fifth of what the world needs. Countries with which the Aussies and Filipinos enjoy excellent relations—primarily the United States and Japan—would get first dibs, but then there would be next to nothing left over. That would remove the countries most capable of stabilizing global cobalt supplies from the list of countries that care about said stabilization of supplies.

Option 2: Someone invades the Democratic Republic of the Congo with a whole lot of troops and seizes control of a route to the mines. Unfortunately, Congo's cobalt is nowhere near the coast, but instead deep in the country's southern jungles. The most expedient solution would be to partner with South Africa and establish a very long corridor all the way up the highland spine of southern Africa. This is precisely the route the Brits followed under the local leadership of Cecil Rhodes around the turn of the last century. After South Africa attained independence in 1915, Johannesburg took over the project at its attendant rail line, maintaining flat-out colonial control over the entire zone—including the portions that crossed through the supposedly independent countries of Zimbabwe and Zambia. Constant imperial intervention kept the route open until apartheid ended in the early 1990s. Since then the rail line has fallen into accelerating disrepair.

Option 3: Figure out the materials chemistry of a better battery that does not require cobalt (or at least not nearly as much). It sounds nice, and lots of smart money is chasing this option, but lots of smart money has been chasing this option for years with few meaningful breakthroughs.[*] There's also the lag of operationalization to consider. If we somehow cracked the code on a better battery as you read this paragraph, it would still take more than a decade to build out the supply chain for mass production. In the best-case scenario, we will be stuck with cobalt at least until the 2030s.

Option 4: Give up on the mass electrification the green transition says is essential.

So take your pick: go old-school imperial on multiple countries in order to strip-mine a specific material while alternatively exploiting or shooting desperate locals who try to get a bite of the action for themselves, or go without and stick to coal and natural gas. The future is full of such fun choices.

As long as we're talking about crappy battery chemistries, let's dive into **lithium.**

Lithium occupies the third spot on the periodic table, which, among other things, means it has but three electrons. Two of those electrons are locked up in an orbital zone called the inner atomic shell, a fancy way of saying they are happy in their home and aren't going anywhere. That leaves one electron with the ability to scoot about within lithium metal, jumping from atom to atom as the mood strikes. Scooting electrons about is a slightly nontechnical way of saying "electricity."

One electron per lithium atom can so scoot. That's pretty piss-poor. Lithium is among the least energy-dense materials we have access to on Earth, one of the reasons why a single Tesla needs 140 *pounds* of it to function—and why making a lithium battery without cobalt is the greentech equivalent of pissing in the wind.

Luckily, the supply system for lithium is considerably less depressing than that of cobalt. The vast bulk of global lithium ore comes from either

---

[*] At the time of this writing in early 2022, Tesla has fielded a no-cobalt battery in China, but only in the very small, nearly zero-internal-storage vehicles that predominate there, which have never found a market niche in the United States.

mines in Australia, or evaporation ponds in Chile and Argentina—none of which should face post-Order issues in production. But, reminiscent of cobalt—and reminiscent of iron ore—the real processing, some 80 percent of the total, occurs in hyperfinanced China. The future of lithium processing will likely resemble that of iron ore: the raw material supply lines are fine, but refining and value-add will need to happen in a new location where power is cheap. As with iron ore, the United States, Sweden, France, and possibly Australia look pretty good.

In the meantime, it is worth absorbing the disturbing fact that the production of lithium, its refining into metal, and the incorporation of that metal into rechargeable battery chassis is among the most energy-intensive industrial processes humanity has ever devised.

Let me smack you with some dirty Green math.

A typical 100-kilowatt-hour Tesla lithium-ion battery is built in China on a largely coal-powered grid. Such an energy- and carbon-intensive manufacturing process releases 13,500 kilograms of carbon dioxide emissions, roughly equivalent to the carbon pollution released by a conventional gasoline-powered car traveling 33,000 miles. That 33,000-miles figure assumes the Tesla is *only* recharged by 100 percent greentech-generated electricity. More realistically? The American grid is powered by 40 percent natural gas and 19 percent coal. This more traditional electricity-generation profile extends the "carbon break-even" point of the Tesla out to 55,000 miles. If anything, this overstates how green-friendly an electric vehicle might be. Most cars—EVs included—are driven during the day. That means they charge at night, when solar-generated electricity cannot be part of the fuel mix.[*]

---

[*]   Nor does this include pesky little details like the fact that we use aluminum in EVs for reasons of weight, but steel in conventional cars for reasons of strength—and, per pound, aluminum takes six times the amount of energy to make compared to steel. Even considering that you need less aluminum by weight to make a vehicle frame, you're still—conservatively—talking double the carbon intensity for an EV frame compared to a traditional vehicle.

But for now, lithium and cobalt are all we have. To date they are the only materials we have sufficiently decoded to make rechargeable batteries out of at scale. We *know* that the "green" path we are on is unsustainable. We just don't have a better one to consider until our materials science improves.

Silver is the great unsung hero of the modern age. We obviously use it in jewelry and fine tableware and government monetary reserves, but silver is also used in often-unnoticed amounts in everything from electronics to photography to catalysts to pharmaceuticals to telecommunication towers to jet engines to electroplatings to solar panels to mirrors to desalination plants to keyboards to reflective coatings on glass. Should our greentech materials science advance enough to make better batteries or long-range power transmission lines a reality, silver will undoubtedly be integral to the superconductors that will make such technologies function.

In terms of supply, there's both some bad and good news. First, the bad. China's hyperindustrialization and hyperfinancing have had a similar impact on the world of silver as they have on the world of industrial materials, writ large. Big local production, big importing of ores, big processing into metals, and big exports.

Now the good. Roughly one-quarter of silver production is from dedicated silver mines, while the remainder is coproduced with lead *or* copper *or* zinc. Silver metal—particularly from jewelry—is also eminently recyclable. In terms of extraction *and* processing *and* refining *and* recycling, silver's production cycle is well distributed geographically. So while China is a big—indeed the biggest—player at all stages of silver supply, it is nowhere near the majority player, nor is it in a position to either by strength or weakness overly threaten silver supply to others.

THE ALWAYS MATERIALS

Humans have always loved **goooold**! Its resistance to corrosion has made it useful to jewelers since the time of the first pharaohs. This association with wealth, combined with its persistent shininess, has made it a perennial favorite as a store of value and backer of currencies right up to the modern age. Until the world wars and the rise of the U.S. dollar, gold was what most countries held to back their economic systems. And even in the age of U.S. dollar supremacy, gold typically ranks third or fourth in most countries' reserves.

In the modern age—more specifically in the *Digital* Age—we've found more prosaic uses as well. The combination of gold's immunity to corrosion and its high electrical conductivity grants it niche applications in the semiconductor space, both for power management and information transmission.

Industrial uses? Check. Personal uses? Check. Government uses? Check. High value? Check? Store of value? Check. Pretty? Double check!

And yet and yet and *yet* gold is absolutely stupid. Nearly alone among all the materials that humanity uses, there is next to no opportunity for useful metallurgy or value-add. You don't mix gold with a better material to get better conductivity, because gold already is *the best* conductor. You don't mix it with a lesser material to degrade its conductivity, because you can get the same result with cheaper substitutes. About the only time gold is alloyed is to make it so your rings don't bend while you wear them. Aside from that, what's gold is gold is gold. Either it is the *only* thing to use for a product, or its use would be pointless. Such perfect uses are so limited that athletic award medals break into the top-ten list for annual demand.

That makes its supply chain . . . simple. Ore is mined, purified, transformed into mostly pure metal, and . . . then you're done. Well, you're done minus one itty-bitty step.

The only way not so much to add value but to establish cachet is to have someone you trust, someone you respect—someone *cool*—turn gold metal into those fancy, commercially traded bars that we've all seen in James Bond films and imagine Fort Knox is full of.* Refiners and recyclers *fly* gold to this final coolification step; there's no slow boat for gold. These cool dudes melt it all down, check for purity, fashion those iconic ingots, and put their personal stamps of guarantee on the final product. Any of these dudes that matter are either Swiss or Emirati. Like I said: *cool.*†

China has been trying to muscle into this final step for decades. At a glance it would seem China has a shot: it *is* the world's largest source of gold ore, and home to many midstream refineries. But people go to China for mass production and counterfeiting, not for exclusivity and authenticity. Barring a series of extremely unfortunate schmelting accidents that kill most of the aforementioned cool dudes, China will not enter this stage of the industry.

In a world without China, the biggest hit would be to ore inflow, and that's not nearly as damning for gold as it would be for anything else. Perhaps gold's most valuable characteristic is that gold is gold is gold; it *never* corrodes. Depending on overall economic circumstances, gold sourced from recycling is anywhere from one-sixth to one-*half* of "production" with that number ballooning in times of economic stress. The harsh light of deglobalization is certainly going to encourage a lot of people to melt down all those class rings. With a global supply chain, a simple refining process, and by far the most technical aspect of gold bar

---

*   It is, by the way.
†   Also, like I said, *dudes*. PAMP, the largest Swiss producer of gold bars, actually produced a gender study report that in essence apologizes for not having very many women working in their gold refineries. The gold makers of United Arab Emirates—in essence a misogynist slave state—felt no need to follow suit.

production happening elsewhere, China could harmlessly be scooped out of the entire supply chain.

Lead has long been a magical substance. Easy to mine. Easy to refine. Easy to shape. Easy to alloy. Easy to incorporate into any chemical mix to manifest whatever properties we want. Lead is particularly resistant to corrosion by water. By the mid–Industrial Age we were using it in cars and paint and roofing and glass and pipes and glazes and coatings and gasoline.

Lead only had one downside: it *makes you CRAZY!* Lead's toxicity generates no end of health complications in the brain, up to and including encouraging dissociative and violent behavior. In the United States we began purging lead from our systems in the 1970s, systematically banning its use in product after product. Over the next half century, the ambient level of lead in our *air* dropped by more than 90 percent. At the same time, instances of violent crimes subsided from record highs to record lows. Correlation? Definitely. Causation? Let's go with a strong maybe.*

Once lead is removed from where it might be ingested, its remaining uses are very, very few: some metal alloys (which don't come into contact with people), ammunition (a product for which lead's toxicity might even be perceived as a bonus), and a bit in ceramics and some glass products. But the big boy is lead-acid batteries, a key component in nearly every motorized vehicle regardless of size. Pre-1970 batteries took less than one-third of all lead. Now they absorb more than four-fifths.

This makes lead a bit of an odd duck from a supply chain point of view.

In advanced countries that have had car cultures for decades, the process of replacing batteries builds in provisions for recycling. In the United States and countries like it, some 90 percent of lead needs are met from recycled lead products.

---

* There's also a dissident strain of thought in archaeology asserting that the extensive use of lead in Rome's aqueducts contributed to imperial mismanagement and disassociation in the late Roman period. True? No idea, but it couldn't have helped.

In more recently industrialized countries, with China at the top of the list, the process is less . . . formalized. Most Chinese car batteries are *collected*, but only one-third are officially *recycled*. The rest seem to fall prey to the country's omnipresent counterfeiting and simply get new labels before being sold on as new product.[*] Considering that old, overused lead batteries tend to leak, and that lead is still freakin' toxic, this is not a good thing.

In any case, such mass lead recycling means the developed world can mosey right on without missing a beat. And should China find itself unable to access imported lead ore, it can at least comfort itself that an improved recycling program would both solve a big chunk of supply constraints and make for healthier living environments.

Next we come to mol-ib-den-im, mol-y-bud-um, mo-lib-de-num, oh fuck me, **M-O-L-Y-B-D-E-N-U-M**—we're just going to call it "moly."

Frustrating name aside, moly is one of those materials that most of us haven't heard of, for good reason. It doesn't tend to pop up in your average car bumper or doorknob. Moly is valued for its ability to weather extreme temperatures without significantly shifting form. Not extreme temperatures like when you are vacationing in Vegas in August, more like extreme temperatures when you are under napalm attack. If done right, moly-alloyed steel even becomes a superalloy, a material that maintains all its normal characteristics even when within easy reach of its actual melting point.

Militaries *love* to use moly in armor and aircraft and carbine barrels. In the civilian sector moly tends to serve in very-high-end industrial equipment and motors, as well as sorts of stainless steels that need to be as tough as physically possible, whether in construction, roll cages, high-end Asian cooking knives, or super-high-end lightbulbs. In powdered form moly is used to . . . fertilize cauliflower?[†]

The future of moly is likely a-okay. Moly is produced in a series of

---

[*]   I say "seem to" because counterfeiters tend to not share their production data.
[†]   Yeah, I got nuttin' for that one.

steps, often different for each different type of source ore, often in different facilities, often in the Western Hemisphere, and often linked to the specific steel foundries that alloy it. The result is a supply system far more segmented and resistant to vertical integration than something like bauxite. No Chinese stranglehold here.

THE FUNKY MATERIALS

Finished **platinum** is so very pretty and as such is often used in high-end jewelry (like my you-are-mine-for-life-so-don't-try-anything-stupid commitment band). Other **platinum-group** metals—palladium, rhodium, and iridium, for example—aren't nearly as shiny, but that hardly means they aren't hella useful.

The entire group are regular stars in anything that requires the facilitation or regulation of chemical reactions. Such uses include, but are hardly limited to, the exhaust systems of anything that burns anything in order to shift emissions profiles in less toxic directions, platings to impede corrosion (particularly at high temperatures), dental work (given time, teeth and human saliva can destroy nearly anything), and any product that needs to be able to selectively encourage or discourage the flow of electricity, most notably semiconductors of all types.

Some three-quarters of the world's platinum-group metals (PGMs) are sourced from a single country—South Africa—where nearly everything comes from a single rock formation, the Bushveld Igneous Complex. Imagine if a six-year-old made a twenty-layer cake and then somehow was able to inject frosting up from the bottom, alternatively adding internal frosting layers as well as frosting . . . explosions. Now do it all with magma.

That's the Bushveld. It's a weird-ass geological hiccup that to our collective knowledge hasn't been replicated anywhere else on Earth, but its odd combination of consistency and variation has made it arguably *the* most valuable mineral deposit humanity has ever discovered. The Bushveld practically leaks chromium, iron ore, tin, and vanadium, but the South Africans brush right by all these world-class deposits to go after the *good* stuff: the platinum-group ores that here—and *only* here—exist in an unadulterated state, unmixed with other, lesser ores. Lesser ores like freakin' titanium.

Everywhere else PGMs are found, they are a by-product of other ores, most commonly copper and nickel. After South Africa, Russia is by far the world's largest producer, with nearly one-fifth of global PGMs coming out of Norilsk, a Soviet-built Arctic penal colony whose workers toil a mile underground. So many things have gone so horribly wrong at Norilsk in recent years that the entire place is a cross between a Superfund site and a frigid Tibetan hell.

Third through last place combined account for the remaining 5 percent of output.

Even if you can source the appropriate ore, you're hardly out of the woods: it takes a minimum of seven *tons* of ore and six *months* of work to extract a *single* troy ounce of platinum or its sister metals.

Simply put, if you want platinum or its sister materials, you deal with the South Africans, or the Russians, or you probably go without. And if you do go without, on a clear, breezy day, your vehicle exhaust will be nastier than the nastiest smog ever recorded. Rarities of rarities: China isn't a top-five producer, importer, or exporter of a single one of the raw or finished PGMs. The technologies that use PGMs are simply beyond the Chinese.

Rare earth elements are simultaneously very complicated and very simple.

Complicated in that there isn't just one "rare earth." As the word "elements" suggests, rare earths are a category of materials that include lanthanum, neodymium, promethium, europium, dysprosium, yttrium, and scandium, among others.

Complicated in that rare earths are used in almost everything in the modern era, from sunglasses to wind turbines to computers to metal alloys to lights to televisions to petroleum refining to cars to computer hard drives to batteries to smartphones to steel to lasers.* Complicated in that modern life *cannot* happen without them. Complicated in that rare earths

---

* *pew pew*

are produced by either uranium decay, or . . . wait for it . . . *exploding stars.*

Yet rare earths are simple. Simple in that several of the rare earth elements are not rare at all; cerium is more common in Earth's crust than copper. Simple in that the ores of rare earths are often a by-product of many other sorts of mining. Simple in that we know precisely how to fish each individual rare earth element out of the mixed ore that is mined, and simple in that the problem is that no one *wants* to do the work.

There are two issues.

First, the refining process requires hundreds—and in some cases thousands—of separation units, a fancy term for vats of mostly acid, to slowly encourage each individual element to move away from its similar-density siblings. Beyond being, you know, incredibly dangerous, even if everything works well, refiners will be left with a lot of waste product. After all, the primary source of rare earths on the actual Earth is from the messy, radioactive decay of uranium. None of this is news to those in the industry. The techniques for rare earth extraction date back to before World War II. No trade secrets there.

Second, China has done all the dirty work for the rest of us. In 2021 some 90 percent of global rare earth production and processing was in the PRC. Chinese environmental regulations would make Louisianans blush, while Chinese hyperfinancing and subsidization schemes mean that no production elsewhere in the world can compete on the numbers. The Chinese started producing rare earths en masse in the late 1980s, and had forced pretty much all other producers out of business by the 2000s.

From some points of view, the Chinese have done us all a favor. After all, they have sucked up all the pollution and all the risk, while providing the world with refined rare earth metals at roughly one-quarter of the pre-1980 cost. Without those cheap and ample supplies, the Digital Revolution would have taken a very different course. Computing and smartphones for the masses may have never occurred.

The question is whether the world has become irrecoverably dependent upon Chinese output, and whether the sudden disappearance of that output—due to either Chinese collapse or dickishness—would doom us all. China first publicly threatened Japanese firms (and implicitly threatened American firms) with rare earths cutoffs back in the 2000s.

I vote "no" on that particular concern. First, the real value of rare earths isn't in the ore (that's pretty common) or even the refining (that process was perfected nearly a century ago), but instead in turning the rare earth metals into components for end products. The Chinese are at best so-so at that. The Chinese have taken all the risks and subsidized all the output, while non-Chinese firms do most of the value-add work and reap most of the rewards.

Second, because the ore isn't rare and because the processing isn't a secret and because the first Chinese threats were more than a decade ago, there are already backup mining and processing facilities in existence in South Africa, the United States, Australia, Malaysia, and France. They just don't see a lot of activity, because the Chinese stuff is still available and still cheaper. If Chinese rare earths were to vanish from global supplies tomorrow, processing facilities on standby would start up right away and likely be able to replace all Chinese exports within a few months. A year on the outside. And any company that uses rare earths led by any person who isn't a complete moron already has months of rare earths stockpiled. Hiccups would abound; Armageddon would not call.

Rare earths are a great example of the world just waiting for China to fall, and for once actually being ready for it.

THE RELIABLE MATERIALS

Nickel is one of those materials that have few uses by themselves but are integral to a single process with a single companion material that makes it absolutely essential to every single economic sector. Standard steel bends and rusts and corrodes and warps and loses some of its coherence with high or low temperatures. But add about 3.5 percent nickel and a splash of chromium to the steel mix, and you get an alloy that is both stronger *and* largely eliminates those concerns. We colloquially know this product as "stainless"—the backbone of nearly all steel used in every single application. The forging of such stainless accounts for more than two-thirds of total global nickel demand. Other nickel metal alloys account for another fifth. One-tenth goes into electroplating, with the balance going into batteries.

As one might expect, China is the world's largest importer, refiner, and user of nickel ore, but the ubiquitous nature of steel in pretty much everything, *everywhere*, means that even China's large-scale, breakneck industrialization and urbanization cannot dominate the *entire* market. Unlike aluminum, where much of the resulting finished metal is exported, the bulk of the nickel ore the Chinese refine and blend into steel is used at home. So whereas China's impact on the aluminum market is an ALL-CAPS issue that has destroyed the capacity of competitors the globe over, China's nickel-related steel habits are "merely" highly distortionary.

Nickel is one of those rare materials where the implosion of global trade will not automatically result in the implosion of the market. Four of the top five producers—Indonesia, the Philippines, Canada, and Australia—are ones that have alternative markets for their nickel sales in their own neighborhoods. The last of the top five—the French territory of New Caledonia—is highly likely to see its output plunge as internal debates over whether it wants to be a failed colony or a failed country override all other thinking.

The number six slot goes to Russia, which produces nearly all its nickel from a single complex near that godawful city of Norilsk. Add in Russia's building geopolitical, financial, demographic, and transport complications, and I'd not count on Norilsk being a major source of global metals supplies a couple of decades from now.

Add it all up and the nickel market might actually achieve something that much of the soon-to-be world will become eminently *un*familiar with: balance.

I'm not going to bother with the more blasé uses for **silicon**. The silicon that goes into glass is typically sourced from normal sand. Purification is required, obviously, but we cracked the code for that process nearly two millennia before Rome, and in modern times it doesn't require a particularly sophisticated industrial base to churn out glass at volume. Nor am I going to look at the other big use for "sand"—part of the input process for unconventional oil production (aka "fracking"). After a few years, the oil services firms discovered that nearly any basic sand will work just fine. No, we're going to instead focus on the silicon products that are much higher up on the value-add scale and more integral to day-to-day life in the modern world.

First, the good news. The *really* good news. Silicon is wildly common, accounting for something like one-quarter of the earth's crust. We think of silicon most commonly as sand because we immediately and emotionally attach sand to beaches and lakes, but in reality most of the world's silicon is locked up in quartz and silica rocks. Such rocks are far better than beach sand because they aren't contaminated with algae, plastics, hypodermic needles, or pee. If you're making glass, 98 percent purity is a-okay, but the absolute lowest grade for silicon as an actual industrial input is 99.95 percent pure. Getting there requires a blast furnace, which typically requires a lot of coal. Overall, the process isn't all that complicated—you basically just bake the quartz until anything that is not silicon burns away—which means some 90 percent of this first-step processing tends to be done in countries like Russia and China, countries with a lot of surplus industrial capacity that don't give two shits about environmental issues.

This quality level is more than fine for most of what we use silicon for. Roughly one-third of production ends up in things we know as sil*icones*—a broad category that includes everything from sealants to kitchen utensils to gaskets to coatings to fake boobs—and sil*icates*, which go into ceramics, cement, and glass. Nearly half is alloyed with aluminum to make the creatively named sil*umins*, which have largely replaced steel in any product where shedding a lot of weight is more important than being able to take a tank shell, most notably in train and automobile frames.*

Such products are both important and omnipresent, but they aren't the sexy part of the story. *That* comes from the final two product categories.

First up are solar panels. The 99.95 percent purity of "standard" silicon isn't anywhere enough. A second round in the blast furnace gets the silicon up to 99.99999 percent pure.† Round two is far more sophisticated than round one's bake-it-pure. China's GCL Group is the only Chinese entity that can manage such precision at scale, making it responsible for one-third of global supply. The rest comes from a smattering of developed-world companies. This pure silicon is incorporated into the solar cells that make solar panels do their thing, with the assembly work more often than not done in China.

Second are semiconductors, with silicon being by far the biggest input by volume. And since some of the newer semiconductors are shaped at nearly the atomic level, the silicon must be 99.99999999 percent pure.‡ No *way* that gets done in China. Once some first-world company makes

---

* There is no improving vehicle mileage without a *lot* of aluminum and silicon. No electronic vehicles, either. Greens take note: Smelting aluminum is power intensive. Forging silicon is power intensive. Alloying them is power intensive. The frame for an EV requires roughly *quintuple* the energy input of a traditional car. That's one of a score of inconveniently non-environmentally friendly details Tesla leaves out of its advertising.

† That's seven 9s.

‡ That's *ten* 9s.

this ultra-rarified, electronic-grade silicon, it is sent on to somewhere in the East Asian Rim to be melted into a clean-room vat and grown into the crystals that form the foundation of all semiconductor manufacture.

In a post-globalized world, all this back-and-forth-and-back-and-forth-and-back-and-forth, with most stuff cycling through China at least twice, will be a solid *no bueno*. Expect the Chinese and Russians to get largely cut out of global processing simply due to issues of security and supply chain simplicity. Anything shy of solar and electronics applications should be more or less okay. The base work isn't technically challenging.

That's where the good news ends. Figure *half* the population of the planet can kiss the very idea of solar panels goodbye. The problem isn't the quartz. We already produce solar-quality quartzes in Australia, Belgium, Canada, Chile, China, France, Germany, Greece, India, Mauritius, Norway, Russia, Thailand, Turkey, and the United States. The problem is the purification: it is *only* done in China, Japan, the United States, Germany, and Italy.

But the *real* problem will be the semiconductors. Some 80 percent of the world's high-quality quartz that ultimately makes up electronic-grade silicon comes from a single mine in North Freakin' Carolina. Want to remain modern? You pretty much *must* get along well with the Americans. They will soon have something they have never had: resource control over *the* base material of the Digital Age. (They're also going to do pretty well dominating the overall high-end semiconductor space, but that particular breakdown is in the next chapter.)

Uranium is a bit nonstandard because until recently a leading source of uranium demand went to efforts to blow up the planet with the push of a button. Humanity certainly still has problems, and with the end of the Order it will have many, many, many more, but at least no one is stockpiling tens of thousands of strategic atomic warheads. The reality is even better than it sounds. Starting in 1993, the Americans and Russians started not only separating their warheads from their delivery systems, but also removing the uranium cores from those warheads and spinning them down into the sort of material that can be transformed into fuel for nuclear power plants. By the time this megatons-to-megawatts program was completed in 2013, the two countries had transformed some twenty *thousand* warheads, leaving each side with "only" about 6,000 apiece.

Great for global peace? Certainly! But the effort skewed the uranium market. The Americans and Russians used this warheads-turned-fuel program to power their civilian nuclear reactors. In the United States, such spun-down weapons material powered 10 percent of the grid for nearly two decades, and since large portions of nuclear power fuel are recyclable, the uranium market will remain distorted for decades to come.

If you're not American or Russian, your only source of nuclear power fuel is to source uranium ore, grind it into a powder called yellowcake, heat it to a gaseous state to separate the uranium from the waste ore, and spin that uranium gas through a series of centrifuges so the different isotopes of uranium at least partially separate. Split them up partially and you get a civilian-grade mix of uranium that is roughly 3–5 percent fissile material, which can be processed into power reactor fuel rods. Spin them up to the 90 percent fissile level for a warhead and the U.S. government is likely to throw you a surprise party complete with some high-caffeinated Special Forces troops and a few thoughtfully live, precision-guided munitions.

In a post-Order world, uranium is likely to become *more* popular as a power fuel. While running a 1-gigawatt coal power plant for a year requires 3.2 *million* metric tons of coal, a 1-gigawatt nuclear power plant requires only 25 metric tons of power-fuel-enriched-uranium metal, making uranium the only electricity input that could theoretically be *flown* to its end user.

There's also unlikely to be all that crazy a shakeup to the world's civilian nuclear fleet, or at least not one due to access restrictions. The world's top four nuclear-power-generating countries are the United States, Japan, France, and China. The United States we've covered. Japan and France both have the capacity to go out and source their needs without assistance. China's uranium comes from neighbors Kazakhstan and Russia. So long as there *is* a China it will be able to get its hands on uranium.

The locations that face the most risk in sourcing sufficient supplies will be those middle powers that both lack the military capacity to source their own inputs and live in geographic locations that utterly preclude safe shipments—Switzerland, Sweden, Taiwan, Finland, Germany, Czech Republic, Slovakia, Bulgaria, Romania, Hungary, Ukraine, and Korea. The likelihood of insufficient supplies increases as you move through the list.

Lowly **zinc** has been with us for a long time. Zinc ore is often found commingled with copper, and smelting them together generates brass. We've been making that stuff (on purpose) for at least four thousand years, although it wasn't until the most recent millennium that we truly understood the physical chemistry of it all (copper and zinc ions can replace one another in the crystal lattice of metal alloys).

What's unique about zinc isn't that it will not corrode—it corrodes very easily—but instead *how* it corrodes. The outer layer of a zinc object oxidizes quickly, forming a patina that prevents oxygen from penetrating any deeper. Voilà! Corrosion generates protection! In some applications, the zinc only needs to be *present* rather than actually bonded to the entirety of the metal object. Bolt or wire a disc of zinc onto a ship's rudder or buried propane tank, for example, and the zinc will corrode away to nothing while protecting the tank or rudder. I know! Freaky!

Fast-forward to the electrical and chemical understandings of the Industrial Age and we've upgraded our use of zinc into a wide range of products.

The same electrical characteristics that protect the aforementioned propane tank make zinc a preferred component in alkaline batteries. We still use a lot of zinc-heavy brass, as it is easier to work and stronger than copper, while maintaining zinc's magical corrosion-management characteristics. It's useful in everything from cellular towers to plumbing to trombones. Zinc isn't only fuss-free in merging with copper, making it a perennial favorite in products that are cold-rolled into sheets or die-cast. We also like to coat it on steel and other industrial metals. Once we decided we wanted as little to do with lead as possible, zinc stepped in as a safe, reliable substitute.

The biggest use—where we put roughly half our zinc—is in galvanization processes where we add that zinc patina. It's a step that is particularly effective at shielding metals from the corrosive effects of weather and seawater. Such uses are in pretty much all the metal you can *see* every day: car bodies, bridges, guardrails, chain-link fencing, metal roofs, and so on.

Altogether zinc is our fourth-favorite metal by use, behind only steel, copper, and aluminum. It will stay in that spot in the decades to come.

Zinc is eminently recyclable. Roughly 30 percent of zinc production is from recycled material, with roughly 80 percent of all zinc capable of making a second go of it. It is found on its own, as well as with lead in many places around the world. China is the largest producer because of course it is, but almost all Chinese zinc is for its own end consumption. Peru, Australia, India, the United States, and Mexico round out the top six. The result is a supply system that is broadly sourced and broadly diversified, offering zinc at a lower price point than better-known metals such as copper. In a world of broken supply systems, at least we'll still have zinc.

Industrial Materials

Material	Value of Production (Million USD)	Primary Uses	Primary Sources	Primary Consumers*
Iron Ore	$280,375	Steel	Australia (38%), Brazil (17%)	China (73%), Japan (6%), Korea (5%)
Bauxite	$4,160	Aluminum	Australia (30%), Guinea (22%), China (16%), Brazil (9%)	China (74%), Ireland (3%), Ukraine (3%), Spain (3%)
Copper	$120,000	Wiring, electronics, plumbing	Chile (29%), Peru (11%), China (9%), DR Congo (7%), United States (6%)	China (56%), Japan (15%), Korea (7%)
Cobalt	$4,200	Batteries, alloys, industrial uses	DR Congo (68%), Russia (5%), Australia (4%)	China (56%), United States (8%), Japan (7%), United Kingdom (4%), Germany (3%)
Lithium	$5,390	Batteries	Australia (49%), Chile (22%), China (17%)	Korea (46%), Japan (41%)
Silver	$14,985	Jewelry, alloys, electronics, industrial uses	Mexico (22%), Peru (14%), China (13%), Russia (7%), Chile (5%)	China (62%), Korea (11.2%)
Gold	$148,500	Jewelry, alloys, non-corrosive and highly-conductive coatings	China (12%), Australia (10%), Russia (9%), United States (6%), Canada (5%), Chile (4%)	Switzerland (34%), United States (12%), China (12%), Turkey (10%), India (9%),
Lead	$10,440	Batteries, alloys, industrial uses	China (43%), Australia (11%), United States (7%), Mexico (5%), Peru (5%)	Korea (36%), China (30%), Netherlands (6%), Germany (6%)
Molybdenum	$7,540	Hardened steel alloys, industrial lubricants	China (40%), Chile (19%), United States (16%)	China (22%), Korea (11%), Japan (10%)
Platinum-group Metals	$20,718	Electronics, metal plating, catalysts	South Africa (50%), Russia (30%)	United States (18%), United Kingdom (15%), China (13%), Japan (11%), Germany (11%)
Rare Earths	$210	Consumer goods and electronics incl. flat panels, smart phones, rechargeable batteries	China (58%), United States (16%), Myanmar (13%)	Japan (49%), Malaysia (17%), Thailand (5%)
Nickel	$29,700	Alloys (stainless steel), metal plating	Indonesia (30%), Philippines (13%), Russia (11%)	China (74%), Canada (6%), Finland (6%)
Silicon	$18,502	Glass, silicone materials, ceramics, coatings, semiconductors, photovoltaic cells	China (68%), Russia (7%), Brazil (4%)	China (34%), Japan (21%), Taiwan (10%), Korea (8%)
Uranium	$2,565	Fuel, weapons, research	Kazakhstan (41%), Australia (31%), Namibia (11%), Canada (8%)	**
Zinc	$35,100	Non-corrosive alloys, pigments, sun screen	China (35%), Peru (11%), Australia (10%)	China (27%), Korea (15%), Belgium (10%), Canada (7%)

* Figures represent end users of refined product. In the case of lithium and rare earths, for example, China is a primary consumer of ores but exports processed and refined materials to other countries that manufacture finished goods.
** Due to the sensitive and strategic nature of uranium usage, publicly reported data does not accurately reflect global consumption
Sources: USGS, OEC, UNCTAD, World Nuclear Association

© 2022 Zeihan on Geopolitics

THIS IS HOW THE WORLD ENDS

For the duration of the Order—that unprecedented, brief, but above all *vital* moment in human history—all these materials and so many, many more have been made available in a largely free-and-fair global market. Their availability isn't simply what our modern life is built upon; it has been a virtuous circle. The Order established stability, which fostered economic growth, which enabled technological advancement, which led to the availability of these materials, which allowed their inclusion into the products, modernity, and lifestyle of the modern age.

In the Order the only competition over materials access was over *market* access. Invading countries for raw materials was expressly forbidden. You simply had to pay for them. Capital-rich systems, therefore, enjoyed the best access. The Asians with their hyperfinance model kind of cheated, with the Chinese ultramegahugehyperfinanced system tending to gobble up anything it could.

Without the rules and constraints of the Order in place, money on its own just isn't going to cut it.

Without the Order it all unwinds.

This is far worse than it sounds.

In the past seventy-five years of the Order, the list of materials critical to what we define as modern life has expanded by far more than an order of magnitude. With the exception of the United States, which will retain full access to the Western Hemisphere and Australia, as well as the military capacity to reach anywhere in the world, *no one* will be able to access all the necessary materials. They are simply too scattered or, alternatively, too concentrated. A few countries with local deposits or militaries with reach can try, but it is a short list: the United Kingdom, France, Turkey,

Japan, and Russia. For the rest, there is a very real risk of reverting not simply to the economic and technological levels that pervaded before 1939, but to before the Industrial Revolution itself. If you lack the industrial inputs, you cannot achieve industrial outcomes. Smuggling of ores, processed materials, and/or finished products will, out of necessity, become a booming business.

Central to this devolution, once again, is American disinterest. The Americans can access what they need without massive military interventions. This will generate not the sort of heavy American involvement most countries would find distasteful, but instead large-scale American *disengagement* that most countries will find terrifying. If the global superpower were involved, at least there would be some rules. Instead we will have erratic intra-regional competitions in which the Americans will largely decline participation. Erratic competition means erratic materials access, which means erratic technological application, which means erratic economic capacity. We are perfectly capable of having increased competition and warfare *while also* experiencing dramatic economic and technological declines.

So this is how it all falls apart. Now let's turn to how we might—*might*—put it all back together.

SECTION VI:
MANUFACTURING

CRAFTING THE WORLD WE KNOW

Calendar year 2021 was an odd one in the age of globalization. We had shortages. Of everything. Toilet tissue. Cellular phones. Lumber. Automobiles. Guacamole. Juice boxes. *The paper needed to print this book!*

It was all COVID's fault.

Every time we had a lockdown or an opening, we changed what we consumed. In lockdown it was more materials for home improvements and electronic gear so we'd have something to do. In openings it was more vacations and restaurant trips. *Each* shift necessitated global industrial retoolings to meet the changed demand profile. *Each* time we got hit with a new variant or a new vaccine or a new anti-vax backlash, our demand profile changed again. *Each* change in our demand profile took a year to work itself out.

It was not enjoyable, and it is nothing compared to what's coming. The supply chain agony of 2021 was primarily about whiplashing *demand*. Deglobalization will instead beat us about the head and shoulders with instability in *supply*.

Consider the vulnerabilities within a "simple" example: blue jeans.

As of 2022, the largest suppliers of denim to the United States are China, Mexico, and Bangladesh. Go back a step and the fabric was likely dyed in Spain or Turkey or Tunisia using chemicals developed and manufactured in Germany. This is to say nothing of where the yarn for the denim cloth comes from. That would be India or China or the United States or Uzbekistan or Brazil. Go a step further back and the cotton was probably sourced from China or Uzbekistan or Azerbaijan or Benin.

But the story doesn't stop—or begin—there. The *design work* behind your favorite pair likely occurred in the United States, France, Italy, or

Japan . . . although many up-and-coming countries are showcasing their design talents. Bangladesh in particular is getting in on the brain work.

Of course there's more to jeans than denim fabric and colors and styles. There are also copper and zinc rivets and buttons. They're *probably* from Germany or Turkey or Mexico (although, honestly, that sort of stuff can come from anywhere). The ore required to forge those bright bits is probably sourced from mines in Brazil, Peru, Namibia, Australia, or, again, China. What about zippers? Japan is the go-to if you want one that won't snag. Three guesses where the snag-prone ones come from. Then there's thread, which phbbbbt . . . *probably* comes from India or Pakistan, but that's another one of those products sourced from shoulder-shrugging ubiquity. Finally, there's the location where workers sew on the "made in" tag. Typically, nothing is actually *made* there. It's more an assembly thing. The average pair of jeans is touched by hands in at least ten countries. And God forbid you use a bedazzler to put sparkly bits on your ass—the input system for that little gadget practically involves space travel.

If you want to get really technical, all this is just the "customer facing" side. Sewing machines don't just pop up naturally out of the earth. They use copper and steel and gears and plastics sourced the world over. Same for the ships that shuttle all this about.

And that's for something made out of cloth that doesn't have to do anything more than be draped across your frame. The average computer has ten *thousand* pieces, some of which are themselves made out of hundreds of components. Modern manufacturing is borderline insane. The more I learn about the sector, the less sure I am as to which side of the border it resides. Modern manufacturing is eminently vulnerable to every facet of every disruption the Disorder is capable of generating.

The technical term for what has made all this and so much more possible is "intermediate goods trade." It is quite literally globalization given physical form.

Historically speaking, intermediate goods trade was a big no-no. That requires some unpacking.

Once again, let's start at the beginning.

STARTING FROM SCRATCH

The first pair of meaningful manufacturing technologies are ones that anyone who has played *Sid Meier's Civilization* knows all too well: pottery and copper. Fired pottery enabled us to store our harvest for the lean seasons, while copper is the first metal we were able to forge into tools—the first of which were sickles to help us harvest wheat. The equipment required to forge this pair of products isn't particularly onerous. Clay can be shaped by hand (or with a pottery wheel if you're extra fancy), whereas copper can be smelted from ore if it is heated in, you guessed it, a clay pot. Once you've got your copper metal, it's simply a matter of beating it—with a rock—into whatever shape you find relevant. Early manufacturing wouldn't have felt all that out of place at a retiree pottery class.

Bit by bit we got better both at working materials and at pioneering the use of new ones. Copper sickles gave way to bronze scythes. Clay pots gave way to ceramics. Bronze spears gave way to iron swords. Wooden mugs gave way to glass bottles. Wool thread gave way to cotton cloth. But in a way, everything from the dawn of civilization right up to the 1700s shared a certain characteristic: organizational simplicity.

There was no Home Depot to run to (repeatedly) to source parts. Most things you made yourself. If you were lucky, you had a blacksmith neighbor, but even his supply system couldn't be confused with complexity. It was one dude, a forge, a hammer, some tongs, and a barrel of water. If he had an eye for the future, he had an assistant and an apprentice . . . and that was about it. Such cottage industries faced extreme limitations. Blacksmiths and skilled folks like them couldn't just go out to the town square and recruit labor; they had to train it. For *years*. There was no rapid technological progress. There were no rapid capacity buildouts.

The Industrial Revolution changed the math in three critical ways.

First, the Industrial Revolution not only gifted us with steel—less brittle, more workable and durable than iron—it gifted us with *huge volumes of steel* so that workers could access the raw metal without having to forge it themselves. With that messy, expensive, dangerous step taken care of, skilled workers could focus on adding value and specializing further. For the first time in human history, specialists in multiple fields could meaningfully collaborate. Interaction brought advancement.

Second, the Industrial Revolution brought us precision manufacturing, both in tools and molds. One of the major drawbacks of cottage industry is that no two parts are exactly the same, so no two finished products are exactly the same. If something breaks, there is no plugging in a replacement piece. Either the entire item had to be chucked or it needed to be taken to a skilled smith to craft a fundamentally new, customized part. In war this was particularly annoying. Muskets were great and all, but if a single piece malfunctioned you were left with an expensive, low-quality club. Advancements in precision did an end run around this restriction. Now identical parts could be made by the dozen. Or thousand. For the first time in human history, manufacturing had scale.

Third, the Industrial Revolution brought us fossil fuels. We've already covered their role in generating power and enabling us to move beyond muscle and water, but there is far more to oil and coal than that. Derivatives of the pair of "power fuels" often have nothing to do with energy at all: paints, pigments, antibiotics, solvents, painkillers, nylon, detergents, glass, inks, fertilizers, and plastics. For the first time in human history, we didn't take a "minor" step forward as we did from bronze to iron; we instead experienced an explosion in materials science applications.

The three improvements dovetail nicely. If skilled workers don't need to master every single step, they can get really good at one or two. Bam! Increasingly diverse skill sets and increasingly complex products. Apply that hyperskill capacity to a larger scale and nearly any product can be produced en masse. Bam! Assembly lines, machinery, automobiles, and telephones. Apply those concepts to dozens of new materials and the entirety of the human condition is remade. Bam! Modern medicine, high-rise cities, advanced agriculture. Taken together, these three improvements—in specialization, in scale, and in product reach—changed the math of the possible, and gave us our first real glimpse of what we today recognize as manufacturing.

There were still plenty of limitations. Not every place had good coal or good iron ore or all the other industrial inputs. And trade remained a dubious business. If you were dependent upon a foreign sovereign for something you needed, it wasn't simply about you trusting him or her in order to get the necessary inputs; it wasn't even about trusting him or her *all the time*. It was about you trusting *all* foreign sovereigns *all* the time. Any power that could reach into any part of any supply chain could wreck the whole thing, often inadvertently. Out of necessity and practicality, all manufacturing of all types was kept in-house.

That naturally benefited certain geographies. Economies of scale are impossible with a skilled labor force of one. Industrialization enabled the development of industrial plants that would (a) enable skilled labor to multiply their efforts by having each worker specialize on a specific task or part, and (b) enable *un*skilled labor to come in and work the assembly lines.

With the industrial code cracked, the questions became: How big could that industrial plant get? Just how specialized could the skilled workers become? How much territory and population could you access within your own system? In sussing that out, the old math of transport came into play. Any geography that could shuttle goods and people about in the preindustrial age could now shuttle about *intermediate* goods. In addition to all their other advantages, the imperial systems with good internal geographies could now generate *manufacturing*, enabling economies of scale that others could only dream of.

The first really big winner was canaled Britain, followed by Germany's Ruhr Valley and ultimately the American Steel Belt. Unsurprisingly, the economic competition among these centers of industry was central to games geopolitical between 1850 and 1945.

But as big and important as the British, German, and American systems were, geopolitics restricted their economies of scale to within their own borders. It took the end of World War II to merge the entire planet into a single system and transform the global ocean into one gigantic safe, navigable waterway. With the United States guaranteeing security for all international commerce *and* preventing the alliance members from either going to war with one another or having colonial empires *and* opening the American consumer market to all interested parties, countries that could have never even dreamed of industrializing suddenly could. All at once, the "safe" locations favored by geography had to compete with heretofore backward, unindustrialized locations.

The rules changed. Manufacturing changed with them. A new set of criteria defined success.

HOW IT WORKS, WHY IT WORKS

One of the fickle things about economic development is that the process isn't the same for everyone. Britain was first, France and the Low Countries mushed together in second place, Germany was third, America roughly fourth, followed by Japan. But because the technologies involved are constantly evolving, even among this first broad batch the paths differed. Britain's process was slow because the Brits were literally making things up as they went along.

Germany's development was far quicker, and not simply because the Brits were kind enough to blaze the path for others. Germany exists in a geopolitical pressure cooker, ringed by strategic and economic competitors. Even worse, the habitable bits of German lands on the Rhine, Danube, Weser, Elbe, and Oder Rivers are—at best—loosely connected. It's easy for Germany's more consolidated neighbors to split it apart. If Germany fails to press every economic development process to the limit, it is overwhelmed. So the German industrialization experience of the late 1800s and early 1900s was absolutely frenetic.

Germany also had some significant geographic advantages over the Brits when it came to capital generation and supply chain establishment. The German river system—in particular the Rhine-Ruhr system of western Germany—is the densest network of naturally navigable waterways in the world. It is perfect for industrialization. In particular, the Ruhr region had some of Europe's best coal deposits (and none of those pesky water table problems that so hindered the Brits). Add it up and German industrialization was less a meander and more a nervous, I-think-someone-is-following-me jog.

On the flip side, the Americans' process was far slower—nearly as slow as the Brits'—but for wildly different reasons. While the German industrialization process didn't really get going until the 1830s, the really intense part was between 1880 and 1915, well under a human lifetime. In the United States the beginning of the process—the start of the railroad era—was similarly in 1830, but American cities were not fully industrialized until the 1930s, and the American countryside not until the 1960s. In many ways the American experience was an inverse image of the German one: there was no geopolitical pressure, so no need to speed things along, and while the Germans had a very dense industrial, riverine, and population footprint, the Americans were all sprawled out. The useful lands of the United States are about twenty-five times the area of the useful lands of pre–World War I Germany, and the Americans didn't have anything resembling a state industrial policy until they were *in* World War II.

For the Americans, everything is—everything *has always been*—rather la-di-da.

Japan was a latecomer to the first round, not really gaining traction until the Meiji Restoration of 1868 gutted the old feudal order, but like the Germans, the Japanese shot ahead quickly out of necessity. The Home Islands are poor in pretty much every imaginable raw material, whether oil or bauxite, so Japan had no choice but to forge an empire in order to secure the materials required for industrialization. Since that meant taking other people's stuff, the Japanese had no choice but to move *very* quickly.

The Koreans were early victims of the Japanese expansion and remained colonized until the Hiroshima and Nagasaki bombings freed them. They then went on to be among the Order's most enthusiastic participants, becoming the vanguard of industrialization's second major wave. Their industrialization path can best be defined as a panicky sprint. The Koreans—even today—are desperate to protect their sovereignty from all things Japanese. The Koreans are the people who lacked a sufficiently large drydock to build a supertanker, so they built the ship in *halves* and then built the drydock *around* the halves to finish the project.

The Southeast Asian states run the gamut. Singapore followed a nearly Korean path for similar reasons, with the part of the Japanese villain being played by Malaysia. Vietnam prioritized political unity over economic development and so remained preindustrialized and poor until the 1990s . . . unless you're in Ho Chi Minh City (aka Saigon), in which case you were industrialized a century ago courtesy of French capital. Even in 2022, Vietnam feels less like two different countries and more like two different planets. Thailand, far more historically confident in its ability to repel invaders (the country's core is ringed by jungle mountains), lies somewhere between both in terms of pacing and outcome.

The point of this little diversion into the practical outcomes of economic theory is that not everyone is at the same level, developmentally speaking, or even proceeding at the same pace. This can be awful, in that countries that are further along tend to have more oomph to their economic systems in terms of productivity, wealth, and diversification and can use that oomph to lord over less advanced systems. Welcome to colonialism, neo- or otherwise.

But this differentiation can also be great, in that if the macrostrategic environment doesn't allow traditional colonialism—like, say, the American-led global Order—there are hefty arguments to be made for manufacturing *integration*.

Between the changed geostrategic environment of the Order and the rise of containerized shipping, the security and cost concerns that had prevented meaningful cross-border integration since the dawn of time had finally unclenched.

In any manufactured product that has more than one piece, there are opportunities for efficiencies. Take something really simple: a wooden top. There's the conical spinny thing and the rodlike spindle, typically glued together. While it is reasonable to expect the cone and the rod to be fashioned by the same woodworker, said woodworker probably didn't make the glue. Two different skill sets. Two different price points. Paint said top and we're already up to three.

Apply that basic concept of specialization to a cell phone: Display screen. Battery. Transformer. Wiring. Sensors. Camera. Modem. Data processor. System on a Chip. (That last is a fancy little gadget that includes a video processor, a display processor, a graphics processor, and the phone's central processing unit.) Nobody would expect one worker to be able to make all of it. Quadruply so for the System on a Chip. Nobody would expect the worker who plugs in the relatively low-tech wiring to be compensated at the same rate as the worker who fine-tunes the sensors. Imagine if all the pieces were made in Japan, a country with a per capita income of some $41,000. That System on a Chip would be pretty fly— and it *should* be, the Japanese excel at complex microelectronic work—but it stretches the mind to think there might be some Japanese dude who loves to run an injection mold system to make phone cases for a dollar an hour. It would be like Lady Gaga teaching piano lessons to four-year-olds. Could she do it? Certainly. I bet she'd do *great*. But no one is going to pay her fifty grand for an hour of her trouble.* The combination of cheap, sacrosanct shipping and nearly endless workforce variety enabled manufacturers to split apart their supply chains into ever more complex, more discrete steps.

If you were to trace the full supply chain of a car, you'd need a bigger budget than I have, but here's the short version:

Metals including platinum and chrome and aluminum, wrapped and soldered wires, a full diagnostic and performance-enhancing computer system, rubber for the tires, synthetic fabrics made from petroleum, plastics for the interior, glass and mirrors, gears and pistons, ball bearings, and injection-molded buttons to turn the radio all the way up to 11. Each of these, and each of the thirty *thousand* other parts that go into

---

* Or at least the Venn diagram overlap between oil sheiks, tiger parents, and hyper-exuberant gay dads is pretty small.

a standard passenger vehicle I didn't list, has its own highly customized workforce and *its own supply chain*. Each part has to be assembled into an intermediate product (air-conditioning, engine, lighting, etc.) by *its own* workforce, and then assembled into another intermediate product (dashboard, car frame) by *its own* workforce, and on and on until the whole mess of stuff reaches final assembly. The supply chains of U.S. auto maker Ford are among the most complex of any firm in existence, tapping more than sixty countries and 1,300 *direct* suppliers that together have more than 4,400 manufacturing sites.*

At each step the need for inputs expands. At each step the differentiation of the input stream expands. At each step the demand for supporting infrastructure expands. At each step the need for petroleum to fuel everything expands. All this occurred in bits and pieces between the Americans and their core Cold War allies throughout the 1950s, 1960s, 1970s, and 1980s, but with the Cold War's end the scope for the differentiation became truly global and the pace accelerated to lightning speeds.

Such increases in complexity and value now play out across every manufactured product. Consequently, in the twenty years following 1996—a period that includes the Great Recession—global maritime trade doubled by volume and tripled by value. Trade that to that point had required five *millennia* to build.

Everything didn't simply get bigger in the post–Cold War globalized world; everything got *faster* as well.

---

*   In reality, we're not quite done. If final assembly happens in Chongqing, China, the vehicle will be shipped down the Yangtze for 8–11 days, dwell at Shanghai for a few days, then get sent on to Los Angeles with a sailing time of 20 days, before getting loaded onto a train en route to a regional distribution center, and finally one of those specialized trucks you see on the interstate that shuttles the final product from the rail yard to the dealership. Even once the car is finished, it still takes about six weeks to get to a point-of-sale. Nor is it "all" about assembly and transport. The insurance for the ship most likely came from London and the regulations that make sure the gas cap won't somehow murder you in your sleep came from the EU. (The EU is more notorious than California for its bizarre regulations.)

JUST-IN-TIME

As recently as the 1970s, about the only way to source intermediate goods was via bulk purchases. In the bad ol' pre-container days, not only was shipping more expensive, it was organizationally clumsy. Time would stretch out between purchases, so it was more cost-effective to purchase a lot at once and maintain a warehouse. Storage wouldn't be cheap, but it would be cheaper than paying for lots of small orders beset by erratic delivery schedules. More important, all that inventory was necessary to prevent the unthinkable: having to halt production because you ran out of a specific widget.

Containerization changed the math by making shipping more reliable, enabling firms to push their inventorying back onto vessels, and enabling smaller orders to be produced at more reasonable costs. Toyota in particular realized that with changed shipping norms, manufacturing could evolve from a big-batch model to more of a steady product stream. This new "just-in-time" inventorying system allows firms to place orders for a few-day supply of widgets as little as a month in advance, with those fresh supplies arriving just as their last orders are running out.

These systems exist for a few reasons.

The most important is to help companies with cash flow. Put simply, the less inventory a company holds, the less cash is tied up at any given time, enabling firms to do other things with the savings: useful investments, capacity expansion, workforce training, R&D, etc. To put this in perspective, consider the iPhone. In 2020, Apple sold 90 million iPhones. A cost savings of just a penny a unit via just-in-time would add up to a cool $1 million savings. In just calendar year 2004 for just U.S. firms, such inventory savings amounted to $80–90 *billion* annually.

In a globalized system, supply chains are not simply about achieving economies of scale; they are about matching each part and process to an economy and workforce that handle the work most efficiently, all in the shortest possible amount of time. One of the many things that makes modern computing and telephony and electronics possible is that the world is awash with workforces and economies at different stages of the development path *while at the same time* the macrostrategic environment enables all those various systems to interact peaceably and smoothly.

Just-in-time is the logical conclusion of humanity producing sufficient surplus foodstuffs to support people who could specialize, like that once-all-important blacksmith. And like intermediate manufactures trade in general, it is possible only because the global transport system has become so reliable.

So that's the how and the why. Let's talk about the where.

THE MAP OF THE PRESENT

GLOBALIZATION PERSONIFIED: MANUFACTURING IN EAST ASIA

First up, East Asia is *the* hub for manufacturing work, largely because of the Order.

Once the Americans made the seas free and safe for all, transport costs dropped so quickly that manufacturing companies didn't just relocate outside the major cities or the old river-based circulatory systems; at least in part *they relocated outside the major economies altogether.* Any country that could build a port and some surrounding infrastructure could participate in the world of low-skill, low-value-added manufacturing, processing foods and producing textiles, cement, cheap electronics, and toys while building out their industrial plant and skill sets. Add in containerization and the process kicked into high gear. In calendar year 1969, the first full year of container service from Japan to California, Japanese exports to the United States increased by nearly a quarter.

The Asians perceived Western consumption as their path to stability and wealth, and all reforged their economic and social norms around export-based manufacturing. Japan vanguarded the process, but it didn't take long for Taiwan, South Korea, Southeast Asia, and China to follow. Decades of exports, growth, and stability enabled most of these players to climb steadily up the value chain. Japan, for example, went from producing cheap stereos[*] to producing some of the most advanced industrial

---

[*] Anyone else have a Sanyo Walkman?

technology in the world. Taiwan was the original land of plastic toys but now makes the world's most advanced computer chips. China only really entered this mix at the turn of the century, but *wow* did it make a splash. China had the benefit of cheaper internal transportation than the other Asian players, more resources to throw into the economy, and a labor base bigger than the rest of Asia put together.

Here's what the Asian manufacturing constellation looks like as of 2022:

Japan, Korea, and Taiwan handle the high value-add in pretty much *all* value-added manufactured products, everything from white goods to automotive to machinery. The trio truly excels at displays and semiconductors, most notably in the design and manufacture of high-capacity chips. The Koreans in particular are scary-good at cellular telephony.

Both the Japanese and Koreans operate via a series of sprawling, vertically integrated conglomerates, the keiretsu and chaebol, respectively. Think Toyota and Mitsubishi, Samsung and LG. Those conglomerates do everything. Let's just pick one: Korea's SK. It is a major player in oil refining, petrochemicals, films, polyester, solar panels, LCD and LED lights, labels, battery components, DRAM and flash memory chips, and *on the side* SK does a booming business in construction, civil engineering, and IT and mobile phone *services* (not to be confused with phone manufacture). Thar be whales here!

Taiwan, in contrast, is a swarm of minnows. Or, considering how hypercompetitive the Taiwanese business environment can be, maybe calling it a swarm of piranhas would be more apt. What few large firms the Taiwanese have fostered—such as semiconductor leader TSMC— are a step above world-class, in part because they tap the skills of thousands of small firms that hyperfocus on one very specific piece of the broader semiconductor industry. In essence, foreign firms or larger Taiwanese firms such as MediaTek subcontract out thousands of micro-improvements to those small firms for each new chip design, and those minnowy piranhas busy themselves with making as solid advances as possible for one tiny bit of the overall process. The larger players then combine the best-in-class outcomes from the whole constellation of Taiwanese R&D to make their best-in-world chips. It does not get higher value-added than that.

At the bottom of the quality and value scale lies China, which despite years of effort and untold billions of dollars invested has to this point not only proven unable to crack the high-end market, it cannot even build the machines that build most of the middle-market stuff. While low-cost labor in China has enabled the Chinese to dominate product assembly, nearly all high-end components (and a fair amount of middle-quality components) are imported from elsewhere. The products China *makes*—as opposed to *assembles*—tend to be on the lower end: steel and plastics and anything that can be die-cast or injection-molded.

By many measures, China is going backward. The country's manufacturing output as a percent of GDP has been *falling* since 2006, which, judging by corporate profitability figures, was probably China's peak year in terms of production efficiency.

China *should* have become a noncompetitive country in manufacturing in the late 2000s because it had exhausted its coastal labor pool. Instead the coast imported at least 300 million—likely as many as 400 million—workers from the interior.* That bought the Chinese economy another fifteen years, but at the cost of hardwiring, both within the coast and between the coast and the interior, massive inequality in income and levels of industrial development.

It also makes the Chinese goal of a domestically oriented, consumption driven, internationally insulated economy flatly impossible to reach. Little of the income from all those Chinese exports went to the workers (especially the workers from the interior), so little can be spent on consumption. China now has a rapidly aging coastal population that has limited consumption needs and—most important—hasn't repopulated. That coastal population is stacked against a seething migrant class from the interior that lives in semi-illegal circumstances in hypercramped,

---

*   The reason for the squishy data is that most internal migration in China is strictly illegal, *far* more so than Central American migration to the United States.

near-slumlike conditions, working grueling hours, and that *cannot* repopulate. It is all located next to an emptied-out interior whose primary source of economic activity is state investments into an industrial plant that is of questionable economic usefulness, populated by a demographic that is too *old* to repopulate. This is all in a country where decades of the One Child Policy have encouraged selective-sex abortions en masse, so there simply are not enough women under forty to repopulate the country in the first place.

The successive waves of hypergrowth—concentrated on the coastal zones where the world can see them—make China's rise seem inevitable. The reality is China has borrowed from its interior regions and its demography in order to achieve what, historically speaking, is a very short-term boost. Never let anyone tell you the Chinese are good at the long game. In 3,500 years of Chinese history, the longest stint one of their empires has gone without massive territorial losses is seventy years. That's. Right. Now. In a geopolitical era created by an outside force that the Chinese cannot shape.

Back to Chinese manufacturing: Yes, the Chinese workforce *has* become more skilled, perhaps doubling, or if you interpret the data kindly, tripling in efficiency since 2000. But because of the country's accelerating demographic collapse, labor costs have gone up by a factor of *fifteen*. The majority of the country's economic growth since the turn of the century has come from hyperfinanced investment rather than exports or consumption.

That hardly makes China irrelevant or backward; it simply shapes what China can and cannot do. Having a billion workers to throw at things and heavily subsidizing *everything* makes China the King of the Low End and the Emperor of Assembly. If you want an Internet of Things meat thermometer that can tell your smartphone how hot your roast is, a cheap chip from China will do just fine. If you want a zippy smartphone so you can post your doctored videos to TikTok, it's best you go with something from the other side of the Taiwan Strait.

Thailand and Malaysia form a middle tier in everything from electronics to automotive to, of course, semiconductors. They do very little assembly and instead focus on the heavy-lift stuff both literally and figuratively. If the Japanese, Koreans, and Taiwanese wire the brains, and the Chinese build the body, the Thais and Malaysians put together the guts, such as wiring, midtier processors, and semiconductors for things like cars and cranes and climate control systems. The Philippines provides the work that is too low-end for even China. At the opposite end, Singapore has evolved into an etheric, otherworldly presence that excels at finance, logistics, advanced petrochemicals, software, and manufacturing so precision-oriented it is used in the internal workings of things like clean labs.

On the edges are newer players looking to find their own niche. Indonesia—with its 250 million people—is lurching bit by bit into China's space. Vietnam is hoping to leverage its dense population clusters, excellent ports, rapidly evolving educational system, and top-down, no-dissent-allowed political system to jump over China completely and become the next Thailand. India, with all its endless internal variation, hopes to take a bite out of *everything*.

If anything, the above vastly understates the Asian system's complexity. Think of the wild variety of economies just within the American state of California. San Francisco is a tourism and finance hub and the most economically unequal urban area in the country. Silicon Valley designs and innovates many of the products produced throughout Asia— even in high-tech Japan—but has to import *everything*: concrete, steel, power, food, water, labor. Los Angeles's urban sprawl disguises a wealth of small-scale industrial production sites. The Central Valley is both an agricultural powerhouse and home to some of the country's poorest communities. And that's just one state.

Similar patterns and diversity hold true throughout Asia, most notably within the broad swath of mainland China. Greater Hong Kong and Greater Shanghai are by far the country's financial and technological hubs. The North China Plain—home to more than half of China's population—is all about bulk over brains. For a point of reference, the per capita income variation in the United States between the richest and poorest states—Maryland and West Virginia—is just under two-to-one. In China the variation between richest and poorest—between ultra-urban coastal Hong Kong and ultra-rural interior Gansu—is nearly ten-to-one. Even that understates the possibilities for synergies. Since 1995, China's major cities have added some 500 *million* people, mostly migrants from the country's ultra-poor interior, absolutely swamping every urban center with ultra-low-cost labor. Multiple, varied cost structures and labor quality abound not just within the country, but within each *city*. No wonder China has become the workshop of the world.

Mesh the multiplicity of options within China with the multiplicity of options across Asia and it should come as no surprise that this corner of the world is home to fully half of the globe's manufacturing supply chain steps—as well as the source of some three-quarters of the world's electronics, cellular, and computing products.

All that's necessary to make it work is a strategic environment that enables ships to sail without risk, enabling the region's myriad labor cost structures to hum along, cranking out products in perfect synergy.

SMARTER, BETTER, FASTER . . . AND FOR EXPORT: MANUFACTURING IN GERMANOCENTRIC EUROPE

In many ways, Europe is a reinterpretation of the East Asian system on a smaller scale and with a bit less diversity. The countries of Europe have always favored a degree of economic egalitarianism within their own borders, reducing the potential benefits of having colocated high- and low-wage structures within the same country.

With a total population of "only" a half billion, Europe doesn't even have the theoretical capacity to generate an economic system as wildly large and divergent as China, with its 1.4 billion souls. But Europe *does* have a Japan, Korea, and Taiwan (Germany, the Netherlands, Austria, and Belgium). It also has its own Thailands and Malaysias (Poland, Hungary, Slovakia, and the Czech Republic).

It even has hangers-on that contribute in uniquely European ways. Romania, Bulgaria, and especially Turkey are a bit like Vietnam in that, yes, they are low-wage, but all (and triply so for Turkey) often surprise to the upside in terms of product quality. Spain handles a lot of the heavy work as regards metal framing.

Italy is, well, Italy. Unlike the Northern Europeans, who integrated their peoples early on by extending government writ up and down river valleys into ever-larger polities and so take to things like supply chains naturally, the Italians were a series of disconnected city-states from the fall of Rome right up to formal unification in the late 1800s. Italian manufacturing is local, and viewed less as an industry and more as a point of artistic pride. Italians don't *do* assembly lines, or even regional integration. They don't manufacture. They *craft*. As such, any products that come out of the Apennine Peninsula are either absolutely, shockingly ridiculous in their quality and beauty (think Lamborghini) or absolutely, shockingly ridiculous in their lack of quality and beauty (think Fiat).

Because it is Europe and so needs to be overcomplicated, the region is home to three other manufacturing circuits:

1. The French *do* pull a bit from the Netherlands and especially Belgium, and they *do* contribute to the Germanic network, but mostly the French obsess about keeping most of their manufacturing separate from the rest of their European partners. Of the European Union's major countries, France is by far the least integrated.
2. Sweden, with a population of just 10 million, kind of kicks ass in its own way. It partners with near-peer wage levels in Denmark and Finland, while relying upon lower-wage structures in Estonia, Lithuania, Poland, and especially Latvia.
3. The United Kingdom is . . . having trouble making up its mind. It voted back in 2015 to leave the EU but didn't complete the process until 2020 . . . and did so without setting up an alternative trading network. The Brits are now seeing long-established supply chain linkages to the Continent shattering without necessarily establishing replacement systems. The result? Shortages. In everything.

There is considerable variety in terms of firm structure as well. The French decided long ago to use a mix of state investment, exclusionary trade practices, and outright espionage to encourage industrial consolidation across the French economy into massive state champions. The Dutch did something similar, minus the exclusionary trade practices and espionage. Those hyperefficient Germans instead favor midsized companies that specialize in specific products—say, heating units or forklifts—and draw upon scads of smaller firms throughout Central Europe to fuel their supply chains. British manufacturing is as hyperspecialized as Turkish manufacturing is hypergeneralized.

Europe's weakest point in the game of manufactures is that its labor cost disconnects between high and low are not as wide as they are in Asia, so the Europeans are not as economically competitive in products that benefit from more varied labor structures. The spread between advanced Germany and less industrialized Turkey is $46K versus $9K, while the Japanese-Vietnamese differential is $40K versus $2.7K. Europe really doesn't have a "low end" in the Asian sense, so a great number of products that rely upon low wages for at least part of their cost structure—and that's everything from basic textiles to advanced computers—are not made in Europe at all. Overall, Europe produces roughly half the total value of manufactured products compared with what comes out of East Asia.

Instead, the Europeans excel at less complicated manufacturing systems. That doesn't mean less advanced *products*—far from it, stuff that comes out of Germany is top-of-class—but instead products that require a narrower cost-input spread between the highest skilled labor required and the lowest (so not so much fancy computer chips down to a boring plastic case, and more high-end transmission down to an integrated, shock-absorbing bumper). Automotive and aerospace figure highly, but what the Germans are exceptionally good at is building the machines that manufacture other things. The bulk of the expansion of China's industrial base since 2005 has been possible only because the Germans built the core machinery that made it happen.

A WORLDFUL OF OPTIONS:
MANUFACTURING IN NORTH AMERICA

The world's third major manufacturing bloc is under the North American Free Trade Agreement, an economic alliance of Canada, Mexico, and the United States. The NAFTA system is utterly unlike its competitors. There is far and away a dominant player—the United States, of course—but that player is also the most technologically advanced. Canada exists at a similar wage and tech level, so what integration exists is largely concentrated where Detroit, Michigan, meets Windsor, Ontario—the core of the northern lobe of North American automotive manufacturing. The single bridge connecting the two cities carries more cargo traffic by value than America's *total* trade with *all* but its top *three* trading partners.

There are two bits of magic in the manufacturing of North America. The first is within the United States itself. America is a big place. In terms of flattish, usable land, it is easily twice the size of either Europe or China, both of which have vast swaths of nigh-useless territories that are mountainous or desert or tundra. Both have built up about as large a population as they can manage, while the Americans could easily double their population and still have loads of spare land (which is precisely what's likely to happen by the end of the twenty-first century). America may not have the *wage* variation that exists throughout Asia and to a lesser degree in Europe, but it more than makes up for it with *geographic* variation. Different parts of the United States have wildly different costs for food, electricity, petroleum products, and land.

Each region has its own unique characteristics:

- **Cascadia** is known for its left-wing politics, hefty regulation, unionized environment, but most important, sky-high urban land costs. Seattle sits on an isthmus, while Portland is squashed between highlands.

Both boast traffic as epic as their property prices. The only saving grace from a cost point of view is the region's cheap electricity.* The only play the Pacific Northwest has in the world of manufacturing is to move upmarket and provide the highest value-add possible. This is the land of Boeing and Microsoft.

- The American **Northeast** is tight tight tight! High land costs. High labor costs. Overloaded infrastructure. High regulatory barriers. Heavily unionized. Densely populated cities. Nearly zero green space to be had. Most manufacturing has long since decamped the region, leaving behind a weird bifurcation. First are the legacy corporations that date back nearly to the country's industrialization, such as GE, Raytheon, and Thermo Fisher Scientific. None produce all that much locally, but corporate headquarters and intensive design work both call Massachusetts home. Second, what stuff is still built here has been shaped by ever-rising costs for siting, labor, and regulatory compliance. It is a merger of industry and brain work: biomedical, systems controls, scientific instruments, aeronautical and navigational devices, electrical systems, and the design, final assembly, and refurbishment of a variety of aerospace, maritime, and naval hardware. Above all, the Northeast is where the *training* takes place for the *brain work* that drives *all* American manufacturing *everywhere*. After all, the Northeast is home to Yale, Harvard, and that most hallowed hall of nerds, the Massachusetts Institute of Technology.

- The **Front Range**—where I hang my hat these days—and the **Arizona Sun Corridor** are a world apart. Land is dirt cheap. Regulations are for the bonfire. But there just aren't all that many people, and the cities are certainly not close together. The combined population of the two zones' urban corridors isn't much more than 10 million, and the drive from Colorado Springs, the southern extreme of the (very-extended)

---

*   Hurray, hydropower!

Denver metro, to Albuquerque is a cool four hours.[*] Between very limited economies of scale and high in-region transport costs, standard manufacturing supply chains are almost out of the question. The solution? Tech servicing and all-in-one manufacturing hubs that don't heavily integrate with the rest of the country unless it makes sense for the product to be *flown*. This is the corner of America getting into high-end semiconductor fabrication of the Japanese and Taiwanese style.

- The **Gulf Coast** is Energy Alley. Petroleum and natural gas are both produced and processed there. The shale revolution has so deluged the region in vast volumes of low-cost, high-quality hydrocarbons that the region is busy expanding its industrial plant to make not just intermediate products like propylene or methanol, but increasingly downmarket products like safety glass, diapers, tires, nylon, plastics, and fertilizer. The biggest problem? Siting can be a bit of a bitch. Big refineries need maritime access and lots of space. Still, this region lucks out in two ways. First, the Texas coast sports an extensive chain of barrier islands that provide it with more shielded port potential than *all* of Asia (and the lower Mississippi in southern Louisiana isn't even remotely shabby, either). Second, most American petrochemical facilities were built with *lots* of standoff distance. (Working with large volumes of oil and natural gas at high temperatures can be dangerous work.) At least some of that empty space can be converted (and *is* being converted) into yet more industrial capacity.

- A region that consistently surprises to the upside is the American **Piedmont**. Sub-average educational system. Semi-rugged terrain that both increases transport and land costs while limiting opportunities for integration and economies of scale. Limited options for river transport. It doesn't feel like the South should be very successful.

---

[*] And even that is only if the traffic is light, the weather is good, and the cops are asleep.

But the locals more than make up for their shortcomings with oppressively felonious levels of charm. Rather than wait for investors to come to them, southerners venture out to potential investors the world over, typically bringing with them their delegation's combined body weight in bourbon to smooth over any cultural barriers.[*] Once the southerners inebriate, er, land an investor, they then set to work back home to create the perfect customized business environment. Infrastructure is expanded, the workforce is exquisitely tailored not just for the investor's business but *for specific jobs*, tax laws are changed, and the southerners do what they do best: make outsiders feel like they're part of the family. Embarrassingly little *American* investment drives the South, but foreign investment? Everywhere. The American South has become a playground for Germany's VW and Mercedes-Benz; Japan's Honda, Mazda, Nissan, and Toyota; Korea's Hyundai and Kia; and Sweden's Volvo. Even persnickety Airbus has facilities in Charleston, South Carolina, and Mobile, Alabama.

- **Florida**. You go to Florida for beaches, Disney World, and retirement— not to manufacture stuff. And we're walking . . .
- The **Great Lakes** region was once known as America's Steel Belt. A bit of canal work in the mid-1800s connected the Northeast to the Great Lakes and Greater Mississippi, making this region the greatest integrated manufacturing zone on the planet. For a time. During the Great Depression the Americans adopted something known as the Jones Act, which forced any cargo shipped between any two American ports to use only vessels that were American built, owned, captained, and crewed. That, put conservatively, increased the cost of water transport in the United States by a factor of five. What made this region special and successful withered. Add in international competition during the globalization age and the region has since been . . . reimagined as the

---

[*]   Fun fact: When hard-drinking American southerners meet with equally hard-drinking Koreans, the result is one of those irresistible-force/immovable-object contests.

Rust Belt, despite arguably having the nation's best educational system. Manufacturing still exists of course. Illinois is home to none other than John Deere, with the bulk of the continent's large farm equipment even today manufactured in the Midwest. Detroit is no slouch, but neither is it the region's norm. Instead of mass-volume, heavily integrated systems, most players are on the small side, heavy into highly technical custom work and often supplying specialty parts to . . .

- **TEXAS!** The Texas Triangle comprises the cities of Houston, Dallas–Fort Worth, Austin, and San Antonio. From a manufacturing point of view, the Triangle has it all: cheap food, cheap power, cheap land, no income tax, minimal corporate tax, hilariously light regulations. And that won't change. Hell, the Texas legislature only meets once *every other* year, for only thirty-five days, and legislators are constitutionally barred from even considering legislation for the first half of that time window. American manufacturers of all types have flocked to the region. The single biggest subsector is automotive, but that oversimplifies a dizzying variety and dynamism. Austin operationalizes Silicon Valley's ideas. Dallas–Fort Worth leverages its banking center to turn Austin's brain work into mass manufacturing. San Antonio mixes lower costs than even the Texas average with the tech of Austin to blow out anything that can be put on an assembly line. But the real star of the Texas game is Houston. It plays with Austin in tech and Dallas–Fort Worth in automation and San Antonio with mass manufacture *and* it is a financial capital *and* it is America's energy hub *and* it is in the Gulf Coast region *and* it is America's biggest port by value *and* it is *really* good at moving around big chunks of metal. That machine work the Germans are so good at? Houston comes in a solid second place globally. No wonder Houston is the country's second-largest concentration for Fortune 500 headquarters.

Most of America's regions would do very well flying solo, but they do not need to. Add in the country's broad-scale road and rail system for transporting intermediate products, and in many ways the American manufacturing system has more variety than even Asia, even without its northern and southern neighbors.

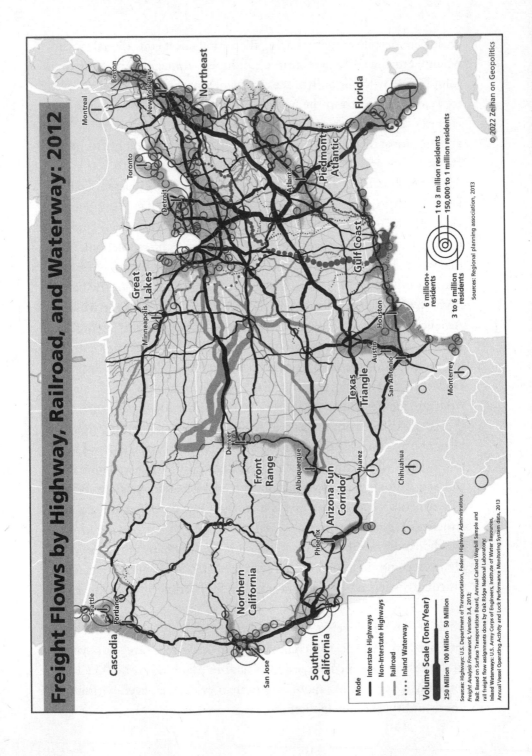

Freight Flows by Highway, Railroad, and Waterway: 2012

© 2022 Zeihan on Geopolitics

Mode
— Interstate Highways
— Non-Interstate Highways
— Railroad
······ Inland Waterway

Volume Scale (Tons/Year)
250 Million 100 Million 50 Million

1 to 3 million residents
150,000 to 1 million residents

6 million+ residents
3 to 6 million residents

Sources: Regional planning association, 2013

Sources: Highways: U.S. Department of Transportation, Federal Highway Administration,
Freight Analysis Framework, Version 3.4, 2013;
Rail: Based on Surface Transportation Board, Annual Carload Waybill Sample and
rail freight flow assignments done by Oak Ridge National Laboratory;
Inland Waterways: U.S. Army Corps of Engineers, Institute of Water Resources,
Annual Vessel Operating Activity and Lock Performance Monitoring System data, 2013

This brings us to the second bit of magic in NAFTA manufacturing. America *does* have a neighbor that complements its system: Mexico. The wage differential between the American and the Mexican average is approximately six-to-one, less than Asia's split, but bigger than Europe's. That doesn't tell the entire story, however. Mexico is a different beast compared to many of the other countries we've covered. Anti-Americanism didn't stop dictating Mexican industrial policy until the 1990s, and Mexico didn't really start playing the industrialization game until 2000—which, incidentally, is a mere heartbeat before China was admitted to the World Trade Organization.

Being a late starter definitely generated some problems, but nothing has held Mexico back more than its topography. Mexico's low latitude puts it firmly in the tropics. The combination of tropical heat and tropical moisture and tropical bugs makes the tropics the most problematic climate possible for industrialization; building materials are compromised, concrete often sets incorrectly due to the humidity, asphalt slides in the heat, and the population must do battle with tropical diseases. Mexicans address these issues by moving up onto the broad plateau between the Sierra Madre mountain chains, but that has generated new problems: Living at altitude means no coastal access and no navigable rivers, necessitating artificial infrastructure that must battle with the terrain at every step. Trains can only carry half their nameplate capacity when on rails that are on as little as a 0.25 percent slope, and there's a lot more than a 0.25 percent slope on most mountains. Everything gets very expensive very quickly.

Another "problem" of moving upmountain is that the higher one climbs, the lower the humidity and the vapor pressure of water. For those of you who live at sea level, that means water not only evaporates quickly, it actually boils at a lower temperature, specifically about 15 degrees lower in Mexico City than in Miami.

These characteristics take us two places. First, Mexico does have an extreme labor-cost variation of the sort that makes East Asia work so well—the country's fractured nature ensures it—but that variation is not easily accessible, making the point more or less moot until such time as Mexico's infrastructure can catch up.

Second, as one moves north from Mexico City, the combination of higher latitudes plus different wind and sea currents and a shifting mountain complexion turns the land to desert. Normally this would be bad. Rainfall is so low that very little non-irrigated agriculture occurs in northern Mexico at all. That means cities are on their own. There are no hinterlands to draw tomorrow's population from.

But that in turn creates an interesting political and economic dynamic. When cities are, in essence, oases, the normal evolution is for a single person or small group of people to assert control over just about everything. If infrastructure or industrial plant needs to be built, someone has to pay for it, and whoever does the paying likes to keep control over it. If the city isn't surrounded by a belt of forest or farms, there really isn't anywhere for rebels to hide. That makes the Mexican system—particularly the northern Mexican cities—fairly oligarchic.

Normally, oligarchic systems are neither wealthy nor dynamic, because the bosses keep the cash to themselves. In the case of northern Mexico, however, these jefes are hard up on the U.S. border and serve as gateways to the world's largest industrial and consumer market. That changes the math. Northern Mexican businesspeople still integrate with one another, at least within their own shared metro region, but it is far more important for them to plug into an American supply system, particularly the wealthy Texas Triangle supply system.

Perhaps best of all, while the United States features the developed world's healthiest demographic structure, Mexico features the best of the advanced *developing* world's. There's plenty of consumption on *both* sides of the border.

End result: the Texas–Mexico axis boasts the technological sophistication of Japan, the wage variation of China, and the integration of Germany with its neighbors, all within the footprint of the world's largest consumption market.

That is where we are now. But now is not the future.

THE MAP OF THE FUTURE

Of the three major manufacturing environments, Asia's is by far the least sustainable.

It is . . . somewhat difficult to know where to begin.

THE END OF ASIA INC.

There's the neighborhood angle:

The four Northeast Asian economies do *not* get along. Only America's two largest overseas military deployments—in South Korea and Japan—keep the locals from being at each other's throats. Only the threat of American naval power prevents the Chinese from trying something cute. Whether because of local historical anger and angst or American departure, in the world unfolding there is no way on Earth the East Asians are capable of the sort of productive cooperation necessary to enable broad-spectrum, multimodal, integrated, and peaceful manufacturing supply chains. The Northeast Asians are politically, strategically, and culturally incapable of the degree of trust required to form their own version of NAFTA, much less the kind of joint decision making that defines the European Union.

There's the demographic angle:

In calendar year 2019, China suffered the greatest decline in its birth rate on record. Sad to say, it was expected. The One Child Policy had depressed China's birth rate for long enough that China is now running out of twenty-somethings, and twenty-somethings are the people who have the kids. Generate fewer young adults and the new generation cannot have many kids. Cram them all into urban condos and even those who *can* have kids don't *want* to.

Worse was soon to come. Data from 2020 data indicated an even greater drop. Instinct credits the drop to coronavirus, but it takes nine months to generate a baby. Most of the 2020 drop, therefore, was due to circumstances and choices made in 2019. Formally, China's birth rate isn't simply the lowest since 1978, birth rates in Shanghai and Beijing—China's largest cities—are now the lowest in the world. At the time of this writing we are still waiting for finalized 2021 data, but anecdotals from throughout China are beyond horrid for the dominant Han population.

They are even worse for the non-Han. Say what you will about Mao, but his version of communism had a bit of a soft spot for China's many minorities* and allowed them exemptions to One Child. But Maoist communism is long dead, replaced by a steely neofascist ultranationalism. As China faces the terror of disintegration in a deglobalized world, the Chinese Communist Party has begun systematic persecution of its minorities to the point of stationing CCP officials *inside people's homes* to prevent them from, among other things, procreating. The Uighirs of Xinjiang saw their birth rate drop by *half* just between 2018 and 2020. Instead of exceptions to One Child, some of China's minorities are now de facto under a Zero Child Policy. Add it up and China is now the world's fastest-aging society.

The demographic situations elsewhere in East Asia aren't quite so graphic, but that's not to say they are much better. Japan is already the world's oldest demography (and was the fastest-aging one until China took up that mantle in 2020). Korea's baby bust started twenty years after Japan's, but has progressed faster. Taiwan and Thailand are roughly a decade behind Korea. Even populous Indonesia and Vietnam, with roughly 400 million people between them, have been bitten by the urbanization bug. Neither is close to that "no return" point, but their demographic structure in 2021 looks remarkably similar to China's in the 1980s.

Rapid aging strikes the Asians with a triple bind: First, aging work-

---

*   In this context, "soft spot" means "did not systematically wipe them all out."

forces may typically be more productive, but they are also more expensive. China's low-skilled labor supply peaked in the early 2000s. China's skilled labor supply is peaking at the time of this writing. The end result is as clear as it is unavoidable: higher labor costs. China is no longer the low-cost producer, and it hasn't moved up the value chain fast enough to be the high-quality producer.

Second, such rapid aging precludes the Asians in general—and the Chinese in particular—from ever breaking away from their export model. There simply isn't enough local consumption to even hope to gobble up everything the Asians produce. And if the Americans no longer empower the Asians to export the world over, the entire Asian model fails overnight. Third and finally, rapidly aging workforces are perfectly capable of collapsing under their own weight via mass retirement.

There's the question of input access:

China imports more than 70 percent of its 14 million barrels of oil it needs every day; Taiwan, Korea, and Japan import more than 95 percent of their 1, 2, and 4 million barrel needs, respectively. More than two-thirds of all their inflows originate in the Persian Gulf, a region not exactly brimming with stability under the Order, much less expecting to become more stable in the aftermath of the American withdrawal. China is the biggest importer of *every* industrial commodity, with the Japanese and Koreans reliably showing up in the top five.

Energy aside, nearly all the industrial commodities in question come from the Southern Hemisphere, with Australia, Brazil, and sub-Saharan Africa being the biggest players. What doesn't come from them comes from Russia, and while I wouldn't put Chinese-Russian conflict at the top of my things-that-can-go-wrong list, it is nowhere near the bottom, either. The Russians, after all, have a time-honored tradition of using resource flows to extract geopolitical concessions.

Perhaps the biggest problem for the Chinese will be . . . the Japanese. China's navy is coastal and near coastal, with only about 10 percent of its surface combatants capable of sailing more than 1,000 miles from shore. Very few can sail more than 2,000 miles. China has no real allies (except maybe North Korea), so projecting power . . . anywhere is a hilarious impossibility. Japan, in contrast, has a navy fully capable of sailing—and fighting—a continent or two away. Should push come to shove, the Japanese can simply dispatch a small task force past Singapore into the Indian Ocean and shut down Chinese resource inflows—and with them, shut down China—remotely.

There's an economies of scale angle:

The secret sauce of the Asian manufacturing model is the region's highly variant labor markets, combined with the American-provided and -subsidized security environment and global trade network. Demographic collapse is upending the former, while the American withdrawal is ending the latter. Anything that drives up costs or increases security concerns reduces the capacity of the East Asians to mount a joint effort in the world of manufacturing. Lose what makes Asia special and there is no reason at all for Asia to continue being the global hub in that most differentiated of manufacturing markets: electronics and computing.

There's a supply chain angle:

Anything that raises the marginal cost of manufacturing or transport, or increases instability and risk in manufacturing or transport, eliminates just-in-time inventorying from even theoretically working. That forces manufacturing closer to end consumption points. Since Asia Inc. is the world's largest manufacturer and *exporter*, it is this part of the world that will suffer the most from the future colocation of manufacturing with consumption. And since the very concept of just-in-time means no one stores much inventory, when it goes down, it'll *all* go down, *all at once*.

If Asian demographics and geopolitics complicate (or, more likely, breach) regional production processes, then there will be no economic reason for the subsectors of electronics, cellular phones, and computing to be monopolized here. Break Asia's chokehold on that market, even a little, and the economies of scale that have kept East Asia the undisputed workshop of the world will erode away.

China specifically faces a follow-on challenge:

China as the workshop of the world is utterly dependent upon imported technology and components. In high-value sectors such as semiconductors, telephony, and aerospace, China has published national plans to become the global leader in *all*, but it has proven broadly incapable of manufacturing high-value-add components like low-nanometer chips or jet engines on its own.* Items most of us just assume the Chinese dominate in—household electronics, office equipment, and computers—actually have more than 90 percent of their value added *outside* of China. For ships the figure is 87 percent. For telecom gear and the guts of most electronic gadgetry it is 83 percent. Even for exceedingly lowbrow work such as paper, plastics, and rubber, upwards of half of the value-add happens elsewhere.†

China's failure to advance has simplified the country's industrial model somewhat: China uses its hyperfinanced model to drive down the costs of the components that it *can* produce; it imports the parts it *cannot* produce, plugs them in, and sends the final product off. But this model only works if external suppliers actively participate. Anything from a security crisis to sanctions ends that pretty quickly. China has already experienced a lockout in cellular tech (Huawei) and aerospace (the C919 passenger jet). Based on how politics unfold, some version of this sort of disruption can (and will) occur in nearly every product category.

Finally, there's a market proximity issue:

The two largest destinations for Asian end products are in faraway America and Europe. The Americans are a cool 7,000 miles across the Pacific, while the Europeans are—depending upon origin, route, and destination—9,000–14,000 miles away. In a post-globalized world it is reasonable to expect *some* trade relations to last—France and North Africa, Turkey and Mesopotamia, Germany and Scandinavia, for example—but locality will be key.

---

*   Or, if we're being brutally honest, to successfully reverse-engineer the products of others.

†   Don't get me wrong: I don't feel great when I see a new story about some Chinese spy successfully funneling American military technology to Beijing. But please keep it in perspective. China didn't figure out how to make a ball-point pen without imported components until 2017. The idea that China can get a set of blueprints and suddenly be able to cobble together a stealth bomber or advanced missile system is a bit of a scream.

The longer the shipping route and the more players that lie along any particular route, the more deals that need to be cut and the more opportunity for interruption. One of the reasons the goods transported via the Silk Roads were so expensive was that no single power controlled the entire route. Typically, *hundreds* of middlemen all added their own fees, inflating the goods cost by a factor of 1,000 or more.

With the possible exception of Japan, there is *no* Asian power that has the naval capacity to reach either of the two large end markets in question, and in a post-globalized system it isn't very likely that Asian product would be very welcome in the first place. Add in the general mutual loathing most Asians feel toward one another and the entire model that has pulled the region out of poverty and war is set to implode. The only question is whether someone will try to go out swinging. And to be crystal clear, "swinging" is exceedingly bad for supply chain security.

THE DISASSEMBLY OF EUROPE

Somewhat similarly, the European system will falter for any number of reasons. The first rationale is both the most obvious and the least manageable: Europe's baby bust started before Asia's, with the Europeans passing the point of demographic no return even before the new millennium. Belgium, Germany, Italy, and Austria will all age into mass retirement in the first half of the 2020s, while nearly every country in a Central European line from Estonia to Bulgaria is aging even faster and will age out in the second half.

Even worse, demographics alone ensure that Europe as we know it will collapse on a similar time schedule. When the Central European states joined the EU in the 2000s, they succeeded in convincing the Western Europeans to open their labor markets. Some one-fourth to one-third of the young worker population of the Central European region decamped for better personal economic prospects to the west. Bottom line: Western Europe's demographic figures are far *worse* than they actually appear. Whether it's because Central Europeans return home when the going gets tough, which robs Western Europe of its workforce, or because *more* Central Europeans head to Western Europe when the going gets tough because those are the only jobs left, the labor balance that has enabled European economic functionality since 2008 is about to evaporate.

The demographic problem haunts in a second way. Europe has aged to the point that it cannot absorb its own products. Europe *must* maintain a high level of exports to maintain its system. The top destination is the United States, a country that is turning ever inward and at the time of this writing is already edging its way into a broad-spectrum trade war with the European Union. The United States is also (again, at the time of this writing) exploring a similarly broad-spectrum trade deal with the United Kingdom. As any future trade peace with the EU will soon require London's sign-off, no one in continental Europe should count on easy rectification.

The European products that do not go to the United States instead travel to the far side of the planet: Northeast Asia. Even if, against all odds, the Northeast Asian system (as well as Northeast Asian demand for European products) survives, the Americans will no longer be guaranteeing freedom of the seas for civilian maritime shipping. The route from Shanghai to Hamburg is a breezy 12,000 nautical miles. At the zippy seventeen miles per hour that modern container ships typically sail at, that's a cool thirty-five-day trip. The fastest any commercial cargo vessel can sail is twenty-five knots. That's still three full weeks—a lot of time to spend sailing through waters infested with pirates, privateers, hostile navies, or some combination of the three.

Perhaps even worse, the part of Europe that maintains the most robust trade relationship with the Chinese is Germany. German product sales to China skew very heavily in the direction of machinery used to make other products . . . products for *export*. Even if, against all odds, Germany and China can maintain a trade relationship in a world where they lack the strategic reach to interact directly, Chinese exports will not be nearly as needed, undermining the base rationale for any sort of German-Chinese interaction.

The same broad strategic issues that face the Asians also face the Europeans, although those particular problems are of less or more concern depending on location and perspective.

First, the "more." Most European countries started industrializing in the 1800s, with even the laggards—largely the former Soviet satellite states—beginning at the latest in the 1950s. That means most mines in Europe have been tapped out for at least a few decades. The Europeans, having been industrialized for at minimum a couple of generations, may not consume as many materials as the Asians, but they produce even fewer. The Chinese might import the vast majority of the materials they need, but typically, the Europeans must import them *all*.

Now, the "less." Most of the industrial commodities required for modern life come from locations far closer to Europe than East Asia—such as the Western Hemisphere and Africa. Several European countries—France and the United Kingdom come to mind, but so too do Spain, the Netherlands, Italy, and Denmark—have sufficient naval capacity to protect occasional shipping to and from the locations in question. Just as good, most sailings from these regions to Europe are unlikely to pass through any particularly contested waters. As to Western Hemispheric sourcing, the Americans are certain to put the kibosh on any sort of piracy or privateering in their hemisphere, and European commerce is unlikely to be barred so long as it remains unmilitarized.

The trick will come from those European countries farther removed from the Continent's far west who lack both access and naval forces. They must source materials from a different "close" location: Russia. Germany cannot maintain its position as a wealthy and free nation without the Americans, but Germany also cannot maintain its position as a *modern industrialized* nation without Russia. The story of all things German and Russian is about alternating chapters of begrudging cooperation and incisive conflict. As searing as that is for the Germans and Russians, it is far worse for the peoples between them—countries essential to Germany's manufacturing supply chains. The Ukraine War is already forcing some tough questions upon all involved.

And of course, even all this assumes nothing goes wrong *within* Europe. Europe suffers from one of those weird geographies where just enough of it is flat and well rivered and easy to walk across that portions of the Continent are convinced that they can and should lead a major consolidated power, while there are just enough bits that are peninsular or mountainous or island to play host to dissident powers that will always dash such dreams. It's only during the Order that global peace and wealth smothered the age-old contest between the two visions. Smothered. Not killed. Despite seventy-five years of healing and growth and safety and security and modernization and freedom and democracy, much internal angst and grievance remains. Brexit, occurring at the very height of globalization, is a case in point. With the American withdrawal, that smothering ends.

Simply put, the Germanocentric system cannot maintain its current position, much less grow, and *no one* in the world has a strategic interest in bailing it out. The challenge for Central Europe will be to keep the Germans from acting like a "normal" country. The last seven times Germany did, things got . . . historical.

A bit of a bright spot: Europe's subsidiary trade networks look more favorable than the Germanocentric system.

The Sweden-centric system might be able to hold together. Northern Europe's supply chains are less exposed to potential threats, its energy supplies are more local, and its demographics are less aged and slower-aging, suggesting a better match between supply and demand that would limit the need for extra-regional imports and exports in the first place. In the North Sea the Scandinavians even have sufficient oil and natural gas to meet nearly all their demand. "All" they need to do is somehow source the various industrial inputs they need from a continent away.

They have two options:

The first is to partner with the French system at least in part. In addition to France boasting sufficient domestic consumption to absorb its own production, it also has sufficient geographic insulation and positioning to reach the needed inputs. Add in a competent expeditionary military and a nearly galactic volume of self-regard, and France can reasonably go its own way. Sweden & Friends would do well to find a way to work alongside the French.

The second option might feel more comfortable to the Scandinavians: work with the Anglos. Scandinavian-British cooperation against all things continental has a centuries-old history. With the Brits moving in with the Americans (organizationally speaking), some interesting possibilities are surfacing. The Americans obviously have a more powerful military and economy than anything the French boast. The Americans similarly also have far greater *reach*—reach to anywhere that might have necessary resources. The American-Mexican market is second to none, while the British market remains the healthiest one (demographically speaking) in Europe outside of France.

THE NORTH AMERICAN CENTURY

When it comes to the fate of the NAFTA system, most indicators look wildly positive.

Let's begin with base structure: part of why American manufacturers feel cheated by globalization is because *that was the plan*. The core precept of the Order is that the United States would sacrifice economic dynamism in order to achieve security control. The American market *was supposed* to be sacrificed. The American worker *was supposed* to be sacrificed. American companies *were supposed* to be sacrificed. Thus anything that the United States still manufactures is a product set for which the American market, worker, and corporate structure are hypercompetitive. Furthermore, the deliberate sacrifice means that most American manufactured products are not for export, but instead for consumption within North America.

That's not how China works. The Chinese make everything that they are technologically capable of making, using subsidies, technology theft, and diplomatic strong-arming to expand the list of products whenever possible. And unlike the United States, many of those products are for export. Put another way, the products the Chinese make are ones that, for whatever reason, the Americans have *chosen* not to make.

China's telecom firm Huawei is a case in point. Huawei directly, and via a branch of the Chinese government, which excels at hacking foreign firms, has pursued a dual strategy for two decades: steal whatever tech is possible, and purchase whatever cannot be replicated. Sanctions enacted by the Trump administration (and doubled down upon by the Biden administration) prevented legal tech transfer to Huawei at the same time American firms wised up to the hacking threat. The result? Huawei's corporate position imploded in less than two years, taking it from being on the cusp of the world's largest cell phone manufacturer to not even being on the top-five list within China. Most Chinese firms simply cannot function without active American participation.

The inverse is not true. Sure, the Americans would need to build out their industrial plant to compensate for lost low-cost suppliers, and that is easier and more quickly said than done, but it isn't like the Americans don't know *how* to do things like smelt aluminum or forge glass or bend steel or craft carburetors or assemble motherboards.

Then there's trade access: add all imports and exports together, and still some three-quarters of the U.S. economy is domestically held, limiting its exposure to all things global. Canada and Mexico are far more integrated, getting roughly two-thirds and three-quarters of their economic heft from trade, but roughly three-quarters of that trade is *with the United States*. Within North America as a unit, more than 8 in 10 dollars (or pesos) of income is generated within the continent. That's by far the most insulated system in the world.

Beyond that, the Americans have already ratified, operationalized, and implemented trade deals with Japan and South Korea, another two of the country's six largest trading partners. Add in a pending deal with the United Kingdom (another of the six) and fully half of the United States' trade portfolio has already been brought into a post-globalized system.

Next up is raw material supply: none of the NAFTA partners are slouches when it comes to industrial commodity or energy production. All generate globally significant volumes of multiple industrial commodities, natural gas, and oil. More is coming. As global maritime civilian transport fails, much of the raw production and intermediate processing that is done on the U.S. Gulf Coast will find its potential for global sales limited, either due to collapsing end markets, lack of security, or both. That will trap more of the output within North America. That's not great if you're an energy producer or processor, but it's *fantastic* news if you are an energy product *user*. As most manufacturers are.

If more supplies of anything are required, South America is a solid starting point. Extra-hemispheric sourcing is obviously more problematic, but unlike all other manufacturing regions, the North Americans have the consumption-based market *and* the capital *and* the fuel *and* the military reach to go out and get what they need.

Let's talk supply chains.

Most studies in the past half decade have indicated that by 2021, most manufacturing processes were *already* cheaper to operate in North America than in either Asia or Europe. That might shock, but it doesn't take a deep dive to understand the conclusions. The North American system sports high labor variation, low energy costs, low transport costs to end consumers, nearly unlimited greenfield siting options, stable industrial input supplies, and high and stable capital supplies.

Even better, the North American continent faces few security threats between its own shores and those of potential suppliers. On average, North American products face less than one-third the supply chain disruptions the Germans are likely to feel, and one-tenth that of the Asians. Now, industrial plant doesn't manifest for free, or overnight, but the sorts of disruptions North American manufacturers are likely to experience are the sort that can be grown through.

That gap between North American manufacturing viability and that of Asian and Europe is only going to increase in the decades to come, in large part because of ongoing evolutions in electricity generation. The United States and Mexico have among the world's *best* greentech options. Wind on the Great Plains, solar in the Southwest. Mexico is pretty good on both as well, particularly in the north, where the greatest integration with the American system occurs.

But perhaps most important of all, not everyone in North America has yet to toss their hat into the manufacturing ring.

First up are the Millennials. For all their many* faults, America's Mil-

---

*   Many, oh-so-very many.

lennials are the largest chunk of population of any developed country that are of working age. Their consumption is driving the North American system now, just as in twenty years their investment will drive it. Because of them, North America faces nothing like the consumption and capital crunches that will soon define Asia and Europe.

Second, America's manufacturing megaregions just aren't very integrated (the sole exceptions are the Gulf Coast and the Texas Triangle). Any future in which global trade is disrupted is one in which the U.S. federal, state, and local governments will have vested interests in improving those interconnections. With those interconnections will come smoother and more efficient integration of domestic manufacturing systems.

Third, not all of Mexico is playing. Yet. The northern Mexican cities have bet whole hog on American integration, but central Mexico is a manufacturing region in and of itself. Integration with the Americans occurs, but it just isn't nearly as all-encompassing as what occurs in northern Mexico. Nor is southern Mexico folded in. The south is Mexico's poorest and least technically advanced region, while also suffering from the worst infrastructure in terms of local roads and rail as well as those that might link the south to the rest of the country.

As the Canadians, Americans, and northern Mexicans build out a more integrated system, that system will naturally extend its integrative reach farther south. The Mexico City core, after all, is home to over 70 million people and is far more linked-up within itself than the northern Mexican cities are to one another. In the world we're devolving into, adding 70 million middle-income people to any system is about as big a win as can be had.

Fourth, there *may* be a pending win that's just a touch bigger. The United Kingdom voted to leave the European Union back in 2016 but didn't actually pull the plug until 2020, and it wasn't until 2021 that London realized it hadn't planned for the aftermath. Like, *at all*. The continental Europeans have shown no propensity to extend the Brits any concessions, and Britain on its own just isn't big or stable or diversified enough to matter. *But* add the United Kingdom and its sophisticated first-world manufacturing capacity to the NAFTA grouping and the math changes significantly. Extending NAFTA-esque trade links deeper into Mexico would be great, but incorporating 66 million Brits? That just might be even better. Both are on deck.

There *is* a problem: that all-important workforce variety. Brits are at a similar skill set and labor cost as Americans and Canadians, while central Mexicans measure up similarly to northern Mexicans. Two decades of moderate growth in Mexico combined with a gently aging demographic means that Mexico now needs a low-cost manufacturing partner. Put another way, Mexico needs . . . a Mexico.

There are two options. The first is . . . iffy. The Central American states of Honduras, Guatemala, El Salvador, Costa Rica, Nicaragua, and Panama are already incorporated into a trade deal with the United States called the Central America Free Trade Agreement. The problem is infrastructure. Running a road and rail network the entire length of Mexico's mountainous terrain in order to connect Central America's low-cost and low-skilled workforce to the American market seems like a stretch. It certainly wouldn't be nearly as lucrative as the relatively short haul between the Texas Triangle and northern Mexico.

That leaves sea connections. The Central American countries are in reality individual cities—one or two per country—surrounded by a lot of bush. The trick is to find an industry in which such labor can achieve sufficient profitability to justify export. It is not clear there is one. Outside of finishing work, even textiles are not likely to be a great match. That limits the region to tropical agricultural production and processing. That's not nothing, but it's also not great. And those sectors certainly cannot employ sufficient numbers of locals to move these countries out of the "nearly failed" category.

A more viable option is Colombia. Like the Central Americans, the Colombians already have a trade deal with the United States. Unlike the Central Americans, the Colombians have a far more skilled labor force at a wage level that's roughly two-thirds that of today's Mexico. The biggest challenge, which is a pretty common challenge throughout Latin America, is infrastructure. Unlike Mexico with its single raised central plateau,

Colombia has a V of highlands with the cities of Medellín and Cali on the western leg and so is more likely to integrate via the country's Pacific ports, while the capital, Bogotá, sits on the eastern leg and is more likely to look north to the Caribbean coast.

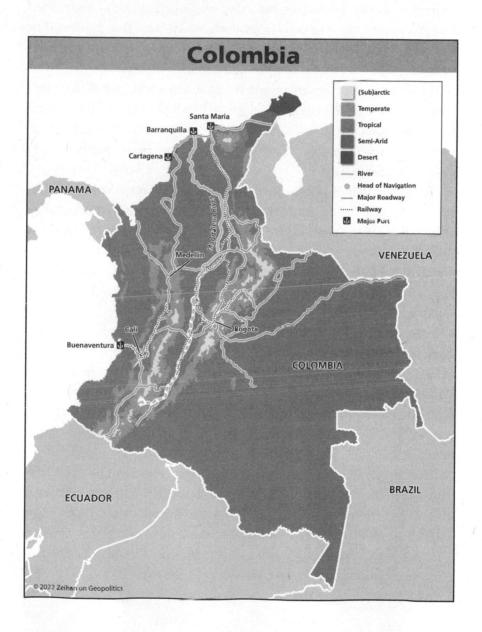

To this point, globalization has . . . crushed Colombia's dreams. The difficulty and cost of lugging stuff up and down Colombia's mountains has prevented meaningful supply chains from manifesting both within the country and between Colombia and the wider world. As such the country is mostly known for exporting oil, superhard coal, and coffee. But in a world where the costs of production skyrocket due to instability, and demand for industrial inputs of all types surges in North America— including *labor*—Colombia may be about to have its day.

If Colombia were located anywhere else in the world, talk of meaningful integration with North America would be a fool's errand. But between Colombia's unique price point, its unique geography, and its relative proximity, it just might be able to play in the North American system in a very Asian way: just-in-time.

The whole basis of just-in-time inventorying is that the stability of the various manufacturing partners is so reliable that you can bet the future of your firm on the next shipment arriving, well, just in time. In most of Asia that entire concept is about to fail. Not so in the NAFTA region. For all their faults, Canada, America, and Mexico face no structural challenges and so can continue to use just-in-time should they choose to do so. So can Colombia.

In addition, while whatever Asian (and European) manufacturing survives is unlikely to be able to tap the economies of scale required for a mass assembly line approach, North America's mix of integrative infrastructure and higher consumption means it can probably continue with both assembly lines and limited applications of automation. The NAFTA trio will simply need a bit of help with some of the lower-value components. Once again, enter Colombia.

Most people think of the Bretton Woods system as a sort of Pax Americana. The American Century, if you will. But that's simply not the case. The entire concept of the Order is that the United States *disadvantages* itself economically in order to purchase the loyalty of a global alliance. That is what globalization *is*. The past several decades haven't been an American Century. They've been an American sacrifice.

Which is over. With the American withdrawal, the various structural, strategic, and economic factors that have artificially propped up the entire Asian and European systems are ending. What consumption remains is concentrated in North America. Only North America sports a demographic profile that doesn't have to immediately adapt to a fundamentally new—and fundamentally unknown—financial reality. And so massive manufacturing reshoring to the American system is already in progress.

The real, actual American Century is only *now* beginning.

That hardly means there won't be manufacturing anywhere else.

A NEW CROP OF HUBS

Some 95 percent of value-added manufacturing occurs in East Asia, Europe, or North America. Most of this is due to the mix of factors we've already churned through: geography, demographics, transport, and globalization.

But part of it is also due to policy.

During the Cold War, two regions largely abstained from globalization writ large. The first abstinence, that of the Soviet Union, was by design. Globalization was created to isolate the Soviets. The second to abstain, the Latin American country of Brazil, held its systems apart for a mix of political and ideological reasons.

When the Cold War ended, both opened themselves up, particularly to the inexpensive electronic and computing products of the East Asian Rim. Shielded as they had been for decades, neither the Russians nor the Brazilians could compete. Adding insult to injury, the Chinese entered both countries to form joint ventures, and proceeded to scrape every bit of intellectual property from every firm they could in a manner that would even make Facebook blush.[*]

By 2005 there was little left for the Chinese to steal. By 2010 the

---

[*]   Briefly.

Chinese had fully incorporated all the stolen technology into their massive manufacturing system and were shoving cheaper products down the throats of both of their former "partners," casually crushing firms that once had been global leaders. Some version of this happened to a lesser degree in much of the developing world. That, more than anything else, is why manufacturing within East Asia makes up some half of global manufacturing, while the powerhouses of Europe and North America comprise almost all of the remainder.

In the world to come, Russia and Brazil *might* experience a bit of a manufacturing renaissance. Anything that encourages supply chains to be shorter, simpler, and closer to consumers will benefit any manufacturing system that is *not* in East Asia or Europe. But even this "might" comes with a pair of major caveats. First, recovery would require the Russians and Brazilians to address a host of unrelated issues, ranging from educational systems to infrastructure. Second, any manufacturing renewal would largely be limited to servicing customers within Russia and Brazil, or at most, countries within arm's reach. That's not nothing, but neither country is even on a theoretical track to becoming the next China, Mexico, or even Vietnam.

The end of China similarly *might* help out the largely nonmanufacturing economies of sub-Saharan Africa. None of them could hope to compete with China-centric manufacturing on cost, but with China gone? There may be some room for local successes. There are still (many) problems. The African continent is composed of a series of stacked plateaus, which all but prevents the various states from linking themselves together with infrastructure and achieving regional economies of scale. Nor do very many of them get along. Nor do any of them enjoy the sort of rich capital structure that might enable them to build much infrastructure on their own. But with China gone from the equation, there is at least a touch of hope. The countries with the most potential for breakout are those whose local geographies enable easier integration within their own systems as well as with the outside world: Senegal, Nigeria, Angola, South Africa, Kenya, and Uganda. Of these, Nigeria—due to population size, young demographics, and ample local energy production—looks best positioned.

On a more upbeat note, there are three regions that *will* be able to take advantage of the changed strategic circumstances to enter or reenter the world of manufacturing in a big way. The same mix of factors—demographic, labor variation, security, resource access, and transport safety—will determine who can pull it off.

The first of these regions is Southeast Asia sans China. It has a number of factors going for it.

- Southeast Asia has labor variation in spades: Singapore is ultra-high-tech and heavy in banking, Vietnam and Indonesia are young, vibrant societies handling the low end, and Thailand and Malaysia occupy the middle ground . . . but this is the *Asian* middle ground. The Thai and Malaysian economies are arguably more technically sophisticated than a sizable minority of European countries and American states.
- The Southeast Asian countries of Indonesia, Malaysia, the Philippines, Thailand, and Vietnam are *very* rapidly urbanizing. The region's hypercrowded cities push down the cost of labor relative to global norms, giving the Southeast Asians a leg up in any sort of apples-to-apples competition.
- The region has reasonable supplies of many industrial inputs; most notably it is nearly self-sufficient for its oil and natural gas needs. Myanmar in particular has loads of minerals that have yet to be industrially produced, while Papua New Guinea practically bleeds useful materials. For what the region cannot produce itself it can rely upon Australia, a world leader in coal, lithium, iron ore, nickel, and uranium.
- While it would be a stretch to say that everyone in the region always gets along, the very nature of the regional geography—heavy on jungles, mountains, peninsulas, and islands—makes it very difficult for the locals to have anything more than a border skirmish. The last meaningful fight was Vietnam's 1980s invasion of Cambodia, and to

be blunt, that conflict didn't move the economic needle at all. Cambodia was a nowhere before, and a nowhere it remains.

The region has a couple of significant weaknesses that, in my opinion, are perfectly manageable.

First, with everyone living in (and continuing to move to) cities, and with tropical soils being of limited fertility, this region has no hope of feeding itself. Luckily, the mass agricultural exporters of Australia and New Zealand are right next door, while the agricultural bounty of the entire Western Hemisphere is a straight shot across the Pacific.

Second, there is no obvious leader within Southeast Asia. Singapore is the richest, but also the smallest. Indonesia is the biggest, but among the poorest. The Thais are the most "with it," unless they're having one of their periodic military coups.* The Vietnamese are the most organized, but that's because their government is borderline dictatorial. This isn't simply an issue of asking who speaks for the region, but also, who can maintain sea-lane security? That task is largely beyond the locals.

Luckily, there's help at hand for this as well. Japan's navy is very long-range capable—blue-water in the vernacular of defense-minded wonks—and could patrol the region fairly easily. It's critical to note that this is *not* the age of Imperial Japan. There will be no imperial invasions. Most of Southeast Asia may be a generation or two behind the Japanese in terms of economic development, but all the countries that matter are fully industrialized. This would be a defense *partnership*, not an occupation.

Next up is India. In the ways that work, India is a bit like China. It is a huge, sprawling country with wild variation among its heavily populated regions. The Bangalore corridor was an early entrant into the world of tech servicing, while the country also excels at petroleum refining, heavy chemicals, generic drug production, and fast-turnaround consumer goods.

---

*   Which seems to be all the frickin' time.

India's problem is that it might be a bit *too* varied and *too* heavily populated. India is not an ethnically defined nation-state like China or Vietnam or France or Poland, in which one group dominates the population and the government, but instead boasts more ethnic and linguistic diversity than any *continent* save Africa. Many of these ethnicities don't simply have their own cultures; they have their own *governments*. These governments often exercise vetoes—sometimes formal, sometimes informal—over national policies. The reverse is often true as well. It isn't a setup that argues for great connections and smooth business relations.

This is what India has looked like for a millennium and a half. Nothing as minor as the collapse of the world we know is going to change it. But if global connections falter, India's trademark snarled bureaucracy just isn't going to be as big a problem as a lack of long-distance maritime transport. At a *minimum* the changed circumstances will enable India to build out its manufacturing capacity to serve its own 1.4 billion strong population. India's size alone means it doesn't have to be a global player to be globally significant.

A common problem for both Southeast Asia and India will be capital supply. Since both players sport relatively young demographics, local capital generation is somewhat thin. Since both suffer from complex and riven terrain—all those jungles and mountains and peninsulas and islands— the need for capital to build compensating infrastructure is high, and the opportunities for land-based infrastructure to link up the region's various workforces are weak at best. Both *will* pick up many pieces of many manufacturing networks as China breaks down and up, but the industrial plant will still need to be built—and that is not free. With the notable exception of Singapore, none of these economies have hard currencies or stable stock markets. Even if they can maintain political and macroeconomic stability, they will not be destinations for capital flight.

What they all need is foreign direct investment (FDI). The concept behind FDI is simple: money to purchase or build specific facilities— typically industrial plant—in order to produce a specific product. The solution to Southeast Asian and Indian capital problems is likely the same: Japan. The Japanese workforce is rapidly aging into obsolescence and

Japanese consumption peaked three decades ago. But the Japanese are still loaded. While their workforce isn't going to be building much by or for themselves, they are still eminently capable of designing products to be manufactured elsewhere and paying for the industrial plant to make it all happen. Combine Japanese tech and military strength and wealth with India and Southeast Asia's manufacturing potential and demographic and industrial inputs and you have one of the great alliances of the twenty-first century.

The question is whether anyone else will be invited to join the party. The Koreans would be a logical choice, but they are just as expert at holding grudges against the Japanese for the 1905–45 occupation of Korea as they are at high-tech manufacturing. It isn't clear that the Koreans, who utterly lack the naval capacity to look after their own needs, will be willing to reach out to the Japanese in a post-American world. Taiwan, in contrast, is a slam-dunk partner. The Taiwanese and Japanese instinctively share a hostile view of Beijing and have been collaborating on all things industrial since the end of the Korean War.

There is one more region worth looking at: Buenos Aires.

For those of you familiar with Argentina, I'm sure you think I've suffered a stroke. Argentina has among the world's most investor-unfriendly regulatory and tariff regimes, and the country's penchant for flat-out confiscating private property has wrecked its local manufacturing base. All true. All relevant . . . for the world that's dying. But in the world that's being born, a world fracturing into regional and even national trade systems, Argentina's socialist-cum-fascist industrial policy will work much better. After all, if cheap manufactured products are no longer easily available from East Asia, the Argentines will either need to go without or make some stuff locally. And the Argentines *hate* going without.

That's likely to lead to a significant regional industrial boom. Argentines are among the world's most educated people, so the issue has never been intellectual capacity. The Buenos Aires region is also within reach of cheaper labor markets in Paraguay, Uruguay, and southern Brazil. The local market of 45 million Argentines is worth going after, and the rest of the Southern Cone—the region that preexisting Argentine infrastructure already links to—adds in nearly a quarter of a billion more. The combined Southern Cone is also a major producer of nearly every agricultural and industrial product under the sun, and there is no one in the Eastern Hemisphere with the capacity of breaking the American security cordon around the Western Hemisphere. In a world that will soon face shortages in everything from foodstuffs to industrial processing to coherent and sustainable manufacturing systems, Argentina & Friends checks all the boxes.

So that's the *where*. Now let's look at the *how*. After all, the world we're devolving into will manufacture things not simply in different places and on different scales, but also in different ways.

MANUFACTURING A NEW WORLD

The longer and more complex the supply chain, the more likely it is to face catastrophic, irrecoverable breakdown.

That single statement contains a *lot* of angst and disruption.

Evolving from the manufacturing norms of the globalized world to the new norms of a deglobalized one will not be like disassembling a car and then reassembling it in a new location. It will be like disassembling a car and then reassembling it as a bread maker, an apple picker, and a Barbie dream jet. The processes we use to manufacture things will change because the environment will change. Global economies of scale will vanish. Many of the technologies we use to manufacture goods under globalization will not prove applicable to the fractured world emerging.

That means that we, today in 2022, have a lot of industrial plant that just won't be relevant much longer.

Consider China: Total manufacturing value-add in China in 2021 was right around $4 trillion, some three-quarters of which were for export. The raw value of the underlying industrial plant is easily ten times that, not counting supporting transport and power infrastructure, nor the thousands of long-range ships that shuttle inputs into and end products out of the country, nor the value of supporting codependent supply systems that involve other countries throughout East Asia.

It is all going to become stranded. Deglobalization—whether triggered by the American withdrawal or demographic collapse—will break the supply links that make most China-centric manufacturing possible, even before consuming nations more jealously protect their home markets. Pretty much the entire export-driven industrial plant (and a not small portion of the domestically driven industrial plant) will be written off. Completely.

Not all of it will need to be replaced. Demographic decline means global consumption peaked back in the golden pre-COVID days of 2019, while the fracturing of the global system will further reduce overall global income and wealth levels. But within many of those smaller fragments, there *will* be a need to build replacement industrial plant. After all, tapping the global market for finished goods will no longer be a viable option.

The characteristics of this new industrial plant will reflect a fundamentally different macroeconomic, strategic, financial, and technological environment. It will be a bit different based on where that plant is located, but some common characteristics will exist across them all.

1. Mass-production assembly lines are largely out. Mass production of any type requires massive economies of scale. Even within the North American market, such production "only" needs to serve about a half billion people, with a combined economy of about $25 trillion. Yes, that's a lot, but it's but one-third of the pre-COVID global total and the NAFTA countries will be producing primarily for themselves, not for the world writ large.

2. Reducing economies of scale reduces the opportunities for automation. Applying new technology to any manufacturing system adds cost, and automation is no exception. It will still happen, but only in targeted applications such as textiles and advanced semiconductors. Such automated applications are already cheaper than human labor.

3. The pace of technological improvement in manufacturing will slow. Let me make that broader: the pace of *all* technological improvement will slow. Rapid tech advancement requires a large body of highly skilled workers, the opportunities for large-scale collaboration among those workers, and a metric butt-ton of capital to pay for the development, operationalization, and application of new ideas. Demographic collapse is gutting the first, deglobalization is fracturing the second, and the combined pair are ending the third.

4. Supply chains will be much shorter. In a disconnected world, any point of exposure is a failure point and any manufacturing system that cannot snuff out its own complexity is one that will not survive. The model of dozens of geographically isolated suppliers feeding into a single, sprawling supply chain will vanish. Instead, successful manufacturing will twist into two new, mutually supportive shapes. The first will carry out more steps within individual locations in order to eliminate as much supply chain risk as possible. This suggests that such core facilities will become far larger. The second sort of manufacturing will be tiny facilities that supply customized parts. Machine shops in particular should thrive. They can quickly absorb capital and technology and new designs and new workers, and crank out customized or rapidly changing parts for use in those larger, core facilities.

5. Production will become colocated with consumption. With the global map fracturing, serving a consumer market means producing goods within that market. For smaller and more isolated markets, this suggests extreme production costs due to an utter lack of economies of scale, as well as difficulty sourcing the necessary range of input materials. Larger systems (NAFTA comes to mind) will do much better. After all, inputs sourced in Utah can be used to build a product in Toronto that can be sold in the Yucatan. "Colocation" is relative.

6. The new systems will put premiums on simplicity and security just as the old system put premiums on cost and efficiency. The death of just-in-time will force manufacturers to do one of two things. Option A is to warehouse masses of product—including finished product—as far forward in the manufacturing process as possible, preferably at the very edge of major population centers. Option B is to abandon as much of the traditional manufacturing process as possible and do all-in manufacturing as physically close to the end consumer as possible. One technology suited to the latter is additive or 3-D manufacturing, the idea being that a powdered or liquefied material is sprayed in thin layers over and over again until a product is "printed." Yes, additive manufacturing is expensive in per-product absolute terms, but the goalposts have moved. Cost is no longer the driving focus, and any 3-D-printed products by definition will have next to zero warehousing costs.

7. The workforce will be very different. Between an alternating emphasis on customization and carrying out multiple manufacturing steps in one location, there isn't much room for people who don't know what they are doing. One of the great gains of the Industrial Age was that low-skilled labor could make a reasonable living working on an assembly line. But now? Demand for the lowest-skilled jobs within the manufacturing space will evaporate, while rewards for the highest-skilled jobs will soar. For poor countries, this will be a disaster. Moving up the value-add scale means starting at the bottom. Between geopolitical devolutions, demographic inversions, and technological changes, most of those jobs will no longer exist. In addition, shorter, simpler supply chains will reduce overall employment in manufacturing in general as measured in terms of jobs per unit of product produced. The end result? Widening inequality both within and among countries.

8. Not everyone can play. Each fractured piece of the world will need to look to its own internal manufacturing system, and many will lack the capacity. The capital requirements for building out industrial plant are steep. Demographic aging will limit options within Europe. Likely restrictions on capital transfers will limit options throughout the non–East Asian developing world. The regions that can best tap outside capital will be those with the best prospects for tapping resources, producing products reliably, and maybe even selling a few out-of-region: Southeast Asia, India, and the Greater Buenos Aires region. The only region likely to be able to fully self-fund its own buildout is NAFTA.

9. Finally, and most depressingly, there are different sorts of losers in this world we are devolving into. It is one thing if your country loses a manufacturing system because someone else has a better Geography of Success for making this or that widget in the age unfolding. Change the map of transport, or finance, or energy, or industrial materials, and the list of winners or losers will shift with it. That's not a happy outcome for the loser, but it isn't the end of the world. Unless it is. There is a difference—a big difference—between a rising *price* of access and an absolute *lack* of access. The first leads to an industrial hollowing out. The second leads to outright deindustrialization. Just as with energy, countries that lose access

to the building blocks of modern industrial society do not just enter recession, they lose the capacity to play the game at all.

Now let's talk products.

There are literally hundreds of subsectors across the manufacturing space, comprising thousands of intermediate and end products *each*. Just a list of them all would slay more trees than this entire book. In the interest of brevity and environmental preservation, we are going to focus on the top eleven in terms of internationally traded value.

The single biggest piece of international manufactures trade is **automotive**. All those 30,000 parts per vehicle have their own supply chains. Since each part has its own labor requirements and cost structure, a *lot* of countries produce a *lot* of steps and often serve as suppliers to one another's brands and markets. It is pretty standard to find a German transmission in a Ford or a Mexican engine block in a Geely or Malaysian wiring in a BMW.

Of course that level of industrial interplay is totally going away. This isn't quite as disastrous as it sounds. Because everyone builds a bit of everything, any place where existing supply chain systems are concentrated generates significant network effects, *assuming there is sufficient consumer demand for the end product*. In China, where vehicle sales peaked in 2018, this is bad. In Europe, where it peaked decades ago, this is worse. But the Texas–Mexico axis is kind of perfect. When 25,000 of the parts are already produced (or assembled) within a fairly tight geography that is within the world's largest car market, the economics of adding each individual remaining part are not particularly daunting.

Heavy vehicle manufacturing—primarily farm, mining, and construction equipment—in many ways follows the same pattern as automotive. Lots of countries produce lots of different pieces and flip their intermediate inputs back and forth. Parts is parts is parts . . .

. . . but only to a point. Where billions of people want a car, not everyone feels the need to rush out and pick up the latest and greatest backhoe. There's also the far from minor point that you cannot finagle something the size of a combine into a standard container unit. Shipping difficulties alone mean that most locations that need farming or mining or construction equipment need to manufacture a lot of it themselves.

Taken together, heavy equipment is a bit like automotive in microcosm. Like automotive, heavy equipment manufacturing exists in the three big manufacturing hubs—East Asia, Europe, and North America—each of which both largely serves its own regional markets, but also provides upwards of one-fifth of components for one another's systems. Secondary powers—think Argentina, Brazil, and Russia—have managed to preserve their own heavy equipment manufacturing systems due to a mix of tariff barriers and necessity.

Moving forward, the German system will be absolutely hosed. Germany's demographics are too terminal to maintain production, it is too integrated with other terminally demographic countries to maintain its supply chains, it is too hooked upon industrial commodities imports to even attempt large-scale manufacturing, and it is too dependent upon extra-continental exports to maintain revenue flows.

Night-and-day-different is Brazil. Easier energy and material access. A largely homegrown industry that builds from the wheels up with minimal exposure to any other country's issues. Add in a hefty need domestically for construction *and* agricultural *and* mining equipment and Brazil might see an *expansion* in sales abroad as other countries fall out of the industry.

Sitting in between the Germans and Brazilians as regard to supply chain sanctity, domestic demand, the security of materials access, and demographic structures are the Italians, French, and Japanese. Italy's output tends toward smaller models for national reasons (smaller farm fields and congested cities require smaller equipment), which coincidentally are easier to export. France's system has captured nearly all domestic sales, but remains heavily export-geared. The French and Japanese models will have their wings clipped if they cannot maintain excellent relations with the Americans, the most popular end destination for both. The challenge is less about need and more about access. China faces a similar, if less intense, version of the same problem (internal demand in China is far higher than in France or Japan).

Still, there's a big difference between having 80 percent of a mining truck and having the whole thing. Luckily, anyone who is pretty good at automotive should be able to prove pretty good at heavy equipment. Many of the same skill sets and infrastructure requirements apply. Within North America, look to the Texas–Mexico axis for mining and construction gear, and Houston in particular. Want farm equipment? It'll still be the Midwest you're after.

The **lumber** industry* straddles the world of agriculture and manufacturing in complex and shifting ways. The value-add process from tree to lumber to pulp—or boards or aromatics or planks—adds up to a cool quarter of a trillion dollars of goods, and even that is before the real work begins that transforms the wood into furniture or veneer or cologne or house guts or charcoal. As you might guess, mapping the lumber industry's future—hell, mapping the lumber industry's *present*—is a snarly process.

So let's focus on the obvious bits:

Everyone uses everything. In different concentrations, of course, but everyone uses wood for construction and furniture and fuel and paper and so on. Wood is a base material for human existence, and it has been so long as there have been . . . humans.

But not everyone can produce wood in volume. The United States, as a large temperate zone country with extensive forested mid- and high altitudes, is by far the world's largest wood producer, but because of its penchant for large, single-family homes packed with furniture, it is also a net importer. Canada and Mexico fill nearly all of America's surplus needs. Forget needing to worry about the changes a post-globalized world will bring to North America; the continent is *already* looking after its own for this subsector.

In a deglobalized world, the industry's problems are threefold:

---

* That's "timber" if you're British.

First, the *United States* is the source for the more important of globally traded manufactured wood products, like agglomerates such as pellets, sawdust, and particleboard; panels like plywood; and pulp for paper. In a fractured world, such high-volume to low-value products just are not going to sail as far. That will be an issue for the forest managers and processors in the American Piedmont, but will largely pass unnoticed throughout the rest of North America. For consumers throughout Europe and Asia, dizzying product price inflation is pretty much a given, especially since nearly all reasonable product substitutes are petroleum based.

Second, what doesn't come from the United States tends to cross those geopolitical stress points I keep yammering on about: wood from heavily forested Southeast Asia goes to Northeast Asia, wood from Russia goes to Central and Western Europe. The variety of disruptions in the wood trade to come will be as varied as the product mixes. About the only flow that will maybe—probably?—be okay will be Scandinavian wood going elsewhere in Europe.

Third, there is a big looming environmental issue. In 2019, wood and various wood by-products accounted for 2.3 percent of Europe's *electricity* generation, mostly because the EU has some epically stupid regulations that consider the burning of wood and wood by-products to be carbon-neutral despite the pretty much undisputed fact that wood burning emits more carbon dioxide than even coal.

More to the point, some half of the trees felled are used as direct fuel, with the vast majority being burned within a day's walk of the forest's edge, particularly in India and sub-Saharan Africa. In a post-globalized world, very little about wood-as-fuel is going to be inhibited. If anything, the opposite will happen. If people cannot source globally traded energy products like natural gas or diesel, they will have a choice between not having heat for cooking or staying warm . . . or burning wood. The scale of the devastation—in terms of carbon emissions, land cover, biodiversity, smog, water quality, and safety—caused by half the world's population reverting to wood burning is difficult to wrap the mind around.

Next up: with the fall of Asia Inc., expect the world of **semiconductors** to look very different.

The fabrication of semiconductors is an exceedingly difficult, expensive, exacting, and—above all—*concentrated* process. Everything from the melting of the silicon dioxide powder, to the drawing of the liquid silicon into crystals, to the slicing of those crystals into wafers, to the etching, doping, and baking of those wafers, to the breaking of those wafers into individual semiconducting bits, to the assembling and packaging of those incredibly delicate bits into protective frames that can be slapped into GameBoys and smart lightbulbs and laptops, is typically *all* done at the same facility. Each step requires clean-room conditions, so rather than ship product multiple times via clean-chain transport, it is safer and more reliable to do it all in the same place.

Taiwan, Japan, and Korea do the really good semiconductors. Malaysia and Thailand handle the midmarket. China has the bargain basement. These facilities just don't move.

Or, at least, they haven't. But the world is changing and now they are moving. Constrained as they are by the need for very highly skilled workers, rock-solid electricity reliability, and a host of at-scale manufacturing support systems, most fab facilities will have little choice but to come to the United States.

This highlights a problem. American manufacturing—especially in the information technology space—is exceedingly high value-add. It can, and does, participate in the mass manufacture of high-end chips that are used in servers, laptops, and smartphones. So much so that even at the height of hollowed-out globalization, the United States remains responsible for roughly half of all chips *by value* despite producing only about one-ninth of chips *by number*.

Unfortunately, the future of manufacturing will still need lots of non-genius-level chips. American workers can only stoop to that level with significant subsidization. Nor can Mexico help: it lacks the culture of large-scale precision education required to generate the necessary workforce. If the goal is to manufacture something that only became digitized in recent decades, this is a mammoth problem. You can say "goodbye" to the Internet of Things.* And we should probably prepare for a generation of vehicles that are more analog than digital.

Of course, there is more to semiconductors than just semiconductors. By themselves, chips are useless. They must be incorporated into wiring harnesses and control boards and whatnot before being installed into other products. That intermediate stage requires eyes and fingers. This not only makes me think about future partnerships with Mexico and Colombia for intermediate manufacturing steps, but also suggests grand partnerships are on deck throughout the industries built around semiconductors in general, specifically computing, smartphones, and consumer electronics.

Computer assembly is surprisingly straightforward (most of the important components are, in fact, semiconductors) and it really just comes down to a question of price point. If it is a lower-quality product and can be done by hand, like, say, assembling motherboards, Mexico will be where it's at. If more precision is required—say, the installation of displays—and so automation is required, look to America.

The first post-globalization decade is going to be rough for **smartphone** users. Right now nearly the entire supply chain system is either in Europe or Asia. The European system is *probably* fine. Most European cell manufactures are in Scandinavia and their regional supply systems are unlikely to face too many challenges. But the Asian system? Phbbbt. Korea is the biggest player, and Korea's ongoing existence not only as a manufacturing or tech power but as a functional country is dependent upon the Koreans making their peace with the Japanese. A significant wrong step and the entire Android operating system will lose most of its hardware.

As for the Apple ecosystem, Apple designs its products in California, but then *entirely* outsources its production to a China-centric network that is certain to implode in the not-too-distant future. That entire manufacturing system will need to be remade from scratch within the United States. Southeast Asian states lack the required scale, while Mexico lacks

---

* Although, honestly, do we really need a digital thermometer that sends its results to your phone, or a clothes dryer that sings?

the precision capabilities. Even in the best-case scenario, once the world cracks we will go years between iPhone models.

Electronics—a very broad category that includes everything from white goods to fax machines to routers to blenders to hair dryers—are a bit like automotive in that every*one* has their fingers in every*thing*. Unlike automotive, however, there isn't much of a secret sauce. No one carries out corporate espionage or threatens war over the IP required to make a ceiling fan or garage door opener.

What defines the electronics space is that all-important feature of Order-era manufacturing: labor differentiation. The skill set—and above all, price point—that makes the casing for an office phone is different from the skill set that wires the cord or builds out the digital interface. The successful electronics manufacturers of the future will be the ones who have multiple labor skill sets and price points within close proximity. Look to both Southeast Asia and the U.S.-Mexican border region. Even more than the other sectors, electronics are a *big* deal. Far more than automotive or computers, electronics are a huge product category and are among the most labor intensive of the manufacturing sectors. It may sound sexy to build semiconductors domestically, but if you want to employ a couple million people, it's electronics you're after.

Another big-ticket subsector is **aerospace**. As with automotive, the big three Order-era manufacturing regions each has its own system: Boeing for North America, Airbus for Europe, and Comac for China. This won't last. Comac, despite decades of forced tech transfers and espionage, has proven unable to build all the required components for a functional jet. Post-Order it simply won't have the capacity to import what it needs and it will simply die.

Airbus isn't much better. Airbus is a multistate conglomerate of aerospace firms from Spain, France, Germany, and . . . the United Kingdom, and the United Kingdom is responsible for little things like wings and engines. In a post-Brexit world, the future of Airbus was already sketchy. Fast-forward to the aftermath of the pending U.S.-British trade deal and British aerospace will be folded into the Boeing family. Even worse, some of the biggest purchasers of Airbus aircraft have been the Persian Gulf long-haul carriers of Etihad, Emirates, and Qatar Air. All their flights originate or terminate in the Persian Gulf. With the Americans abandoning the Persian Gulf region to its own fate, there is *no way in hell* that civilian aviation will continue to operate in the area. If Airbus has a future, it will be in reinventing itself as a military supplier for a Europe that can no longer rely upon American strategic overwatch.

In the aftermath, Boeing will take over global aviation. The global aviation market will be much smaller, but there's something to be said for being the last man standing.

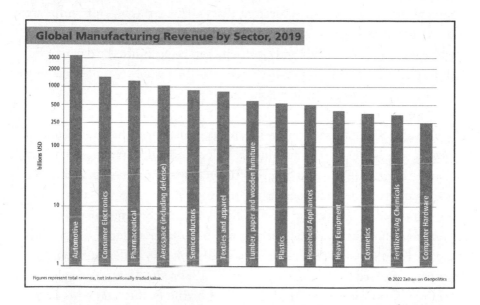

Global Manufacturing Revenue by Sector, 2019

Figures represent total revenue, not internationally traded value.

© 2022 Zeihan on Geopolitics

Machinery is where things get sketchy, and not simply because no one really puts machinery into a specific category for data collection. Germany is hands-down the world's best because the German cultural penchant for anal-retentive precision is precisely what makes for good machinery. Unfortunately for the world, culture cannot be transferred. No matter how much cash is splurged on it. Just ask the Chinese, whose efforts to pirate German designs and mimic German output have consistently met with failure.

This leads us to three outcomes. First, the United States will be okay. Mostly. While Americans aren't as good at this sort of thing as Germans, Houstonians come reasonably close. Second, the Chinese industrial position is utterly screwed. Even if nothing else goes wrong, the Chinese are utterly dependent upon German machinery to maintain their entire industrial behemoth. Third, the world writ large will experience a technological slowdown. Without the Germans doggedly pushing the envelope for what good machinery looks like, expect technical advancement in the space—which is required to manufacture everything else—to stall.

That's the high end. A complete reorganization on the low end is imminent as well. The two subsectors that will see the biggest shifts are **textiles** and **wiring**. Textiles is a low-skilled, labor-intensive industry while wiring is low-skilled and electricity intensive. Since the dawn of the Industrial Age, these sectors have been go-tos for newly industrializing countries trying to get their foot in the door.

No more.

Advances in automation now mean that most yarn, thread, cloth, and clothes can be made via machine in a developed country more cheaply than by semiskilled human hands in Bangladesh. Expect cloth and clothing made from natural fibers to relocate to where the wool and cotton are harvested: in particular, look to the American South, Australia, and New Zealand. For synthetic fibers, it will be difficult to top the U.S. Gulf Coast. Keep in mind that these "jobs" will look very different upon their return compared to their departure in the 1980s and 1990s. A single systems engineer can maintain an *acre*-sized textile facility all by his or her lonesome.

As to wiring, the U.S. shale revolution has granted the United States the cheapest electricity in the world. Not only is metals smelting coming back to the United States, so too is the next step in the process: wiring. Human hands will still be needed for finishing work in textiles and the fabrication of wiring harnesses for follow-on manufacturing, but what used to be a foot-in-the-door industry has irrevocably changed.

There's more at stake here than just a few stray socks. Textiles and footwear and wiring are typically among the earliest steps in the development process. Poorer countries use these subsectors not simply to gain income and begin urbanization, but also to build the sort of organizational and training experience to move up the value-added chain into more sophisticated manufacturing and systems. The relocation of these subsectors to more advanced economies in general, and their increasing automation in specific, denies countries that have not yet begun the development process the opportunity to access what has typically proven to be the bottom rung of the process. Whether the country in question is Bolivia or Laos or Congo, the risk is not of devolving to a world that predates 1939, but to one that predates 1800.

BREAKING DOWN THE BREAKDOWNS

If anything, this chapter *under*states the impacts that will reverberate through and break apart the world of manufacturing. Anything that raises the marginal cost of transport increases friction throughout the system. Simply a 1 percent increase in the cost of a subsidiary part largely obliterates the economics of an existing supply chain. Most locations will count themselves fortunate if their transport costs increase by only one *hundred* percent.

This is the world we're moving into. Changes in transport, finance, energy, and access to industrial inputs will make it poorer and more fractured, and will dial back much of the progress we've come to associate with the modern era. And even that assumes everyone can continue to source their needs, and in doing so survive as modern nations at all.

Unfortunately, that is not the end of the story. Now we have to discuss who will be around to see this future. Now we have to discuss who gets to engage in the one activity that supersedes all others: *eating*.

Now we have to discuss agriculture.

SECTION VII:
AGRICULTURE

WHAT'S AT STAKE

This section is the most important by far. If you can't get a widget, sure, you might not be able to manufacture a car. If the gas station runs out of fuel, sure, your life is going to be thrown into a tailspin. But if there isn't enough to eat, you die. Your neighbors die. Everyone in your town dies. Your country dies. Far more governments have fallen due to food failures than war or disease or political infighting combined. And it almost seems like a sick joke, but food is perishable. The one thing we absolutely must have is the one thing that can rot away in a matter of months, even if we are careful. Days if we are not. Food is fleeting, but hunger is forever.

If anything, the long term is even more crushing. If the food supply system breaks down for any reason, you cannot simply manufacture more. Even quick-grow oats need three months from planting to harvest. Corn takes six. Six months is typically also the soonest a hog goes to slaughter. Nine for cattle, although twelve is better—and that assumes feed lots and not free-range. Want to go organic and free-range? You're now talking twenty-four months. Minimum. Orchards typically don't produce for the first three years. Some take eight.

Nor can everyone play. One of the most difficult-to-move bulk products is *water*. Opposite sides of individual water molecules have strong negative and positive electrical charges, which make the molecules cling to everything, even each other.* Pumped water must overcome this friction, and that can only be done by constantly expending energy. It is the single largest reason why some half of the Earth's nonfrozen land surface is unsuitable for agriculture, and why meaningful cultivation of nearly

---

* It's called hydrogen bonding, for you chemistry nerds out there.

half of the lands we *do* farm first required the pumping technologies of the Industrial Age. Deindustrialization doesn't simply mean an end to industry; it means an end to large-scale food production and the return of large-scale famine.

If anything, I'm sugarcoating the challenges facing food production in a post-globalized world. To understand just how dire the future truly is, we need to have one final, one truly *brutal* chapter. We need to understand who will be fortunate enough to be able to *eat* in our disorderly future.

We need to go back the beginning, one last time.

BUILDING THE BOUNTY

Long ago, in a land far, far away,* humans domesticated their first plant: wheat. With that one achievement, everything else became possible. Pottery. Metals. Writing. Homes. Roads. Computers. Light sabers. *Everything*.

As food crops go, wheat is kind of perfect. It grows fairly quickly, making it a staple regardless of the growing season's length. It is easily hybridized to adapt to different elevations, temperatures, and humidity levels. Some varieties can be planted in autumn and harvested in the spring, taking the edge off the starving season. But above all, wheat just isn't particularly finicky. As many farmers half-joke, "wheat is a weed." Frosts late or early, flood or drought: when the weather isn't cooperative, sometimes wheat is the only thing that grows. As such, wheat has long been the grain of choice for most of humanity. As the years ticked by into millennia, nearly every culture, everywhere, grew wheat in significant volume, with most placing it at the center of the food experience.

Wheat did more than merely feed us. It changed us. Wheat's biological characteristics shaped our species' technological, geopolitical, and eco-

---

* Certainly predating the tenth millennia BCE in what is today Iraqi Kurdistan, for those of you keeping track.

nomic outcomes. Wheat's generally unfussy attitude isn't just about climate; it also doesn't require babysitting. Once the wheat seeds are tossed on the ground, you are pretty much done until harvest time. And if the wheat tends to itself, then farmers can do other things for 90 percent of the year.

There were other ancient grains—farro, millet, amaranth, teff—but all required either more land or water or labor (or typically all three) than wheat—in order to generate fewer calories. That's great for contemporary diets, whereby we are all getting a little pudgy, but less so for the preindustrial world, where starvation was the constant wolf at the door. For non-wheat-based cultures, contact with a group that ate wheat was often the kiss of death. The wheaties had more bodies that could be thrown into a conflict, not simply because more calories meant a bigger population, but also because they could press spears into farmers' hands for a high proportion of the year. The wheaties had access to more and more reliable calories because farmers could use their "free time" to grow *additional* crops, leading to even more calories that could support even larger populations. Sheep were particularly popular in the Middle East, with cows being the go-to for Europeans.* All that free time meant greater labor differentiation and from that, faster technological progress. The non-wheat-eaters just couldn't keep up.

If *unmanaged* wheat production—little more than tossing seeds on the ground—generated geopolitical power, *managed* wheat production elevated wheat-based cultures to dizzying heights. The secret is in the often-glossed-over concept of irrigation. We all understand that plants need water and sun, but most of us do not internalize the sort of miracles that can come from not simply water management, but water *control*.

I'm from Iowa, a place where it rains regularly, soil moisture is lush, and irrigation is almost unheard-of. Iowa agriculture is productive and robust and regular. Nothing too crazy there.

---

* Yup. That's right. Wheat brought us *cheese*!

One of my favorite places to visit is the interior of Washington State because of topography and people and culture—okay, *fine*, I go for the wine. The bulk of interior Washington is arid-to-desert. Annual rainfall is comparable to the Chihuahuan Desert. Winter temperatures rarely dip below freezing, while summer temperatures often top 100 degrees. Soil moisture is hysterically low.

Under preindustrial circumstances, very little could grow there. But runoff from the Cascades and Rockies form the Yakima, Snake, and Columbia Rivers, all of which flow through and merge in the region. The result is a sprawling series of sinewy greenbelts in the heart of one of the Western Hemisphere's driest regions. Full sun. Almost every day. Irrigation sourced from the largest-flow water system in North America. Check it out on Google Earth: the rough triangle connecting Yakima to Walla Walla to Moses Lake is either lush green from irrigation in the flats of the river valleys, or dead brown desert.*

Iowa is optimized for corn and soy—high-humidity, single-season, temperate crops. You get a "standard" six-to-eight-month growing season before winter descends. But in Washington you can grow almost *anything*: corn, soy, nuts, apples, pears, stone fruits, wheat, potatoes, grapes, sugar beets, hops, mint, and pretty much any vegetable under the sun. Productivity per acre is insane because all crops get blazing sun nearly every day *while also* getting as much water as they could possibly want. Product options are nearly limitless, and producers can grow things nearly all year round. Desert is death. Temperate is seasonal. But desert plus irrigation is *kablam*!

Ancient Mesopotamia, Egypt, and the Indus River basin all had sufficient tracts of *flat* in their river valleys, so no industrial-level technologies were required; preindustrial diversion channels did the trick just fine. For the era it was absolutely the perfect Geography of Success. All of the First Three civilizations married the potential of wheat to irrigation to generate

---

* California's Central Valley follows a very similar pattern for very similar reasons.

the world's first large-scale food surpluses, necessitating pottery to store the surpluses, roads to collect the surpluses, writing and arithmetic to keep track of the food surpluses, and cities full of nonfarmers to eat the surpluses. And so the Mesopotamians expanded into Anatolia and the Zagros, Egypt into Sudan and the Levant, and the people of the Indus from the Mahi to the Oxus to the mouth of the Persian Gulf.

As the technologies of civilization leaked out of the First Three into the broad reaches of the ancient world, the combination of managed and unmanaged wheat production turned many colonies into daughter cultures with their own food surpluses, which in turn spawned granddaughter cultures. In all cases, however, food availability remained a common restriction, placing an absolute cap on population, urbanization, technological progress, and cultural expansion. And while wheat was a willing partner, the grain still demanded labor for sowing and harvesting (and a whole lot of labor for managed irrigation systems).

The solution to this constraint proved deceptively simple: conquer someone with large-scale managed wheat production and put their people to work growing food for your growing empire. In most cases, that "someone" was the world's lands with the best-*managed* wheat systems, where the bulk of the population existed in wheat-growing slavery: the founding civilizations of humanity.

In the sixth century BCE, the Persians of the Achaemenid Empire, led by Cyrus the Great, conquered their Mesopotamian predecessors, initiating the Mesopotamian-Persian rivalry, which continues to the current day. Shortly after, Cyrus's descendants—Cambyses and Darius—added Egypt and the Indus to the empire. The Achaemenid expansion then stopped for the simple reason that all the food production that was worth having had already been conquered. Stalled military campaigns led to infighting, which led to the tender mercies of Xerxes,* which led to rebellion, which led to the fourth-century BCE rise of the Macedonians under

---

*   For Sparta!

Alexander the Great, who, like the Achaemenids before him, conquered the entirety of the known (fed) world. And, like the Achaemenids before him, Alexander too largely stopped once the great granaries of the First Three were under his control.*

And so history unfolded: the rise of empires for the next 2,500 years revolved around the securing of lands that could feed expansion. Spain for the Romans, Ukraine for the Russians, Poland for the Germans, South Africa for the British, Egypt for pretty much everyone at some point.

Three broad developments broke the wheel of wheat-induced conquering.

First, the industrial era introduced humanity to synthetic agricultural inputs, most importantly fertilizers, but also pesticides, herbicides, and fungicides. Lands already used for agriculture doubled their output in short order, but subpar lands that had been passed over throughout history could experience quadrupling (or more) of their preindustrial output levels. Farm fields crept across the Earth. In the new technological era, the Geography of Success changed. Lands that had once lain fallow became breadbaskets. Cool, wet, low-sun northern Germany suddenly became a food producer nearly on par with northern France, while the ability to grow crops in Siberia made life in Russia a tiny bit less miserable.

Empires still conquered Egypt,† but with access to industrial technologies, many cultures could now control reliable, large-scale food production within their own territories. Locations that were once imperial marches quickly matured into legitimate challengers to the more established players. It took decades for the older powers to come to grips with such profoundly altered power balances. We know this come-to-grips era as the German unification wars of the 1800s and the far greater conflicts that followed soon after.

Nor are industrial inputs merely about fertilizers and fungicides. Electricity and steel are technologies of industrialized agriculture as well. Put

---

*   Also, he died at age thirty-two. So there's that.

†   Because it was *so* easy.

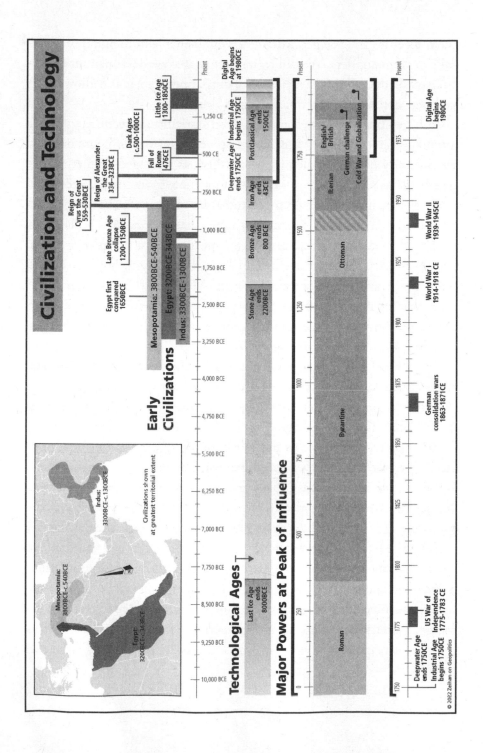

Civilization and Technology

Early Civilizations

Technological Ages

Major Powers at Peak of Influence

Reign of Cyrus the Great 559-530BCE

Reign of Alexander the Great 336-323BCE

Dark Ages c.500-1000CE

Little Ice Age 1300-1850CE

Fall of Rome 476CE

Digital Age begins 1980CE

Late Bronze Age collapse 1200-1150BCE

Egypt first conquered 1650BCE

Mesopotamia: 3800BCE-540BCE

Egypt: 3200BCE-343BCE

Indus: 3300BCE-1300BCE

Deepwater Age / Industrial Age ends 1750CE / begins 1750CE

Postclassical Age ends 1500CE

Iron Age ends 43CE

Bronze Age ends 800 BCE

Stone Age ends 2200BCE

Last Ice Age ends 8000BCE

Civilizations shown at greatest territorial extent

Indus: 3300BCE-c.1300BCE

Mesopotamia: 3800BCE-c.540BCE

Egypt: 3200BCE-c.343BCE

Present

1,250 CE

500 CE

250 BCE

1,000 BCE

1,750 BCE

2,500 BCE

3,250 BCE

4,000 BCE

4,750 BCE

5,500 BCE

6,250 BCE

7,000 BCE

7,750 BCE

8,500 BCE

9,250 BCE

10,000 BCE

Iberian

Ottoman

Byzantine

Roman

English/British

German challenge

Cold War and Globalization

Digital Age begins 1980CE

World War II 1939-1945CE

World War I 1914-1918 CE

German consolidation wars 1863-1871CE

US War of Independence 1775-1783 CE

Deepwater Age ends 1750CE / Industrial Age begins 1750CE

1750 250 500 725 1000 1250 1500 1750 1975 Present

© 2022 Zeihan on Geopolitics

them together and you get hydraulics, which enable us to pump water up hills or from aquifers. We can *create* fresh water via desalination. Industrialization doesn't simply increase our output per acre; it also allows us to produce foodstuffs on previously barren lands.

Refrigeration too is an industrial-level agricultural technology that's a not-so-minor miracle. Meats now last weeks instead of hours or days. Perishability hasn't so much been banished, as managed. Something as perishable as an apple, once subjected to some very industrial-era tricks that involve a near-freezing-temperature, blacked-out warehouse that had all the oxygen pumped out, can last more than a *year*. When placed in cool, dark, sealed, desiccated storage, wheat can last up to *eight* years. For fresh stuff, modern genetics improves durability to both withstand temperature variations and delay spoilage. Mix this all into a geopolitical salad that involves industrial transport options that have become *so* cheap and *so* reliable, we regularly ship anything, anywhere in the world on a regular basis. We even ship *hay*.

The second factor that broke the world of wheat was, shocker, the Order. By making the seas safe for all and banning imperial expansions, the Americans overturned the previous millennia of agriculturally driven conquering. The lands of the First Three all achieved and/or consolidated their independence from their imperial masters. Once-marginal lands the world over experienced explosive growth as imported technologies and inputs transformed the natures of their possibles. This "Green Revolution" ultimately proved responsible for nearly quadrupling the agricultural bounty of what we know today as the developing world. By far the biggest winners of this shift were the countries of South, Southeast, and East Asia, home to half the global population. The Order, combined with the dissemination of industrial technologies, has shifted 3 *billion* people from living on the razor's edge to being food-secure. Better modern inputs, fewer imperial-era restrictions, more farms on more acreage, larger yields of a greater variety of products. Wins all around.

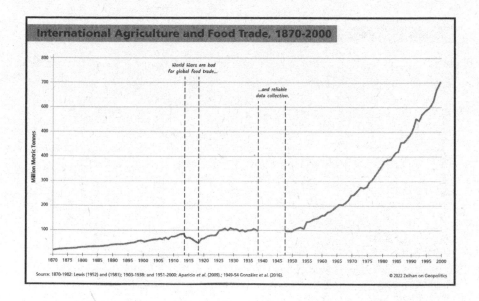

International Agriculture and Food Trade, 1870-2000

World Wars are bad
for global food trade...

...and reliable
data collection.

Source: 1870-1902: Lewis (1952) and (1981); 1903-1938: and 1951-2000: Aparicio et al. (2009).; 1949-54 González et al. (2016).

© 2022 Zeihan on Geopolitics

That greater variety is the third and arguably the most important factor that ended the Wheat Age: people chose to simply *stop growing wheat.*

In the long-lived Imperial Age, control of the high-output wheat-producing zones was the very definition of success. Reliable food supply directly led to reliable population growth and reliable military expansion. But in the era of the industrialized Order, the strategic calculus changed radically. Global trade softened the imperative of needing to obsess about wheat self-sufficiency. American strategic overwatch removed the paranoia of needing to prepare for imperial assault. The new inputs combined with the Green Revolution meant global wheat security had been achieved. So agriculturalists the world over got down to the business of reshuffling the geography of global food production, with a particular focus on serious specialization.

Higher calorie and protein-content products such as corn, soy, lentils, or oats spread like weeds. The world's better rangeland shifted over to animal husbandry. Irrigated lands—whether in Iraq or California's Central Valley—took up orcharding at industrial scales.

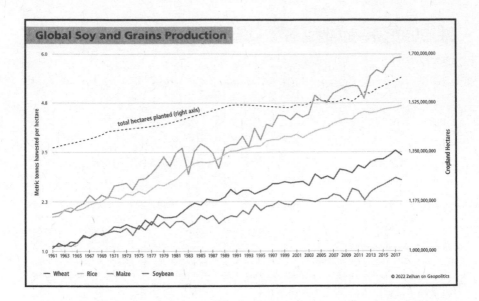

Global Soy and Grains Production

© 2022 Zeihan on Geopolitics

In the developing world, where the industrial technologies were new, the result was a massive expansion of food production of all types, with wheat still a central player. Wheat was simply more likely to be planted on land that in the preindustrial period had been useless.

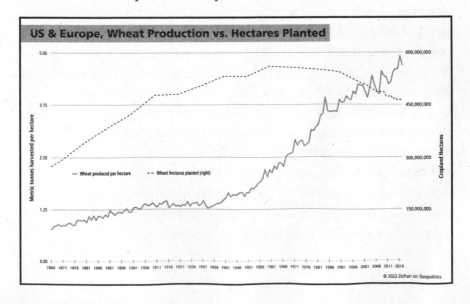

US & Europe, Wheat Production vs. Hectares Planted

© 2022 Zeihan on Geopolitics

In the advanced world, where the industrial technologies were more established, wheat was steadily pushed to the margins while more productive lands were used for everything else. *Anything* else.

The Order's encouragement of economies of scale means every patch of land and microclimate tends to produce the single thing that it does best, as prompted by the needs of a fully unified global market. Corn and soy demand heat and humidity, placing them in continental interiors. A single frost can destroy a citrus crop, pushing citrus into the subtropics. Rice doesn't just like heat and humidity; most versions need to be *drowned* at various stages of growth—perfect for warm, wet lands. Oats and barley like it cooler and drier, shifting them to higher latitudes. *All* grains need a dry period to ripen before harvest. As a rule, the upper latitudes are simply too cold for anything except specific wheat varieties or maybe beets,* while the tropics don't get cool or dry enough for most crops to germinate and dry properly—encouraging the adoption of completely different crop sets: everything from mangos to yams.

Diets changed. As peoples of the developing world gained access to international trade, they did what you would expect: improved agricultural output at home, got a bigger cut of their raw materials extraction than they did as colonies, urbanized, diversified into manufacturing, earned more money, and ate more and better foods, which increasingly came from farther and farther away. In East Asia this has meant incremental shifts from rice to wheat, and a massive surge in demand for pork. In Iran it has meant more rice as a supplement to wheat. In northeast China, the Caribbean, and sub-Saharan Africa this has meant incrementally less sorghum and millet and root crops, and incrementally more rice, chicken, and beef.

With basic food security taken care of, "agriculture" today means much more than just staples, and in many cases doesn't even mean food. We now not only produce corn and wheat and soy and rice, but also potatoes

---

*   *Bletch!*

and lentils and apples and cherries and hazelnuts and almonds and avocados and strawberries and blueberries and quinoa and hops and timber and cotton and flax and flowers and cannabis. Each has its own preferred temperature and humidity zone and soil type, and the Order enabled each region to maximize its advantages, produce at scale, and sell to a hungry, wealthy, growing global market. Massive product displacements from wheat are now the norm.

Consider two countries with nearly nothing in common in regard to geography or history or climate or culture or economic structure: New Zealand and Egypt. New Zealand is a very wet country, while densely populated Egypt has lots of extra labor to tend to plants. In contemporary times both *could* easily grow sufficient volumes of wheat for their needs. In fact, if they chose to, they would be among the world's most lucrative wheat producers.

Neither plays that game.

Instead, the pair produce products more customized to their environmental and labor conditions—products in ravenously high demand globally. New Zealand's ultra-mild climate makes it the world's most efficient dairy, timber, and fruit producer, with cow paddocks, industrial forests, and orchards crowding out less profitable wheat fields. Similarly, Egypt grows cotton and citrus for export rather that wheat for local consumption. Both countries export their ag products for top dollar, and then import cheaper foodstuffs—like wheat—that they could have grown themselves had global agronomics pushed them in a more autarkic direction.

This banishing of wheat to the periphery means the bulk of the world's wheat is grown in just a handful of places: the American Great Plains, the Canadian Prairie Provinces, Australia's Murray-Darling Basin plus the continent's southwestern fringes, the drylands of central Argentina, southeast England, the endless small fields of highly protectionist France, dumpling country in northern China, Pakistan and India to feed the teeming masses and limit the need for imports, and the great expanses of the Russian wheat belt, a zone that includes Belarus, Ukraine, and Kazakhstan. (Of these, only France, Pakistan, and India grow wheat in areas that could grow lots of other things more efficiently, but for these three, efficiency isn't what governments are targeting.)

The industrialized Order hasn't simply enabled us to increase the total calories grown by a factor of seven since 1945; it has enabled vast swaths of the planet to have large populations when geography alone wouldn't previously support them. Populations in North Africa are up by over a factor of *five* since 1950, Iran over six, while Saudi Arabia and Yemen have increased by over a factor of *ten*. Bulk food shipments originating a continent (or more) away are now a commonality.

For agriculture, industrial technologies changed the *where* and *how much* of the possible, the Order changed the *access* and *reach* of the possible, while mass displacement changed the *what* and *variety* of the possible. More land, some 11.5 billion acres, is under cultivation than at any other time in human history. More crops—in 2020, total agricultural output was worth about $8 trillion—are in production than any time in human history. That's roughly 10 percent of *global* GDP, the largest value of any economic sector. More of those foods, over one-third by value, are internationally traded than at any other time in human history. Even much of the remainder isn't consumed locally (just how many Florida oranges can Floridians eat?).

If the goal is efficiency and rising standards of living, this all makes sense. But it doesn't take much of a shift in the mechanics of global trade to shatter this interlinked system. If the geography of access shrinks, what makes the "most sense" changes drastically.

Manufacturing and energy and finance are cool and all. They have collectively brought the entirety of humanity into the modern age. But agriculture? It is *the* first step along the path from the misty terrors of yesteryear to the world we know. Should contemporary agriculture unwind, it will mean a massive contraction in volumes and varieties and availabilities and reliabilities of foodstuffs. It will mean that entire countries that have used modern agricultural technologies and markets to pull themselves out of the preindustrial age will now fall backward into the preindustrial past. At preindustrial *population levels*.

THE GEOPOLITICS OF VULNERABILITY

Let's reexamine everything else from this project so far, but from an agricultural point of view.

Let's begin with **manufacturing**.

The Order's emphasis on efficiencies, economies of scale, and expanding the reach of industrial technologies shapes not simply where certain crops are grown, but *how* they are grown. Of largest consequence are the row crops, products that can be grown in an industrial manner via the use of heavy equipment to plant, fertilize, weed, and harvest them.

The largest of the row crops by volume produced are wheat, soy, corn, potato, canola, beans, peas, buckwheat, sugar beets, flax, sunflower, and safflower. Because operating heavy equipment on slopes or near wetlands generates impressively expensive industrial accidents, the marriage of such equipment and row crops really only works in agricultural zones that are both flat and large, making such equipment absolutely critical throughout Canada, the United States, Brazil, Argentina, Australia, South Africa, the Netherlands, Poland, Romania, Bulgaria, Belarus, Ukraine, and Russia, and making it regionally important within the United Kingdom, France, Germany, Spain, Belgium, Algeria, Bolivia, Mexico, China, and New Zealand. Collectively these row crops in these countries account for about one-quarter of all global food production by mass. Larger farms mean larger, more specialized equipment. Specialized equipment means specialized manufacturing supply chains. And specialized supply chains are woefully vulnerable to disruption.

For mass row-crop *producers*, the list of would-be equipment suppliers is exceedingly short.

In the late globalization period there are but four places that produce the relevant equipment for mass row-crop agriculture in both bulk and quality. Europe's manufacturing capacity is multinational and subject to the coherence (or lack thereof) of the European Union. China's equipment is on the small side. The average size of a Chinese wheat or corn field is typically about one acre, less than 1/350 the size of its American equivalents. North America's manufacturing capacity is intact but heavily relies on East Asia for computing components. The Brazilians have some limited production capacity, largely for their own market, but with a smattering of exports to South Asia and sub-Saharan Africa.

In a deglobalized world, European supply chains face severe constraints. German-made farm equipment requires the same supply chain linkages throughout Central Europe as German automotive, as well as global markets for sales. Neither is possible moving forward. French equipment manufacturing capacity is likely to pass through the needle successfully, due to both its total capture of its home market and less complicated access to North America. Chinese farm equipment production and exports are simply a dead letter, from both production and export angles. Look to Brazil to pick up some of the slack.

For *all* agricultural producers, the question will be whether they can tie themselves into one of the remaining equipment suppliers. Luckily, the list of big-field row-croppers disconnected from manufacturing centers is a short one. It would be surprising if the regional geopolitic breaks against Algeria and Bulgaria and Poland and Romania and Spain and the United Kingdom, but it would be *more* surprising if it breaks against *none* of them. Australia, New Zealand, and South Africa are not at all proximate to their equipment sources, but they also do not face supply routes nearly as gauntlety.

Outside of the big Cadillac-style mega machines necessary for row cropping, South and Southeast Asia use smaller equipment for their smaller fields. With China out of the mix as a supplier there is no clean substitute. India *does* make a lot of small work trucks and tractors, but its supply chain sourcing spans the globe (and includes China). Everyone who sports largely internal supply chains and makes appropriately sized kit—Brazil and Italy come to mind—is a *looooong* way away. Probably better for Thailand and Malaysia to retool some of their automotive sector to plug the looming gaps. That will not—that *cannot*—occur overnight.

The worst of the impacts will be felt in the former Soviet states of Russia, Ukraine, Kazakhstan, and Belarus. Sure, as with most heavy equipment manufacture, most is made close to home. But every joke you've ever heard about Russian tractors is more fact than fiction. Russia's fall from grace has been so hard that few farmers have *ever* been able to purchase new equipment in the post-Soviet era. What they operate is *old*. And as much as the former Soviet space is known for manufacturing subpar equipment, it is more known for shoehorning foreign parts into local gear to keep it running. Even worse, the most successful and productive farms in the FSU are the large ones . . . that import their equipment from elsewhere. Whether it is because the old stuff finally breaks down or the new stuff is unavailable, agriculture in this corner of the world is going to turn desperate indeed. The pain will not stay bottled up. In the late-Order period, these countries are the origin of some 40 percent of the world's wheat exports.

The picture darkens considerably once one starts looking at the world of **transport**.

The bulk nature of most agricultural outputs necessitates giant bulk shipping vessels. The specialized nature of large farm equipment necessitates specialized shipping systems (there's no shoving a massive combine into an itty-bitty shipping container). The Order's penchant for maximized production of specialized products combined with the input-intensive nature of contemporary agricultural production requires endless merchant fleets. While "only" 20–25 percent of grains and soy are transported internationally, some 80 percent of the *inputs* are.

These flows—*all* these flows—will be endangered to one degree or another, and *any* interruption in *any* of them will have devastating knock-on effects up and down the supply systems, indeed all the way to the dinner table. If a carburetor is delayed three months in getting to the assembly location, the car can still be finished—just with a delay of three months. If pesticide or fertilizer or diesel fuel or raw soy or a refrigeration unit is delayed three months, much of the food product itself will be *lost* somewhere along the chain of planting-growth-harvesting-processing-shipment.

There's the hardly minor issue of planetary geography. Roughly two-thirds of the human population lives in the temperate and near-temperate zones of the Northern Hemisphere. This hemisphere is a net food *importer*. About the only good news is that the Southern Hemispheric temperate zones—regions highly resistant to the coming geopolitical storm—are very lightly populated compared to the Northern Hemisphere. That makes the countries of the global South big food exporters. But considering that the collective size of their agricultural regions is less than one-fifth that of the Northern Hemisphere . . . the global South can only help so much. Any Northern Hemispheric disruptions to either food production directly, or supporting industries indirectly, immediately turn into food shortages on a scale humanity has never before experienced.

There's another level to all this:

Under the globalized Order, most countries specialize in producing nonfood products of various sorts—for example, light manufacturing for Ireland, cotton for Uzbekistan, oil for Algeria, electronics for Japan—and then use export sales to purchase internationally traded foodstuffs. For most countries these sorts of swaps will no longer be nearly as available. Hit *any* part of this system—tankers for oil or fuel, LNG tankers or pipelines for natural gas, jets for high-value products like semiconductors, containerized shipping for automobiles, bulk cargo vessels for potash, finished fertilizer or raw grains—and it quickly ripples not simply to the core of agricultural production on the front end, but to the ability of food importers to pay for those imports on the back end.

The greatest pains will be felt in the same regions and in the same sectors we keep returning to:

- Manufactured products out of East Asia and Northern Europe,
- Processed industrial commodities out of the Persian Gulf, East Asia, and Northern Europe,
- Food products inbound to North Africa, Northeast Asia, the Persian Gulf, and South Asia,

- Energy shipments on the Persian Gulf and the Red, Baltic, Black, South China, and East China Seas.

Of these, the most critical are those for the inputs that translate not simply into fuels, but into the sorts of products that make everything else in the Industrial Age possible.

This brings us to **energy** disruptions.

Part of this is painfully obvious. Oil and oil-derived products are critical to all things agricultural. If they aren't present in sufficient volumes, the tractors, combines, trucks, trains, terminals, and ships that are central to producing and transporting foodstuffs and their input streams simply do not function. And forget the electric vehicle craze. Leaving aside the minor details that, come harvest time, farmers are out in the fields eighteen hours a day (or more) and that there is *no* battery system in the world that can handle that sort of out-charge with only six (or fewer) hours of in-charge, as well as the less minor detail that an EV ship could not recharge *in the middle of the freakin' ocean*, electrification technology does not yet exist that can manage the high power-to-size requirements for either heavy equipment or long-range oceanic shipping. There simply is neither an existing technology nor an imminent technological revolution that can replace oil and natural gas in the agricultural sector.

And how's this for a Throwback Thursday? One of the great technological advances that brought us not simply the modern age but basic civilization itself was the ability to capture energy from moving water and air via watermills and windmills in order to grind grains into flour. We now manage said grinding with *electric* mills. In a world suffering circumscribed access to the basic energy inputs *that generate electricity*, good luck maintaining not simply an industrial lifestyle, but a *post-waterwheel lifestyle*. Think all the way back to the first chapter. How many of the world's varied geographies have good geographies for waterwheels? You think there's enough of them to grind flour for 8 *billion* people???

Also, unfortunately, the energy question is about a lot more than "merely" fuel. To explain that, we need to jump to the next restriction on agriculture: **industrial commodities**.

Remember how there's more to oil and natural gas than simply moving things around? Oil is typically *the* primary ingredient for pesticides, herbicides, and fungicides, while most fertilizers' base materials also include natural gas. The collective adoption of such chemical inputs in the late 1800s in the advanced world increased grain output by roughly a factor of four, with the developing world participating in such bounty in the decades after World War II and especially after the Cold War. Without such inputs, the reverse will be true.

Every soil type—every crop—demands not only different amounts of fertilizer, but different *types* as well. Each fertilizer has its own grab bag of geopolitical complications, resulting in a dizzying mix of implications.

Natural gas is central to nearly all aspects of the fabrication of nitrogen-type fertilizers. Nitrogen is the go-to nutrient if the goal is leafy growth, making nitrogen-type fertilizers key both for grasses such as corn and wheat as well as fruits and vegetables (flowers are specialized "leaves"). Anyone who cannot source crude for domestic refining cannot produce nitrogen fertilizers.

This will be a problem nearly everywhere in the Eastern Hemisphere, but as with the broader energy question, the complications will be particularly intense in Korea, Central Europe, and the bulk of sub-Saharan Africa. The country that will certainly face the biggest declines in agriculture output will be China. Not only do the Chinese grow pretty much *everything* at scale, but Chinese soil and water quality is so low that Chinese farmers generally use more fertilizer per calorie produced than any other country—*five times* the global average in the case of nitrogen fertilizers.

More interested in crops than locations? Consider that at least two of the top five producers of this entire list of products will face chronic nitrogen fertilizer shortages:

Almonds, apples, beans, blueberries, broccoli, cabbage, carrots, cashews, cassava, cauliflower, cherries, coconuts, corn, cucumbers, currants, eggplant, figs, fonio, grapes, green beans, kiwifruit, lettuce, millet, oats, okra, olives, onions, peaches, peas, pineapples, plums, potatoes, pulses, quince, quinoa, raspberries, rice, rye, sesame, squashes, strawberries, sweet potatoes, turnips, wheat, and yams.

This—all this—is unfortunately just the opener for this particular hellscape.

There is a lot more to fertilizer than simply oil or natural gas. There's a second classification of fertilizer based on a material called phosphate. Phosphate is, in essence, fossilized bird poop, which serves as a suitable substitute to . . . human poop. I'm slightly oversimplifying here, but the mined bird poop is treated with acid, ground to a powder, and tossed on plants. Its commodification and production in industrial volumes has proven absolutely critical to the rise of industrialized agriculture, especially because a) there are a *lot* more people who need food now than there were in 1945, and b) most of humanity agrees that storing and spreading our *own* poop is something we would really rather not do. Testament to these facts? Phosphate-based fertilizers experienced an eightfold increase in production and application since 1960.

Regardless of your feelings on the topics of population,* the world's biggest phosphate suppliers are the United States, Russia, China, and Morocco. Hopefully by now you know what I think is going to happen to supplies out of America (hoarded for regional use) and Russia (say "goodbye" to anything that once emerged from the empire of broken dreams). China's production comes from its deep inland western provinces, which are in most cases secessionist, so keeping Chinese production internationalized requires China threading not one needle, but instead three.

That leaves Morocco as the world's great hope, and for once there *is* actual hope. In addition to its already-productive phosphate assets, Morocco occupies a territory called the Western Sahara, which has the world's largest *undeveloped* phosphate supplies, most of which are located

---

*   Or poop.

within a few miles of the coast.* Even should Russian and Chinese sup-
plies fall off the market completely, the United States plus an enlarged
Morocco should be able to supply sufficient volumes for all of North
America, South America, Europe, and Africa. That's *great* for them.
And . . . wretched for everyone else.

This is actually worse than it sounds. One of the many complications
the world of hyperspecialized globalized agriculture has created for itself
is that we now grow or raise each plant or animal where it makes the most
economic sense within a holistic system. For example, cattle have shifted
into the Great Plains, while corn and soy dominate the Midwest. In the
pre-Order days, the two would have been more or less colocated. In that
pre-Order system, the farmers would use cattle manure to provide phos-
phorus for their fields. Without immediate proximate supplies of animal
poop, farmers now have no choice but to use artificial, phosphate-type
fertilizers. That has required both international supply chains to source
and process the phosphates, and gasoline and diesel to get the fertilizer to
the field. This entire model collapses in a post-globalized system.

But as critical as nitrogen and phosphate fertilizers are, they cannot
hold a candle to potassium fertilizers. On the outcome side, most plants
at harvest are between 0.5 percent and 2.0 percent potassium by weight,
with the most potassium-heavy bits being the parts that feed into the
human supply chain. *Every* crop needs a *lot* of potassium every year. On
the sourcing side, nearly all the world's potassium comes from a mineral known as potash, and internationally traded potash comes from just
six places: Jordan, Israel, Germany, Russia, Belarus, and Canada. Jordan
is a borderline failed state even with unlimited American security and
economic support and de facto Israeli management. In a post-American

---

* There's a tedious, drawn-out saga within Africa on whether Western Sahara is a
  Moroccan province, a disputed territory, or an independent nation. Considering
  that Morocco has controlled the WS as long as I've been alive, and that this is a
  chapter about how much of the world is going to soon be starving in the dark, you
  can imagine how much I care about such minutiae.

Middle East, Israel will be many things, but a "trade hub" will not be one of them. German supplies are insufficient to help out any country beyond those which Germany borders. Russia and Belarus are already on the other side of a new Iron Curtain. That just leaves Canada. *Thank God for Canada!* South America and Australia—the continents that produce and export the greatest volumes of foodstuffs relative to their populations—have almost no potash. China imports half its needs. South Asia, Europe, and sub-Saharan Africa are painfully shy of both potash *and* phosphates.

There is one itty-bitty ray of hope in the coming global fertilizer—and from that, food—shortage: most studies by most agricultural scientists suggest that most farmers have been overfertilizing for decades, especially when it comes to potassium fertilizers. This would suggest that at present most farms in most places have a potassium surplus baked into the soil. This would further suggest that most farmers can reduce their inputs of fertilizer without sacrificing yields by all that much. The question is, for how long? Most data suggest up to a decade. That might seem insufficient. It is not. It is *wildly* insufficient. But it does suggest that perhaps we will have a bit of time to scramble for solutions rather than jumping directly into continental-sized famines the first time someone hijacks a cargo ship.

Let's end this cheery discussion with a look at the interaction between agriculture and **finance**. This might sound obvious, but agriculturalists tend to not get paid for their product until they . . . deliver it. This might sound even more obvious, but agriculturalists cannot work double shifts or odd hours or opposite seasons to generate more product. Stuff is planted or born when seasonal weather allows it. Stuff is grown or raised while the weather of a different season enables it. Stuff is harvested or slaughtered once it reaches maturity, almost certainly in yet another season. *And only then* are agriculturalists paid.

But we've come a long way from preindustrial days, when the only inputs for farming were a few bags of unmilled wheat that had been held back from the last harvest, or when the only cost for raising animals was an easily distracted, stargazing shepherd boy. Contemporary industrialized agriculture has a dizzying array of inputs. They fall into three general categories.

Raw stock. Seeds for planting sounds simple, but in many cases hybridized, genetically modified, or otherwise specialized seeds are far more expensive than simply holding back some of the previous year's harvest. Such specialized seeds easily lead to harvests triple of what could be grown the old-fashioned way. In 2021, seeds for a single acre of corn plantings ran about $111. Tree stock for orchards needs to be purchased. The never-ending process of selective breeding to generate bigger, more productive, and tastier meat products requires a never-ending effort to secure the perfect stud. In the pre-COVID low-inflation days of 2019, a basic stud sheep easily set back a rancher $600, while a run-of-the-mill horny bull went for $1,500. In the everything-shortage economy at the time of this writing, those numbers have doubled. Should you want something special, top-notch Black Angus breeding stock can easily set you back seven grand at auction.

Growth inputs. These include fertilizers, herbicides, pesticides, fungicides, and possibly irrigation for plant crops, and silage, grazing rights, and medical inputs for animal husbandry. Such expenses are not once-and-done. Whether you are engaged in plant or animal husbandry, pretty much everything but wheat requires a degree of attention—and inputs—all season long.

Equipment. A modern combine will set a farmer back a cool half million. Dairy cows not only must be shielded from the weather, but they require facilities capable of milking them multiple times a day. Most of the newer, low-labor, mostly automated facilities have installation costs in excess of $10 million. As global demographics age and labor costs rise, orcharders have even invested in labor-saving machines that spray trees, automate irrigation tasks, and pick, separate, clean, and even pack fruits.

All of this is in addition to more baseline costs such as fuel and labor.

A typical 200-acre corn farm in Minnesota can expect input outlays of about $85,000 every year. A typical 5,500-acre family corporation wheat

Average Productivity and Cost of Inputs by Crop

	Continuous Corn	Rotation Corn	Rotation Soybeans	Wheat	Double-Crop Soybeans
Average yield per acre (bushels)	169	180	55	77	38
Harvest Price	$3.80	$3.80	$10.10	$5.70	$10.10
Annual Revenue	$642	$684	$556	$439	$394
Less Variable Costs					
Fertilizer	120	111	47	71	35
Seed	111	111	67	44	78
Pesticides	58	58	50	30	45
Dryer Fuel	33	27	0	0	5
Machinery Fuel	12	12	8	8	5
Machinery Repairs	22	22	18	18	15
Hauling	17	18	6	8	4
Interest	12	11	7	6	6
Insurance and Miscellaneous	38	38	34	9	9
Total Variable costs	$423	$408	$237	$194	$202
Net profit per acre	$219	$276	$319	$245	$192

Source: Purdue Crop Cost and Return Guide, 2020   All prices in USD   © 2022 Zeihan on Geopolitics

farm in Montana can expect that annual figure to top $1 million. None of that would be possible unless *everything* was financed. Disrupt that finance and the entire system collapses.

Among the advanced economies, the financialization of the agricultural system is often integrated directly into governing systems in order to smooth out the process and protect farmers and ranchers from the vulgarities of cycles financial, economic, and climatic. For example, the Farm Credit System, which supports American agricultural producers, enjoys a direct congressional charter and is one of the United States' largest financial institutions.

Most countries lack that sort of organizational and financial heft, and are far more subject to the whims and trends of global financial availability. From 1990 through 2020, that wasn't much of a problem. Capital flight from the former Soviet world, hyperfinancialization out of China, and heavy agricultural subsidies out of Europe and Japan, combined with the ridiculously available and cheap credit made possible by the Boomer Bulge, has deluged agriculturalists the world over with all the financing they could stomach. But between deglobalization and the global demographic inversion, that environment is turning inside out. Borrowing costs will rise even as borrowing terms tighten and liquidity vanishes. Agricultural producers will suffer right along with everyone else, but when agricultural producers cannot source financing, there are food shortages.*

Simply put, disruption in nearly any sector immediately translates into a disruption of agricultural production with catastrophic outcomes.

---

* Love organic products and think they can help solve these issues? You must suck at math. Their inputs are *much* higher. Specialized seeds. Higher volumes of water. Nonchemical pesticides and herbicides and such are more expensive as well as bulkier to transport and store and apply. The far lower effectiveness of organic inputs necessitates at least quadruple the passes over fields that synthetics require, necessitating yet more labor and fuel. All that extra activity on a field encourages higher soil erosion and water contamination than traditional farming, which in turn demand more inputs. The leading organic "fertilizer" for orcharding is *chicken parts not suitable for human consumption*. It doesn't take much imagination to visualize the gooey, pungent logistics chain for shredded chicken guts, which, of course, require a refrigeration chain to prevent utterly decadent levels of nastiness, drastically increasing organics' carbon footprint. And at the back end, the result is far lower yields per acre, meaning even *more* land with even *more* low-effectiveness inputs required to generate the same volume of food as more conventional practices. You can have organic foods or environmentally friendly foods. You cannot have both.

AVOIDING—OR ACCEPTING— THE WORST

Let's do some rank ordering.

The first category of food-exporting countries are those whose supply systems for everything from finance to fertilizers to fuels are sufficiently in-house that they can continue producing their current product set with only minor adjustments. France, the United States, and Canada are the *only* countries on the planet that check all the boxes. Russia is a near miss. Russian farm vehicles are, well, *Russian*. Saddled with an aging and collapsing population, Russia simply doesn't have the labor to maintain ag output with anything less than the sort of mammoth field equipment that Russia is incapable of manufacturing for itself.

Next up are those exporting countries that have most of the pieces in place *regionally*. They will still require access to a sort of friends-and-family network in order to meet all their input needs, but even in a Disorderly world this should be manageable.

Ranked from those facing the least to greatest challenges: New Zealand, Sweden, Argentina, Australia, Turkey, Nigeria, India, Uruguay, Paraguay, Thailand, Vietnam, Myanmar, Italy, and Spain. All have shortcomings—most notably in accessing equipment, fertilizers, and energy—but none are likely to face the sort of extreme supply or security challenges that will wreck production in more vulnerable locations.

Belarus, Kazakhstan, and Ukraine are in this category as well. In addition to input shortages, there's an open question whether any excess food output can be exported anywhere useful as Russia reasserts greater control over them. Keep in mind that Russia grows a lot of wheat on its *marginal* territories. In poor harvest years at the height of the Order, Russia *already* interfered with exports out of the other three wheat-belt states in order to ensure its own people sufficient food supplies.

The third category are those exporters that simply cannot maintain the input flows required to keep things going without a perfect constellation of unlikely geopolitical factors that are largely beyond their capacity to shape. They won't face catastrophic production declines, but they'll have to get used to agriculture becoming intermingled with geopolitical threats—and in some years that means crops simply won't perform to snuff. This is the future for Brazil, Croatia, Denmark, Finland, the Netherlands, Pakistan, and South Africa.

Fourth among the exporters are those places that have carved out a place for themselves among the agricultural powers of the Order but have zero chance of playing a significant role in the Disorder. Most of their supply chains lie outside of territories they can reach, and most face security concerns that will make it impossible for them to maintain what has become their business as usual: Bulgaria, Estonia, Czech Republic, Ethiopia, Finland, Germany, Hungary, Latvia, Lithuania, Mali, Romania, Slovakia, Zambia, and Zimbabwe.

The real desperation is on the importers' side of the ledger.

The first category are those who are close enough to exporters both geographically and diplomatically that they need not overworry about getting cut off: Chile, Colombia, Ecuador, Iceland, Indonesia, Malaysia, Mexico, Norway, Peru, the Philippines, Portugal, Singapore, and the United Kingdom. Japan also falls into this category not because it is close to food suppliers, but because it has the naval reach to go out and secure what it needs.

The second group of importers is where things get uncomfortable. Food will be available, but at a price—and not one that is entirely denominated purely in financial terms. These importers will need to bend to their suppliers' will. Should they not, foodstuffs will be directed elsewhere:

- Russia will use this food "diplomacy" to help consolidate control over Mongolia, Tajikistan, Turkmenistan, and Kyrgyzstan. Based upon how quickly the rivers of Central Asia dry up over the next one to

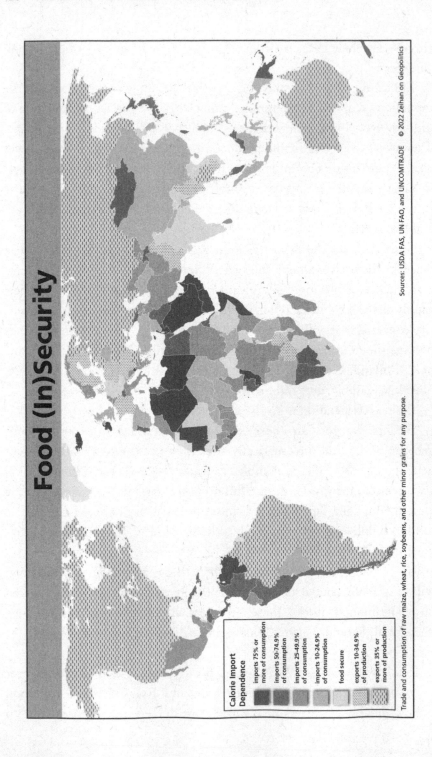

Food (In)Security

Calorie Import Dependence

- imports 75% or more of consumption
- imports 50-74.9% of consumption
- imports 25-49.9% of consumption
- imports 10-24.9% of consumption
- food secure
- exports 10-34.9% of production
- exports 35% or more of production

Sources: USDA FAS, UN FAO, and UNCOMTRADE   © 2022 Zeihan on Geopolitics

Trade and consumption of raw maize, wheat, rice, soybeans, and other minor grains for any purpose.

three decades, the Russians could find themselves either competing with Uzbekistan for Central Asian dominance or overwhelming a desperate, perma-drought-stricken Uzbekistan.*

- Hyper food-secure France is going to get all neocolonial. Paris will establish a suzerain relationship with Belgium, will attempt one with Switzerland, and will firm up links with a willing Morocco and Tunisia and an unwilling Algeria. The French will also establish as many dependencies as possible in the oil-rich states that are part of what was once known in imperial days as French West Africa, most notably Gabon, Congo (Brazzaville), and Chad.

- India will spend some food to *own* Bangladesh, which will find itself in the worst of all worlds. Less precipitation in the southern Himalayas means the overall productivity of Bangladeshi rice paddies will drop. But what water flows the country receives are more likely to be in the spring, when they could well *over*flood rice production, dealing local food production a double blow.

- Nigeria, the only African nation that can maintain its agricultural output without extensive outside assistance, will establish a sphere of influence that includes Equatorial Guinea, Cameroon, Chad, Niger, Burkina Faso, Ghana, Togo, and Benin. In a bit of turnabout-is-fair-play, oil- and natural-gas-rich Nigeria will find itself sparring, neocolonial-style, with the French throughout West Africa, and doing reasonably well in the contest.

- Turkey was already going to emerge as the master of the Eastern Mediterranean. It will use its superior land quality, mild climate, and command of the region's oil and trade flows not only to keep its agricultural system running, but also to extract geopolitical concessions from Azerbaijan, Georgia, Greece, Iraq, Israel, Lebanon, and Syria.

- The United States will trade food for cooperation on a variety of issues with the Central American states and the Caribbean nations and

---

* Or *both*.

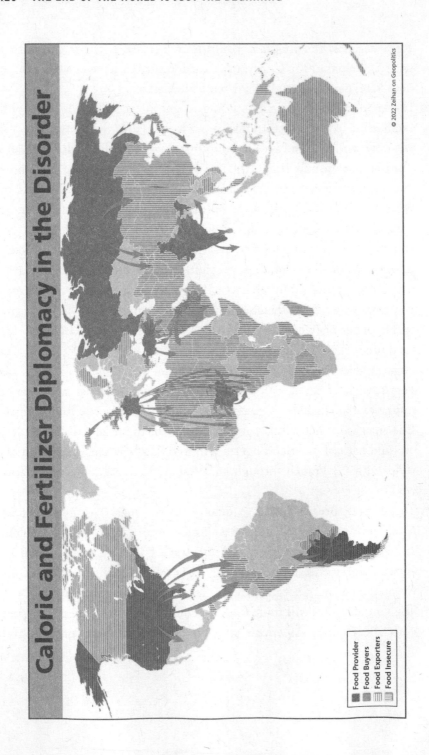

Caloric and Fertilizer Diplomacy in the Disorder

Food Provider
Food Buyers
Food Exporters
Food Insecure

© 2022 Zeihan on Geopolitics

islands, including Cuba. On less friendly terms, the Americans will use food as one of the levers to force Venezuela into a shape more to its liking. On more friendly terms, American food diplomacy will steadily transform Colombia into one of America's fastest friends and allies.

- Even though both will need to bring in food from farther abroad, Japan and the United Kingdom will likely bundle it into the array of tools used to force their wills upon Korea and Ireland, respectively.

As for the rest, there just won't be enough food to go around. Expanding domestic production even under the Order never enabled these places to be self-sufficient. What food imports might arrive will either be part of a severe quid pro quo or will represent a happy constellational alignment that can neither be planned for nor relied upon. Everyone not already mentioned in the Middle East (the region most overpopulated relative to its agricultural capacity) and sub-Saharan Africa is more or less on their own, and with global agricultural inputs no longer reliable, downward population shifts are inevitable.

If anything, this hit list is overly . . . rosy. Since 1945 and especially since 1992 the world has been living in extreme calorie surplus. A good rule of thumb is that it takes about nine times as many inputs to generate a calorie from animals as it does from plants, and the post–World War II era has enabled the vast bulk of humanity to drastically up their animal consumption. Yet all of us are well aware that even in this time of plenty, some locations do not have enough to go around. The issue is economic—or economic as shaped by the Order.

Haiti, a chronically undeveloped country, is a quintessential example. Until the mid-1980s, the Haitian diet was primarily root crops, maize, and some wheat, crops that were either not particularly calorie dense or were broadly inappropriate to Haiti's tropical climate. The Haitian population often flirted with famine. But Haiti sits off the coast of the world's agricultural superpower and by 2010, American-grown rice became *the* single largest component of the Haitian diet. Not only was U.S. rice more reliable and caloric than homegrown options, but also, because of the economics of America's industrialized agriculture,

American rice was also *cheaper* than anything the Haitians could grow themselves.

This price point disconnect contributed to three follow-on impacts. First, reliably cheaper food that arrived more reliably largely destroyed Haitian agriculture, both in terms of production directly and in the preservation of the skill sets required to reboot that production at a future date. Second, the sudden collapse of livelihoods throughout a largely agrarian system contributed to the vast denuding of the country's forests as the increasingly destitute population sought to build rafts and paddle to the United States. And yet, third, the Haitian population doubled, in large part *because food was so cheap*.

Haiti isn't even the extreme case. Many states are worse managed, are suffering greater agricultural collapses, or *both*. I'm particularly concerned, in no particular order, about Afghanistan, Cuba, North Korea, Iran, Venezuela, Yemen, Syria, Libya, Zimbabwe, Honduras, Guatemala, Laos, Turkmenistan, Iraq, Sudan, South Sudan, Niger, and Mali. All have experienced population booms beyond their systems' capacity to feed them, while simultaneously losing command of the preindustrial skill sets that sustained their pre-Order populations. For many of these places, the pre-Order, preindustrial struggle for subsistence will soon be thought of as a *high* point that cannot be returned to.

Should something—should anything—happen to those imported food flows, civilizational collapse into anarchy complete with a population "correction" isn't simply a distinct possibility, it is *the most likely outcome*. After all, a government that cannot feed its population is a government that falls.

That's the story of the biggest losers in relative terms. In absolute terms the biggest loser by far will be China. China sits at the end of the world's longest supply routes for nearly everything it imports, including roughly 80 percent of its oil needs. China's navy lacks the range necessary to secure, via trade or conquest, agricultural products—or even the inputs to grow and raise its own.

China's demographic collapse suggests imminent labor force *and* capital-supplies collapses. And China's existing, Order-era agricultural system is already the most hyperfinanced sector in history's most hyper-financed economy. There is nothing about this that will work in the world to come. There will be no shortage of famines in the post-Order world. Likely in excess of 1 billion people will starve to death, and another 2 billion will suffer chronic malnutrition. Some two-thirds of China's population faces one of those two fates. And remember, China is also history's most quickly *aging* society. The people who will be called upon to manage—or suffer through—mass malnutrition and famine are going to be *old*.

MITIGATING FAMINE

There really aren't many ways to avoid the sort of mass carnage that this chapter is laying out. Luckily, "not many" is not synonymous with "none."

THE ART AND SCIENCE OF INPUTS

The first way to prevent famine is to contribute some thing or technology that wasn't being added previously, in order to increase yields. There are precious few places where this is possible at the time of this writing in 2022, much less in the future, when the various preexisting inputs will have become more difficult to source. In fact, I can only really come up with one place where this is a pure play according to the rules of Industrial Age agriculture: Myanmar.

As the Imperial Age wound down in the early twentieth century, Myanmar, then known as Burma, was among the most technologically backward of the Europeans' Asian colonies. It was largely unindustrialized when the Japanese seized it from the British during World War II. The British never really went back. Formal independence came in 1948. Then a coup in 1962 ejected the democratically elected government. The new junta decided that people without electricity and cars would be less likely to revolt, and so purposefully followed a policy of *de*industrialization. A brief resurgence of democracy in the late 2010s was squelched with another coup in 2021. Simply put, if the world falls apart, it will end up looking a lot more like 2021 Myanmar, while Myanmar will look . . . more or less the same.

But Myanmar has some of the world's best rice-producing terrain and cheapest labor, and a navigable river—the Irrawaddy—running right through the most promising agricultural zone. At present, the Western world has made the whole country persona non grata for diplomatic reasons, but it doesn't take much imagination to think someone, somewhere will look at this perfect agricultural setup and think, "Hey, we could get a bunch more rice out of there if someone could ship in a few bags of fertilizer." "All" that needs to happen is for some outside countries to be willing to stomach Myanmar's authoritarian and borderline genocidal domestic policies. That probably won't be a problem in the case of India or Thailand. Both countries (a) are Myanmar's neighbors, (b) possess sufficient industrial bases and energy-sourcing options to supply some agricultural needs, and (c) barely have a problem with Myanmar *today*. Toss in global food shortages and both will likely engage Myanmar aggressively. Perhaps even cooperatively.

There's another sort of input that might at least partially replace the missing components of equipment and fertilizer and such: labor. The country to watch most closely in this regard is China.

Before the country's post-Mao modernization began in 1979, there were next to no tractors and such in the Chinese countryside. Nor was there much of anything in the realm of artificial fertilizers and the like.* Instead, the rural population had been politically, economically, spiritually, and nutritionally gutted by the Cultural Revolution, which was, in essence, a full national purge of anyone who did anything in any way aside from what matched up with whatever twisted thought was running through Mao's brain at the time. The point is that the population was basically a crushed peasantry, working small-plot fields by hand, giving individual attention to every individual plant, bereft of any of the technologies that had been developed in the past two centuries. Technically it wasn't farming at all. It was *gardening*.

Preindustrial gardening isn't stupid. In reality, it is actually wildly productive. It's just that in the advanced world, we consider it as a hobby or supplement. But if gardening is a *full-time job* and if it is the *only method*

---

*   Mao (in)famously decided that many fertilizers were too expensive and barred their use.

of food production and if the *labor is bottomless and free*, it can actually give some forms of industrialized agriculture a run for their money in output levels per acre.

In the world China is about to find itself in, the Chinese will need to make some seriously difficult choices. Oil for automobiles or for tractors? Natural gas for electricity or for fertilizers? Labor for mass manufacturing, for which there are no customers, or for food production? None of these are pleasant topics, but neither is national disintegration or famine. China's best bet will likely be a brutal, state-organized *de*urbanization campaign that somewhat resembles the Cultural Revolution, to turn a half billion people or so back into gardeners. We'll know soon whether the PRC's hyperurbanization campaign of the past four decades has squeezed all food-production-related skills out of the population. Regardless, deurbanization will be nowhere near enough to head off national famine—China simply cannot maintain its current population without full access to the global system to provide foodstuffs and agricultural inputs—but mass deurbanization just might—might—generate enough food to preserve the concept of China as a political entity.

Schmaybe.

Some version of deurbanization to free up more labor for agriculture is likely to happen in the other parts of the world that face mass famine as well, with perhaps Egypt at the top of that dreary list. Much of sub-Saharan Africa won't be far behind. In this the sub-Saharan Africans probably face a slightly less scary future than the Egyptians. About half the Egyptian population lives on desert that was reclaimed by *Industrial Age technologies*. Should anything happen to the electricity-driven pumps that turn portions of the Egyptian Sahara green, well then, pzzzzzzt. Agricultural lands in sub-Saharan Africa may not be (anywhere close to) the world's best, but at least most of them get *rain*.

There's another sort of "input" that is highly likely to prove useful in a completely different sort of geography. The world's best temperate zone farmlands, the ones largely confined to advanced countries unlikely to experience severe disruptions, will be able to apply *digital* technologies to agriculture.

Normally when we think of digitization we're thinking of online applications for loans or working from home during COVID or blah-blah-blahing away on smartphones, but digitization also applies to a few techs that are extremely ag-centric.

First, the obvious application: genomics. We've all heard of genetically modified organisms, the culmination of a series of digital technologies that allow us to modify characteristics of plants to make them more resistant to salt, drought, heat, cold, pests, and/or fungus. There's also something called "gene editing," which is pretty similar to the making of GMOs, but the tweaks to the genome are more targeted and could—theoretically at least—occur naturally or via more traditional methods such as crossbreeding. Gene editing simply speeds up the process from dozens of generations to one.

The bottom line is that technologies now exist to hack plants and get them to spend more energy on propagating (that is, growing the bits that humans ultimately eat). That increases yields while reducing input requirements. Perhaps the best example of what can be achieved with everything from crossbreeding to selective breeding to genetic modification and genetic editing is contemporary corn.

The plant we know as corn (or maize if you are European) is descended from a group of grasses known as teosintes. The edible portions of wild varieties are a hard, tough, roughly one-inch spike of kernels encased in tough, shell-like seed cases. Unsurprisingly, these were by far the least productive of ancient plantings in terms of per-acre yields. Fast-forward through roughly eleven thousand years of human tinkering to today, add in Industrial Age inputs, and corn consistently generates the greatest output per acre. In a soon-to-be world of reduced yields and input availability, you can see the advantages.

Second, the less obvious application: facial recognition. In democracies, the most common use is to unlock your phone. In China, the most common use is for the government to know where you are, who you are with, and what you're doing at any given second. In *agriculture* the emerging use is for a tractor-mounted computer to individually evaluate *every single plant* as the tractor rolls through the field, first to identify it, and then to determine what should be done to or for it, and finally to signal an attached apparatus to take action. Is the plant a weed? Squirt of herbicide. Is the plant infested with bugs? Squirt of pesticide. Is it yellow? Squirt of fertilizer. No longer will farmers have to use broadcast sprays over their entire fields, one pass per spray type. Now they can simply reload a bunch of canisters with the various inputs and make a single pass giving customized, on-the-fly attention to each individual plant via a rig that more or less drives itself. It isn't so much industrial farming as it is *digital gardening*, where every plant gets dedicated attention . . . just not from a human.

Taken together, genetically tweaked seeds plus digital gardening promise to—at a minimum—double crop yields per acre by 2030, while simultaneously reducing chemical inputs and fuel needs by up to three-quarters.

However, this assumes that farmers will be able to afford to apply the new inputs. Farm equipment is already among the most expensive gear civilians can purchase, and the new digital gardening equipment undoubtedly will cost triple to purchase and far more than triple to maintain as compared to its nondigitized industrial forebears. Such investments only make sense for row crops where the farms are huge and capital supplies ample: United States, Canada, and Australia are *it* for large-scale application. There are a few large row-crop farms in France, Germany, the Netherlands, and New Zealand that *might* qualify. A handful of politically well-connected Brazilian megafarms might be able to play. Argentina will be a slam dunk *if* the Argentine government can admit it has no hope of manufacturing this sort of equipment domestically and so allow for low-tariff imports.

But that . . . that is *everyone* who might be able to experience input-related improvements.

UNWINDING "PROGRESS"

The second means of mitigating famine is to grow products more in line with local, rather than global, demand. Many of those displacement crops that have contributed to global health and wealth these past few decades will go away.

Expect three patterns to manifest, based on climate, geography, and culture.

First, large-scale, export-driven monoculture will give way to small-scale, local-driven polyculture. That will (hopefully) help serve the caloric and nutritional needs of local communities, but it will come at the cost of economies of scale. Whether you look at it from the point of view of inputs or reach or tech or capital or planting preferences, the volume of foods produced on Earth in aggregate *must* decline.

Second, wheat plantings will come back in a very big way . . . after they disappear in a very big way.

The same input math that was in play for all agricultural crops in the Industrial Age—better financing, better equipment, synthetic fertilizers, pesticides, and herbicides—applies to wheat as well. Combine wheat's utter lack of persnicketiness with the high-octane industrial inputs and you have the reason why global wheat output has soared for decades. Such consistently high supplies have driven wheat prices down. That makes the grain decidedly unsexy, but since nearly all wheat is grown on marginal land, few wheat farmers have the option of growing something else.

Now fold in all the other lessons of this book: in transport, in finance, in energy, in industrial materials, in manufacturing. Most wheat is grown *only* in places where *only* wheat can grow, but it can *only* grow in those places *so long as the input streams are not interrupted*. Deglobalization tells us that in most such locations, there will be a helluva disruption. Globally, we are on the verge of a shortage in humanity's number one foodstuff.

And not just that one. A lack of inputs makes most for-export or cash-crops nonviable even before global transport breakdowns prevent such crops from making it to end buyers. Whether because you cannot import wheat or because you can only eat so many avocados, farmers the world over will have no choice but to shift plantings. Wide-scale wheat, augmented by climatically dictated staples such as oats, barley, and rye in cooler climates, and cassava in the tropics, is the wave of the future.

Consider this: countries like the United Kingdom, Russia, the UAE,

Poland, and Mongolia are currently at the apex of their historical culinary diversity. In coming years, unless they can join someone else's trading network, they risk at best going back to the diets of the mid-nineteenth century, but *without* the imports they used to be able to access from their respective colonial involvements and trade relationships to augment meagre domestic production options. Gruels, porridges, and mush beckon—with a little cabbage on Sundays.

Third, this is a recipe for gross rural poverty. Removing monoculture reduces economies of scale. Returning to wheat removes cash crops and the income that comes from them. Since 1945 the number of people involved in agriculture has plunged by 80 percent while gross rural incomes have increased. Not rural incomes per person, but instead rural incomes per *acre*. In per capita terms agricultural lands have experienced some of the greatest income increases in human history. Without internationalized input flows or international export options, much of this will now unwind.

Extend the earlier Kiwi and Egyptian examples, which neatly bracket the extremes of future yield reductions, crop shifting, and rural impacts:

- Shatter Pacific trade norms and the Kiwis will be left with more dairy and fruit than they can sell, and not enough wheat to make bread. Shatter trade norms in the Mediterranean and the Egyptians will have lots of extra cotton—and starve.[*]
- The regional geography matters, too: New Zealand enjoys easy access to food supplies from food-rich regions in Australia and the Western Hemisphere, enabling a reasonable degree of continued specialization and food product trade. Australia and New Zealand are, in particular, well tailored to continue being each other's most reliable trading partner. Compare that to Egypt, located where the Mediterranean meets East Africa—both regions that are already food-poor.

---

[*] I love oranges as much as the next guy, but while they can be part of a balanced diet, they cannot *be* your diet.

- Demographics comes into play as well: from a regional food-supply point of view, New Zealand's population of 5 million isn't much more than a rounding error, while supporting 100+ million Egyptians will be like a cat swallowing a cannonball. Egypt's population is now so large that even if the country were able to maintain industrial inputs and it shifted *all* its productive lands over to wheat cultivation, it still wouldn't be enough to provide enough calories. But the Egyptians have to try. The alternative is to simply die.
- This coming rush to wheat by definition means that other products will face drastic production reductions. In the case of Egypt specifically, this means less cotton and citrus for international markets. But they aren't the big boys. In terms of internationally traded crops, cotton and citrus rank seventeenth and sixteenth. Far more important are the three crops that, along with wheat, provide the bulk of humanity's food intake.

EXPANDING THE DIET, SHRINKING THE DIET

Let's begin with corn and soy, which rank fourth and first among internationally traded food commodities, respectively.

Like wheat, corn and soy were both first cultivated and domesticated deep in prehistory. Hundreds of generations of selective breeding enabled corn to power the Mayan and Aztec empires, while soy . . . bounced around a lot. It was definitely domesticated somewhere in Northeast Asia,* but then it wandered the world with pretty much every known trade route right up to the Columbus expeditions. At that point soy was introduced to the Western Hemisphere for the first time, and that changed everything.

Both corn and soy have peculiar quirks that make them quintessential contemporary Western Hemispheric crops.

- Corn loves heat and loves humidity. It thrives in the American Midwest, the Argentine Pampas, and the Brazilian Cerrado far better than in Europe or Northeast Asia, regions that tend to be cooler or drier or both.
- Both corn and soy are quintessential row crops. That encourages the use of mechanization, which in turn pushes for larger and larger fields to pay for the equipment. Simply by happenstance, there just aren't all that many appropriate horizon-spanning fields in the Eastern Hemisphere. (Most of the Eastern Hemisphere's large fields are in Australia or Russia, countries whose lands are either too dry or too wet or too cold for soy.)
- Corn needs help propagating. Historically, domesticated corn required

---

* The Chinese, Japanese, and Koreans are capable of *lively* debates over the details.

artificial pollination, while contemporary hybrids require managed pollination via a process called detasseling. In essence, a portion of corn plants in a field must have their flowers (aka the tassels) removed so the correct genetic mix can contribute to the fruit (the cob). It is sharply seasonal work that broadly matches up with the large farms, young demographic-structure, small-town culture, and labor economics of New World agriculture.* Even if Russia or Australia had the climate, they would still lack the rural population density to supply the labor.

- Soy is biologically wired to flower when the number of daylight hours drops below about 12.8, but, like corn, it also craves heat and humidity. About the only locations with this perfect mix of heat and humidity and seasonal variation in the Eastern Hemisphere are on the western and northern shores of the Black Sea. But *all* the soy farmland in that region amounts to less than 7 percent of the soy-matching climate zones in the Western Hemisphere, most notably in Argentina's Cordoba, America's Iowa, and Brazil's Parana. Unsurprisingly, something like 70 percent of the world's corn exports and 85 percent of its soy exports come from three countries: Argentina, Brazil, and the United States.

- The biggest Eastern Hemispheric exporter for both corn and soy is Ukraine, a country the world should not depend upon. Issues abound. The country is too poor to afford the mechanization that corn and soy require, while the country's energy, refining, and manufacturing capacity is thin. But security trumps everything. At the time of this paragraph's tweaking on February 28, 2022, the Russians are eyeballs-deep in their invasion of Ukraine. The war may unfold in many ways, but at a minimum, the 2022 planting season will be disrupted, giving the world a preview of the food shortages of the future. The previous instance of disruptions of agricultural exports from the former Soviet space occurred in 2010. The price of wheat doubled. One outcome, among many, was the cavalcade of protests, government collapses, and wars of the Arab Spring. Far worse lies ahead.

---

* De-tasselling also happens to be hot, tedious, sweaty, itchy work and the need to get away from it is probably the biggest reason why I went to college. No corn, no book!

For the most part, this specific displacement and differentiation will prove to be a positive. Western Hemispheric supply chains are broadly self-contained within the hemisphere, suggesting that any disruptions should be limited and manageable. That in turn means deglobalization will not force a collapse in the world's production profile for corn and soy.

This is *not* to say that profile will not change. It will. It will change drastically, but not because of the pain and shock of deglobalization interrupting input access. Rather, it will change because of a change in market *demand*.

Corn is, in a word, screwed. That corn on the cob you buy for grilling or steaming is *not* the stuff that blankets the never-ending fields of Nebraska, Iowa, and Illinois. The stuff you eat is called *sweet* corn; it makes up less than 1 percent of the corn grown in the United States. What you see across the Midwest is something called *field* or *dent* corn. Via a process called nixtamalization, which uses heat and some sort of alkaline solution, field corn *can* be turned into a food like masa, but for most people, corn has different uses than direct consumption.

The world's biggest and most creative field corn consumers are the Americans, who produce field corn in such prodigious quantities, they feel it reasonable to process it into thousands of products, ranging from high-fructose corn syrup to faux-plastic bottles to sparkplug ceramics to schoolhouse chalk. The biggest volume of those products by far is the biofuel colloquially known as ethanol. A mix of subsidies and mandates requires American gasoline to contain 10–15 percent of the corn-based product, which doesn't sound like too much until you realize that at ethanol's peak, some half of the American corn harvest was being turned into a gasoline additive. The mandate absorbed so much corn it drove up not just corn prices, but the prices of pretty much *all* crops by displacing farm acres *to* corn: wheat, soy, cotton, and hay got decidedly perky from the competition, as did pork and beef due to the higher costs for feed.

For the rest of the world, serving as animal feed *is* corn's primary purpose.

In the late-globalization era of rising incomes, this is just fine. As people earn more money, they want to eat more meat. But in a post-globalized era of collapsing incomes, most people in most of the world will not be wealthy enough to enjoy animal protein on a daily basis. Expect corn *demand* to collapse right along with large-scale animal husbandry in any country whose production does not serve regional demand *or* that relies upon imported corn to fatten up its animals. That will hit meat producers like Uruguay and Australia in the first category, and meat consumers like Korea and China in the second.

What corn loses, soy gains. Soy is also an animal fodder. In fact, due to its higher protein content, in many cases soy is the superior input. Unlike field corn, however, soy easily can be processed for human consumption. And since soy is a plant, soy-based protein is cheap compared to hamburgers and pork chops. In a deglobalized, disconnected world there simply isn't going to be the same giant pool of upwardly mobile meat-eaters required to sustain animal husbandry on its current, global scale. This shift from high-cost animal protein to low-cost plant protein is a necessary transformation that will probably save a billion people or so from starving to death.* If you don't live in the Western Hemisphere, Europe, or Australasia, it's time to up your tofu game.

However, there is a distinct probability that even with large-scale corn production giving way to ever-larger-scale soy production, we *still* won't even have enough soy. The problem is Brazil, the largest soy exporter of the late globalized period. Brazil holds that mantle due to five factors:

1. Brazilian scientists hacked soy's genome to tweak the daylight-hours requirement so the plant can flower and mature in the country's more equatorially located farmlands. (Near the equator, summer and winter have nearly identical day lengths, so soy never knew what to do and wouldn't mature.) This scientific feat enabled Brazil to expand soy production beyond its southern, more temperate provinces such as

---

* This means that if the switch doesn't happen, we're looking at *two* billion people dying of famine.

Rio Grande do Sul to its more equatorial and tropical provinces, such as Mato Grosso. This one tweak is responsible for some one-third of *global* soy exports.

2. Brazil's soy exports are as physically far from Asian markets as is possible on the planet. They need to be sailed either around the tip of South America or across the South Atlantic to the Cape of Good Hope, before crossing the Pacific or Indian Ocean along the longest possible crossing. Most foods are very low value compared to their weight or volume. Fifty pounds of gold is worth about $25,000 and you can hold it in your hands. Fifty pounds of aluminum is worth about $50 and you can fit it into a bucket. Fifty pounds of soy would run you about $10 and require a wheelbarrow. Unless you were one of those lucky Imperial Centers with good internal water transport options, most of humanity didn't even consider sourcing food from more than a few miles from production sites until the eighteenth century. In the industrialized Order, this doesn't matter. Long-haul, low-cost shipping has become ubiquitous.

3. Brazil's near-tropical soils are extraordinarily nutrient-poor and Brazil's primary soy-producing regions do not experience winter bug kills. On the upside, the lack of winter means most Brazilian soy (and corn) farmers can double- (and even triple-!) crop. On the downside, not only are insects, weeds, and molds a constant problem, but the clear-cutting of forests to create farmland has removed most natural pressures, so the various bugs can focus their genetic efforts on resisting agricultural chemicals. Pesticides, herbicides, and fungicides that must be reformulated every decade or so in the American Midwest require overhauls every two to three years in Brazil. Consequently, Brazilian row-crop agriculture has the world's highest input costs in fertilizer, pesticides, herbicides, and fungicides per unit of output. In the globalized period of easy input supply and easier product sales, this is but a footnote.

4. Like soy production in Argentina and the United States, the majority of Brazil's soy production is deep inland. Unlike Argentina or the United States, Brazil lacks the flat-to-the-coast geography that enables a cheap rail-and-river transport system to ship out its agricultural bounty. Most of Brazil's soy is moved by truck. That necessitates vast volumes of cheap,

imported capital to fund the necessary infrastructure. In the capital-omnipresent era of the Boomer Bulge and Chinese hyperfinancing, this isn't an issue.

5. All crops go through cycles of oversupply and underdemand, but if there is a commonality in the post-1990 world, it has been that the global population has consistently gotten bigger *and* richer, and that means it wants more and better foods. The biggest single component of this bigger-and-richer is price-insensitive China. The preferred luxury food of the Chinese is pork, the Chinese hog herd is larger than the rest of the world's combined, China's own farmland is woefully inadequate to the task of feeding it, and the fastest way to fatten up a pig is to feed it soy. Unsurprisingly, Brazilian soy has been on a tear since 2000.

With the exception of the genetic brain work, *all* these factors will break the other way for the Brazilians in a deglobalized world. That hardly means Brazilian agricultural output will collapse, but it does mean that output *will* shrink, that Brazil's output *will* be far less reliable, that Brazil's output *will* be far more cyclical, and that the Brazilians *will* struggle with internal transport issues in ways the Argentines and Americans simply cannot comprehend.

Next up is rice. In terms of international trade, rice is "only" ranked ninth by value, but that belies its importance as the world's second-most-popular grain after wheat. At issue is that there are many different varieties, ranging from the Arborio used in risotto to the basmati of Indian cuisine to the sticky of Indonesia to the jasmine of Thailand to the black of China. The Asians think of rice the same way Americans think of barbecue. There's a right way, and then there's *horror*. The attitude tends to reduce the volume traded.

The world's collective rice varietals are not nearly as storied as wheat, largely because in many ways rice is wheat's polar opposite. Rice is a difficult and expensive crop to grow, demanding more in inputs, labor, machinery, and processing than any of the other major foods that humanity consumes.

Rice is demanding of both water and labor, to the point that its cultivation profoundly shapes—and hobbles—the cultures that use it. Wheat is a once-and-done. Well, maybe twice-and-done if you consider threshing. Rice? Fat chance. It is all about water management.

Nearly all the world's rices are *not* row crops, but are instead grown in paddies. Rice paddies must be dug out and lined with clay so they don't leak. Paddies are less fields and more gigantic open-air pots. In a separate location, rice seeds must be grown into seedlings. In most cases these seedlings are planted by hand into flooded paddies for early growth, and after a few days the paddies are drained to enable the young rice plants to breathe, get enough sunshine, establish root pegging, and grow.

Then begins the water dance: fields are repeatedly flooded to drown out terrestrial weeds and bugs, and then drained to kill aquatic weeds and bugs. Too much water at any stage drowns the crop. Too little results in dirt-caked desiccation. Depending on cultivar, this flooding-then-draining cycle must be repeated up to four times before a final drying that precedes harvest. After harvest, the rice stalks must be dried again. Rice must be threshed *twice*—once to separate the grains from the stalks, and a second time to remove the husks from the grains. And that's just for *brown* rice. To get *white* rice, the grains must be polished to remove the bran.

There is no tossing some seeds on the ground and coming back in a few months. Rice farming is a near-full-time job. When a wheat power goes to war, so long as the farmers are back for harvest, all is good. When a rice power goes to war, a year of starvation is baked into the decision making.

Considering how many rice varietals there are, it should come as little surprise that there's a *lot* of variation type by type and region by region. The monsoonal climates of the Indian subcontinent have very wet seasons that are good for rice and very dry seasons that are good for wheat (but a paddy is a paddy and so farmers must choose what to prepare their lands for). Japan tends to use machinery to plant seedlings. In Mississippi, rice is a row crop under incessant, heavy, and heavily controlled irrigation. California plants its rice via *airplane*.

The Order didn't transform the world of rice nearly as much as it did the world of wheat. Wheat grows anywhere, so the Order banished it to places only wheat can grow. But rice cultivation requires very specific conditions that must be *created*, an ultra-low-cost labor force that does very little else, and *lots* of water, typically for more than one season. Regardless of what the Order did to everything and everywhere else, it did not result in a mass upheaval in the hows and especially the wheres of rice cultivation: RiceWorld has long been a fairly contained crescent of lands from South Asia through Southeast Asia into East Asia. This arc comprises roughly 90 percent of total rice production, nearly all of which is paddy-style.

Looking forward, RiceWorld faces two challenges.

First, poop.

With the notable exceptions of Japan, Hong Kong, and Singapore, very few spots in South, Southeast, or East Asia had industrialized before 1945. As such, most rice production used human and animal poop as its primary fertilizers. Considering that rice laborers were wading around in poop water all day, you can imagine the impact upon life spans.[*]

In China the horrors of the Cultural Revolution unwound most early progress in introducing fertilizer, forcing Chinese peasants to return to poop. It really wasn't until the 1990s that poop really vanished as an input. Add in a few other industrial techs as regards harvesting and irrigation, and many Chinese ricers finally enjoyed sufficient food security that they could up and leave paddy life for the city en masse. Incomes rose. Disease rates plunged. Life spans expanded.

Unwind that process, deny access to imported inputs, and RiceWorld will find itself in serious trouble.

Without those phosphate fertilizers, rice cannot be grown in the necessary volume *anywhere* in RiceWorld. Decades of massive urbanization have separated the sources of poop from the paddies. That means either 2 billion people need to give up on rice, or these regions need to *de*urbanize far more quickly than they urbanized so "natural" fertilizer can once again be colocated with rice production.

---

[*]   For those of you who love to get into the nitty-gross-gritty, google "schistosomiasis." Warning: do *not* do so right after a big lunch.

On this point, China has the possibility of being okay*ish*. Unlike the vast bulk of East and Southeast Asia, the Chinese can source phosphates internally, although only so long as China remains fully intact. All of China's phosphate mines are in its far west—specifically Tibet and Xinjiang, regions where the CCP has been carrying out ethnic-based genocides with various degrees of intensity and brutality since the 1950s. Such regions also happen to be a thousand-plus miles of nothing from the country's densely populated Han-supermajority regions, where the rice is grown. Should China crack for any reason, its only hope for reasonable rice yields is to shift back to a poop-powered circle of life.

The knock-on effects of such mass relocations for manufacturing capacity should be obvious. The labor will simply be in the wrong place, doing something unrelated to widget making. The knock-on effects for rice output are somewhat less obvious. China's breakneck urbanization means its population has aged so quickly that there are not a lot of strong backs to relocate to the farms in the first place. And the knock-on effects for *population size* are simply terrifying. Nearly all population gains in China that occurred between 1980 and 2020—roughly 500 million people—are from *health* gains extending life spans, not from new births. This means that should China need to switch away from synthetic fertilizers to something more . . . natural, the country's life span gains—*the country's last forty years of population increases*—will be lost in just a couple of decades even if nothing else goes wrong.

The second challenge to RiceWorld is less gross, but perhaps even more problematic: water access.

Rice's finicky, water-intensive nature means that, unlike with wheat, there is *no* growing of rice on marginal land. This finickiness makes rice incredibly vulnerable to climatic shifts. Change a region's hydrology, even a little, and rice output tanks.

China's most prolific rice production is located along the lower Yangtze, the zone where rice was first domesticated ten *millennia* ago. As China urbanized, cities along the river expanded, absorbing what used to be paddy-rice territory. What's left for rice production are upland territories that rely nearly exclusively upon irrigation. That makes Yangtze rice dependent upon rainfall in myriad climate zones of the upper Yangtze basin—many of which are desertifying. Southern China—another big rice region—is far wetter, but also packed with microclimates due to its ruggedness. Even if the overall amount of rainfall in the area doesn't change, pockets of wet and dry will emerge, leading to pockets of insufficient or malplaced water. Normally, small differences in microclimes wouldn't justify my attention. But there are 1.4 billion people in China and rice is so very finicky.

The water issues facing China specifically are really just a microcosm of the broader issues of climate change, and *that* is a far bigger topic.

AGRICULTURE AND CLIMATE CHANGE

Let's start this section with a few squirmworthy facts.

First, peace is exceedingly bad for the planet. When the Americans crafted their Order, they didn't simply create an alliance to fight the Soviets. That strategic decision also enabled the vast mass of humanity to start down the road toward industrialization, generating an explosion in greenhouse gas emissions as most of humanity started using coal, oil, and natural gas en masse.

Second, the post–Cold War expansion of the Order to, well, everyone, accelerated emissions increases. It was bad enough when the world's major industrialized systems included France and Germany and Japan and Korea and Taiwan. It was quite another when Indonesia and India and Nigeria and China joined the club. Countries that couldn't even consider beginning the industrialization process before World War II are now responsible for more than half of current emissions, with total emissions *seven times* what they were in 1945.

Third, now that most of humanity has experienced things like electricity, it bears consideration that people will not consciously choose to go back to a preindustrial lifestyle, *even if globalization collapses*. Something the modern environmental movement often misses is that oil and natural gas are not only the world's low-carbon fossil fuels, they are also the fuels that are *internationally traded*. In a post-globalized world, the primary fuel most countries can source locally is coal. And not just any coal, but low-caloric, low-temperature burning, high-contaminant soft or brown coal that generates far more carbon emissions than burning . . . almost anything else. We are completely capable as a species of devolving into a fractured, dark, poor, hungry world while *still* increasing greenhouse gas emissions.

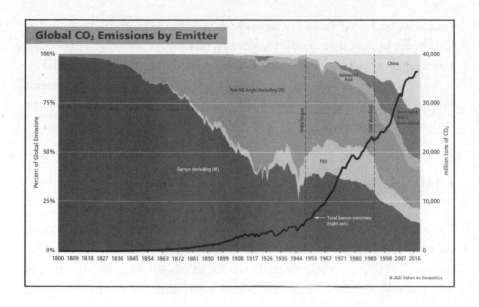

Fourth, our capacity to forecast climate impacts tends to be embarrassingly off.

The best recent example is the United States in mid-2021. A high-pressure system locked some warm air over the Pacific Northwest. Some of that air then descended from the Cascades, triggering compression effects. The result? Normally cloudy, rainy, grungy locales mutated into open ovens for weeks. Portland, Oregon, repeatedly clocked temperatures above 120 degrees. I've seen many climate models that suggest the inevitability of hotter deserts or a hotter American South, but none have projected that Portland—freakin' Portland—would end up being hotter than Las Vegas has ever been.

The reason for such a fundamental miss is simple: we do not at present have good enough data to project climate change down to the zip code level. Anyone who tries is at most making an educated guess.

I don't like guessing. Whenever possible, I don't. So I don't look at many climate forecasts, but instead turn to weather data. Not current or future weather data—*past* data. The weather record is based on hundreds of thousands of reporting locations the world over, taken dozens of times a day, stretching back well over a century. The data isn't controversial. It isn't political. It isn't a projection. And if there is a trend line of change, you know that the needle has moved *already*, and you just need to follow it forward a bit.

For purposes of this project, I'm using 120-year weather data trend lines to project forward a mere thirty additional years. Think that's not very sexy? Think again.

A TALE OF TWO LANDS

Consider two very real-world examples involving two first-world regions for which we have excellent data: the southwest Pacific country of Australia (specifically, the country's southeastern third, where most of its people live and most of its agricultural output is produced) and the American midwestern state of Illinois.

On average, temperatures in both places have risen 1.1 degree Celsius since 1900. We also have—again, from hard real-world data—a solid idea of what this temperature increase hath wrought in both places. The impacts don't even remotely match up.

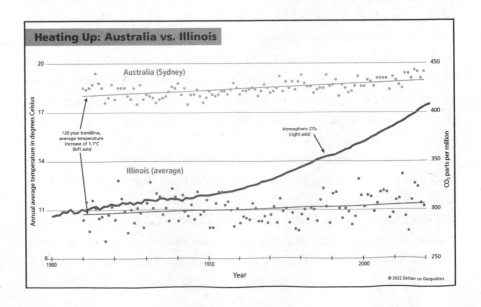

Higher temperatures in Australia have manifested as hotter, drier summer days. In the summer of 2019–20 Australia experienced a drought, complete with borderline apocalyptic bush fires that burned down one-fifth of the country's forests, killing something like a billion animals and destroying roughly one-seventh of the country's rangelands. In contrast, in Illinois, higher temperatures have manifested as increased *moisture*, with the summers of 2019 and 2020 being no exceptions. Instead of fires, Illinois has experienced incrementally *higher* corn and soy output.

Why such stark differences? In a word: geography.

A swirl of a dozen major ocean currents surrounds the Australian continent. Some warm. Some cold. Some seasonal. Australia's far north is firmly in the tropics. The far southeast edges into the cold side of the temperate zone. The result is a land of contrasts. Not only is the middle three-quarters of the Australian continent hard desert, but wild climatic variations from season to season and year to year curse Australia with a jagged flood-and-drought pattern. It is as if the great Australian deserts pulse like a heart, with precipitation patterns surging into and away from the interior every few years. The Aussies, in that wonderful way they have with words, call these phases the Big Wet and the Big Dry. Such patterns were well documented long before the accelerating carbon builds in Earth's atmosphere of the post-1990 world, or even before the Aussies began industrializing. This isn't climate change. This is *Australia*.

Now add in that 1.1-degree Celsius temperature increase. Australia's topographical layout makes it arid. Dry air heats quickly, but also cools quickly. Most of Australia's temperature increase, therefore, manifests as higher *day*time temperatures. That raises the dew point, making rain less likely. This dries the country out and makes it drought- and fire-prone, *decreasing* agricultural potential. Many of Australia's agricultural regions—most notably the western slopes of the Blue Mountains in the country's east, and significant portions of the Murray-Darling Basin in the southeast—are likely to degrade into dust bowls. The fires of 2019–20 have a very harbinger-of-the-Apocalypse feel to them.

Compare this to the Illinoisan geography. Illinois is deep in the continental interior, and so experiences the full four seasons with near-clockwork regularity. Illinois is smack dab in the middle of the temperate zone and receives fairly consistent precipitation month to month, with the driest month (February) rarely receiving less than two inches of water, while the wettest month (May) rarely receives more than five inches.

Some of that rain begins as tropical weather systems in the Gulf of Mexico. We know—again, from real-world temperature measurements—that the air above the Gulf has been steadily warming for decades. Warmer air can carry more moisture, making Illinois more likely to receive rainfall from tropical storm systems, but Illinois's deeply continental nature means it experiences these storms as simple rainfall, rather than mobile-home-relocating hurricanes. The extra moisture as compared to the first half of the twentieth century, somewhere between three and nine inches a year based on where in the state you are, means Illinoisan agriculture is bursting at the seams with greater and greater output.

But what about those temperature increases? So far they have been a . . . positive. Illinois's topographic layout makes it humid. Wetter air heats more slowly and holds its heat longer. Most of Illinois's temperature increase, therefore, manifests as higher *night*time temperatures. That reduces the number of nights with crop-damaging frosts, *increasing* agricultural potential. If warming trends hold, at some point in the 2020s most of Illinois will experience so many frost-free nights that farmers will be able to plant two crops a year.

The conventional wisdom on climate change asserts that Australia's predicament is obvious, predictable, and therefore avoidable. But reality has sucker-punched the conventional wisdom when it comes to Illinois. Different geographies result in different climatic outcomes, even when the net energy increase is identical. It stretches the mind to come up with a positive aspect of the Australian evolutions, and it equally stretches the mind to come up with a *negative* aspect of the evolution in Illinois.

That disconnect is precisely the point.

While we cannot make specific, localized predictions independent of weather data, we *can* use weather data to make some slightly more than broad-stroke statements that are more than dramatic enough for my taste. *All* impact the world of agriculture.

MAKING SENSE OF CLIMATE CHANGE, PART I: IT'S NOT THE HEAT, IT'S THE HUMIDITY

The first more-than-broad stroke involves basic chemistry: while warmer air can hold more water, warmer air also means more moisture is required to generate precipitation. In low-humidity areas, hotter air will typically mean less rainfall (Australia), but in high-humidity areas it will typically mean more rainfall (Illinois). This makes the most difference on the extremes. Most deserts will get hotter and drier (and bigger), most already-arid zones risk desertification, and increased rainfall in the tropics will turn flatter zones into wetlands. Deserts and wetlands are rubbish for growing food.

A temperature difference of only a few degrees will change humidity patterns by only a few percentage points. That doesn't seem like much. It *isn't* much. But remember, we're also dealing with a world in which transport and supply chains will be weakening, or in some places breaking completely. Adding just a bit more stress to agricultural systems in *that* environment will have outsized effects. The hit list isn't an encouraging one. The regions likely to feel the biggest brunt of climatic shifts from this first factor include:

- Mato Grosso, Brazil's Soy Central, the world's densest soy production zone.
- The Levant, the Sahel, and Central America, already the world's most food-insecure regions.
- Southern Ukraine, arguably *the* most productive part of the Russian wheat belt.
- California's Central Valley, in dollar terms *the* most productive agricultural zone on the planet.
- The Ganges Basin, the world's most densely populated river system, home to some half a billion people.
- Argentina's Mendoza wine region, where actual physical *joy* comes from.

MAKING SENSE OF CLIMATE CHANGE, PART II: WATCH THOSE WINDS

The second more-than-broad stroke is that the world is warming *unevenly*, with the poles heating at roughly triple the rate of the tropics. Temperature differentiation generates wind, and greater temperature differentiation generates *more* wind. Whether this is good, bad, or otherwise depends upon what the Earth looks like between you and the equator. If there's a big body of tropical water, expect the stronger winds to bring you more rain. A *lot* more rain.

Japan, Taiwan, the Koreas, Mexico, and China should brace for more rainfall. In all six cases, water *management* is likely to prove a problem because all suffer from extremely rugged topographies in the zones likely to experience additional moisture. Japan, Taiwan, and South Korea are highly developed countries that already boast robust water management systems and might enjoy something a bit like an Illinois-style output kick.

Mexico, China, and North Korea are unlikely to be so fortunate. Mexico's southwest coast isn't going to get so much spritzed as drenched, but most of Mexico is rugged and high-altitude. Any gain to agriculture will likely be matched by destruction via mudslide. Southern China, the part of the country likely to get the most additional warmth and water, is already the country's warmest and wettest area. It is more likely to see torrential floods and lingering wetlands of the type that will overload the region's rice-growing efforts, *reducing* rather than increasing harvests. North Korea already suffers from regular catastrophic flooding. The last batch in the 1990s contributed to the famine-induced death of nearly 2 million people.

Changing rainfall patterns impact water flows, especially when those water flows have already been impinged upon by human activity. Among the world's major rivers, the one that has seen the greatest changes to its volume and flows in recent years is the Mekong, in Southeast Asia. The Chinese have tapped its upper reaches to irrigate fields on the Tibetan Plateau, the Laotians and Thais are building dams like mad to generate hydropower, the Cambodians have centered their civilization on the intersection of the Mekong and their seasonally flooded lowlands, while the Vietnamese have turned the Mekong's entire delta into one gigantic rice paddy. Deltas being where rivers meet ocean, you can see the problem. Even marginally lower river flows lead to both the land sinking a bit and the sea pushing inland. Even a minor shift in sea or land levels means vast swaths of the Mekong Delta will become exposed to seawater, and . . . no rice will grow. More than 100 million people depend upon the delta for their food supply.

I'm also worried about the Indian subcontinent, a region with boatloads of people and whose near-equatorial location will generate a different sort of wind condition. Rising temperatures in the Indian Ocean mean the temperature differential between sea and land is shrinking. Less temperature variation means less intense winds, which means that the century-old and very well documented weakening of the monsoonal winds will continue. This weakening has already reduced rainfall on the subcontinent by 10–20 percent over the last century.

Normally such a limited figure over a lengthy time frame wouldn't overbother me. The technologies of the Green Revolution combined with the materials access of the Order have more than compensated. But those techs and materials will not be as reliably available in the future. Of even greater concern, one-third of India's population already lives in semiarid regions, while India's population has quadrupled during the past century, making it already the world's most water-poor country in per capita terms. Weaker monsoons mean less rainfall in the Hindu Belt as well as less snowpack in the southern Himalayas. That last bit is particularly bad news for Pakistan, which relies upon Himalayan snowmelt to irrigate *everything*. Opposite Pakistan on the subcontinent is Bangladesh, a country that *is* the Ganges Delta. Weaker outflows from the Ganges suggest the entire country of Bangladesh, some 160 million people, could suffer a fate akin to the Mekong Delta. There isn't a lot of margin for error in this part of the world . . . especially since less rain means less rice.

The Mediterranean isn't nearly big or tropical enough to generate the moisture effect. Instead, stronger equator-polar wind patterns are already pushing some of Northern Europe's rain-generating fronts out to sea. From eastern France all the way to western Ukraine, Northern Europe has been drying out bit by bit for six decades. Under the Order this hasn't been a problem. Europe simply shifted to producing specialty products that it then sells at top dollar to a wealthy, interconnected world. It is unclear whether the Continent *can* shift back, and even if it succeeds, doing so would remove a *lot* of food products from the market as the Europeans preference local needs.*

The eastern three-quarters of the Russian wheat belt is north of interior continental *deserts*. Stronger equatorial-polar wind currents will dehydrate the eastern half of the Russian wheat belt, particularly the portion in northern Kazakhstan. Even worse, any wind-driven drying will intensify a completely different in-progress climate disaster:

The Soviet Union diverted the waters of the Amu and Syr Darya river systems to irrigate cotton fields in the Central Asian deserts, an effort that has all but destroyed the Aral Sea, the region's primary source of humidity. Even without climate-change-induced temperature increases, the region's ongoing desiccation was already going to *eliminate* the snowpack of the western Tian Shan and western Pamir Mountains within a couple of decades. No snowpack, no regional rivers, and the entire region reverts to hard desert. That spells the end of nearly all agriculture in Turkmenistan, Uzbekistan, Tajikistan, Kyrgyzstan, southern Kazakhstan, and northern Afghanistan. As in any desert location where agriculture is fully irrigation-dependent, when the water goes away, so too does the food. And the people.

The hands-down winner of these shifts in wind patterns is the American Midwest. It is this equatorial-polar phenomenon that is at least in part responsible for why Illinois is having such a good time at climate

---

* Incidentally, there's ample paleontological evidence indicating that not only has this sort of European drying happened on multiple occasions, but that at times the entire Mediterranean Basin has withered into a Brobdingnagian version of Death Valley.

change to date. That's wonderful if you're in Iowa or Indiana, less so if you're on the Gulf Coast, where hurricanes are a very real, annual threat.

MAKING SENSE OF CLIMATE CHANGE, PART III: TWO IS BETTER THAN ONE

Two sources of rainfall, that is. Part of what makes American midwestern agriculture so reliable is that it receives rainfall not only from the monsoonal systems coming off the Gulf of Mexico, but also from North America's west-to-east jet stream. It is exceedingly rare for both moisture systems to fail to deliver in the same year.

What is true for the American Midwest in general, however, is not true for all of America. As a rule, the west-to-east jet stream, which dominates most of the United States' weather patterns, overpowers tropical storm flows at roughly the 100th meridian, preventing them from proceeding any farther west.

In the increasingly climate-shifted world we are edging toward, anything east of that line is likely to experience *more* precipitation. Anything west, however, was already dry and will now be even drier. Most Great Plains agricultural communities are irrigation-dependent, clustered along river valleys made possible by highly seasonal snowfall in the eastern Rockies . . . snowfall that in the future is likely to arrive less often, less intensely, and to melt off much more quickly.

But what is likely to be . . . sad in the American Great Plains will be crushing in India or Brazil or Australia or Southeast Asia, which are all primarily monsoonal, or the former Soviet Union or sub-Saharan Africa, which are primarily jet stream driven.

In fact, aside from the American Midwest, only three places in the world benefit from both jet stream and monsoonal moisture systems: France, Argentina, and New Zealand—agricultural powerhouses all. None are likely to experience too awful a time sourcing inputs, whether in the form of equipment or oil. Better yet, none are likely to experience any meaningful security threats that might compromise life in general or

The American Climate

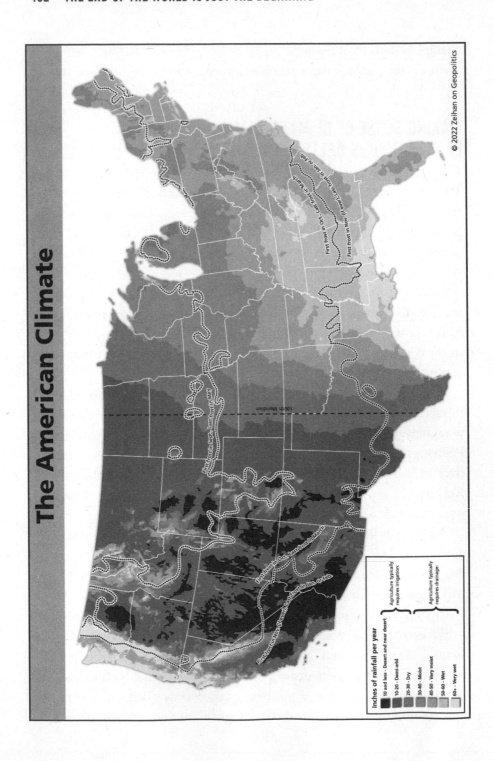

© 2022 Zeihan on Geopolitics

First frost in Oct., last frost in Jan. or Feb.

First frost in Nov. (if ever), last frost in March

First frost in Sept., last frost in May

First frost in Oct., last frost in March

First frost in Oct., last frost in May

First frost in Nov. (if ever), last frost in Jan. or Feb.

100th Meridian

Inches of rainfall per year

10 and less - Desert and near desert
10-20 - Demi-arid
20-30 - Dry
30-40 - Moist
40-50 - Very moist
50-60 - Wet
60+ - Very wet

Agriculture typically requires irrigation:

Agriculture typically requires drainage:

agricultural production in specific. All are likely to see significant output *increases* due to a mix of shifting geopolitical and climatic norms.

But those increases will be nowhere near enough to feed 8 billion people.

And that's before taking into account the fourth and final more-than-broad stroke.

MAKING SENSE OF CLIMATE CHANGE, PART IV: THE END OF THE MARGINS

The areas that will suffer the greatest impact on agricultural capacity will be those that were *already* marginal: arid but not desert, hot and wet but still serviceable. The pain will be felt more acutely in the dry locations rather than the wet ones for the simple reason that it is far easier in terms of energy and infrastructure to drain overly wet regions than to provide water to overly dry ones.

Such marginal lands face a double blow. It took industrial technologies to turn these marginal lands green, and it took the Order to enable the industrial technologies to reach many of these marginal lands in the first place. Any of these locales that lack the river or aquifer access required for mass irrigation—and that is most of them—face stark reductions in productive acres as well as catastrophic reductions in agricultural output per acre of what's left.

This, unfortunately, represents a ginormous proportion of the Earth's surface, including agricultural powerhouses ranging from Bolivia to Brazil to Paraguay to Italy to Spain to Portugal to Algeria to Nigeria to Congo to Pakistan to India to Thailand to China to Vietnam to Indonesia to Australia to Mexico to South Africa. Conservatively, that adds climatic challenges to the agricultural production zones feeding some 4 *billion* people.

This brings us back to wheat. Wheat today is mostly grown on marginal lands, particularly on lands that are marginal because they are already too dry for any other crop. The key word there is "dry." One of the things we have discovered in the past thirty years is that most plants are like most people: they are fairly temperature hardy *so long as they can access more water.* This balance between water and heat is everything in agriculture. Eastern Wyoming and eastern Montana have the same precipitation profile, but Wyoming is just a touch warmer and so cannot grow anything, while Montana is firmly in the Wheat Belt. Heat stress is fairly manageable with sufficient irrigation. But if today's wheat regions *had* extra water, they'd be growing something more valuable than wheat. Think back to interior Washington State. The very river access that enables the region to be an agricultural cornucopia is the same factor that has largely squeezed wheat out of the local production mix.

In rich locations with ample electricity generation, desalination *might* be a partial option. The tech behind desalination has steadily improved in recent years, to the point that the power cost is but one-third of what it was as recently as 2005. But there aren't a lot of oceans near marginal territories that grow wheat—most are fairly far inland. A lack of water is precisely what most of these already dry, already marginal lands will soon face, regardless of whether those lands are in Saskatchewan or Kansas or Luhansk or South Australia or Krasnodar or Shewa or Gaziantep or Santa Cruz or either of the Punjabs.

If anything, this is far worse than it sounds. The two most important crops for humanity are the ones facing the gravest danger: rice because of disruption to water cycles, and wheat because it is grown in already-dry areas that are about to become drier.

A BIT FURTHER FORWARD

This—*all* of this—is from that same rather short-term projection from the weather data. Will deeper climate change occur in the years and decades after? Maybe. Probably. Okay, almost certainly. I lack the data to provide specifics, so I won't. But I *can* cast a look back in time to help prime the mind. After all, climate change is not new to the human experience.

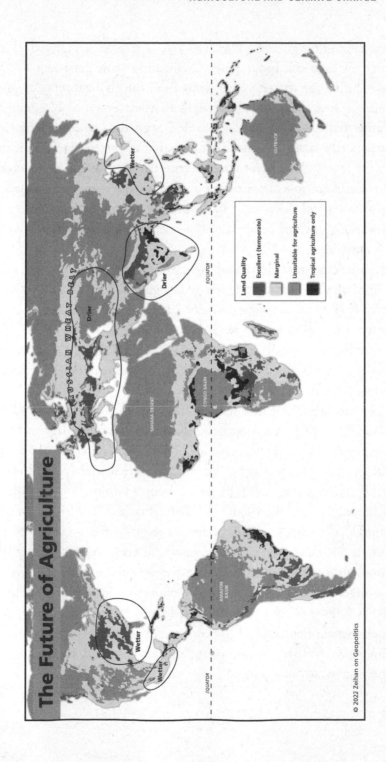

The Future of Agriculture

Land Quality
- Excellent (temperate)
- Marginal
- Unsuitable for agriculture
- Tropical agriculture only

RUSSIAN WHEAT BELT

Wetter

Drier

Drier

Wetter

Wetter

Wetter

OUTBACK

SAHARA DESERT

CONGO BASIN

AMAZON BASIN

EQUATOR

EQUATOR

© 2022 Zeihan on Geopolitics

- The best guess of today's archaeologists is that a regional climate shift smacked the Indus River Civilization with persistent flooding that shifted the Indus's course away from the civilization's city-states, followed by a multi-decade drought that left everyone high and dry. Rather than banding together to deal with the challenge, the civilization's city-states descended into a buffet of internecine cannibalism that so wholly destroyed their collective culture, we *didn't even discover that the Indus civilization existed* until the Brits stumbled across some ruins in central Pakistan in the 1800s. We didn't understand the significance of the find until excavations near the modern city of Harappa a century later.

- In earlier chapters I referenced the Late Bronze Age Collapse, a period of (probably volcanically triggered) drought between roughly 1200 and 1150 BCE. Humans were advanced enough at that point to be able to write things down, so we have some idea as to the effects of the climatic shifts. Apparently it was *really* rough; nearly every civilization on the planet buckled, including *all* the forebears of what we know as Western Civilization.

- More recently, the Little Ice Age was a period from about 1300 to 1850 CE in which temperatures dipped by roughly 0.3 degrees Celsius compared to the earlier era (and about 0.8 degrees C cooler than 1900). The greatest pain was felt in zones that were already cool. There are plenty of (relatively recent) historical records chronicling the difficulty of life in places like Scotland, Sweden, Russia, China, Korea, and Japan. Documented instances of entire regions suffering years "without summer" abound. You can guess how well everyone ate. One of those summerless years in particular—1816—was abnormally cold even for the time. Locales as far south as Connecticut dropped into the low 40s in August, while London received six inches of snow in July. Mary Shelley spent her days locked inside to shelter against the endless cold rain, sleet, and snow while pounding out that airy, buoyant tale we know today as *Frankenstein*.

FEEDING A NEW WORLD

Moving beyond the Big Four crops of wheat, soy, corn, and rice, there is a whole worldful of other food products, each with its own future. We're going to break down the top *seventeen*.

The biggest impacts to the world of agriculture will be felt in animal husbandry, at least in relative terms. The domestication of critters is *the* original human invention, predating even the farming of wheat and rice. And the same technological tree that brought us man's best friend and whiskered watching of grain stores is responsible for everything from hamburgers to chicken wings to bacon to foie gras. But, just as with pretty much everything else, it took the Industrial Revolution combined with the globalized Order to bring meat to the masses.

In the preindustrial era, would-be meat-eaters faced three challenges. First, animals were raised for the home. Scales were small because input limitations prevented rapid animal growth. You gave scraps to the chickens; cows grazed and produced milk. Animal protein was a *supplement* to our diets, and with the possible exception of milk and eggs, not something we had every day. It took the fertilizer-amped agricultural achievements of the Industrial Age to generate sufficient excess soy and grain production to provide fodder for animals.

The second challenge, as always, was transport. Shipping *live* animals long distances in bulk was a no-no because they would need to be fed. The sole exception was sheep, the critter that makes the best metabolic use of grass and so can be fattened up on the graze. But even here, the sheep (and shepherd) would have to *walk* to town. Railways and steamships and trucks sped things up, but the real shift didn't occur until the twentieth century, with the rise of inexpensive refrigerated shipping. Animals could now be butchered and chilled before being shipped, and carcasses don't have to be fed.

Third was cost. Getting the same mix of protein and calories from animals takes roughly nine times the input of getting them from plants. Move off the farm and animal protein becomes the ultimate luxury good. But in the era of the Order, incomes skyrocketed right along with the overall population. Demand for all sorts of meat exploded, particularly after 1990.

None of this, of course, is sustainable in a post-globalized world. Production of the crops used for fodder—most notably corn—will dip. Transport that brings corn and soy to the feedlots and meat to the world will falter. Global income will crater, returning animal protein to the realm of luxury for the bulk of the human population. The key word there is "bulk." The New World writ large will still enjoy massive grain and soy surpluses, enabling it to continue following the industrial agricultural model as regards animal husbandry.

That's the biggest big picture. There are plenty of smaller ones that are still pretty big, though.

The most traded meat is **pork** (the third-largest internationally traded agricultural product by value), and its story is painfully simple. Pork is the preferred animal protein for East Asia. Half of the global hog herd is raised in China, and recently China became the world's largest pork importer as well. Anyone who has bet the farm on long-term demand *from* China will lose the farm. Secondary centers of pork production in Denmark and Spain will continue to exist—they are far enough away from the mess that will be Central and Eastern Europe to be unduly disrupted by security issues—but rising costs for inputs will curtail future output. That leaves it to the Americans to dominate the rest of the market, most notably in Southeast Asia, where the locals love pork just as much as the Chinese (in per capita terms, the Vietnamese already eat *more*).

Next up is **chicken** (the tenth-largest internationally traded agricultural product by value). It is by far the cheapest and least finicky of the animal proteins, but only because of Industrial Age inputs. Historically chickens have been small and scrawny because their diet was table scraps, bugs, and grass seeds, but feed them grain in bulk and they get yuuuge. Some criticize the American chicken industry for the mass use of enclosures, but if the goal is to keep chicken as the cheapest of the animal proteins, that is the only way to raise them. (True free-range chickens cost more per pound than most steaks, with boneless/skinless chicken breasts costing more per pound than all steak cuts save filet mignon itself.*) Those American enclosures explain why the United States is the only significant exporter of chicken meat, and why chicken prices outside of America tend to be triple or more the price within.

This simplifies things from a forecasting point of view. There is nothing about American chicken production that will be adversely impacted by deglobalization. For many, American chicken may be the only imported meat that remains within reach.

Dairy milk (8th by value) has been central to the human diet for millennia, particularly in South Asia, the parts of Africa that are now northern Nigeria and Kenya, and throughout the Western world. Due to its extreme perishability, milk rarely leaves the country in which it is produced, with the sole (and large) exception of the EU's single market, which has become . . . odd. The EU has a Common Agricultural Policy (CAP), a program of subsidies that is by far the EU's largest budgetary line item. The CAP has not only helped keep noncompetitive agricultural producers in business but has also inadvertently encouraged large dairies to spring up in countries that historically had not been major dairy producers, most notably the Netherlands, Germany, and Poland. The result is massive overinvestment, overproduction, and product dumping on a global scale of all sorts of dairy products, most notably **cheese** (5th by value). But remove the EU and you remove the CAP and you remove the bulk of Europe's excess dairy and cheese production.

The United States as a rule has higher-quality and cheaper dairy milk than the Europeans, but the perishability issue limits American dairy exports to low-value milk powder. Americans just haven't developed a cheese culture like, say, France. The French and Italians—while big

---

*   Want to treat foreigners to a superfancy American meal they could not get at home? Don't take them to a steak house. Take them to KFC.

beneficiaries of the CAP—have focused on producing high-quality, wildly desirable niche cheeses. Demand for them will persist no matter what happens to the EU. I will see to it *personally*. Their sales reach will undoubtedly shrink, but they'll still be able to access North America and North Africa quite easily.

The real future of global dairy is New Zealand. The Kiwis enjoy a mild climate with cool summers and warm winters and lots of rain and no predators, so their cows do not require shelter—*or even fodder*. Kiwi dairy has a cost structure that's even lower than the Americans, they produce milk of higher quality than the Americans, and they are well into developing a French-style cheese culture that is insanely value added.[*] One more thing: when a dairy cow is no longer productive, it is sent to slaughter. That little detail has made New Zealand the world's fifth-largest exporter of . . .

Beef (11th by value). Along with the Kiwis, the major players in global beef are the United States, Australia, the Netherlands, Canada, and Ireland. Of these six, the United States is in the best position, primarily because it has vast tracts of federal land that beef producers can lease for grazing.[†] On the flip side, Australia's climatic instability will make it the least reliable of the major exporters over the long term. Beef out of the Netherlands and Ireland is possible only with CAP-related income support.

Technically, India and Brazil are major producers and exporters as well, although—again, technically—their "beef" isn't from cattle, but instead from a critter called the zebu, which is more acclimated to the sultriness of the tropics. This pushes their product into a lower quality category, but there's no reason to expect it to go away in a deglobalized world. If anything, infrastructure constraints in Brazil will trap soy in

---

[*]   If you ever want your mind blown, get a hold of a wheel of Kapiti Kikorangi—a Kiwi cheese that combines the best characteristics of gorgonzola and Camembert. Nomtastic!

[†]   Everybody loves free!

the Brazilian interior and encourage the production and export of *more* zebu since it will have a higher value-add than raw soy. Zebu may be low quality by beef standards, but in a cost-constrained world, cheaper meat will have an attraction all its own.

For everyone else who wants beef, options are slim. Like literally, *slim*. Typical American (and Canadian and Aussie and Brazilian) beef cattle are *massive* beasts that regularly weigh in at over a ton at the time of slaughter. Also, they grow to that size in a matter of months, largely because they are fed a steady diet of corn and soy, as well as getting regular injections of antibiotics and hormones to encourage bulking and survival rates. More traditional beef cattle that are range fed and less manipulated take three to five times as long to mature, end up a foot shorter at the shoulder, and typically have a slaughter weight less than one-third that of their more manipulated peers—which incidentally makes them *the* highest-cost animal protein. Such "heritage" cows may taste better to some mouths, but in a world of constrained trade and access, their far lower productivity levels will elevate beef for the bulk of humanity from a sometimes food to an almost-never food.

My world cannot function without **coffee** (7th by value) and I am . . . concerned. Coffee is a lot like cocaine . . . in terms of where it can be grown. It demands a very specific mix of elevation, temperature, and moisture conditions. Too dry and the crop shrivels. Too wet and it rots. Too hot and it is bitter. Too cold and it won't flower. Roughly 7,500 feet is the ideal elevation, putting it well above most lines of human habitation and making servicing and transport tricky. Mass coffee culture is only possible in a globalized system in which the inputs can access such often-near-inaccessible areas. The Arabica coffee you get at everything from McDonald's to your favorite espresso bar faces the greatest challenges, while the robusta coffee that goes into instant is far more heat and drought tolerant. The combination of deglobalization and climate change suggests that most of the world is about to get a coffee downgrade.

Palm oil (6th by value) is ubiquitous. In nonfood items it shows up in soaps, shampoos, deodorants, and toothpastes. It is also in nearly every processed food product imaginable. Whereas butter and olive oil may be used in small-batch food preparation for local distribution, barring some cutting-edge processing technologies, dairy and olive tend to spoil and/or turn bitter when subjected to excessive heat or movement. And anyhow, palm oil is cheaper than both. That necessitates an input switch to palm oil to protect texture and extend shelf life, particularly if the product is spreadable. No palm oil would mean no margarine, pizza dough, instant noodles, ice cream, or—gasp—Nutella!

Palm requires fertile soil, absolutely no cold, and loads of water *all the time*, making it ideal for coastal tropics. The biggest producers by far are in Southeast Asia. The primary problem moving forward will be soil fertility. The Southeast Asians engage in slash-and-burn agriculture to generate the necessary soil nutrients, but that can only really be done once. After that, it is fertilize or bust, and Southeast Asia is likely to experience shortages of fertilizers, most notably the potassium and phosphate types.

There are a few patches. What makes palm oil work is its fat: add hydrogen to the carbon atoms that make up the hydrocarbon backbone of an oil molecule and it becomes a solid at room temperature (this is the "hydrogenated" bit you see on the ingredients label of most processed food). While palm oil is the best (and cheapest!) for this, it *can* be done with soy, corn, or cottonseed oil as well. It isn't as tasty—as many Europeans will discuss at length when lamenting soy-oil- and corn-oil-heavy American processed food—but it still works. Move outside of the temperate zone world, however, and these options become more difficult—especially if global trade is breaking down.

A loss of palm oil trade for the advanced world is a very first-world problem: it is about taste and texture. For the developing world it is about *shelf life*, and that rapidly translates from convenience into terror. Many may think of universal access to processed food as a root cause of obesity, and they are not wrong. But such access is also one of the glories of the Order. Most of the developing world has *zero* experience in maintaining large populations without shelf-stable food. Remove palm oil from areas that cannot produce their own cooking oil and seasonal famines are absolutely guaranteed.

After the Iberians broke the Silk Roads with their naval-powered spice trade, many of the European empires turned to squabbling over **sugar** (12th by value). Cane sugar is very fussy. It needs constant water, but also heat, and prefers alluvial floodplains and no salt. There are very few spots on the planet that meet such criteria. Most are in Brazil and the Caribbean. In the 1800s the Germans were sparring with the Brits, and in doing so they lost access to all things from warm places. Their solution was to hack local plants and crossbreed into existence what we now know as sugar beets. Sugar beets are just fine in colder climates, just like normal beets.* This suggests that any reasonably cool, temperate-zone climate—and that includes Germany, Russia, Turkey, Canada, France, and the northern United States—should be able to source beet sugar.

The king of *cane* sugar—which, let's face it, tastes *much* better than beet sugar—is Cuba, which has the perfect climate for what is normally a picky product. Any country able to sustain normal economic relations with the Cubans will enjoy a tsunami of the sweet stuff . . . which would absolutely wreck the economics of more expensive, lower-quality beet sugar.†

Tobacco (14th by value) is a nightshade, demanding warmth and moisture without getting too hot or wet. That means a narrow list of locales: the Carolinas, Anatolia, the drier portions of Brazil and Indonesia, a strip of the cooler portions of Africa's Great Rift highlands, pockets of coastal India, and China's Yunnan, Hunan, and Sichuan regions. Without global reach there is not only no global oil or global manufacturing, there is no global tobacco. If you are hooked on cigarettes and lack near-immediate access to one of those production zones, deglobalization is about to help you quit. French, Polish, and Russian nicotine fiends will face particular difficulty in accessing cancer-causing sticks of death.

Bananas (18th by value) vary wildly in terms of type, but all have

---

*   Yuck!
†   I'm looking at you, America.

three key characteristics. First, they need the full tropics and the high heat, high humidity, constant water, and lack of winter that come with them.

Second, cultivating and harvesting bananas is arguably the most labor-intensive *and* fertilizer-intensive agricultural process. You don't simply need the tropics; you need a very poor, very densely populated country with reliable international access.

Third, bananas—especially the Cavendish variety Americans enjoy—are clones, making them eminently, dangerously vulnerable to pests and especially fungal diseases. Should a single banana tree get infected, typically the entire plantation must be razed. For those of you organic buffs out there who refuse to eat anything that's been touched with anything artificial, know that a roughly half-mile radius around organic banana plantations is practically nuked with (eminently *non*-organic) pesticides and herbicides and fungicides to protect your proclivities. Organics also tend to be grown at higher, drier elevations to somewhat limit pests, which means the bananas need massive irrigation to grow. The result is the food product with *the* highest chemical and carbon footprint, as well as the highest staff turnovers from *death* in any product set in any industry. Happy eating.

Cotton (17th by value) is a weird plant in that it needs loads of water *and* sun and there just aren't that many places on the planet that are swampy . . . deserts. The solution, of course, is irrigation. The Egyptians tap the Nile, the Pakistanis tap the Indus, and the Turkmen and Uzbeks tap the Amu and Syr. Deglobalization alone will force the four peoples to shift from cotton they can sell abroad to crops they can eat, and even if deglobalization does *not* occur, a touch of climate change will reduce the water the four have available for irrigation.

Chinese cotton faces even bigger issues, not (simply) because it is grown in the genocidal internment-hellscape-slavocracy of Xinjiang, but because the rivers of Xinjiang flow not to the ocean but into the internal, terminal, long-ago desertified Tarim Basin. It would take painfully little shifts in climate norms for those rivers to dry to the point of pointlessness, taking any hope for irrigating Xinjiang's thirsty cotton fields with them. Indian cotton will likely be more sustainable, but it is all monsoon dependent, so its production is certain to lose reliability.

No matter how you knit this blanket, we *will* have a global cotton shortage.

There are only two large-scale producers that can continue to play: the Western Hemispheric countries of Brazil and the United States. Their cotton might not be the long-staple variety the world prefers, but it is produced in the safer hemisphere *and* it doesn't require nearly as much irrigation, making Brazilian and American supplies far more reliable in the world to come.

Citrus (16th) is a bit like cotton in its desire for a lot of heat and water. Luckily, it also likes a lot of humidity, expanding where cultivation is possible. The future of citrus is pretty clear. In locations where the climate is appropriate, sporting enough rainfall that irrigation isn't required—primarily Florida and northern Brazil—everything looks peachy. But in those places where the quintessential effects of the Order have enabled cultivation via the mass application of capital, fertilizer, and *irrigation*—most notably Egypt and Spain—you should kiss your oranges and grapefruits goodbye.

Anything juicy and on a vine needs consistent, controlled watering, whether it be table or wine **grapes** (20th by value). Too little water and they shrivel. Too much and they split. The key is *control*, and that means dry climates plus the capacity for irrigation. Some of the world's best grapes come from the arid regions and especially deserts of California, Italy, Spain, Argentina, Australia, Chile, Iran, and Washington State's Greater Columbia River Valley.

Supply *will* drop. Irrigation requires capital, which in the world of wine hasn't been a problem the last three decades. Soon it will be. But supply will drop only a bit. Most producers are either New World or—like South Africa and France—at least partially immune to the chaos to come.

Demand, in contrast, will drop *more*. Break global economic growth and global demand for high-cost tipple will break with it. On balance, wine is one of those rare agricultural products that might get cheaper. Whether the wine gets any *better* is unfortunately something I am not well suited to forecasting.*

The preferred climate for both **sunflowers** (19th by value) and **canola** (23rd)—row crops that are crushed for their oil—is in cooler, semiarid zones. Among the world's biggest suppliers are Ukraine, which is likely to fall off the market, and Canada's Prairie Provinces, which ship almost all their output to China, a market that will implode. Luckily for the Canadians, most sunflower and canola territory can be repurposed to wheat production.

Apples and pears (collectively 21st by value) used to be the easy crop, but in the globalized Order we all decided apples the size of tennis balls just wouldn't cut it. If you want an apple the size of your head, you need fertilizer and irrigation. The result has been a wild degree of market segmentation not just among countries, but within them. Much of this variety requires access to different microclimes, and in a world where we aren't interacting as much, that variety will be necessarily limited. The biggest gross exporters that will vanish from global markets are those who simply cannot get their product out: most notably the bulk of the European countries and China (whose apples are a touch nasty anyway). The big growth markets in Southeast Asia and Latin America should be fine; that's great news for growers in the United States, Argentina, and Chile.

Finally, we come to what makes glorious, glorious chocolate possible: **cocoa** (22nd by value). Think of it as a more heat-tolerant, lower-elevation version of coffee, with a preference for tropical humidity. It pretty much only comes from two places: West African output faces constraints in security and trade access and material inputs and capital sourcing (and likely, climate), while Mexico looks . . . completely fine. If you prefer

---

* Although I'd be happy to assist with the after-action evaluation process.

the slightly fruity Central American varieties, you'll be in good shape. But if your idea of chocolate is the ultra-dense, sledgehammer-heavy, knock-you-on-your-ass, give-me-chocolate-or-give-me-death *now* sensation for which West African cocoa is known, life is about to get a lot less sweet.

Value of Primary Global Agricultural Trade, 2020

Product	Value (in billions USD)
Soybeans	64.3
Wheat	44.8
Pork	37.0
Maize (corn)	36.6
Cheese	32.8
Palm Oil	32.5
Coffee	30.4
Dairy Milk	28.9
Rice	25.5
Poultry	24.5
Beef	23.3
Sugar	23.1
Berries	19.5
Tobacco	19.2
Nuts	18.1
Citrus	16.0
Cotton	14.1
Bananas	13.7
Sunflower oil	13.4
Grapes	10.6
Apples & Pears	10.0
Cocoa beans	9.3
Canola oil	4.0

Source: UNCTAD   © 2022 Zeihan on Geopolitics

THE LONG RIDE OF THE THIRD HORSEMAN

In between periods of existential dread during the 2020 COVID lockdown, I was tallying up my work experience of the past decade and came to the conclusion that I had given more than six hundred presentations. Different topics. Different audiences. Different countries. Across such widely varying swaths of themes and places, one question popped up time and again: What keeps you up at night?

I've always found the question . . . curious. I am *not* known as the guy who brings rays of sunshine and rivers of unicorns to a room.

Anywho, at its core, this chapter is my answer to the question.

The same webwork of sacrosanct interconnections that has brought us everything from quick mortgages to smartphones to on-demand electricity has not only also filled 8 billion bellies, it has done so with the odd out-of-season avocado. That's now largely behind us. The web is failing. Just past the horizon looms a world of lower and less reliable agricultural yields, marred by less variety. A world with less energy or fewer manufactured goods is the difference between wealth and security or poverty and conflict. But a world with fewer foodstuffs is one with fewer *people*.

More than war, more than disease, *famine* is the ultimate country killer. And it is not something the human condition can adjust to quickly or easily.

It is the magic mix of industrialization and urbanization that makes modernity possible, and it is precisely those intertwined factors that are under such extreme threat. Weaken the pair, much less break them down, and it will take at bare minimum a generation to rebuild a mix of financial access and manufacturing supply chains and technological evolutions and labor forces that are capable of feeding 8 billion people. And in the time it takes to do *that* . . . we will no longer *have* 8 billion people.

The history of the next fifty years will be the story of how we deal with—or fail to deal with—the coming food shortages. How those shortages—some continental in scope—will create their own changes in circumstance. How political and economic systems the world over will grapple with the one shortfall that matters more than everything else combined.

That is what keeps me up at night.

EPILOGUE

So . . . that's the short version. Thanks for sticking with me.

The (much) longer version is the rest of my work life, expanding on this or that bit of the future for audiences large and small. Hopefully with a bit of humor (gallows or otherwise) to keep the topic's self-generating pessimism in check.

I've had a few stops on my road to *The End of the World*, but the most personally consequential one involves the tucking away of my beliefs.

As a student of history, I feel I appreciate the vast improvements of the past seventy-five years more than the average Jane or Joe. As an internationalist, I believe I understand just how far we've come. As a Green, I think I see a path forward, even if it isn't the one most Greens are convinced of. And as a democrat (little *d*), I *know* popular participation is the "least bad form of government." Believe it or not, I consider myself an optimist.

But that matters little to what I do. Forecasting is hard because checking your personal preferences and ideologies at the door is hard. My job is to inform about what *will* happen. Not what I *want* to happen. Doesn't really matter what crowd. Government, military, or civilian. Manufacturing, financing, or agriculture. I don't enjoy giving people bad news, and I (often) make folks unhappy.

It *has* gotten easier. The telling. Not the news.

Courtesy of the depressing, impressively disengaged leadership of Barack Obama and the equally depressing, impressively disconnected leadership of Donald Trump, we are so far off from the world that I *want* to see, it has gotten easier for me to bury my personal preferences and get on with the work of assessing the state of the world. And write this book.

This is not a call to action. In my opinion, we missed a chance to go down a separate road—a better road—well over a decade ago. And even if I had a viable plan for today, Americans who are interested in playing a constructive role in recrafting the world with an eye toward a brighter future have lost the last eight presidential elections. I might say the singular exception was the most recent one. In the Trump-Biden contest, internationalists like myself didn't even have a guy in the race.

Nor is this project a lamentation for the world that could have been. When the Cold War ended, the Americans had the opportunity to do nearly anything. Instead, both on the Left and the Right, we started a lazy descent into narcissistic populism. The presidential election record that brought us Clinton and W Bush and Obama and Trump and Biden isn't an aberration, but instead a pattern of active disinterest in the wider world. It *is* our new norm. This book is about where that norm leads.

Nor is there leadership beyond America. There is no new hegemon-in-waiting, nor countries that will rise to support a common vision. There is no savior waiting in the wings. Instead, the world's secondary powers have already fallen back into their old habits of mutual antagonism.

The Europeans, in the most peaceful and wealthy period in their history, have proven incapable of coming together for a common cheese policy, a common banking policy, a common foreign policy, or a common refugee policy—much less a common strategic policy. Without globalization, nearly three generations of achievement will boil away. Perhaps the European response to the Ukraine War will prove me wrong. I hope so.

China and Russia have already fallen back on instinct, heedless of the lessons of their own long sagas. In the post–Cold War era, the pair benefited the most by far from American engagement, as the Order prevented the powers that had impoverished, shattered, and conquered them through the centuries from fully exerting themselves, while simultaneously creating the circumstances for the greatest economic stability they have ever known. Instead of seeking rapprochement with the Americans to preserve their magical moment, they instead worked diligently—almost pathologically—to disrupt what remained of global structures. Future history will be as merciless to them as their dark and dangerous pasts.

If anything, humanity's next chapter will be even more grim, for now we have the demographic angle to fold into the mix. In most countries, the point of no return passed around *1980*. That's when masses of twenty- and thirty-somethings simply stopped having children. Fast-forward four decades to the present and this childless generation is now retiring. Most of the developed world faces imminent, simultaneous consumption, production, *and* financial collapses. The advanced developing world—China included—is, if anything, worse off. There, urbanization and industrialization happened much more quickly, so birth rates crumpled all the faster. Their even-faster aging dictates an even-faster collapse. The numbers tell us that it all *must* happen in this decade. The numbers tell us it was *always* going to happen in this decade.

I cannot provide you with a better way forward. Nor can I provide you with a eulogy for something that never happened. Geography does not change. Demographics do not lie. And we have a historyful of history as to how countries and peoples react to their environment.

What I can do, however, is provide you a map. In book form.

Forewarned is forearmed.

Alrighty then! Enough with the dark clouds. Let's talk about the map's silver linings.

A running theme through all my work, including my three previous books, is that our particular point in history—the unwinding of globalization—is little more than a momentary transition period. An interregnum, as it were. Such historical periods are (in)famous for their instability as the old gives way to the new. The interregnum between the British-German competition and the Cold War included the world wars and the Great Depression. The interregnum between the French-German competition and the British-German competition included Napoleon. When old structures fall, or "merely" persevere in the face of extreme challenge, stuff breaks. Lots of stuff.

The 2020s and 2030s will be exceedingly uncomfortable for many, but this too will pass. Best of all, we can already see the sun starting to burn through the clouds. A few things to consider:

Capital availability is a function of demographics. The Boomer generation's mass retirement in the 2020s is to our detriment. They are taking their money with them. But by 2040, the *youngest* Millennials will be in their forties, and *their* money will have made the system flush once more.

On the topic of demographics, the 2040s will host two simultaneous beneficial outcomes. The kids of the youngest Millennials will be entering the workforce, heralding a sort of a return to "normal" for the American labor market. Nearly as important, Mexico's demographic structure will be shaped a bit like a chimney, similar to that of the United States in 2000. That was a magic moment in America when we had a similar number of children and young workers and mature workers, making the United States capital rich *and* consumer rich *and* productivity rich while *still* having a future generation to plan and hope for. ¡Viva Mexico!

Between now and 2040, America's reindustrialization will be complete. Mexican-American linkages will prove to be far tighter and far more consequential than anything the United States ever achieved with its northern neighbor. Most American refineries will be using North American–produced crude rather than extracontinental imports. The inflation and systemic stress that come from quickly doubling your industrial plant will be firmly in the past. We'll think of the deglobalization shock in much the same way we think of the 2007 subprime crisis: as little more than an uncomfortable memory. The 2040s should be a great time to be in North America.

Also by 2040, the agricultural community will have worked all the kinks out of precision farming techniques. A mix of digital, genetic, automation, and engineering advances will have enabled American farmers to triple their caloric output. We may still well be picking cherries and asparagus by hand, but automation will be the rule in nearly every other aspect of food production and processing. It will not be enough to erase the memory of the Eastern Hemisphere's food shortage horrors of the 2020s and 2030s, but collectively these advances and more will provide a stable baseline moving forward.

There's even a far-better-than-average hope we will have made massive strides in materials science, which *should* prove sufficient to land us with both better batteries than ones composed of lithium, as well as far superior long-range electricity transmission capacity. Pair that with the fact that the 2040s will be the decade when most natural-gas-burning, electricity-generating facilities will be ready for retirement. Old trusty fossil fuel facilities out, new trusty greentech systems in. Hopefully—and everything I have an even number of is crossed as I type this—the price points for these new technologies will prove low enough that they can be applied en masse across the globe. We will finally be able to *begin* the *real* energy transition.

Perhaps best of all, the above *assumes* that a great many things do not go very . . . well. Much of this book—much of *all* my books—chronicles the not-very-well bits of future history that lie ahead. Collapses capital and agricultural and cultural. Fractures transport and manufacturing and national. But the North American continent stands apart both geographically and demographically from much of the approaching chaos. It will serve as both a repository of the gains of ages past and a laboratory for the age to come.

The real question—the real mystery—is what happens *then*? Never before in human history has an interregnum smashed so many countries and cultures across such a wide swath of the planet. Even the Late Bronze Age Collapse wasn't so complete. We called the twentieth century "the American Century" because the United States emerged globally predominant in 1945. In the coming age, the gap between North America and the bulk of the world will be, if anything, starker. Never before in human history has the premier power from the previous era emerged so unassailably dominant at the beginning of the next.

Challenges and opportunities beckon. Cultural. Economic. Technological. Climatic. Demographic. Geopolitical. Exploring *that* future— exploring that brave new world—will be a hell of a project.

Maybe that's what I'll do next.

ACKNOWLEDGMENTS

This was a *big* project. I've been working on the text in bits and pieces for at least the past five years, and absolutely everything in my professional career has contributed to it in ways big and small, loud and subtle.

Which means this isn't all my work. Not by a long shot. I'm not so much standing on the shoulders of the giants who have come before as standing on *everyone's* shoulders. My work touches everything. And not just the ins and outs of transport and finance and energy and manufacturing and industrial commodities and agriculture, but *everything*. If I cited everyone who in some way has informed or contributed to this work, the bibliography would be longer than the entire text you just soldiered through.

That said, some contributions to this book have been more equal than others. So, please allow me to slather on some particularly effusive thanks.

Let's start with the people responsible for tabulating and updating details about the biggest of the big: the United States. Endless thank-yous to the U.S. Bureau of Transportation and the U.S. Army Corps of Engineers for the information on everything from road and rail transport statistics to the maps and upkeep!—of the U.S. river-based transport network. Gratitude to America's various Port Authorities not only for promoting the United States' geographical advantages in maritime trade but for sharing trade the statistics and insights they have.

I'm a particular fan of the folks at the U.S. Department of Labor, especially the number crunchers at the Bureau of Labor Statistics, as well as the U.S. Federal Reserve and the U.S. Internal Revenue Service, for their invaluable insights into the inner workings of . . . work. The largest economy in the world and the mainstay currency of global trade aren't easy things to quantify, and I'm thankful that they do much of the heavy lifting for us.

Demographics is a key component of my geopolitical understandings. I owe a huge debt of brain cells saved to the wizards at the UN Population Division and the U.S. Census Bureau. Offering so much more than just a simple count of the American or global populations, they provide reliable, quality information on the makeup of individual societies, historical trends, and future projections. Simply put, they collect and maintain the data on "us."

Adding context and flavor to the demographic data are a whole host of international state agencies and nonprofit organizations. My team has conversed with and relied upon oh so many, but a special call-out to the helpfulness and responsiveness of Statistics Canada, the Statistics Bureau of Japan, Statistics Korea, Eurostat, and the Australian Bureau of Statistics. Your employees work tirelessly to compile information on how things work in your respective countries, and we appreciate the candor and willingness to engage with our many information requests—even in the rare, painful instances where you couldn't provide what we were looking for.

Special thanks to Richard Hokenson—whose work started me down the road to marrying demographics to economics so many years ago—and Paul Morland for writing *The Human Tide*, arguably *the* best book *ever* on the intersection of demographics, history, and national power.

If you ever find yourself needing to stress test an energy-related theory, Vaclav Smil of the University of Manitoba serves as a one-stop shop. That's not quite right. The guy has written more books on the reality of energy than I have socks, and my sock game handily exceeds that of the Canadian prime minister. His works most useful to this project: *Energy and Civilization: A History* and *Prime Movers of Globalization*. Similarly helpful is Jean-Paul Rodrigue of Hofstra University, the author of *The Geography of Transport Systems*, far and away the densest book on an information-to-page ratio that I have ever perused.

Need energy data? No way you are getting anywhere without the U.S. Energy Information Agency, which provides statistics on everything from conventional and shale production to refinery output to historical electricity production data to how much wood is used in biomass power generation in Wisconsin.

Beyond American shores, the International Energy Agency, the BP *Statistical Review of World Energy*, the UN's Joint Oil Database Initiative, and OPEC provide invaluable insights into global production and consumption trends. There are as many ways of tracking energy statistics as there are bodies that track them, but the teams behind these resources provide a compelling look into what fuels . . . everything.

Much appreciation to the teams at Xcel Energy and Southern Company for their efforts—and patience—in communicating the ins and outs and yeses and nos of what does and does not make for a functional power system. (Electricity is *hard*!)

More interested in stuff than electrons? Then it's the U.S. Geological Survey and the National Minerals Information Center that you need in your life. The pair not only track domestic and international production of nearly every minable resource, but also their uses.

Questions on agriculture and manufacturing are limited only by the world's appetite for food and stuff, and you can feast on a buffet of information from the World Bank, the Bank of International Settlements, the Organization for Economic Cooperation and Development, UN Comtrade, the Food and Agriculture Organization of the United Nations, IBISWorld, and MIT's Observatory of Economic Complexity. Collectively, they keep tabs on all the myriad tiny and enormous things and price tags that accompany the human experience. Special thanks to everyone at Farm Credit as well as the U.S. Department of Agriculture's Economic Research Service, and especially Nathan Childs and Michael McConnell for the graciousness of their time.

Eric Snodgrass—that's Dr. Snodgrass to you—is a meteorologist turned college professor turned agricultural economist who just happens to be freakin' *hilarious*. In addition to making me bust a gut every time I'm in his presence, he is the guy responsible for much of my thinking on what we can and cannot predict about climate change, and how observable trends backed by decades of existing data records are *already* playing out. In particular, the Australia versus Illinois comparison within the agriculture section is undeniably his.

A bit closer to home:

As the team was closing down work on *The End of the World* we took on a new researcher—Quinn Carter—who quickly got down to the dirty business of telling me how I'm wrong. *Grrrr.* Welcome to the crazy train, Quinn!

Melissa Taylor served as my head of research for six years. One of her last projects before moving on to her life's next chapter was to assemble the base draft for what evolved into this book's transport section. I shiver at the thought of what that chapter would have looked like without her. I shiver at the thought of what a lot of my recent work would have looked like without her.

Adam Smith has been handling my graphic needs for years. While I'm hugely appreciative of his ability to make everything bright and snazzy, an even greater service is the one he provides to my clients and readers. His common sense is often the first line of defense between my busy, scattered mind and normal people. He protects you from *soooooooo* much.

Wayne Watters and I have been together for eighteen years now, which in gay years is longer than Joe Biden has been alive. Sounding board and soulmate, best friend and bookkeeper, I can't imagine my life without him in it. He may not have been a direct part of the book team, but without him *I* would not have been a direct part of the book team.

Thomas Rehnquist came and went while we were mid–*End of the World*, but in his few months with us he made a seriously oversized splash. In addition to handling the primary fact-check, Tom's work provided the backbone for the entire industrial commodities chapters. I'm happy/angry to say his work has kept me from making an oversized fool of myself.

Susan Copeland is . . . what can I say about Susan? I've been working with her in some capacity for fifteen years. Technically, she's my admin, but so much more than that. She's the organizational and emotional connective tissue that keeps all of us here at Zeihan on Geopolitics safe and sane. I'm *so* blessed that she hasn't yet gotten bored.

Last, but most certainly not least, Michael Nayebi-Oskoui. I've worked with Michael for more than a decade now. This is the third book he's helped me with. He's become more than my chief of staff. It has been a pleasure to watch him evolve into a just as versatile and frazzled analyst as me. The agriculture section flat-out could not have happened without him, and he provided much of the intellectual scaffolding that made finance and manufacturing possible as well.

I have nothing but bottomless thanks to all the folks at Harper Business—most notably Eric Nelson and James Neidhardt—for allowing me to make some well-past-the-last-minute adjustments and additions (such as this note) to address late-breaking developments. Anywhere in the text you see a reference to the Ukraine War or February 2022 is courtesy of their flexibility. Those changes are nowhere near sufficient, considering the scale of upheaval I know to be already in progress, but, considering our production and logistical constraints, I'm thrilled with the updates we were able to include.

One final thanks to you, the reader (or listener if you're part of the Kindle Krowd). Whether you're using my book to help inform your life and business decisions or simply looking for opportunities to prove me wrong, I heartily appreciate having you along for the ride. As a good-bye gift, I'd like to point you to my website. It isn't so much that there's a newsletter there you can sign up for (although there is), but instead that all the graphics from within this book can be found there in high definition and full color. Head to www.zeihan.com/end-of-the-world-maps and you will find them in the full glory in which Adam intended.

And, that, as they say, is that.

INDEX

ABOUT THE AUTHOR

PETER ZEIHAN is a geopolitical strategist and the founder of the consulting firm Zeihan on Geopolitics. His clients include energy corporations, financial institutions, business associations, agricultural interests, universities, and the U.S. military. He is the author of *The Accidental Superpower, The Absent Superpower,* and *Disunited Nations.* He lives in Colorado.